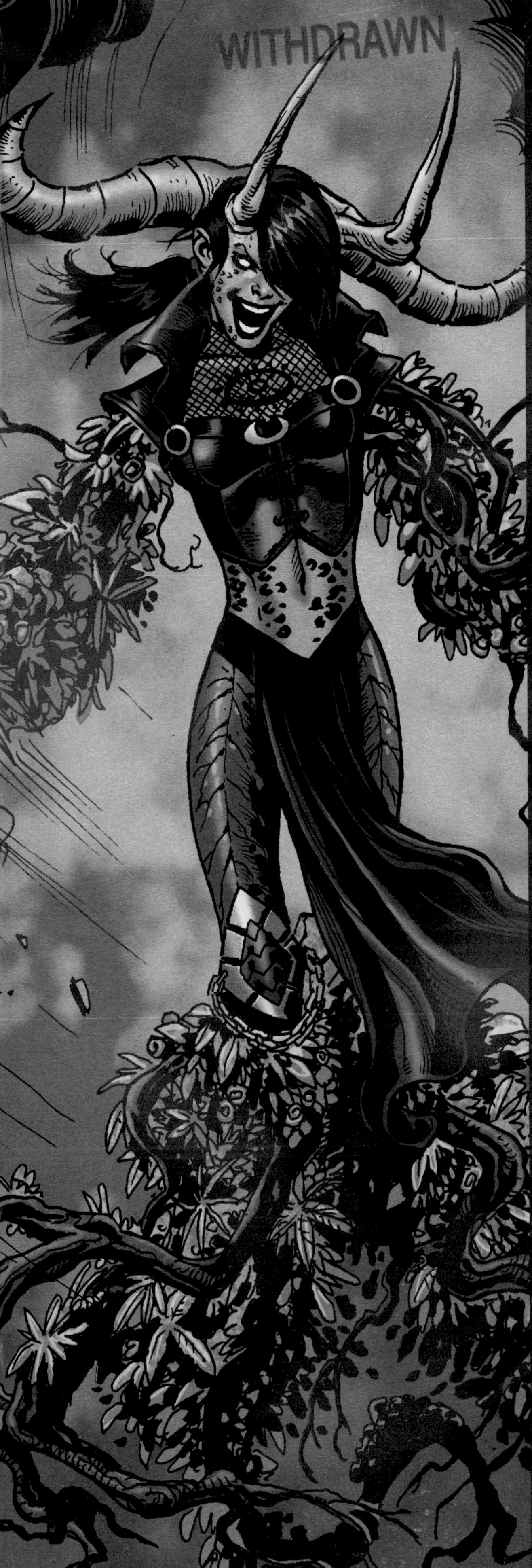

SECRET SIX

VOLUME 2
THE GAUNTLET

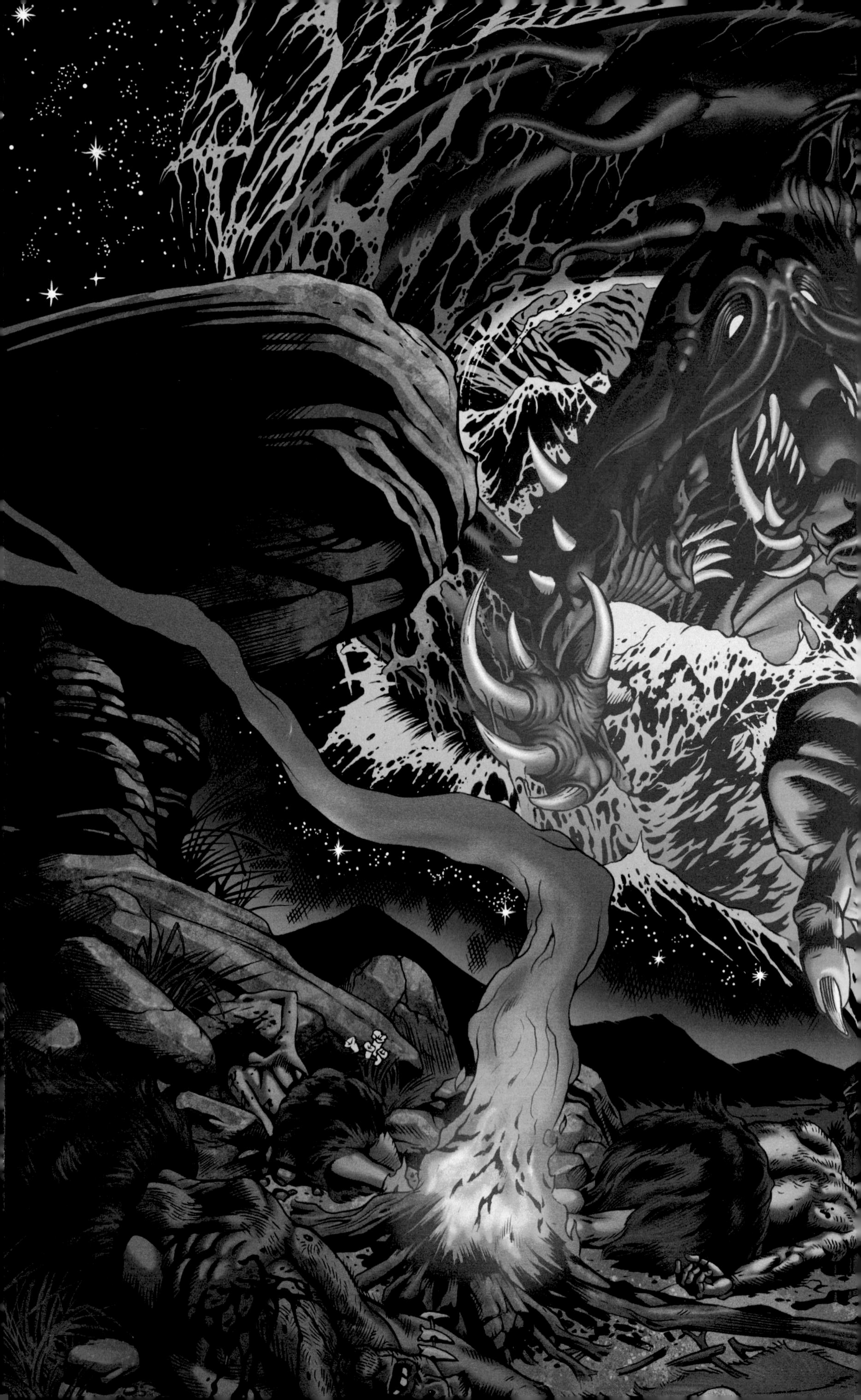

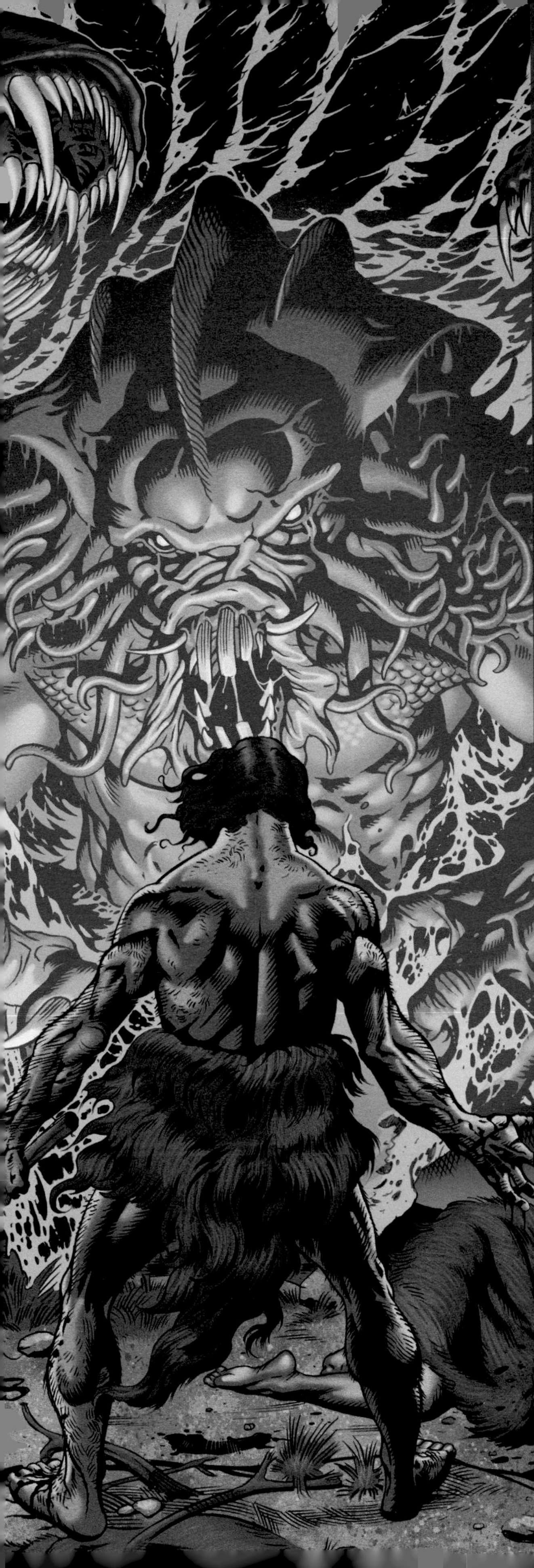

SECRET SIX

VOLUME 2
THE GAUNTLET

WRITTEN BY
GAIL SIMONE

ART BY
TOM DERENICK
DALE EAGLESHAM

COLOR BY
JASON WRIGHT
REX LOKUS

LETTERS BY
TRAVIS LANHAM

COLLECTION COVER ART BY
DALE EAGLESHAM
AND JASON WRIGHT

SUPERMAN CREATED BY
JERRY SIEGEL
AND JOE SHUSTER
BY SPECIAL ARRANGEMENT
WITH THE JERRY SIEGEL FAMILY

JIM CHADWICK KRISTY QUINN Editors – Original Series
DAVID PIÑA Assistant Editor – Original Series
JEB WOODARD Group Editor – Collected Editions
LIZ ERICKSON Editor – Collected Edition
STEVE COOK Design Director – Books
DAMIAN RYLAND Publication Design

BOB HARRAS Senior VP – Editor-in-Chief, DC Comics

DIANE NELSON President
DAN DiDIO Publisher
JIM LEE Publisher
GEOFF JOHNS President & Chief Creative Officer
AMIT DESAI Executive VP – Business & Marketing Strategy,
Direct to Consumer & Global Franchise Management
SAM ADES Senior VP – Direct to Consumer
BOBBIE CHASE VP – Talent Development
MARK CHIARELLO Senior VP – Art, Design & Collected Editions
JOHN CUNNINGHAM Senior VP – Sales & Trade Marketing
ANNE DePIES Senior VP – Business Strategy, Finance & Administration
DON FALLETTI VP – Manufacturing Operations
LAWRENCE GANEM VP – Editorial Administration & Talent Relations
ALISON GILL Senior VP – Manufacturing & Operations
HANK KANALZ Senior VP – Editorial Strategy & Administration
JAY KOGAN VP – Legal Affairs
THOMAS LOFTUS VP – Business Affairs
JACK MAHAN VP – Business Affairs
NICK J. NAPOLITANO VP – Manufacturing Administration
EDDIE SCANNELL VP – Consumer Marketing
COURTNEY SIMMONS Senior VP – Publicity & Communications
JIM (SKI) SOKOLOWSKI VP – Comic Book Specialty Sales & Trade Marketing
NANCY SPEARS VP – Mass, Book, Digital Sales & Trade Marketing

SECRET SIX VOLUME 2: THE GAUNTLET

DC Comics, 2900 West Alameda Avenue, Burbank, CA 91505
Printed by LSC Communications, Salem, VA, USA. 11/25/16. First Printing.
ISBN: 978-1-4012-6453-6

Library of Congress Cataloging-in-Publication Data is available.

PEFC Certified

Printed on paper from
sustainably managed
forests, controlled
sources

PEFC/29-31-337   www.pefc.org

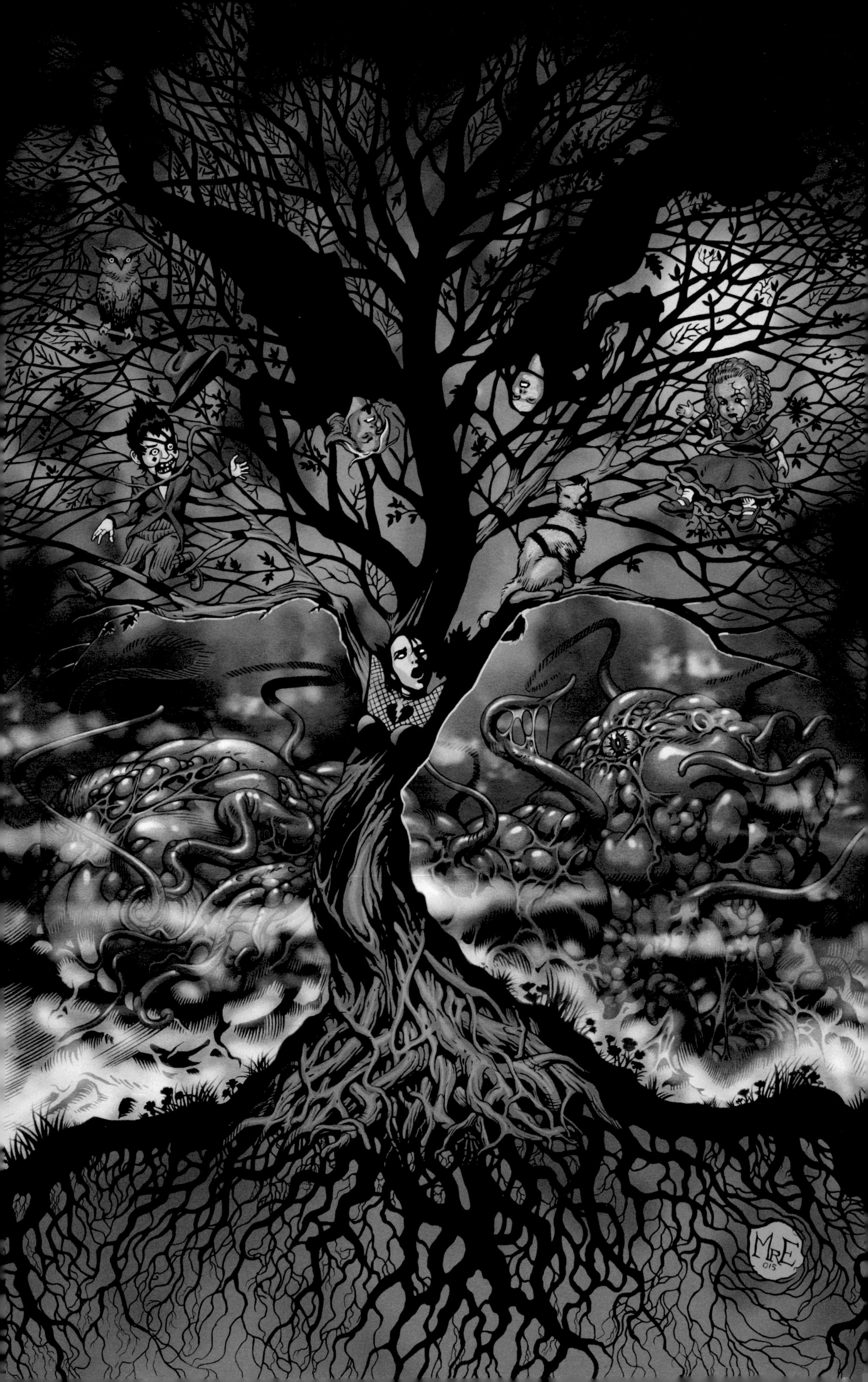
MrE
015

GAIL SIMONE writer DALE EAGLESHAM TOM DERENICK artists JASON WRIGHT colorist TRAVIS LANHAM letterer
cover by DALE EAGLESHAM & JASON WRIGHT

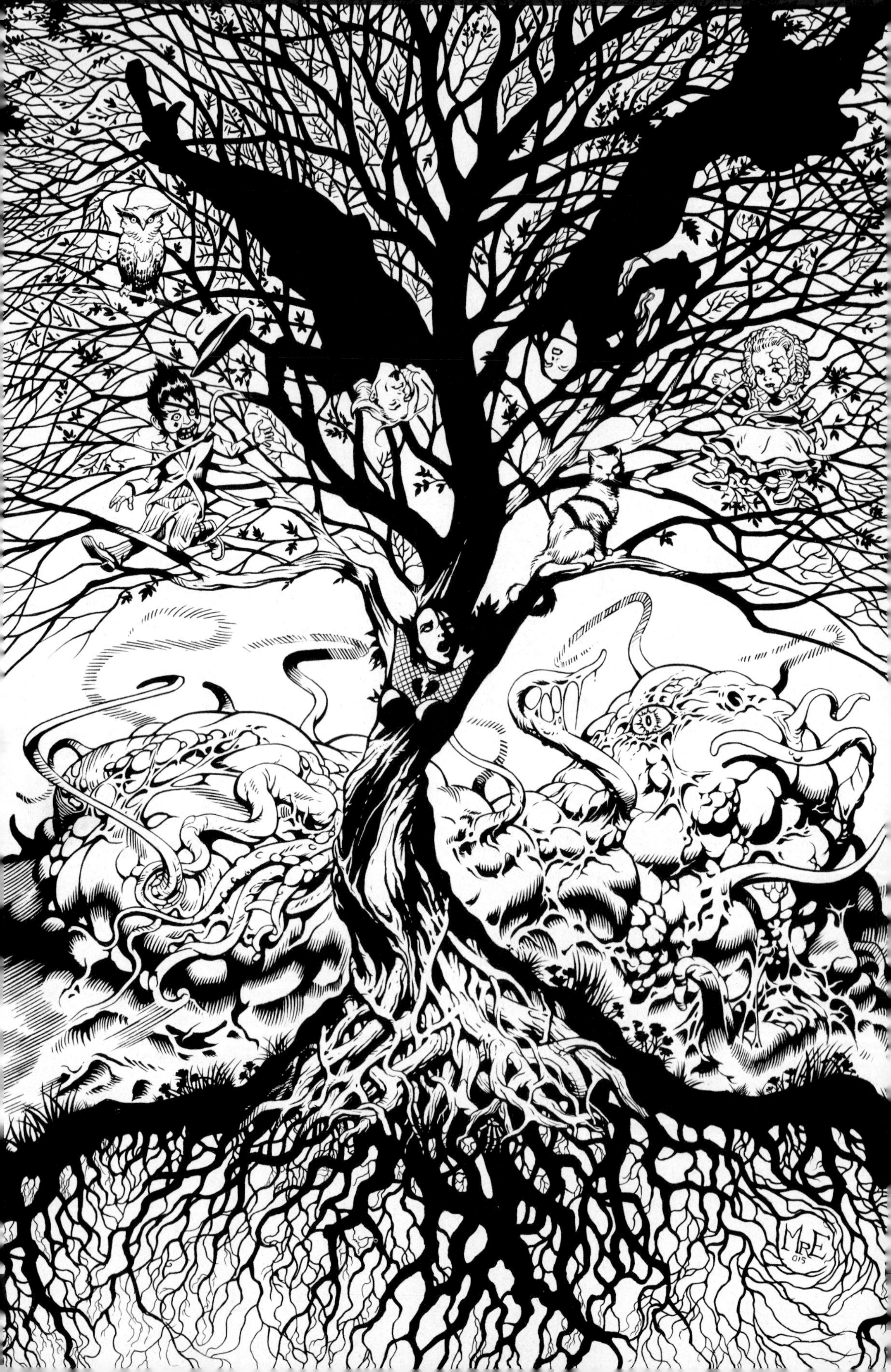

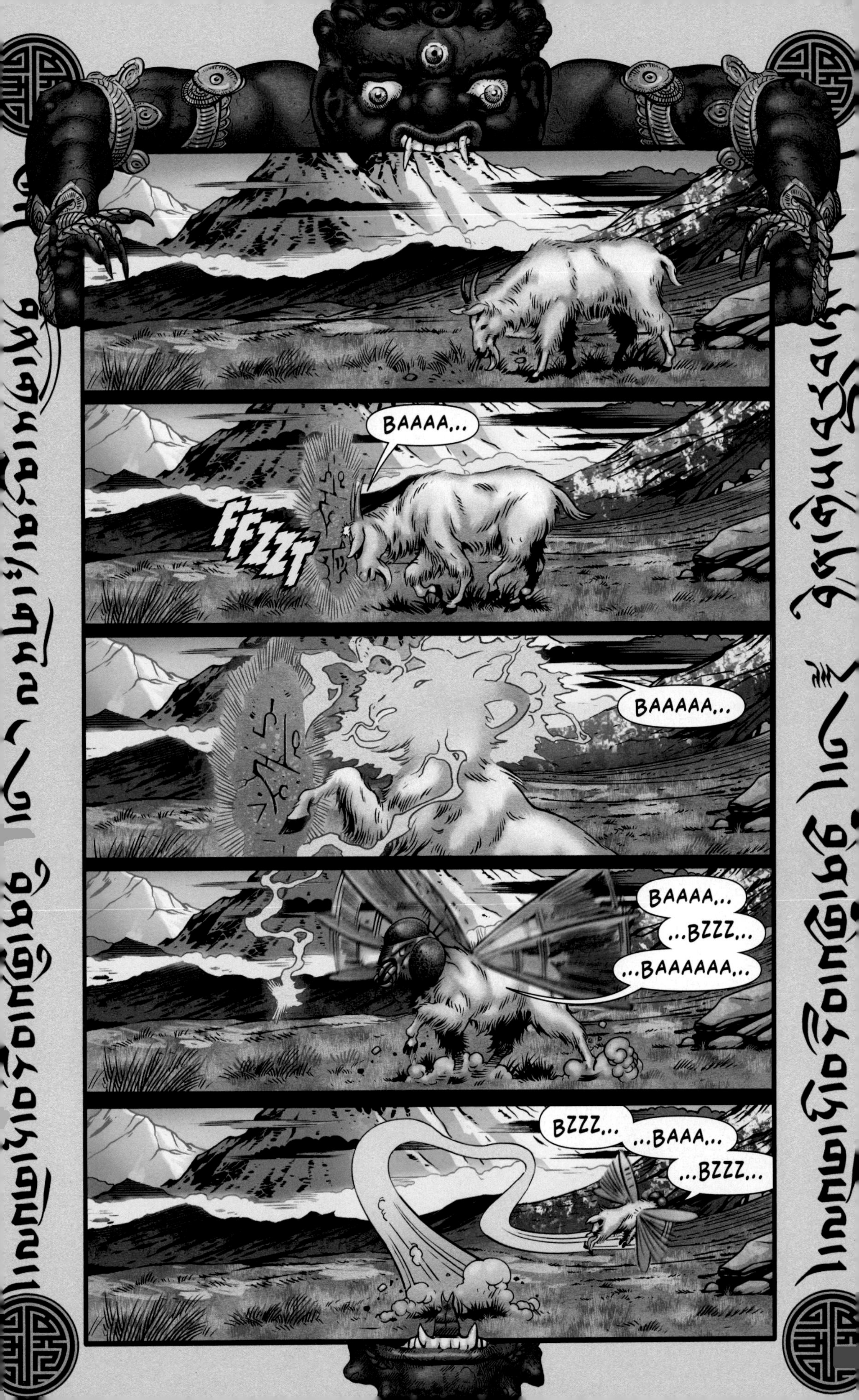
BAAAA...
FFZZZT
BAAAAA...
BAAAA...
...BZZZ...
...BAAAAAA...
BZZZ...
...BAAA...
...BZZZ...

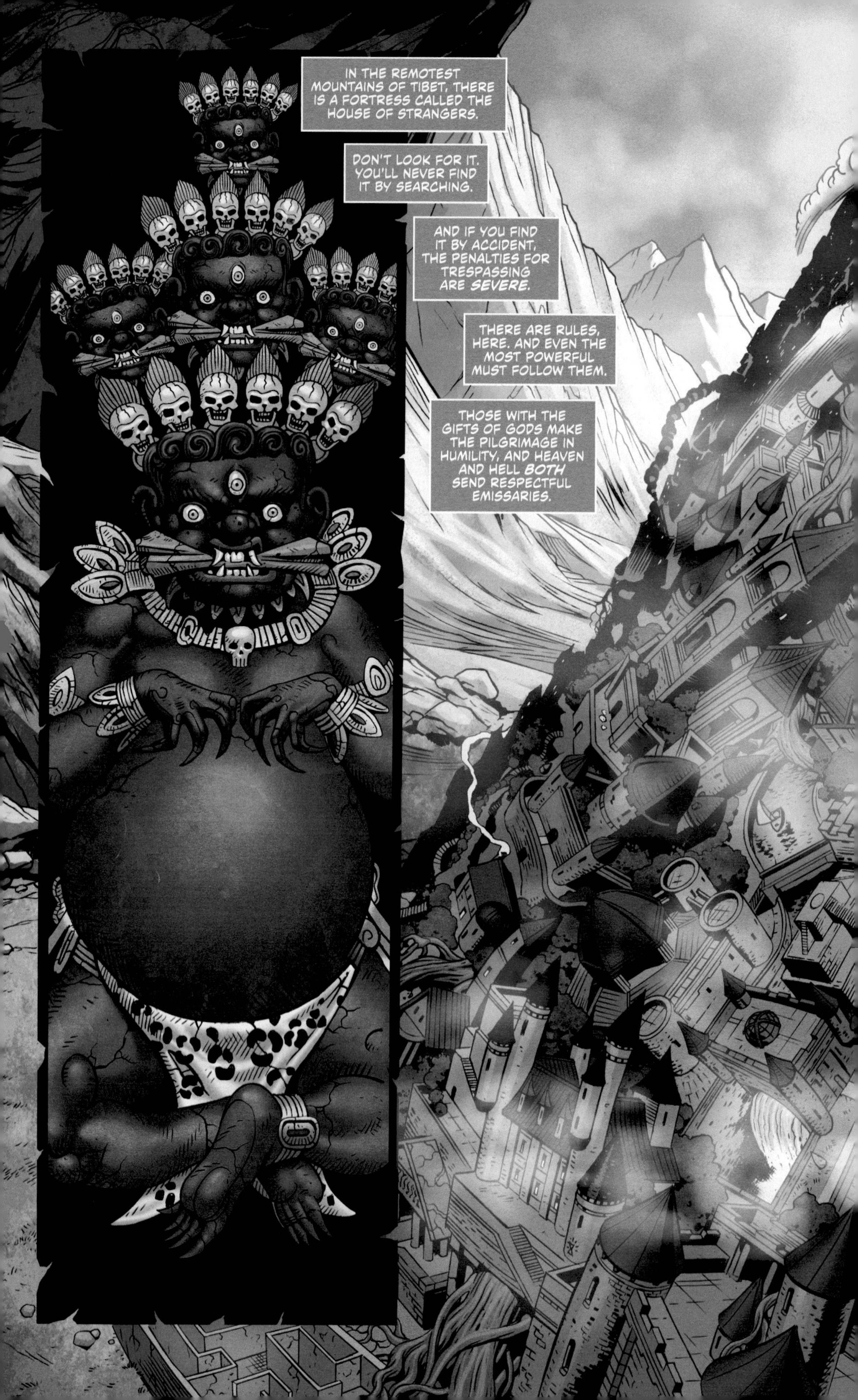
IN THE REMOTEST MOUNTAINS OF TIBET, THERE IS A FORTRESS CALLED THE HOUSE OF STRANGERS.
DON'T LOOK FOR IT. YOU'LL NEVER FIND IT BY SEARCHING.
AND IF YOU FIND IT BY ACCIDENT, THE PENALTIES FOR TRESPASSING ARE *SEVERE*.
THERE ARE RULES, HERE. AND EVEN THE MOST POWERFUL MUST FOLLOW THEM.
THOSE WITH THE GIFTS OF GODS MAKE THE PILGRIMAGE IN HUMILITY, AND HEAVEN AND HELL *BOTH* SEND RESPECTFUL EMISSARIES.

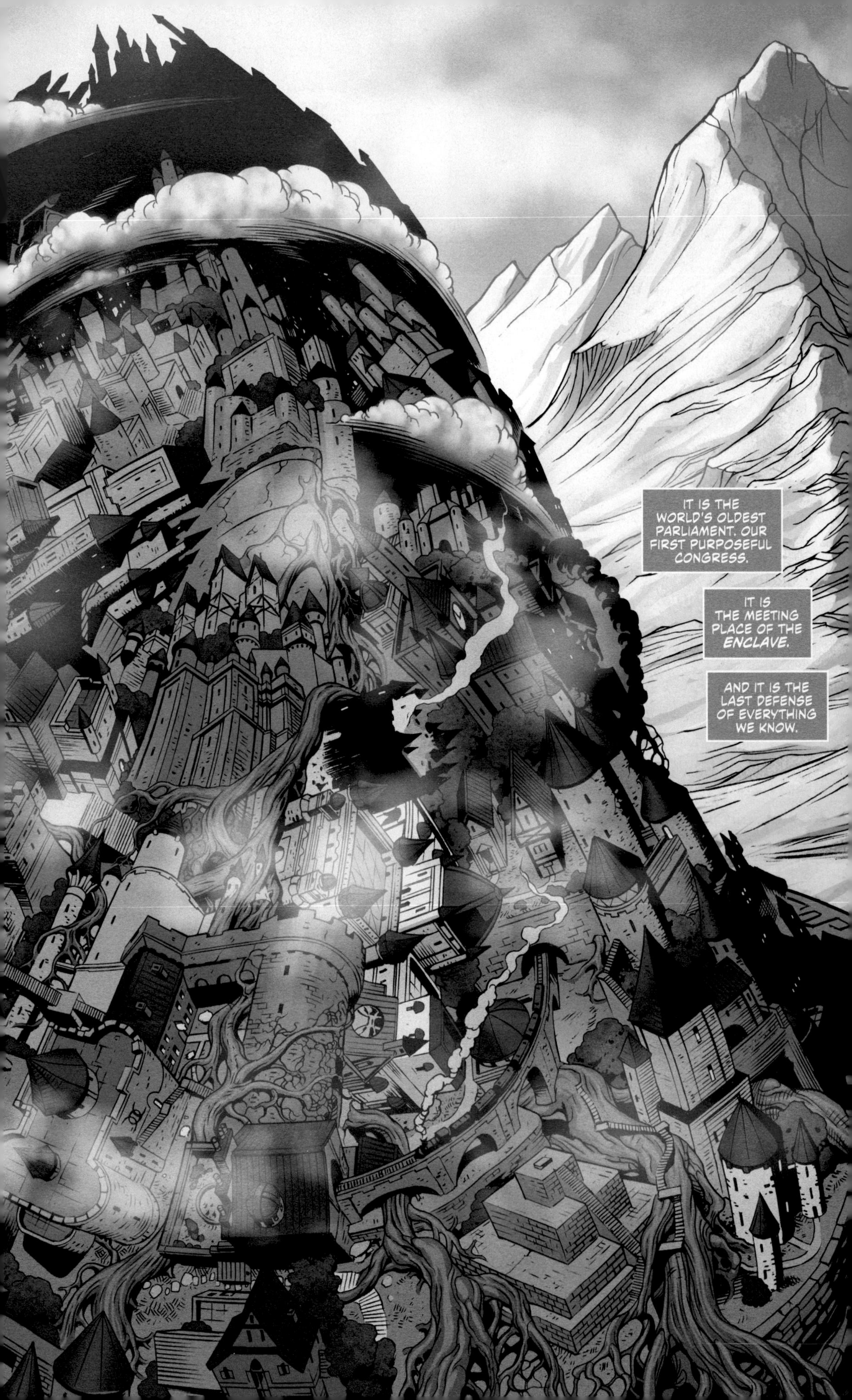
IT IS THE WORLD'S OLDEST PARLIAMENT. OUR FIRST PURPOSEFUL CONGRESS.
IT IS THE MEETING PLACE OF THE *ENCLAVE*.
AND IT IS THE LAST DEFENSE OF EVERYTHING WE KNOW.

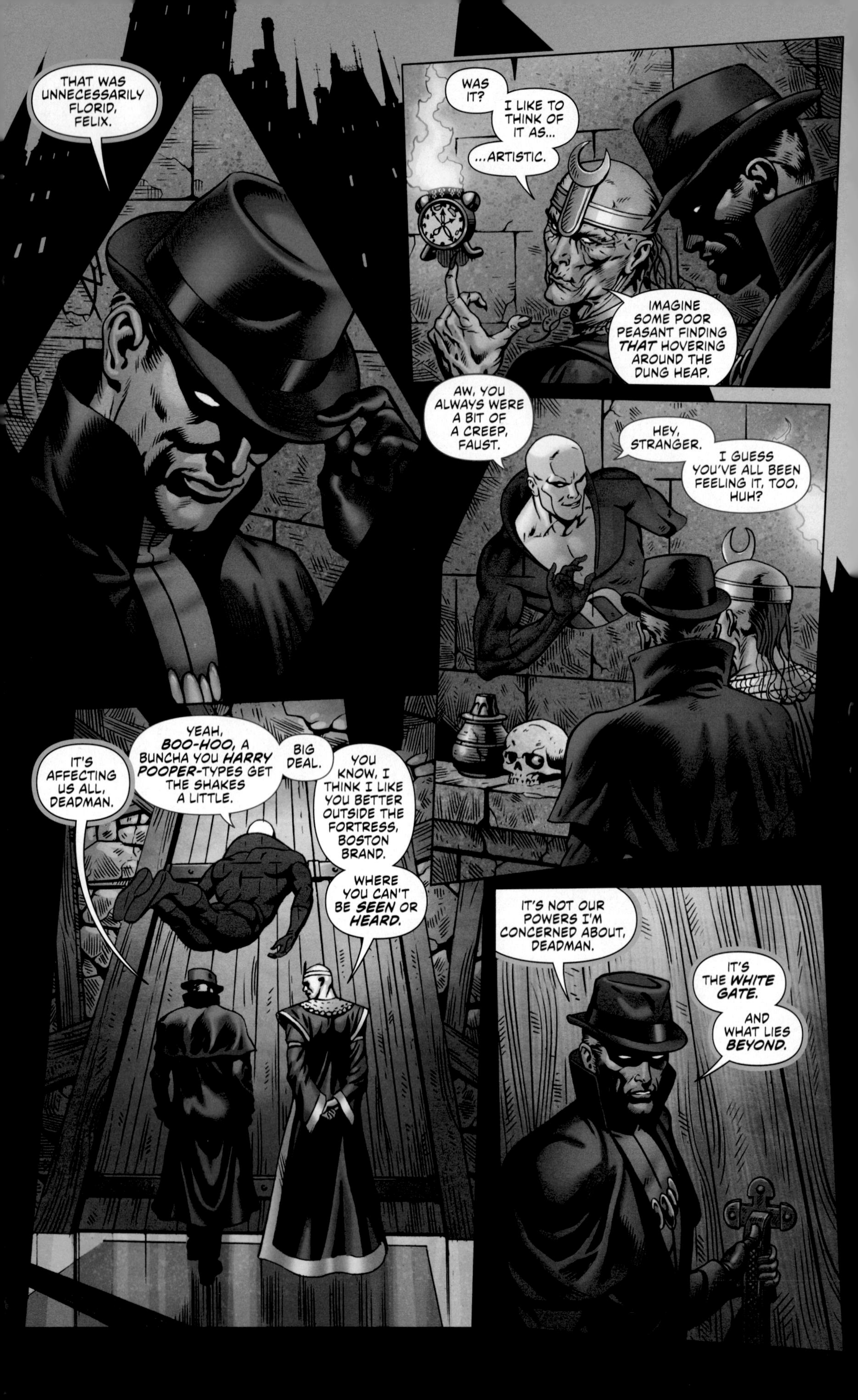
THAT WAS UNNECESSARILY FLORID, FELIX.
WAS IT?
I LIKE TO THINK OF IT AS...
...ARTISTIC.
IMAGINE SOME POOR PEASANT FINDING *THAT* HOVERING AROUND THE DUNG HEAP.
AW, YOU ALWAYS WERE A BIT OF A CREEP, FAUST.
HEY, STRANGER.
I GUESS YOU'VE ALL BEEN FEELING IT, TOO, HUH?
IT'S AFFECTING US ALL, DEADMAN.
YEAH, *BOO-HOO*, A BUNCHA YOU *HARRY POOPER*-TYPES GET THE SHAKES A LITTLE.
BIG DEAL.
YOU KNOW, I THINK I LIKE YOU BETTER OUTSIDE THE FORTRESS, BOSTON BRAND.
WHERE YOU CAN'T BE *SEEN* OR *HEARD.*
IT'S NOT OUR POWERS I'M CONCERNED ABOUT, DEADMAN.
IT'S THE *WHITE GATE.*
AND WHAT LIES *BEYOND.*

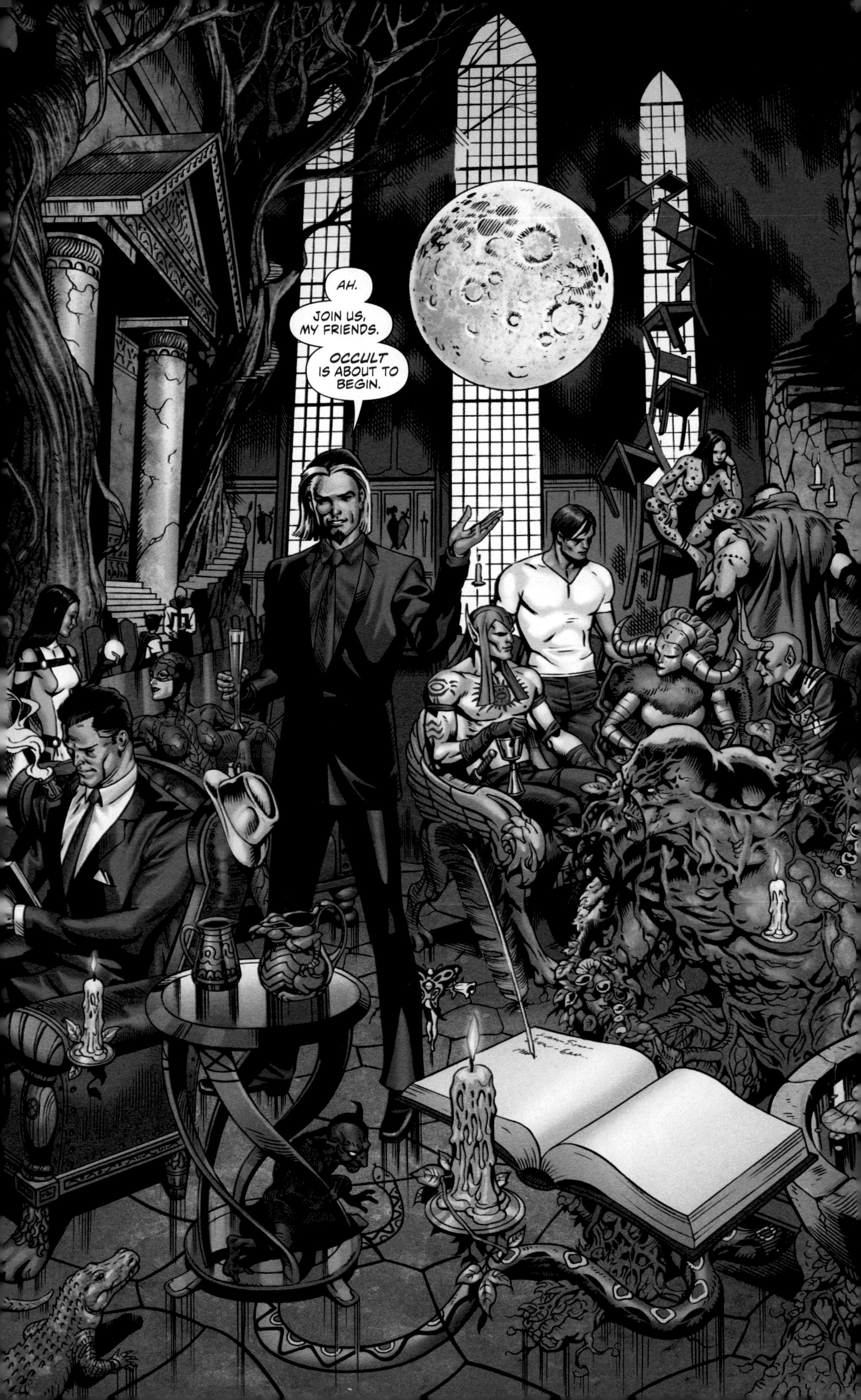
AH.
JOIN US, MY FRIENDS.
OCCULT IS ABOUT TO BEGIN.

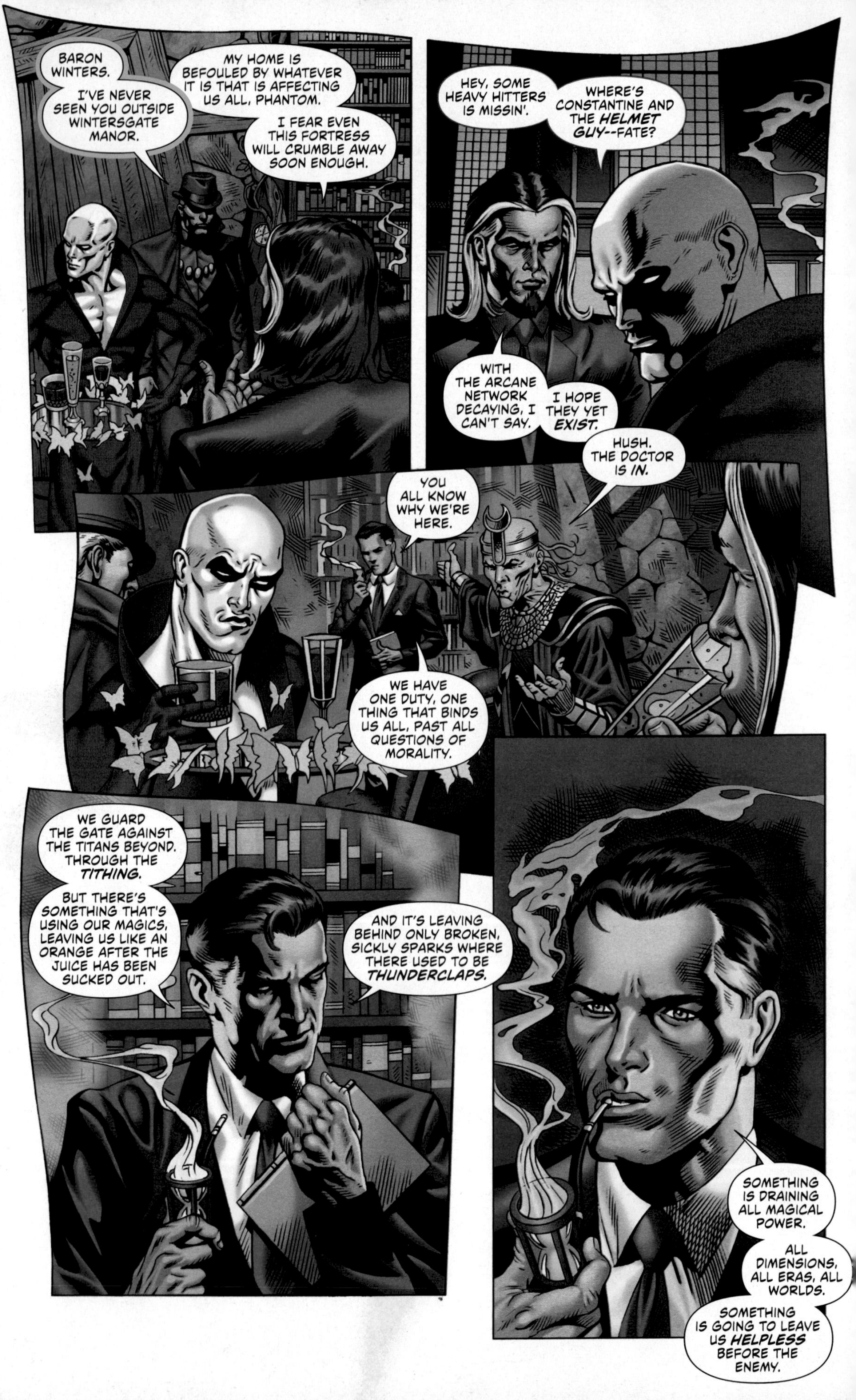
BARON WINTERS.
I'VE NEVER SEEN YOU OUTSIDE WINTERSGATE MANOR.
MY HOME IS BEFOULED BY WHATEVER IT IS THAT IS AFFECTING US ALL, PHANTOM.
I FEAR EVEN THIS FORTRESS WILL CRUMBLE AWAY SOON ENOUGH.
HEY, SOME HEAVY HITTERS IS MISSIN'.
WHERE'S CONSTANTINE AND THE HELMET GUY--FATE?
WITH THE ARCANE NETWORK DECAYING, I CAN'T SAY.
I HOPE THEY YET EXIST.
HUSH. THE DOCTOR IS IN.
YOU ALL KNOW WHY WE'RE HERE.
WE HAVE ONE DUTY, ONE THING THAT BINDS US ALL, PAST ALL QUESTIONS OF MORALITY.
WE GUARD THE GATE AGAINST THE TITANS BEYOND. THROUGH THE TITHING.
BUT THERE'S SOMETHING THAT'S USING OUR MAGICS, LEAVING US LIKE AN ORANGE AFTER THE JUICE HAS BEEN SUCKED OUT.
AND IT'S LEAVING BEHIND ONLY BROKEN, SICKLY SPARKS WHERE THERE USED TO BE THUNDERCLAPS.
SOMETHING IS DRAINING ALL MAGICAL POWER.
ALL DIMENSIONS, ALL ERAS, ALL WORLDS.
SOMETHING IS GOING TO LEAVE US HELPLESS BEFORE THE ENEMY.

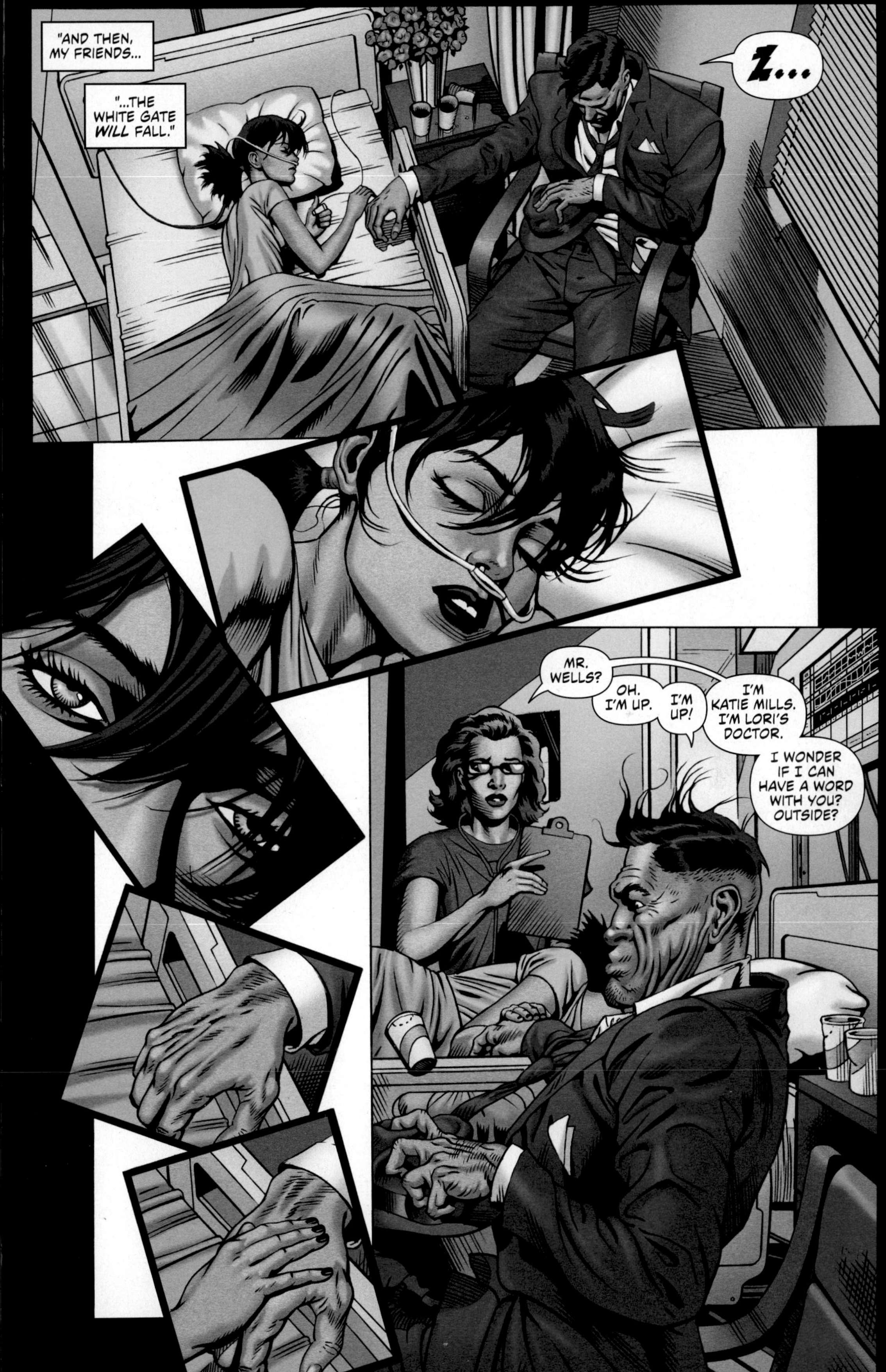

"AND THEN, MY FRIENDS...
"...THE WHITE GATE WILL FALL."
Z...
MR. WELLS?
OH. I'M UP.
I'M UP!
I'M KATIE MILLS. I'M LORI'S DOCTOR.
I WONDER IF I CAN HAVE A WORD WITH YOU? OUTSIDE?

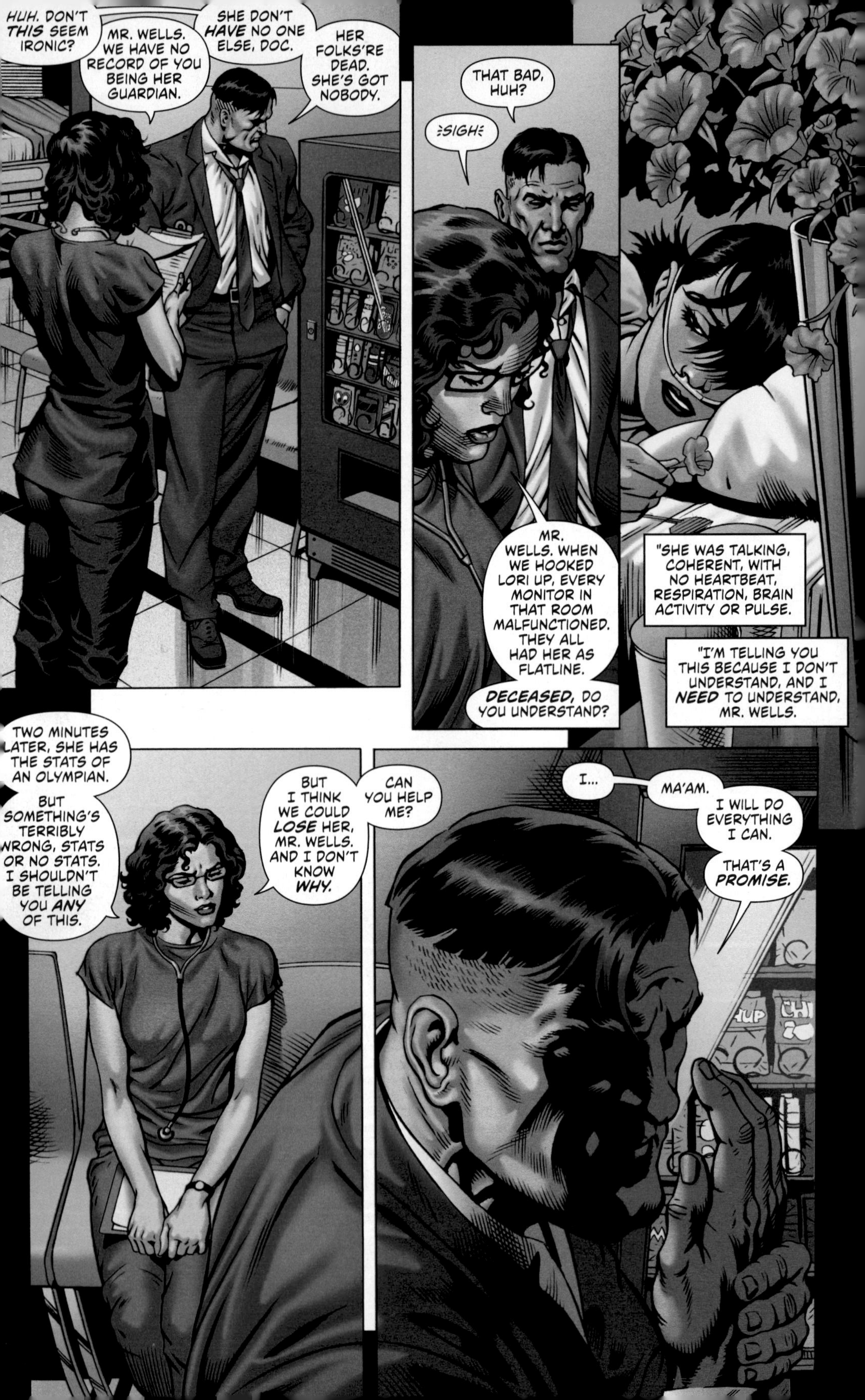
HUH. DON'T THIS SEEM IRONIC?
MR. WELLS. WE HAVE NO RECORD OF YOU BEING HER GUARDIAN.
SHE DON'T HAVE NO ONE ELSE, DOC.
HER FOLKS'RE DEAD. SHE'S GOT NOBODY.
THAT BAD, HUH?
SIGH
MR. WELLS. WHEN WE HOOKED LORI UP, EVERY MONITOR IN THAT ROOM MALFUNCTIONED. THEY ALL HAD HER AS FLATLINE.
DECEASED, DO YOU UNDERSTAND?
"SHE WAS TALKING, COHERENT, WITH NO HEARTBEAT, RESPIRATION, BRAIN ACTIVITY OR PULSE.
"I'M TELLING YOU THIS BECAUSE I DON'T UNDERSTAND, AND I NEED TO UNDERSTAND, MR. WELLS.
TWO MINUTES LATER, SHE HAS THE STATS OF AN OLYMPIAN.
BUT SOMETHING'S TERRIBLY WRONG, STATS OR NO STATS. I SHOULDN'T BE TELLING YOU ANY OF THIS.
BUT I THINK WE COULD LOSE HER, MR. WELLS. AND I DON'T KNOW WHY.
CAN YOU HELP ME?
I...
MA'AM.
I WILL DO EVERYTHING I CAN.
THAT'S A PROMISE.

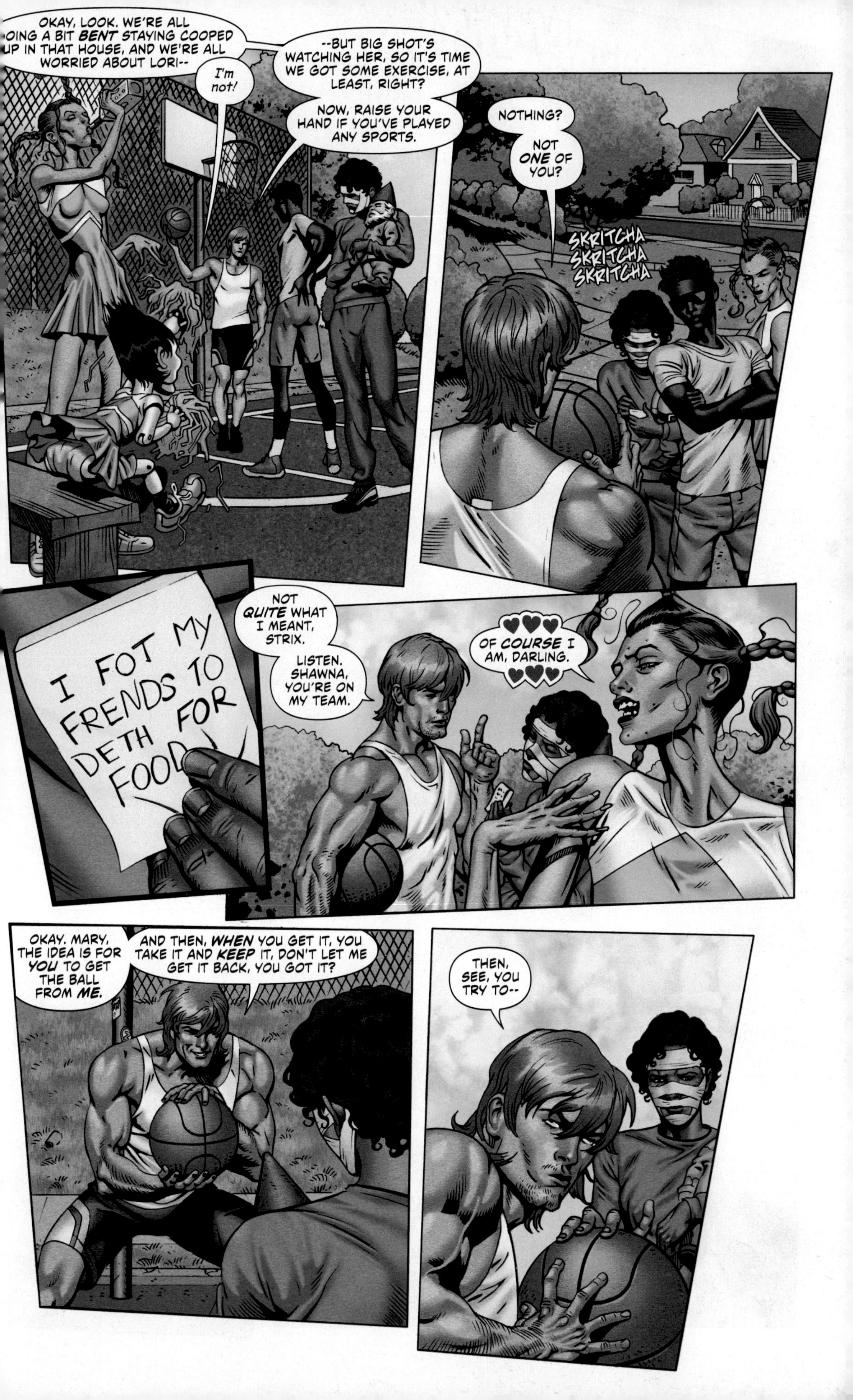
OKAY, LOOK. WE'RE ALL GOING A BIT BENT STAYING COOPED UP IN THAT HOUSE, AND WE'RE ALL WORRIED ABOUT LORI--
I'm not!
--BUT BIG SHOT'S WATCHING HER, SO IT'S TIME WE GOT SOME EXERCISE, AT LEAST, RIGHT?
NOW, RAISE YOUR HAND IF YOU'VE PLAYED ANY SPORTS.
NOTHING?
NOT ONE OF YOU?
SKRITCHA SKRITCHA SKRITCHA
I FOT MY FRENDS TO DETH FOR FOOD
NOT QUITE WHAT I MEANT, STRIX.
LISTEN. SHAWNA, YOU'RE ON MY TEAM.
OF COURSE I AM, DARLING.
OKAY. MARY, THE IDEA IS FOR YOU TO GET THE BALL FROM ME.
AND THEN, WHEN YOU GET IT, YOU TAKE IT AND KEEP IT, DON'T LET ME GET IT BACK, YOU GOT IT?
THEN, SEE, YOU TRY TO--

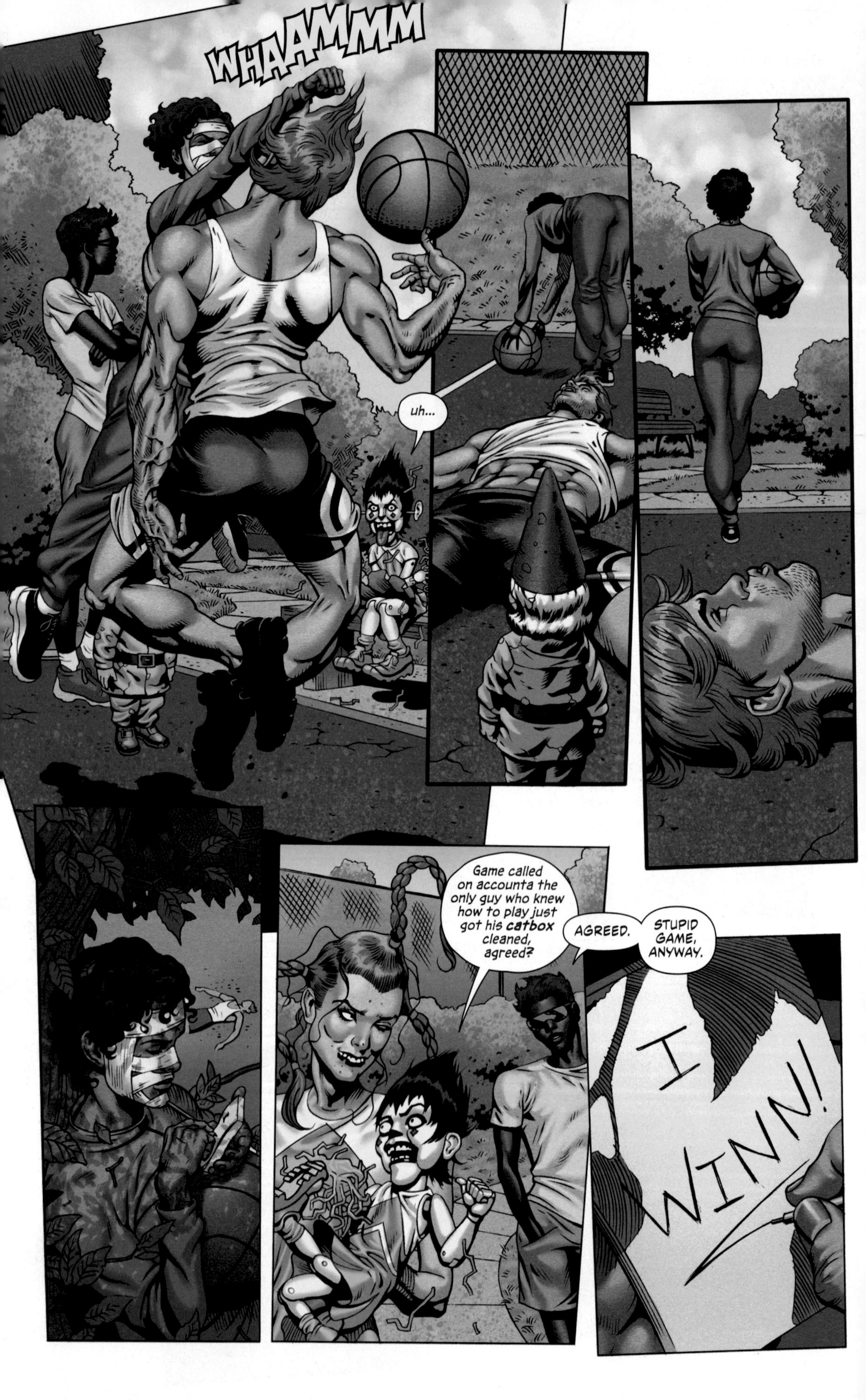
WHAAMMM
uh...
Game called on accounta the only guy who knew how to play just got his catbox cleaned, agreed?
AGREED.
STUPID GAME, ANYWAY.
I WINN!

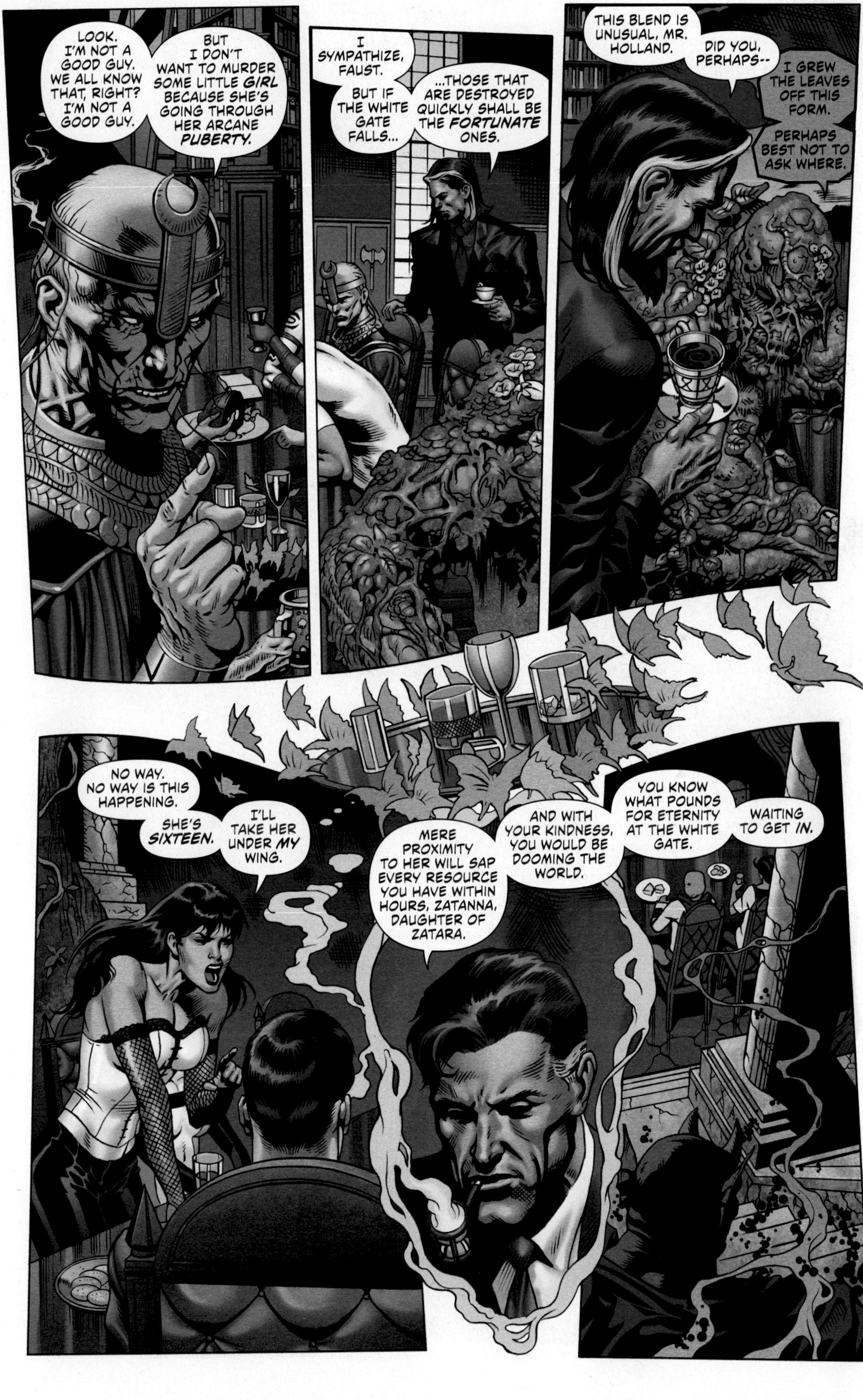
LOOK. I'M NOT A GOOD GUY. WE ALL KNOW THAT, RIGHT? I'M NOT A GOOD GUY.
BUT I DON'T WANT TO MURDER SOME LITTLE GIRL BECAUSE SHE'S GOING THROUGH HER ARCANE PUBERTY.
I SYMPATHIZE, FAUST.
BUT IF THE WHITE GATE FALLS...
...THOSE THAT ARE DESTROYED QUICKLY SHALL BE THE FORTUNATE ONES.
THIS BLEND IS UNUSUAL, MR. HOLLAND.
DID YOU, PERHAPS--
I GREW THE LEAVES OFF THIS FORM.
PERHAPS BEST NOT TO ASK WHERE.
NO WAY. NO WAY IS THIS HAPPENING.
SHE'S SIXTEEN.
I'LL TAKE HER UNDER MY WING.
MERE PROXIMITY TO HER WILL SAP EVERY RESOURCE YOU HAVE WITHIN HOURS, ZATANNA, DAUGHTER OF ZATARA.
AND WITH YOUR KINDNESS, YOU WOULD BE DOOMING THE WORLD.
YOU KNOW WHAT POUNDS FOR ETERNITY AT THE WHITE GATE.
WAITING TO GET IN.

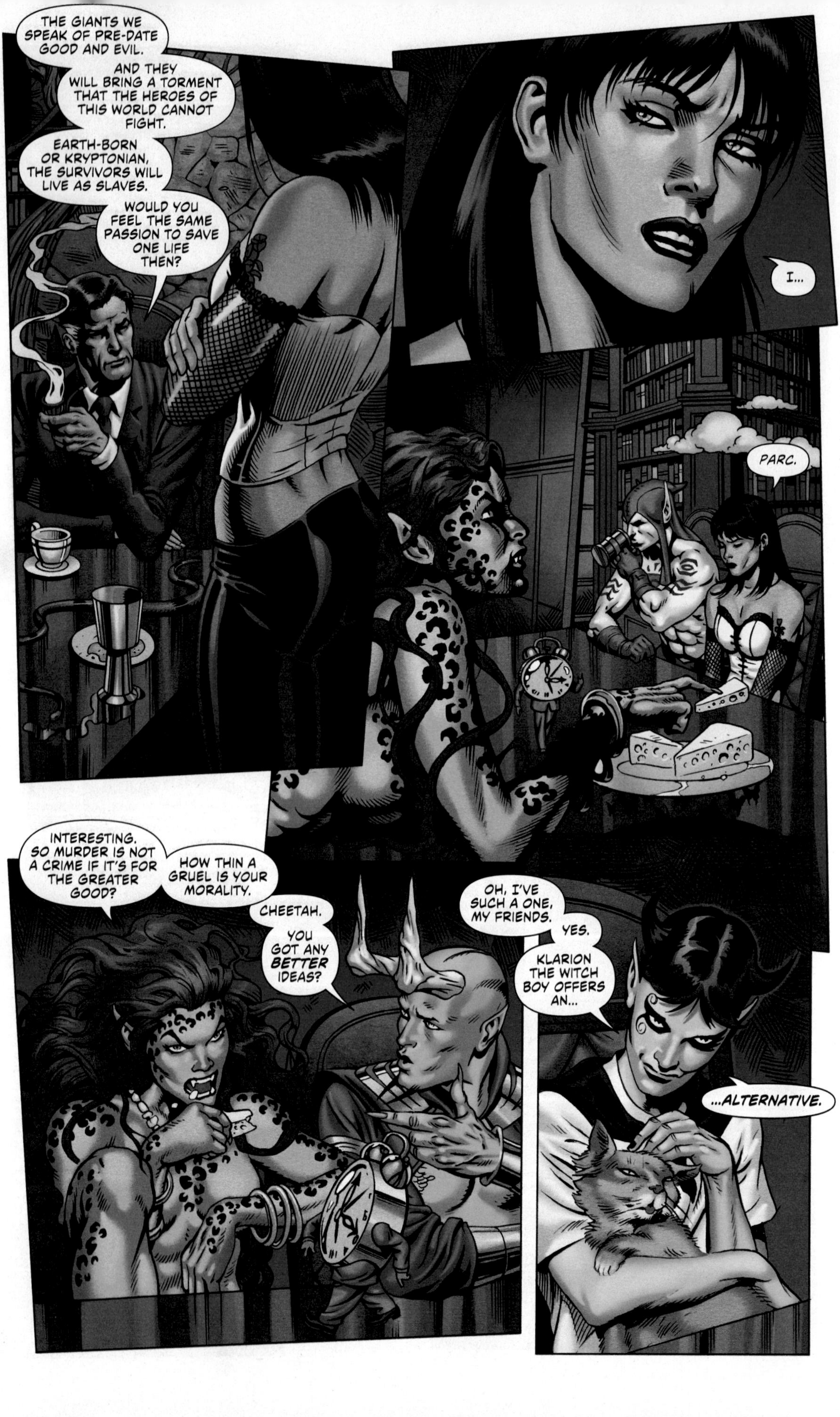
THE GIANTS WE SPEAK OF PRE-DATE GOOD AND EVIL.
AND THEY WILL BRING A TORMENT THAT THE HEROES OF THIS WORLD CANNOT FIGHT.
EARTH-BORN OR KRYPTONIAN, THE SURVIVORS WILL LIVE AS SLAVES.
WOULD YOU FEEL THE SAME PASSION TO SAVE ONE LIFE THEN?
I...
PARC.
INTERESTING. SO MURDER IS NOT A CRIME IF IT'S FOR THE GREATER GOOD?
HOW THIN A GRUEL IS YOUR MORALITY.
CHEETAH.
YOU GOT ANY BETTER IDEAS?
OH, I'VE SUCH A ONE, MY FRIENDS.
YES.
KLARION THE WITCH BOY OFFERS AN...
...ALTERNATIVE.

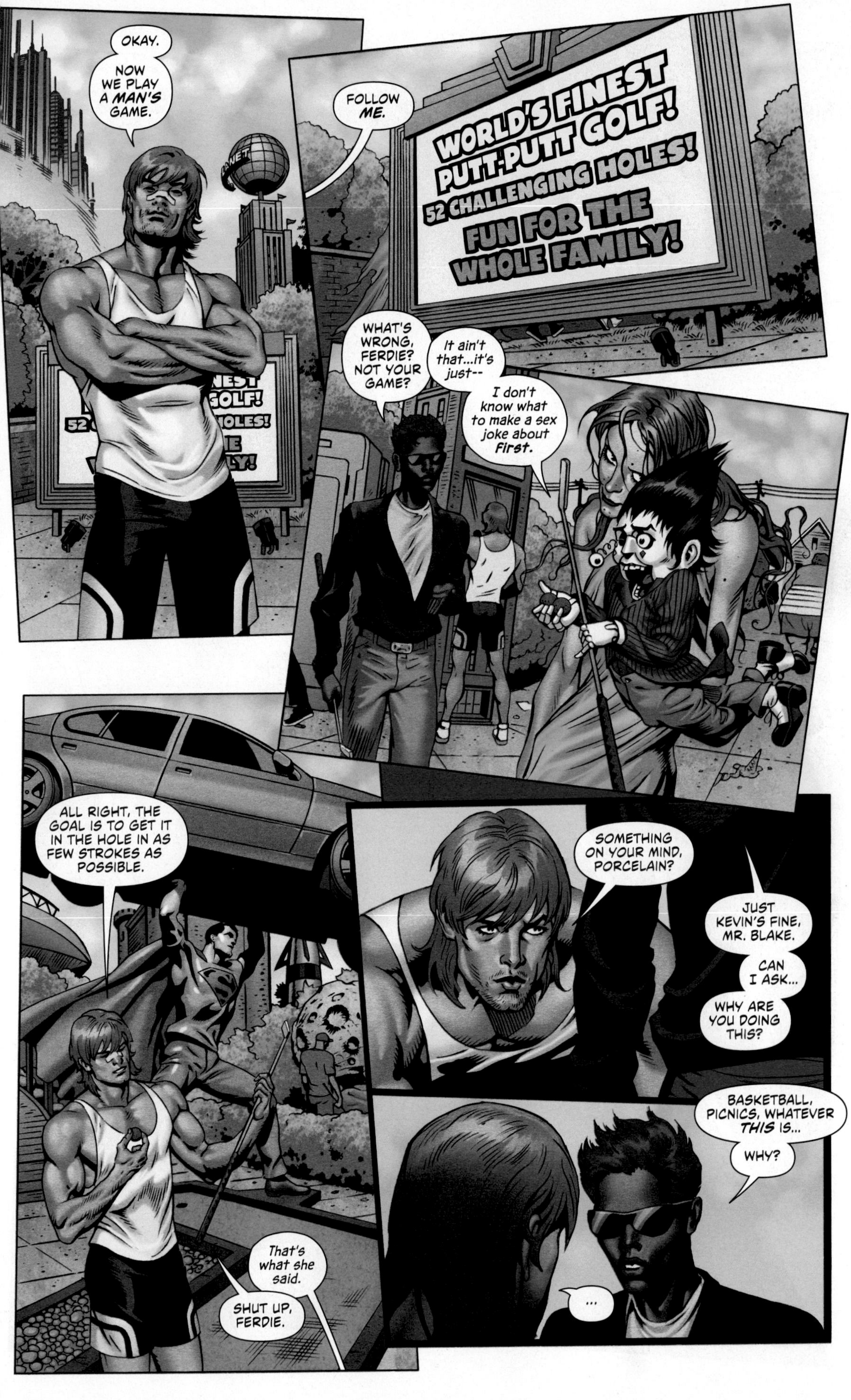
OKAY.
NOW WE PLAY A MAN'S GAME.
FOLLOW ME.
WORLD'S FINEST PUTT-PUTT GOLF! 52 CHALLENGING HOLES! FUN FOR THE WHOLE FAMILY!
WHAT'S WRONG, FERDIE? NOT YOUR GAME?
It ain't that...it's just--
I don't know what to make a sex joke about first.
ALL RIGHT, THE GOAL IS TO GET IT IN THE HOLE IN AS FEW STROKES AS POSSIBLE.
That's what she said.
SHUT UP, FERDIE.
SOMETHING ON YOUR MIND, PORCELAIN?
JUST KEVIN'S FINE, MR. BLAKE.
CAN I ASK...
WHY ARE YOU DOING THIS?
BASKETBALL, PICNICS, WHATEVER THIS IS...
WHY?
...

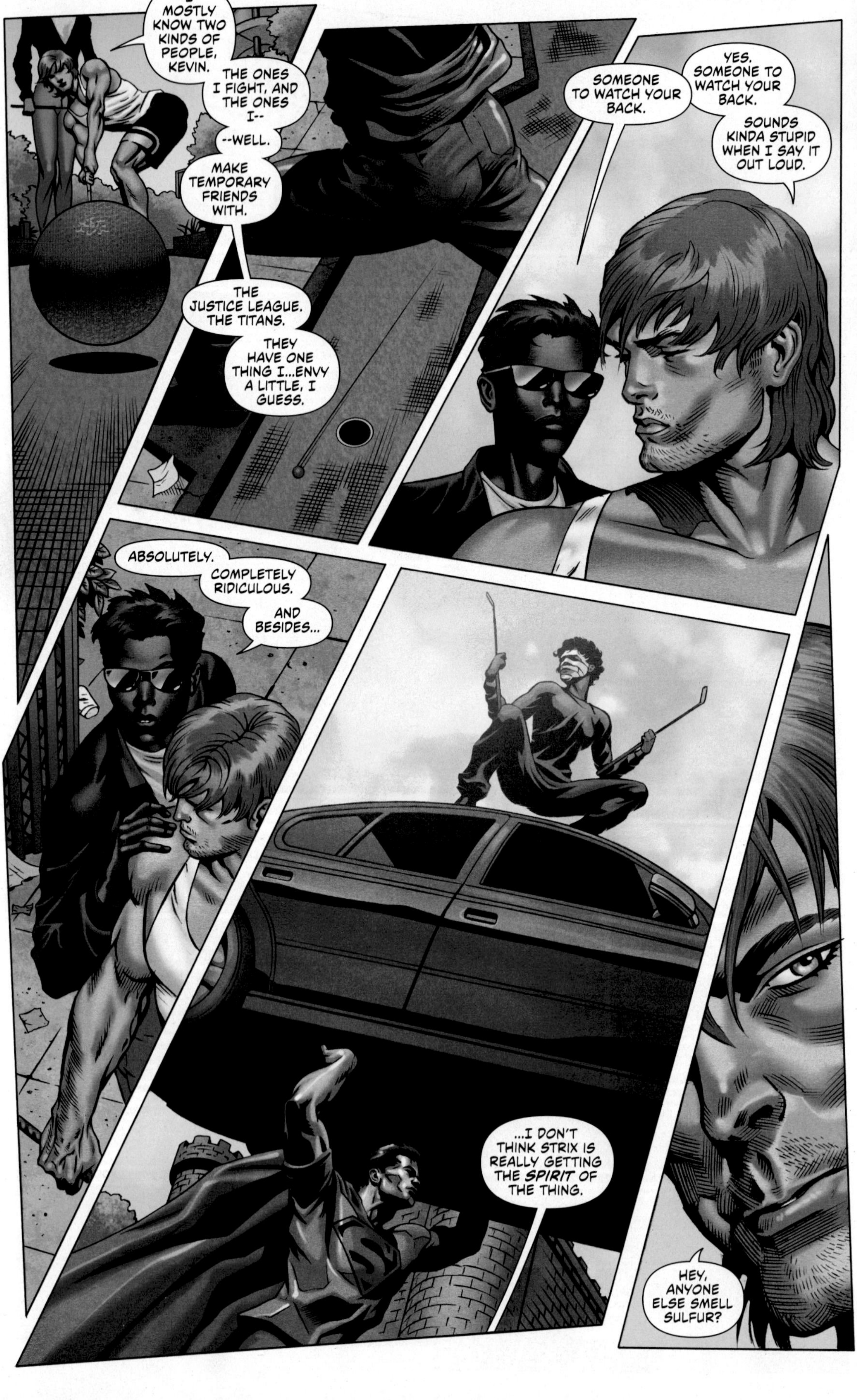

I MOSTLY KNOW TWO KINDS OF PEOPLE, KEVIN.
THE ONES I FIGHT, AND THE ONES I--
--WELL.
MAKE TEMPORARY FRIENDS WITH.
THE JUSTICE LEAGUE. THE TITANS.
THEY HAVE ONE THING I...ENVY A LITTLE, I GUESS.
SOMEONE TO WATCH YOUR BACK.
YES. SOMEONE TO WATCH YOUR BACK.
SOUNDS KINDA STUPID WHEN I SAY IT OUT LOUD.
ABSOLUTELY.
COMPLETELY RIDICULOUS.
AND BESIDES...
...I DON'T THINK STRIX IS REALLY GETTING THE *SPIRIT* OF THE THING.
HEY, ANYONE ELSE SMELL SULFUR?

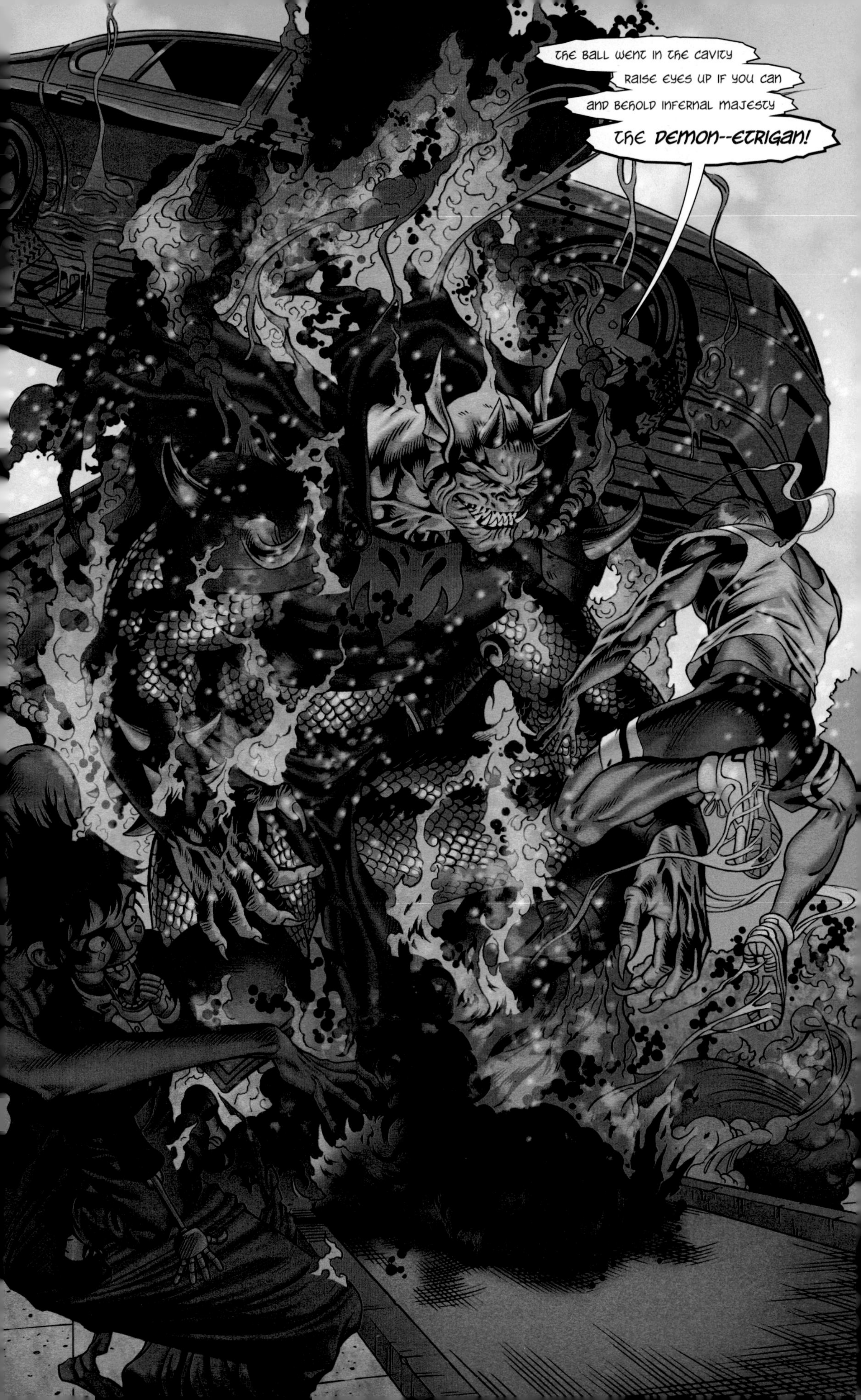
THE BALL WENT IN THE CAVITY
RAISE EYES UP IF YOU CAN
AND BEHOLD INFERNAL MAJESTY
THE DEMON--ETRIGAN!

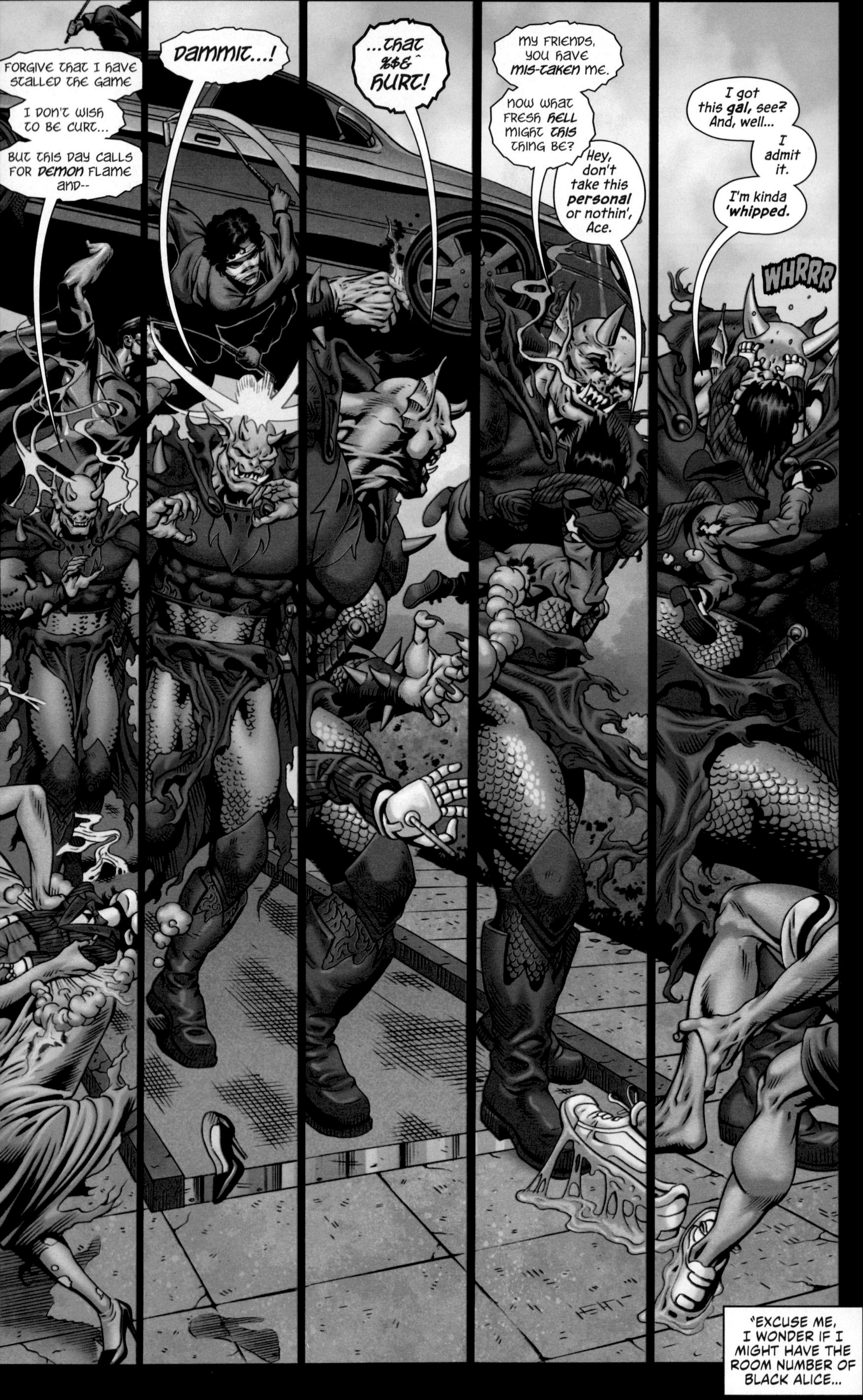
FORGIVE THAT I HAVE STALLED THE GAME
I DON'T WISH TO BE CURT...
BUT THIS DAY CALLS FOR DEMON FLAME AND--
DAMMIT...!
...THAT %$&^ HURT!
MY FRIENDS, YOU HAVE MIS-TAKEN ME.
NOW WHAT FRESH HELL MIGHT THIS THING BE?
Hey, don't take this personal or nothin', Ace.
I got this gal, see? And, well...
I admit it.
I'm kinda 'whipped.
WHRRR
"EXCUSE ME, I WONDER IF I MIGHT HAVE THE ROOM NUMBER OF BLACK ALICE...

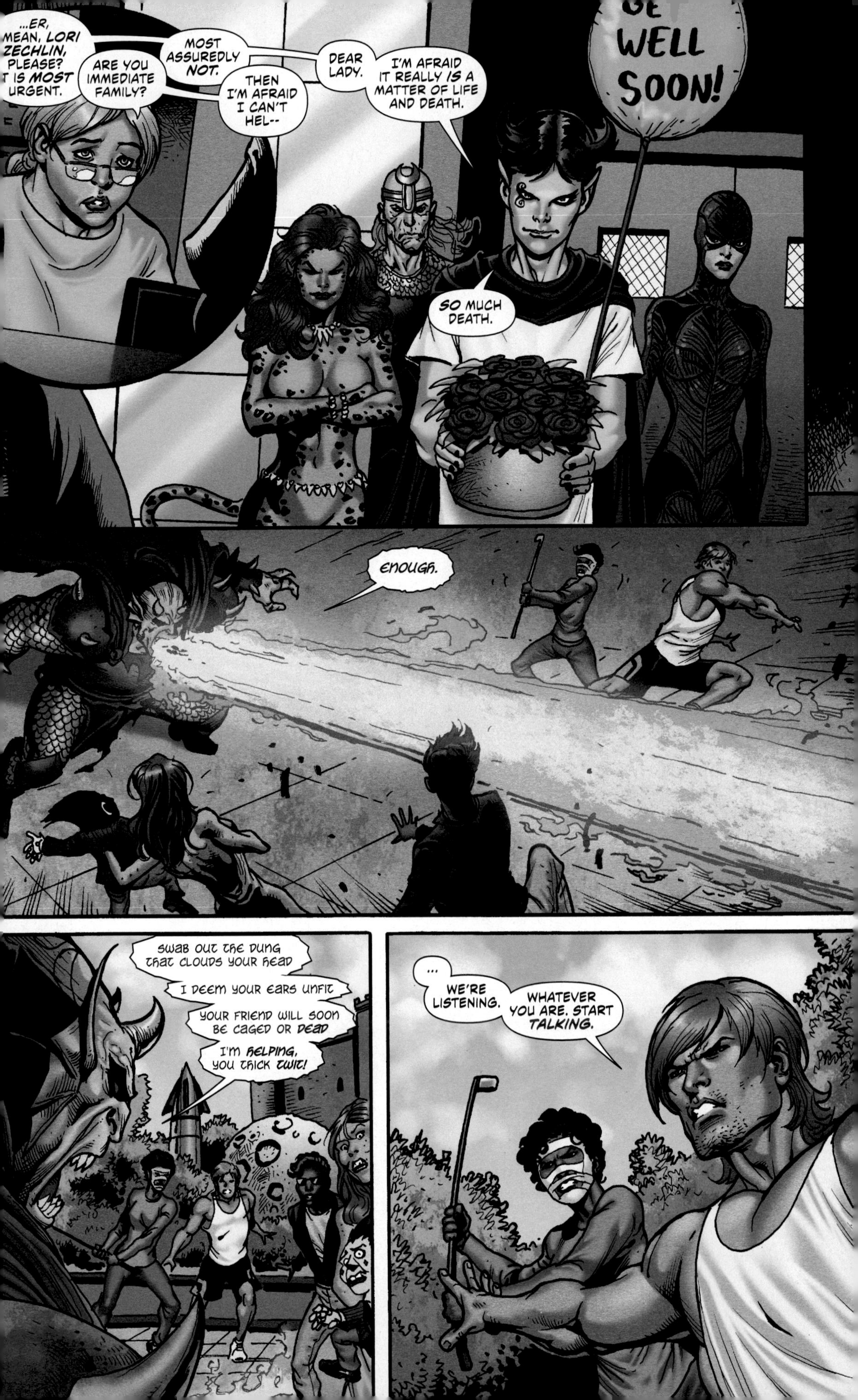
...ER,
MEAN, LORI
ZECHLIN,
PLEASE?
T IS MOST
URGENT.
ARE YOU IMMEDIATE FAMILY?
MOST ASSUREDLY NOT.
THEN I'M AFRAID I CAN'T HEL--
DEAR LADY.
I'M AFRAID IT REALLY IS A MATTER OF LIFE AND DEATH.
WELL SOON!
SO MUCH DEATH.
ENOUGH.
SWAB OUT THE DUNG THAT CLOUDS YOUR HEAD
I DEEM YOUR EARS UNFIT
YOUR FRIEND WILL SOON BE CAGED OR DEAD
I'M HELPING, YOU THICK TWIT!
...
WE'RE LISTENING.
WHATEVER YOU ARE. START TALKING.

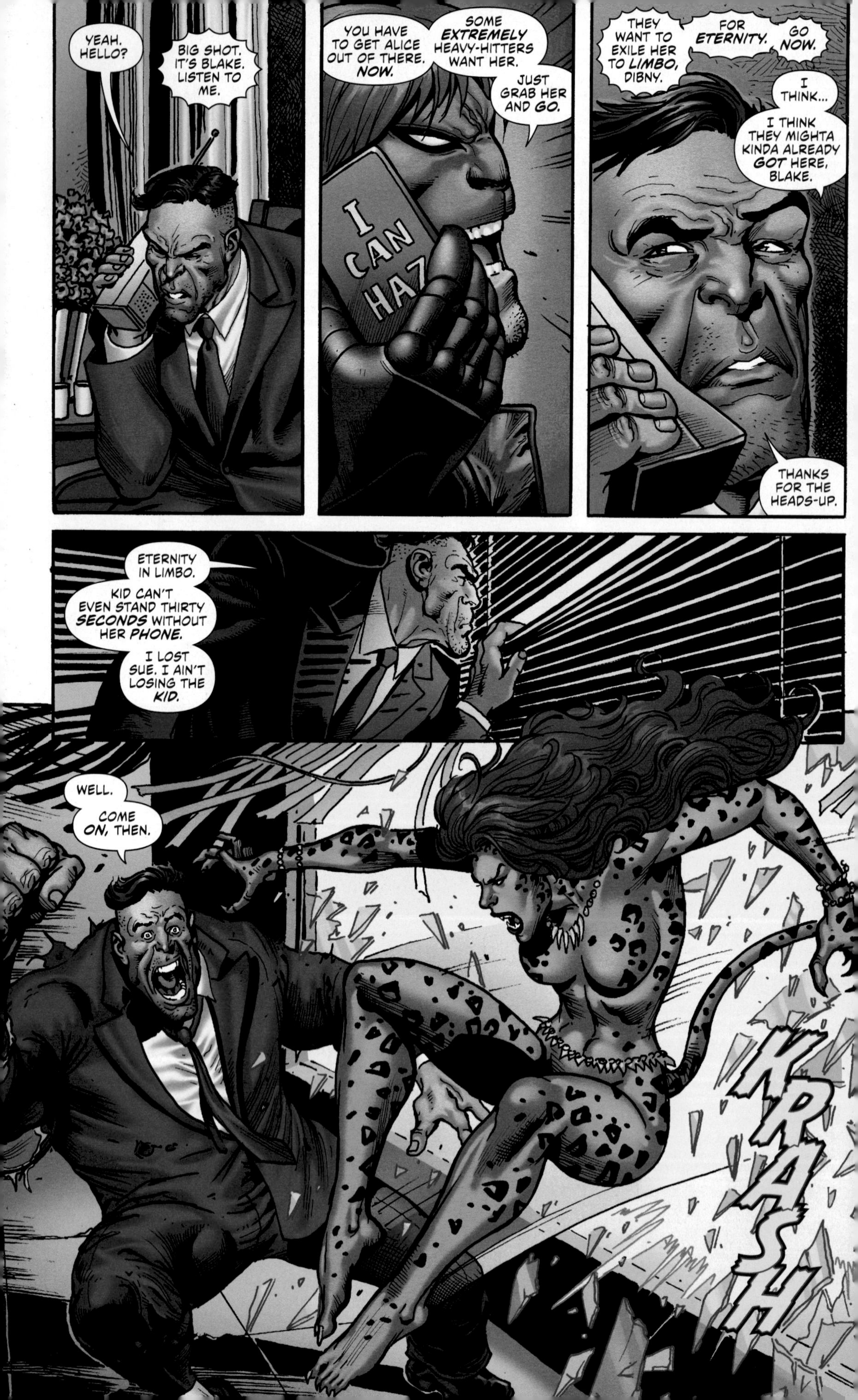
YEAH. HELLO?
BIG SHOT. IT'S BLAKE. LISTEN TO ME.
YOU HAVE TO GET ALICE OUT OF THERE. NOW.
SOME EXTREMELY HEAVY-HITTERS WANT HER.
JUST GRAB HER AND GO.
I CAN HAZ
THEY WANT TO EXILE HER TO LIMBO, DIBNY.
FOR ETERNITY.
GO NOW.
I THINK...
I THINK THEY MIGHTA KINDA ALREADY GOT HERE, BLAKE.
THANKS FOR THE HEADS-UP.
ETERNITY IN LIMBO.
KID CAN'T EVEN STAND THIRTY SECONDS WITHOUT HER PHONE.
I LOST SUE. I AIN'T LOSING THE KID.
WELL.
COME ON, THEN.
KRASH

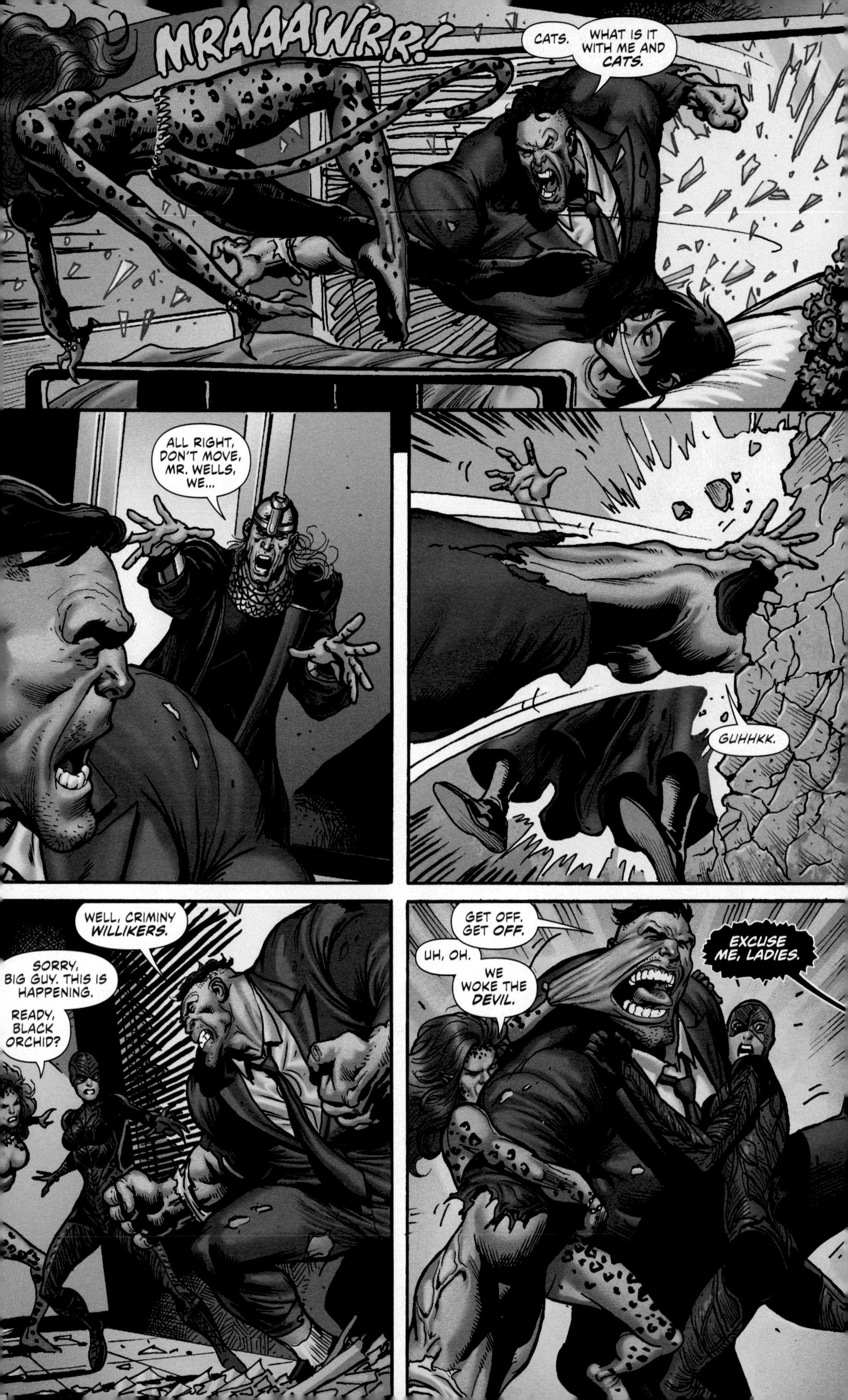
MRAAAWRR!
CATS.
WHAT IS IT WITH ME AND CATS.
ALL RIGHT, DON'T MOVE, MR. WELLS, WE...
GUHHKK.
WELL, CRIMINY WILLIKERS.
SORRY, BIG GUY. THIS IS HAPPENING.
READY, BLACK ORCHID?
GET OFF. GET OFF.
UH, OH.
WE WOKE THE DEVIL.
EXCUSE ME, LADIES.

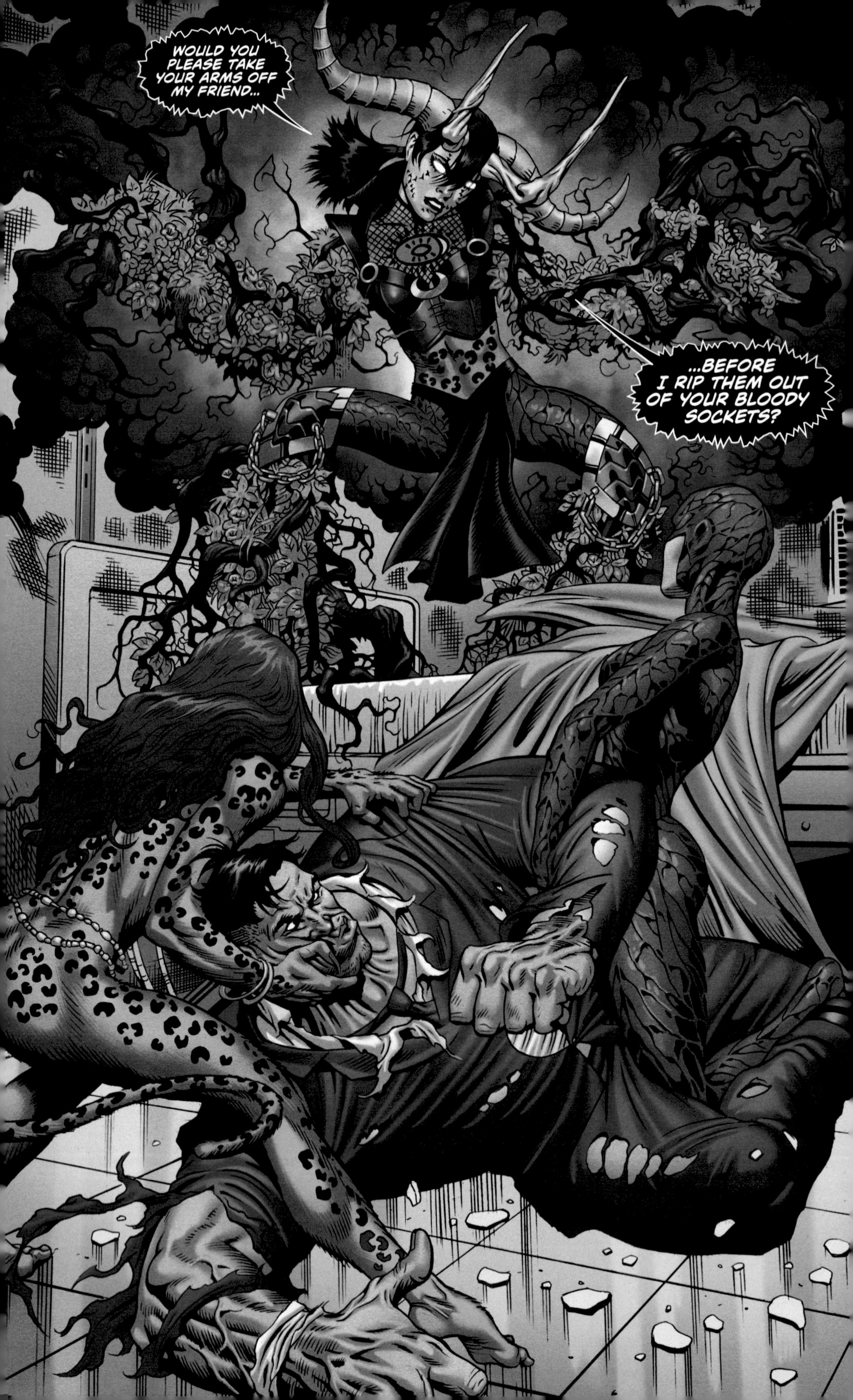
WOULD YOU PLEASE TAKE YOUR ARMS OFF MY FRIEND...
...BEFORE I RIP THEM OUT OF YOUR BLOODY SOCKETS?

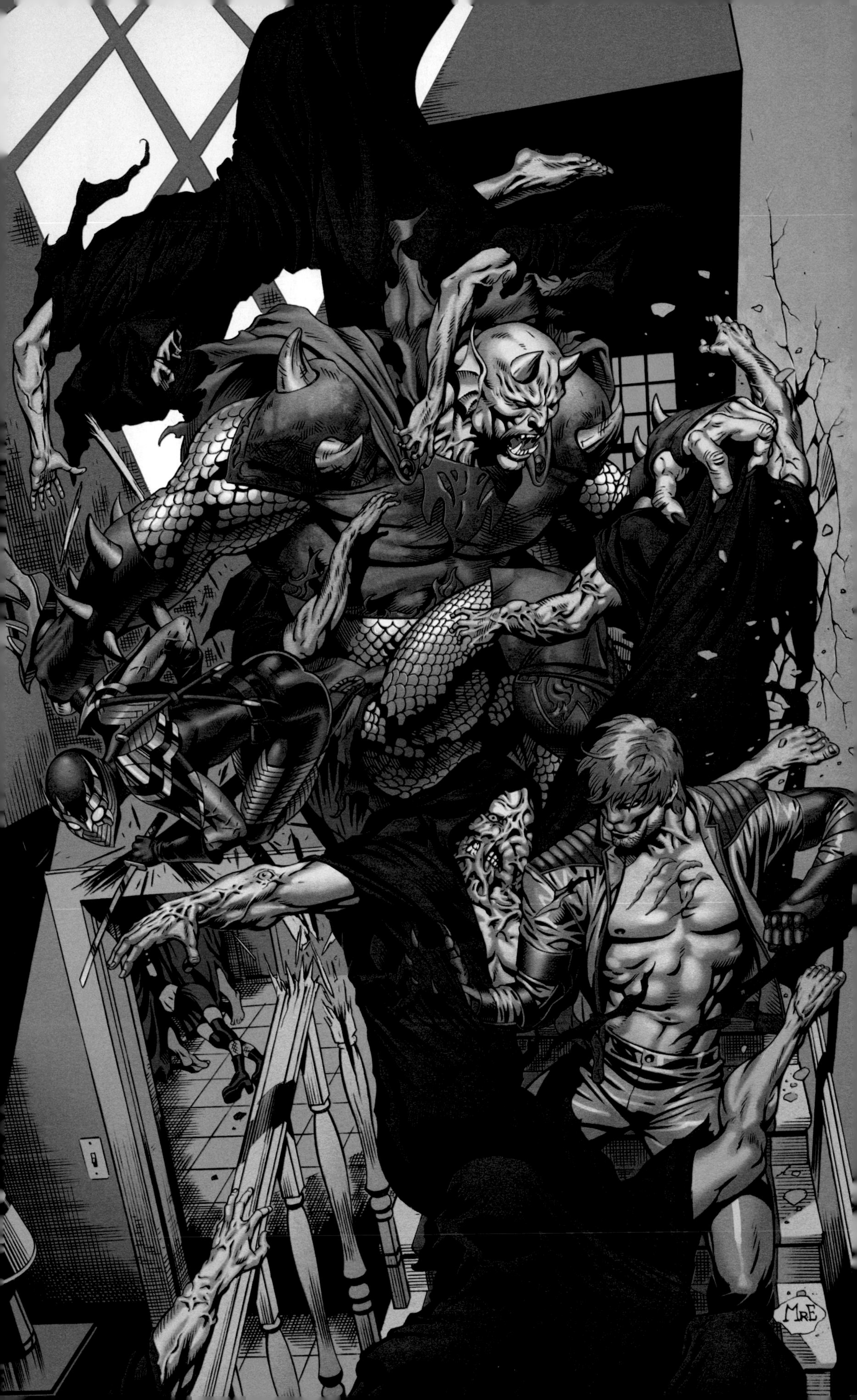

GAIL SIMONE writer DALE EAGLESHAM TOM DERENICK artists JASON WRIGHT colorist TRAVIS LANHAM letterer
cover by DALE EAGLESHAM & JASON WRIGHT

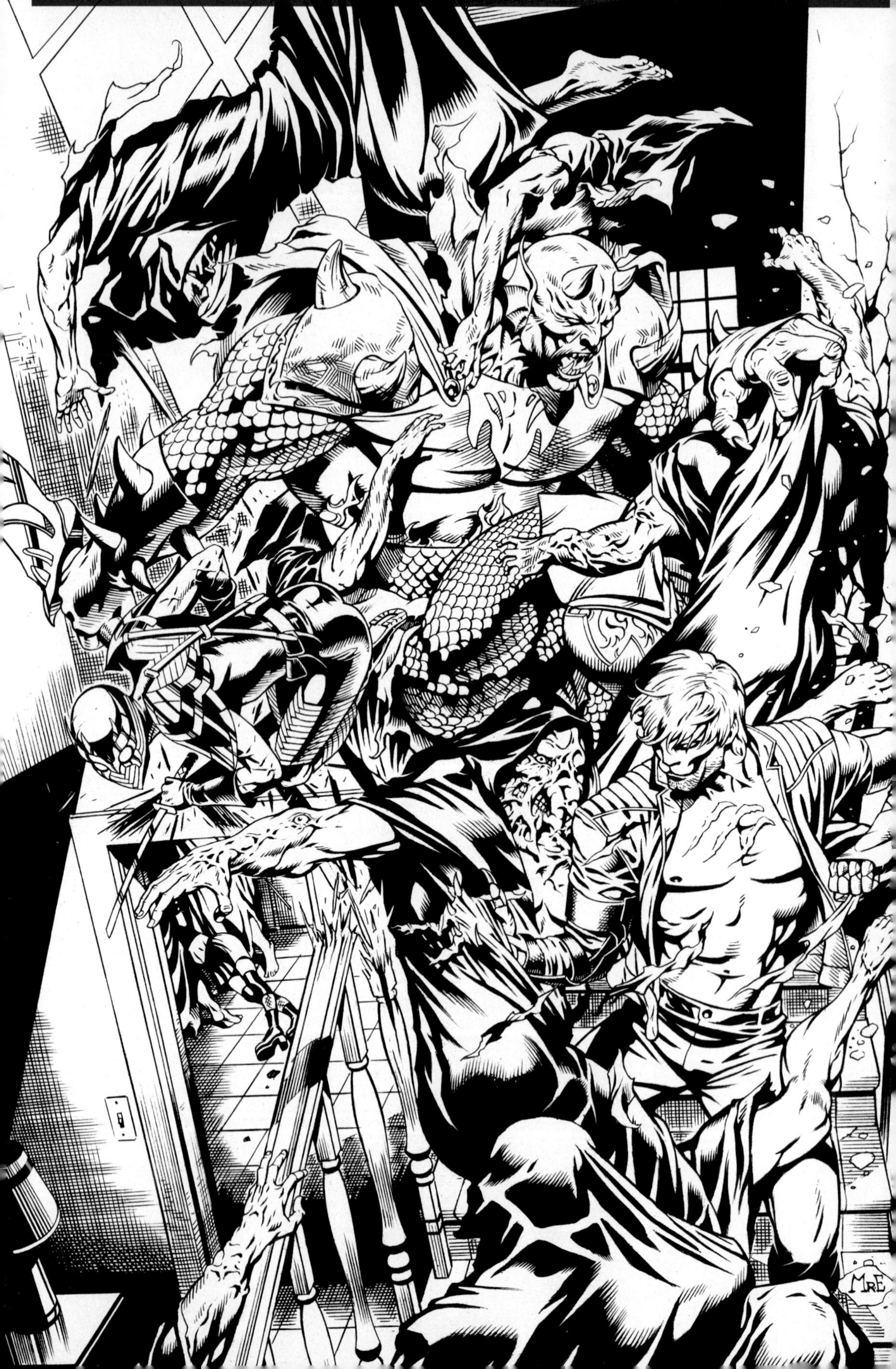

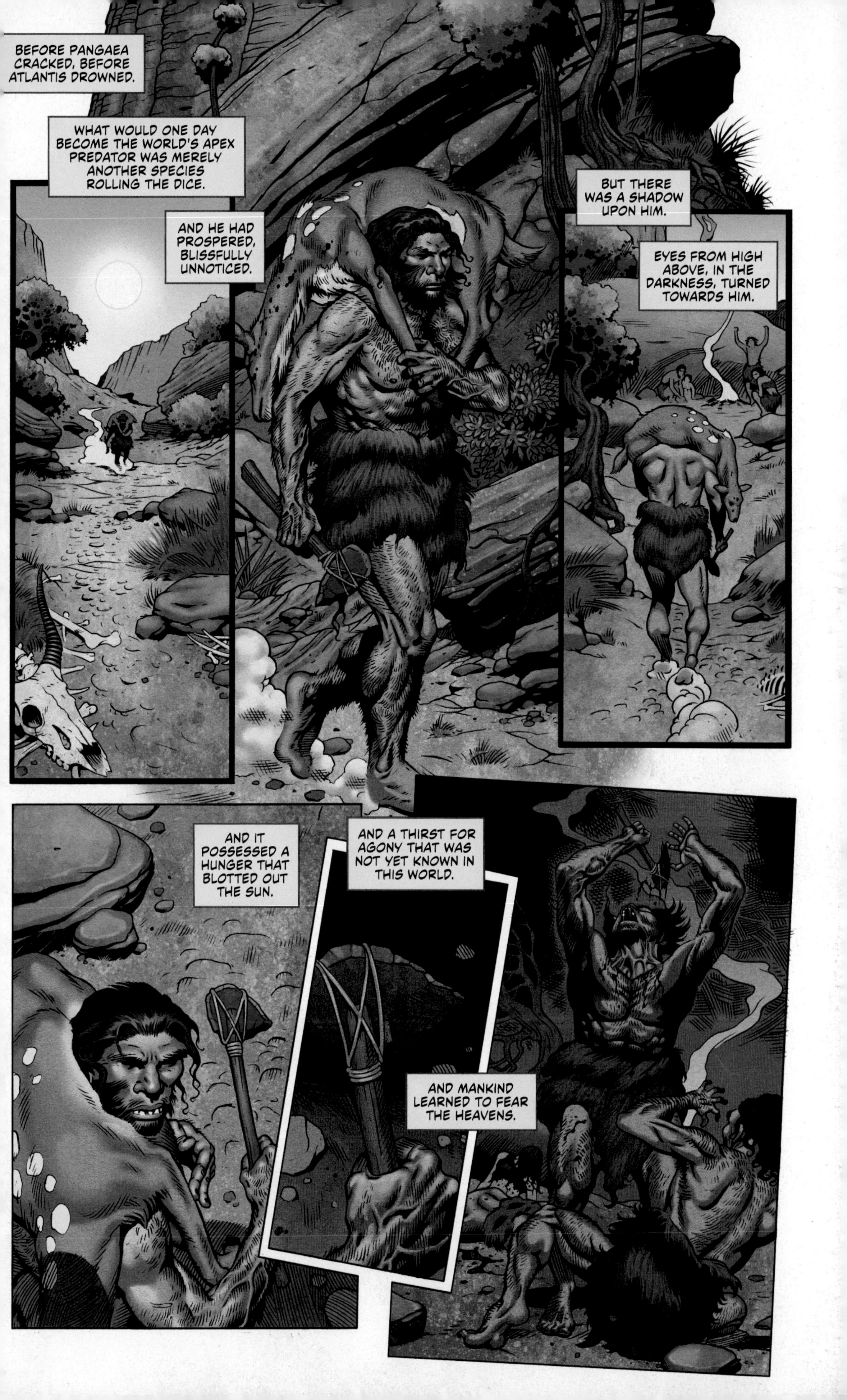
BEFORE PANGAEA CRACKED, BEFORE ATLANTIS DROWNED.
WHAT WOULD ONE DAY BECOME THE WORLD'S APEX PREDATOR WAS MERELY ANOTHER SPECIES ROLLING THE DICE.
AND HE HAD PROSPERED, BLISSFULLY UNNOTICED.
BUT THERE WAS A SHADOW UPON HIM.
EYES FROM HIGH ABOVE, IN THE DARKNESS, TURNED TOWARDS HIM.
AND IT POSSESSED A HUNGER THAT BLOTTED OUT THE SUN.
AND A THIRST FOR AGONY THAT WAS NOT YET KNOWN IN THIS WORLD.
AND MANKIND LEARNED TO FEAR THE HEAVENS.

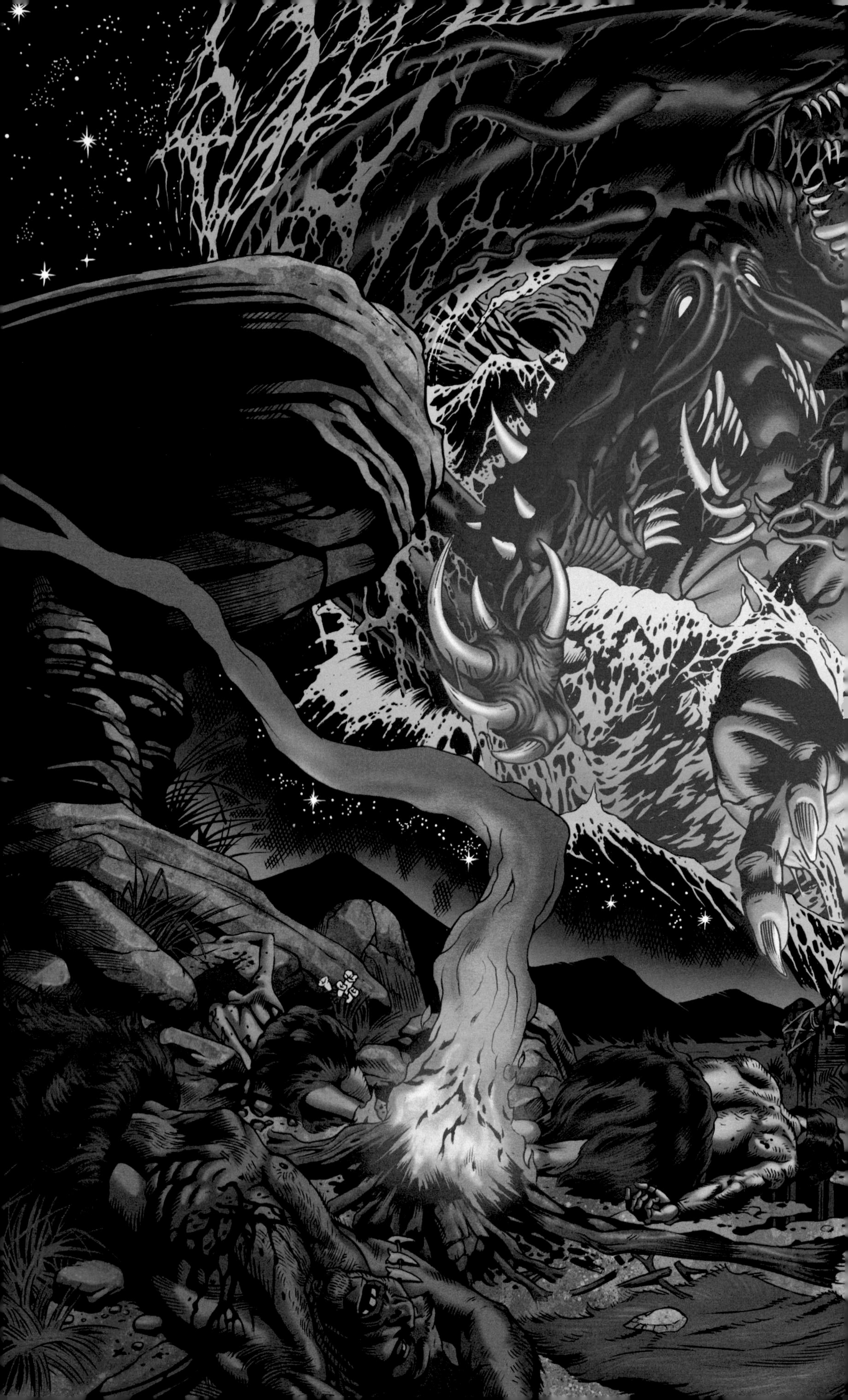

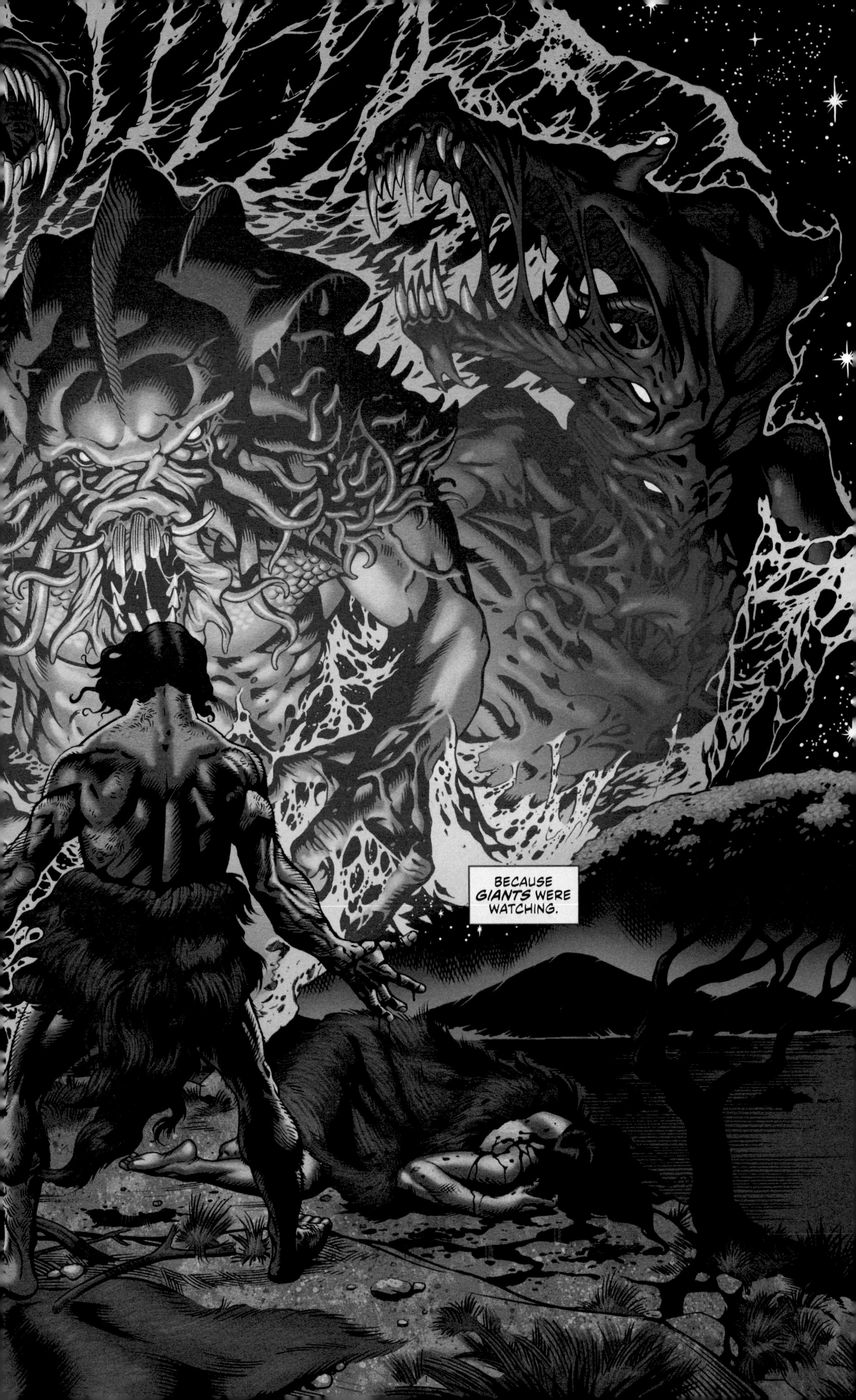
BECAUSE GIANTS WERE WATCHING.

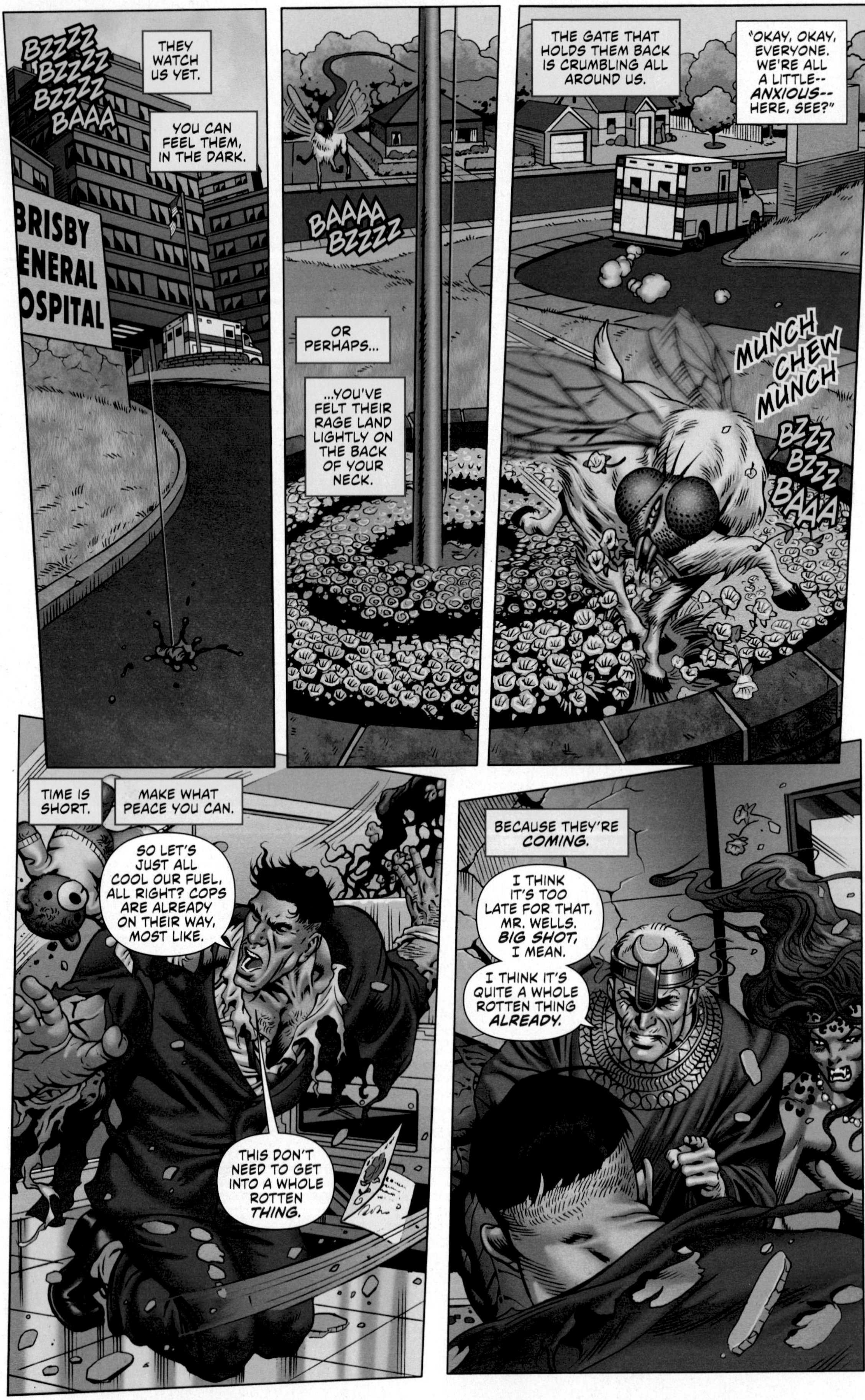
BZZZZ BZZZZ BZZZZ BAAA
THEY WATCH US YET.
YOU CAN FEEL THEM, IN THE DARK.
BRISBY
ENERAL
OSPITAL
BAAAA BZZZZ
OR PERHAPS...
...YOU'VE FELT THEIR RAGE LAND LIGHTLY ON THE BACK OF YOUR NECK.
THE GATE THAT HOLDS THEM BACK IS CRUMBLING ALL AROUND US.
"OKAY, OKAY, EVERYONE. WE'RE ALL A LITTLE-- ANXIOUS-- HERE, SEE?"
MUNCH CHEW MUNCH
BZZZ BZZZ BAAA
TIME IS SHORT.
MAKE WHAT PEACE YOU CAN.
SO LET'S JUST ALL COOL OUR FUEL, ALL RIGHT? COPS ARE ALREADY ON THEIR WAY, MOST LIKE.
THIS DON'T NEED TO GET INTO A WHOLE ROTTEN THING.
BECAUSE THEY'RE COMING.
I THINK IT'S TOO LATE FOR THAT, MR. WELLS. BIG SHOT, I MEAN.
I THINK IT'S QUITE A WHOLE ROTTEN THING ALREADY.

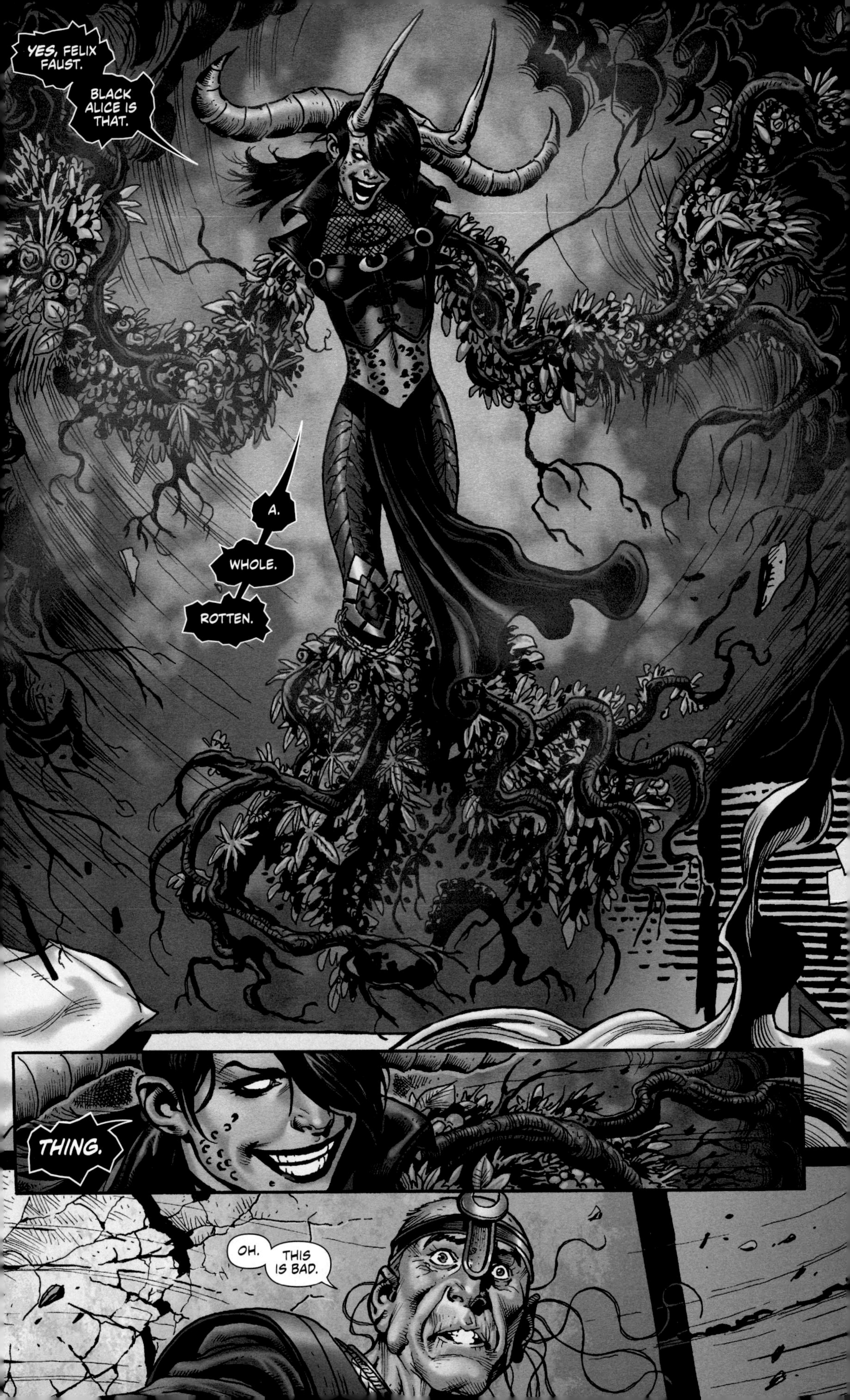
YES, FELIX FAUST.
BLACK ALICE IS THAT.
A.
WHOLE.
ROTTEN.
THING.
OH.
THIS IS BAD.

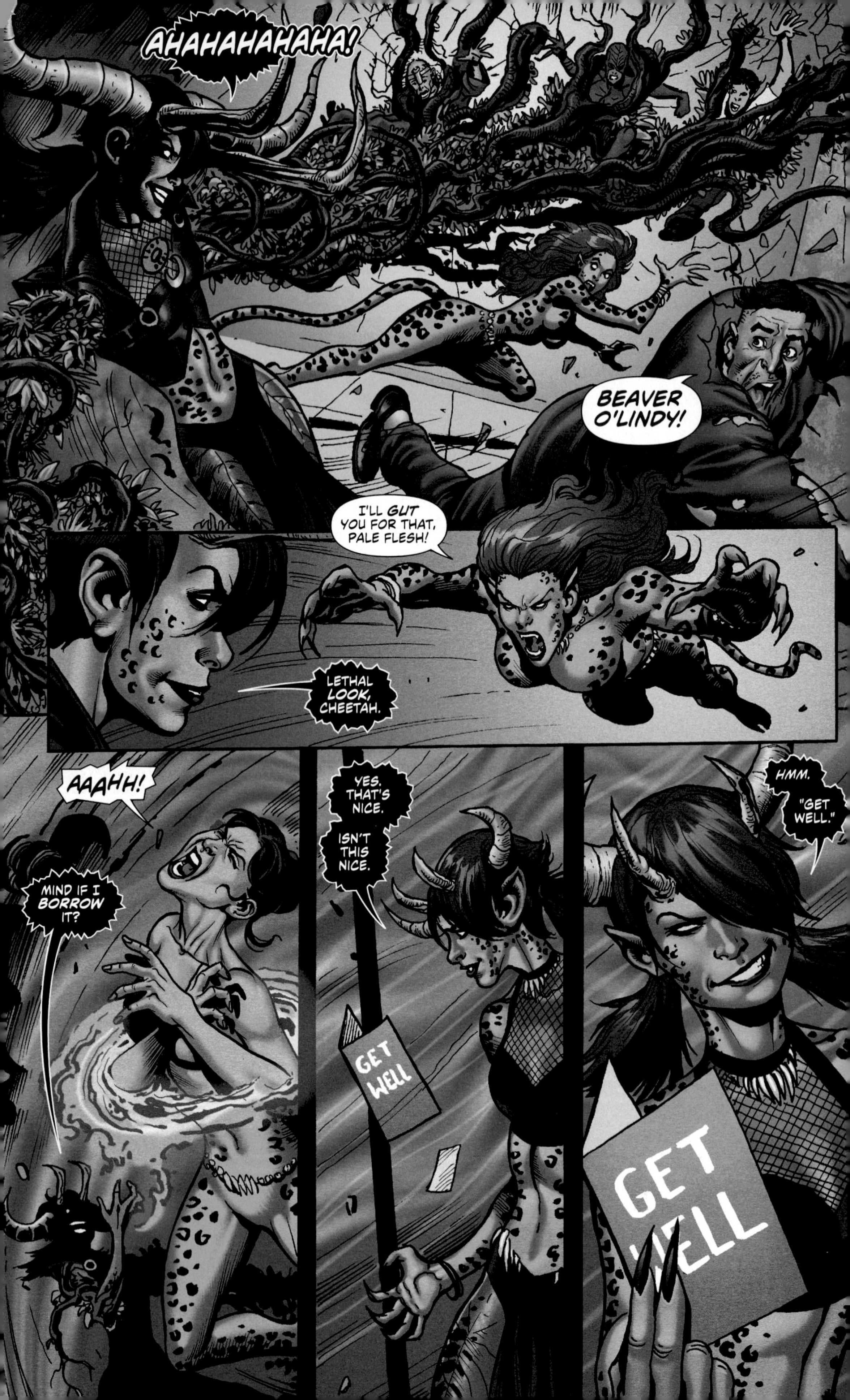
AHAHAHAHAHA!
BEAVER O'LINDY!
I'LL GUT YOU FOR THAT, PALE FLESH!
LETHAL LOOK, CHEETAH.
AAAHH!
MIND IF I BORROW IT?
YES. THAT'S NICE.
ISN'T THIS NICE.
GET WELL
HMM.
"GET WELL."
GET WELL

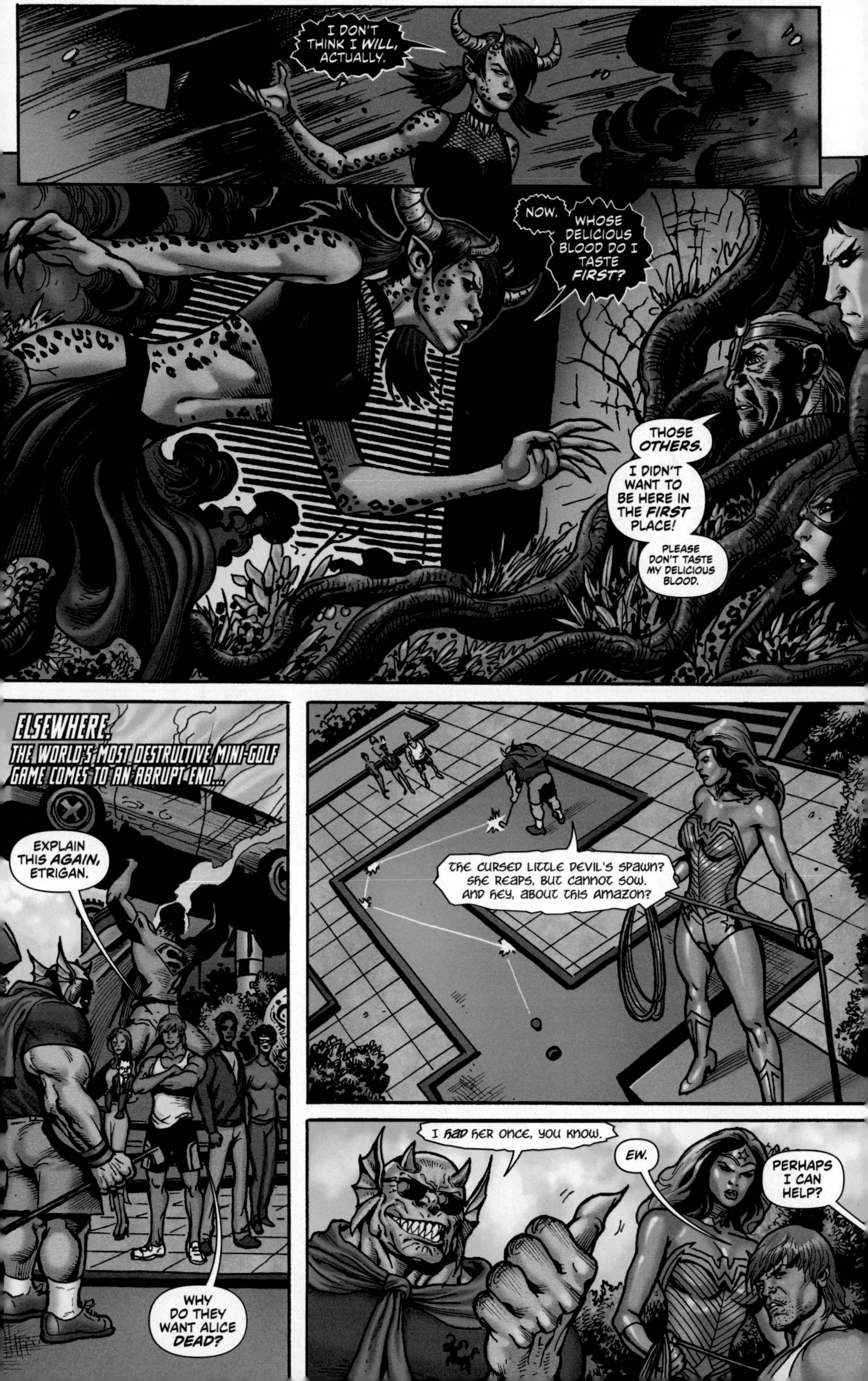
I DON'T THINK I WILL, ACTUALLY.
NOW.
WHOSE DELICIOUS BLOOD DO I TASTE FIRST?
THOSE OTHERS.
I DIDN'T WANT TO BE HERE IN THE FIRST PLACE!
PLEASE DON'T TASTE MY DELICIOUS BLOOD.
ELSEWHERE.
THE WORLD'S MOST DESTRUCTIVE MINI-GOLF GAME COMES TO AN ABRUPT END...
EXPLAIN THIS AGAIN, ETRIGAN.
WHY DO THEY WANT ALICE DEAD?
THE CURSED LITTLE DEVIL'S SPAWN? SHE REAPS, BUT CANNOT SOW. AND HEY, ABOUT THIS AMAZON?
I HAD HER ONCE, YOU KNOW.
EW.
PERHAPS I CAN HELP?

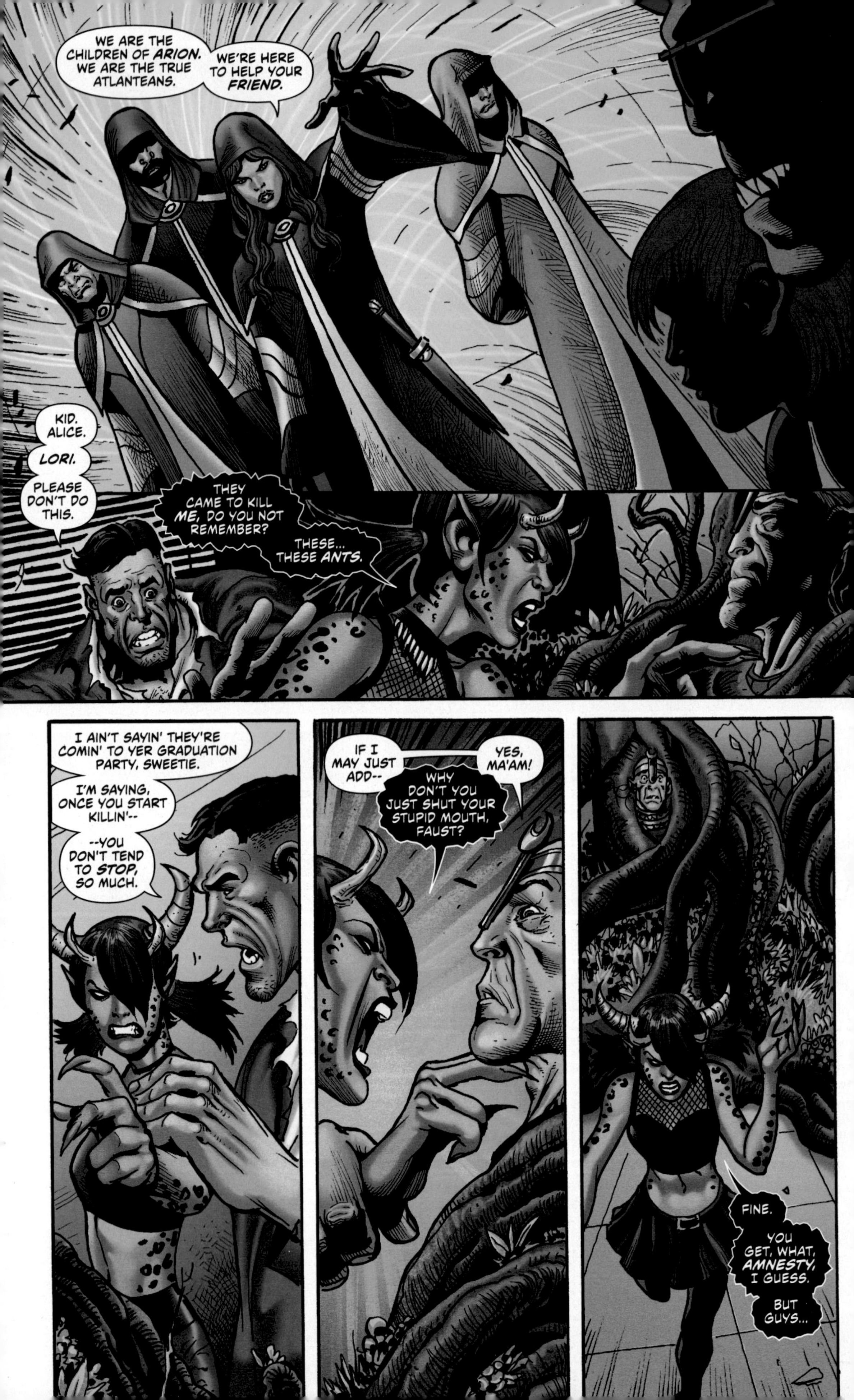
WE ARE THE CHILDREN OF ARION. WE ARE THE TRUE ATLANTEANS.
WE'RE HERE TO HELP YOUR FRIEND.
KID. ALICE.
LORI.
PLEASE DON'T DO THIS.
THEY CAME TO KILL ME, DO YOU NOT REMEMBER?
THESE... THESE ANTS.
I AIN'T SAYIN' THEY'RE COMIN' TO YER GRADUATION PARTY, SWEETIE.
I'M SAYING, ONCE YOU START KILLIN'--
--YOU DON'T TEND TO STOP, SO MUCH.
IF I MAY JUST ADD--
WHY DON'T YOU JUST SHUT YOUR STUPID MOUTH, FAUST?
YES, MA'AM!
FINE.
YOU GET, WHAT, AMNESTY, I GUESS.
BUT GUYS...

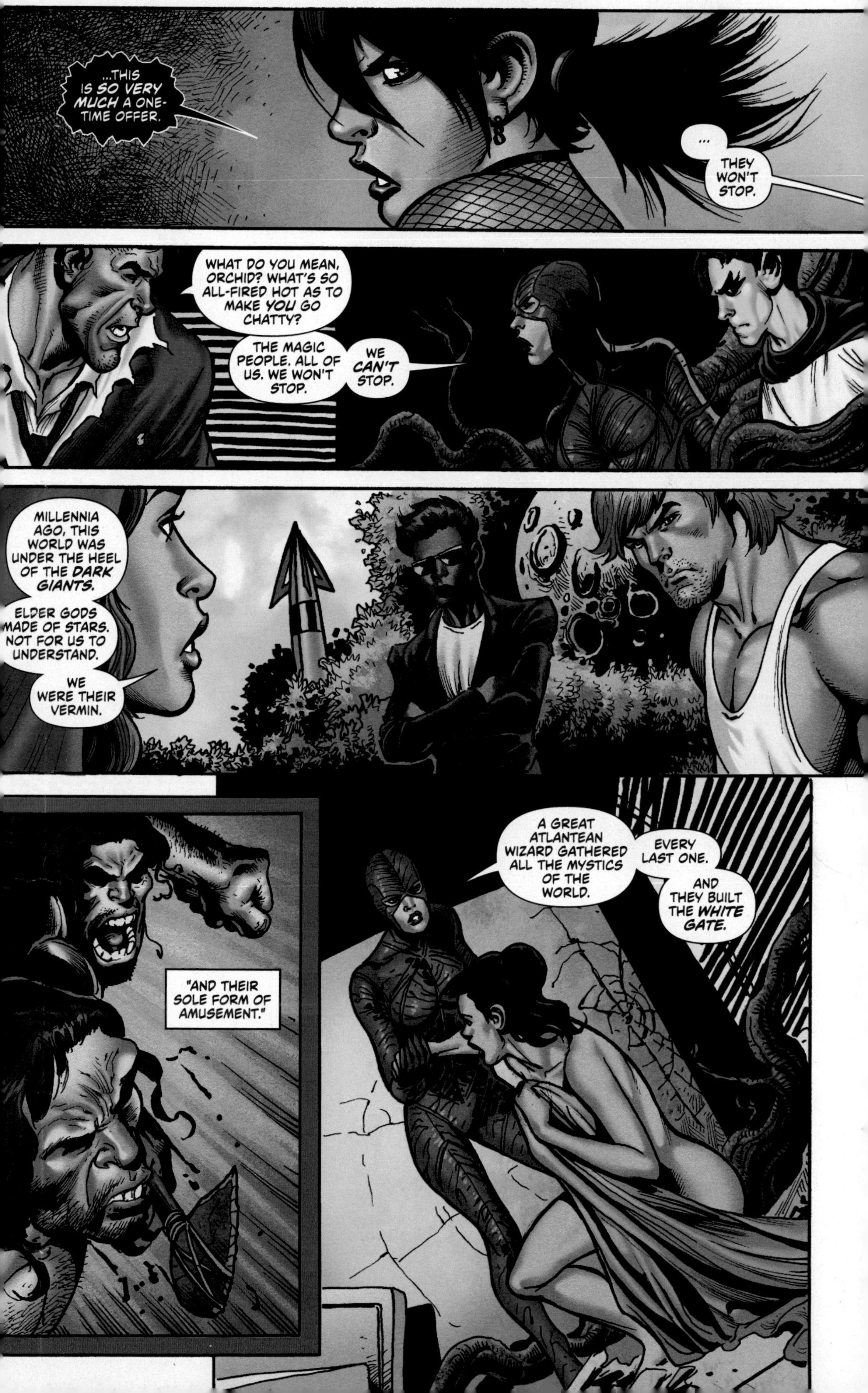

...THIS IS SO VERY MUCH A ONE-TIME OFFER.
... THEY WON'T STOP.
WHAT DO YOU MEAN, ORCHID? WHAT'S SO ALL-FIRED HOT AS TO MAKE YOU GO CHATTY?
THE MAGIC PEOPLE. ALL OF US. WE WON'T STOP.
WE CAN'T STOP.
MILLENNIA AGO, THIS WORLD WAS UNDER THE HEEL OF THE DARK GIANTS.
ELDER GODS MADE OF STARS. NOT FOR US TO UNDERSTAND.
WE WERE THEIR VERMIN.
"AND THEIR SOLE FORM OF AMUSEMENT."
A GREAT ATLANTEAN WIZARD GATHERED ALL THE MYSTICS OF THE WORLD.
EVERY LAST ONE.
AND THEY BUILT THE WHITE GATE.

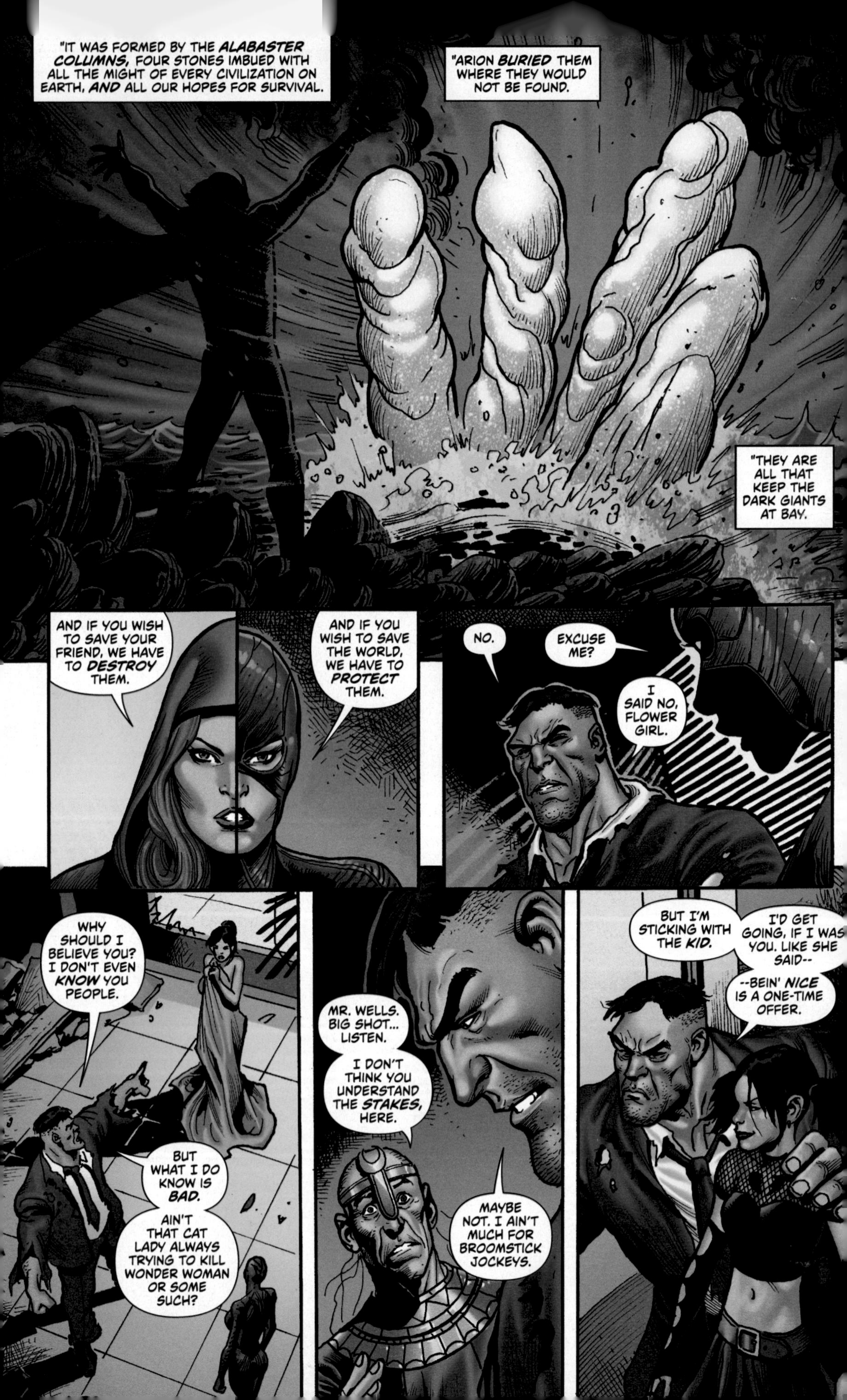
"IT WAS FORMED BY THE ALABASTER COLUMNS, FOUR STONES IMBUED WITH ALL THE MIGHT OF EVERY CIVILIZATION ON EARTH, AND ALL OUR HOPES FOR SURVIVAL.
"ARION BURIED THEM WHERE THEY WOULD NOT BE FOUND.
"THEY ARE ALL THAT KEEP THE DARK GIANTS AT BAY.
AND IF YOU WISH TO SAVE YOUR FRIEND, WE HAVE TO DESTROY THEM.
AND IF YOU WISH TO SAVE THE WORLD, WE HAVE TO PROTECT THEM.
NO.
EXCUSE ME?
I SAID NO, FLOWER GIRL.
WHY SHOULD I BELIEVE YOU? I DON'T EVEN KNOW YOU PEOPLE.
BUT WHAT I DO KNOW IS BAD.
AIN'T THAT CAT LADY ALWAYS TRYING TO KILL WONDER WOMAN OR SOME SUCH?
MR. WELLS. BIG SHOT... LISTEN.
I DON'T THINK YOU UNDERSTAND THE STAKES, HERE.
MAYBE NOT. I AIN'T MUCH FOR BROOMSTICK JOCKEYS.
BUT I'M STICKING WITH THE KID.
I'D GET GOING, IF I WAS YOU. LIKE SHE SAID--
--BEIN' NICE IS A ONE-TIME OFFER.

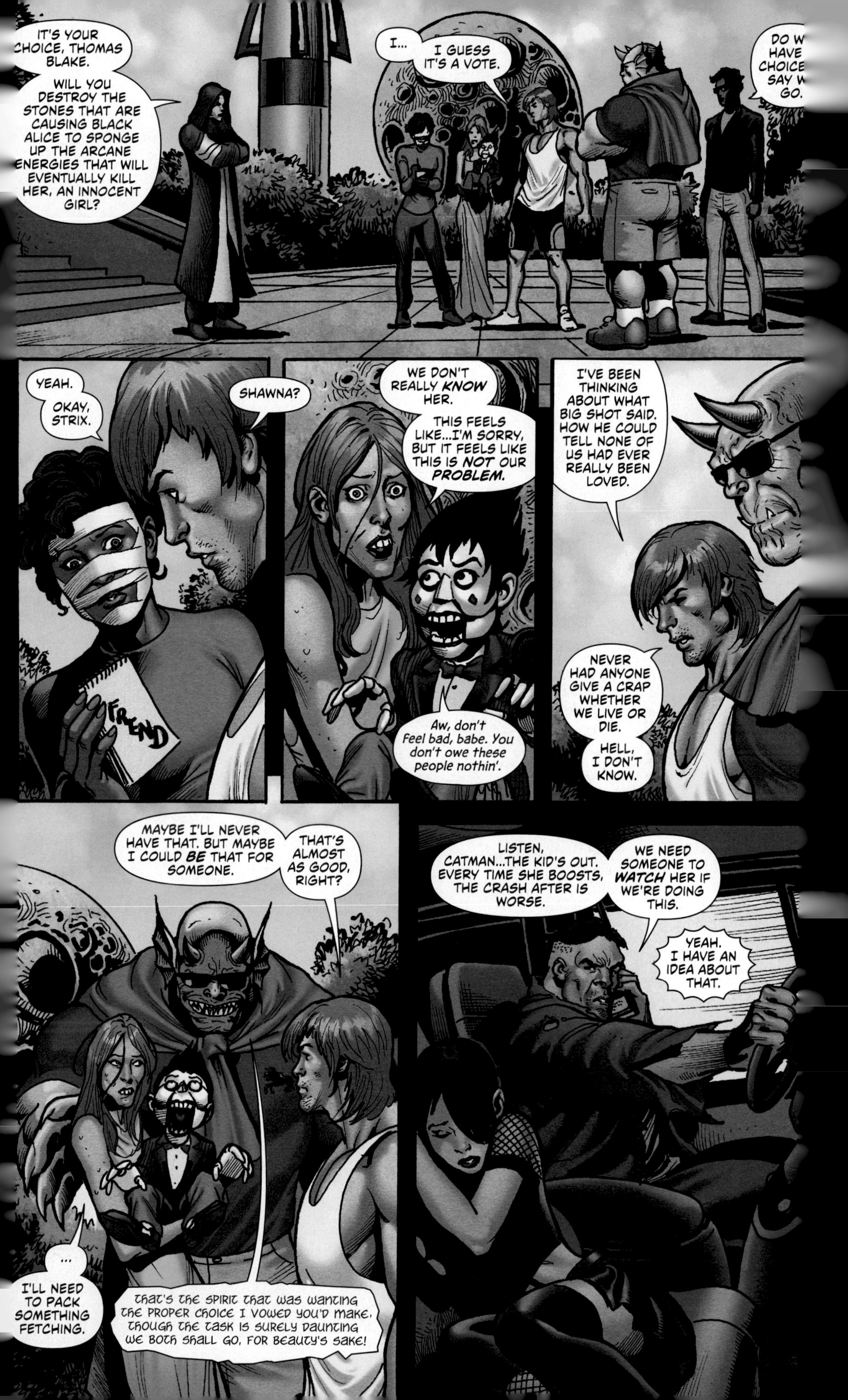
IT'S YOUR CHOICE, THOMAS BLAKE.
WILL YOU DESTROY THE STONES THAT ARE CAUSING BLACK ALICE TO SPONGE UP THE ARCANE ENERGIES THAT WILL EVENTUALLY KILL HER, AN INNOCENT GIRL?
I...
I GUESS IT'S A VOTE.
YEAH.
OKAY, STRIX.
SHAWNA?
WE DON'T REALLY KNOW HER.
THIS FEELS LIKE...I'M SORRY, BUT IT FEELS LIKE THIS IS NOT OUR PROBLEM.
Aw, don't feel bad, babe. You don't owe these people nothin'.
I'VE BEEN THINKING ABOUT WHAT BIG SHOT SAID. HOW HE COULD TELL NONE OF US HAD EVER REALLY BEEN LOVED.
NEVER HAD ANYONE GIVE A CRAP WHETHER WE LIVE OR DIE.
HELL, I DON'T KNOW.
MAYBE I'LL NEVER HAVE THAT. BUT MAYBE I COULD BE THAT FOR SOMEONE.
THAT'S ALMOST AS GOOD, RIGHT?
...
I'LL NEED TO PACK SOMETHING FETCHING.
THAT'S THE SPIRIT THAT WAS WANTING THE PROPER CHOICE I VOWED YOU'D MAKE. THOUGH THE TASK IS SURELY DAUNTING WE BOTH SHALL GO, FOR BEAUTY'S SAKE!
LISTEN, CATMAN...THE KID'S OUT. EVERY TIME SHE BOOSTS, THE CRASH AFTER IS WORSE.
WE NEED SOMEONE TO WATCH HER IF WE'RE DOING THIS.
YEAH. I HAVE AN IDEA ABOUT THAT.

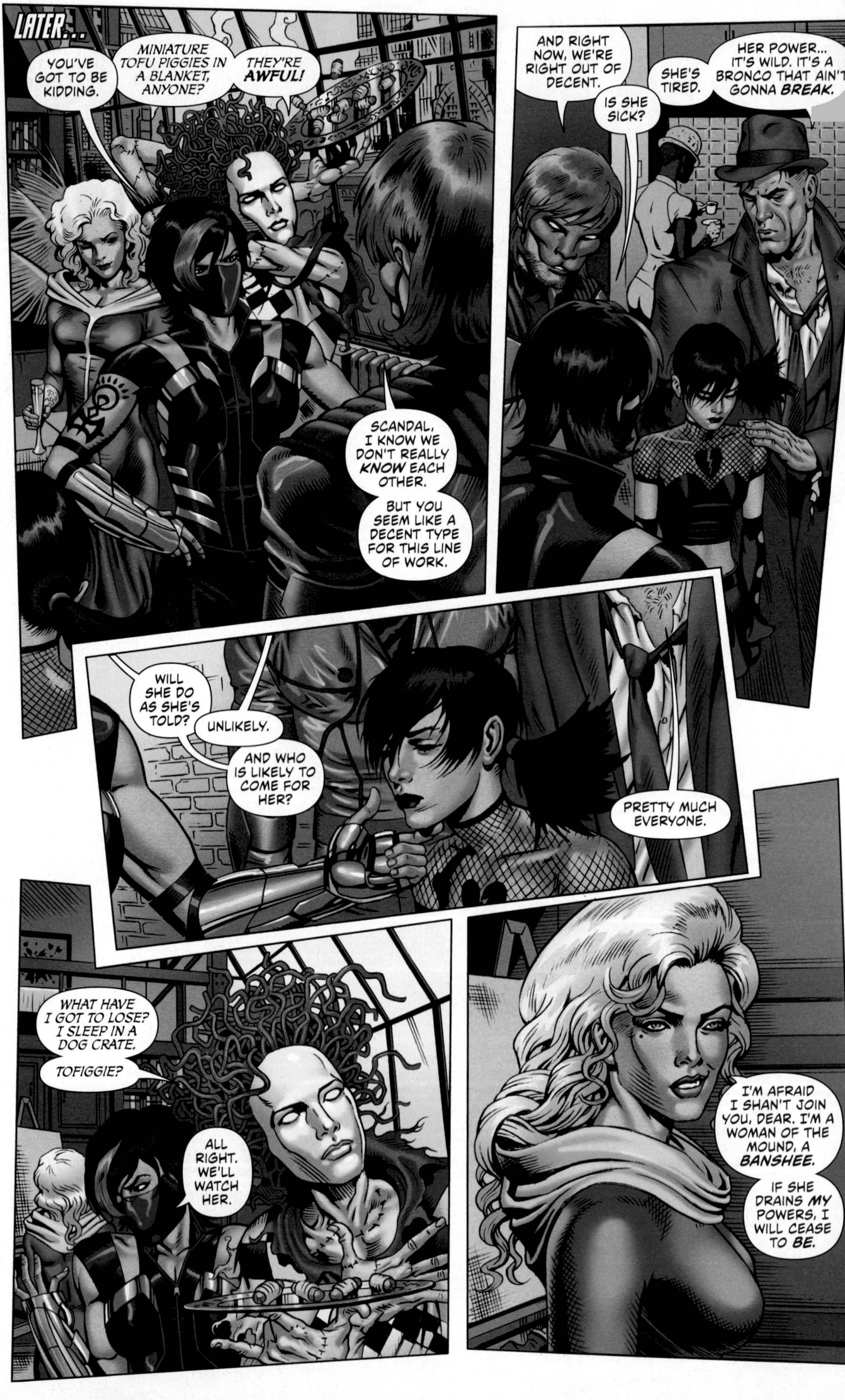
LATER...
YOU'VE GOT TO BE KIDDING.
MINIATURE TOFU PIGGIES IN A BLANKET, ANYONE?
THEY'RE **AWFUL!**
SCANDAL, I KNOW WE DON'T REALLY **KNOW** EACH OTHER.
BUT YOU SEEM LIKE A DECENT TYPE FOR THIS LINE OF WORK.
AND RIGHT NOW, WE'RE RIGHT OUT OF DECENT.
IS SHE SICK?
SHE'S TIRED.
HER POWER... IT'S WILD. IT'S A BRONCO THAT AIN'T GONNA **BREAK.**
WILL SHE DO AS SHE'S TOLD?
UNLIKELY.
AND WHO IS LIKELY TO COME FOR HER?
PRETTY MUCH EVERYONE.
WHAT HAVE I GOT TO LOSE? I SLEEP IN A DOG CRATE.
TOFIGGIE?
ALL RIGHT. WE'LL WATCH HER.
I'M AFRAID I SHAN'T JOIN YOU, DEAR. I'M A WOMAN OF THE MOUND, A **BANSHEE.**
IF SHE DRAINS **MY** POWERS, I WILL CEASE TO **BE.**

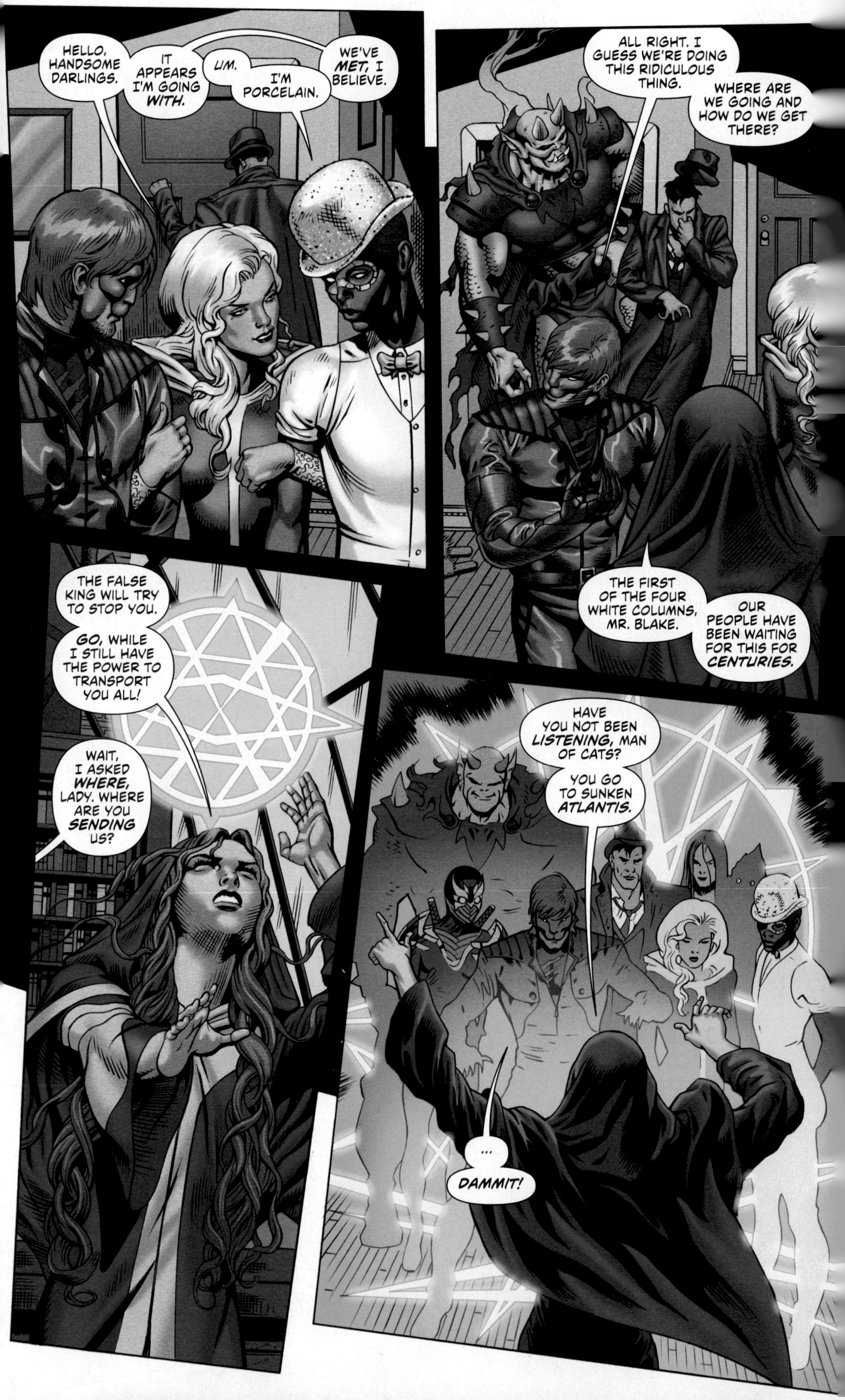

HELLO, HANDSOME DARLINGS.
IT APPEARS I'M GOING WITH.
UM.
I'M PORCELAIN.
WE'VE MET, I BELIEVE.
ALL RIGHT. I GUESS WE'RE DOING THIS RIDICULOUS THING.
WHERE ARE WE GOING AND HOW DO WE GET THERE?
THE FIRST OF THE FOUR WHITE COLUMNS, MR. BLAKE.
OUR PEOPLE HAVE BEEN WAITING FOR THIS FOR CENTURIES.
THE FALSE KING WILL TRY TO STOP YOU.
GO, WHILE I STILL HAVE THE POWER TO TRANSPORT YOU ALL!
WAIT, I ASKED WHERE, LADY. WHERE ARE YOU SENDING US?
HAVE YOU NOT BEEN LISTENING, MAN OF CATS?
YOU GO TO SUNKEN ATLANTIS.
...
DAMMIT!

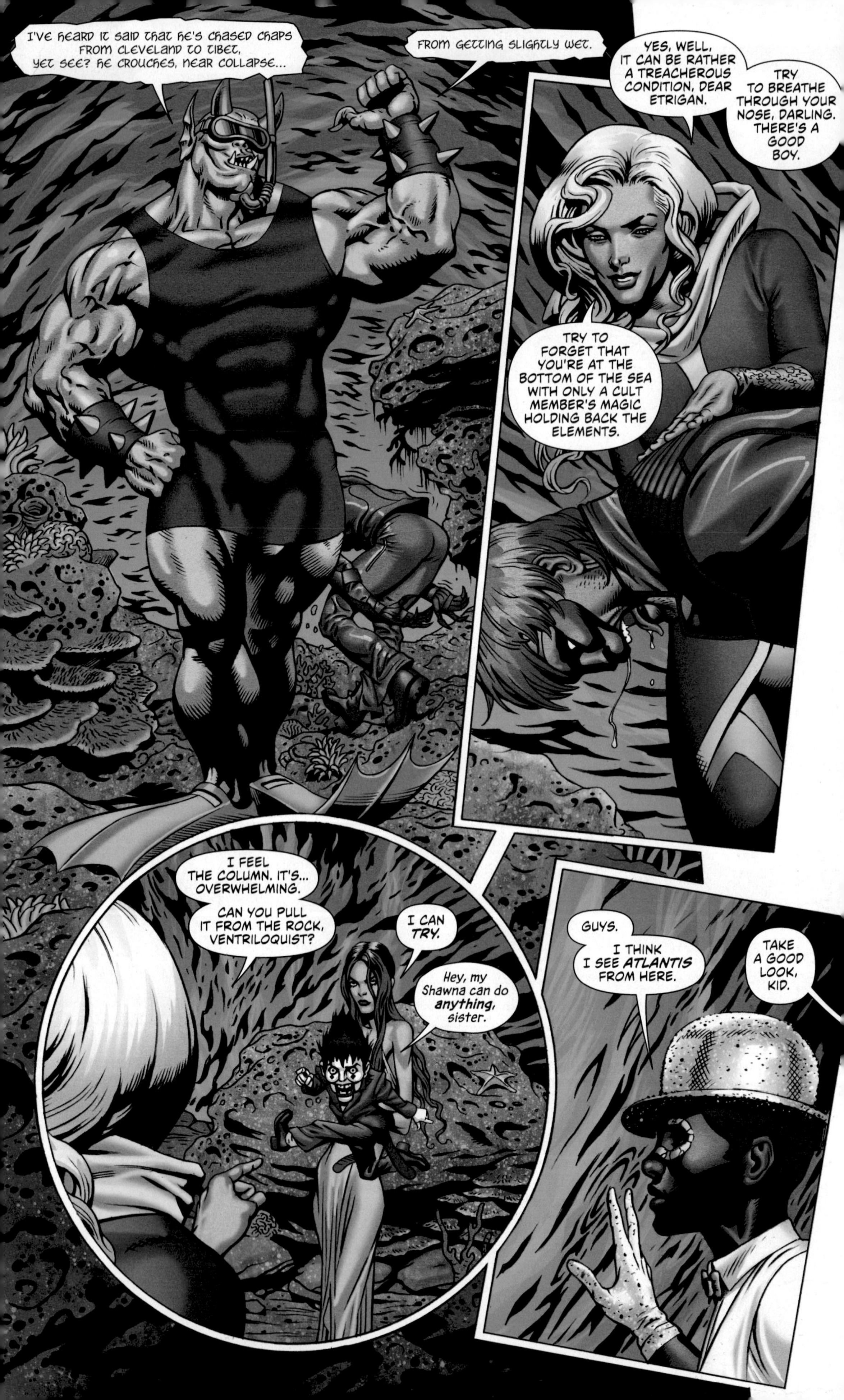
I'VE HEARD IT SAID THAT HE'S CHASED CHAPS FROM CLEVELAND TO TIBET, YET SEE? HE CROUCHES, NEAR COLLAPSE...
FROM GETTING SLIGHTLY WET.
YES, WELL, IT CAN BE RATHER A TREACHEROUS CONDITION, DEAR ETRIGAN.
TRY TO BREATHE THROUGH YOUR NOSE, DARLING. THERE'S A GOOD BOY.
TRY TO FORGET THAT YOU'RE AT THE BOTTOM OF THE SEA WITH ONLY A CULT MEMBER'S MAGIC HOLDING BACK THE ELEMENTS.
I FEEL THE COLUMN. IT'S... OVERWHELMING.
CAN YOU PULL IT FROM THE ROCK, VENTRILOQUIST?
I CAN *TRY.*
Hey, my Shawna can do **anything,** sister.
GUYS.
I THINK I SEE ***ATLANTIS*** FROM HERE.
TAKE A GOOD LOOK, KID.

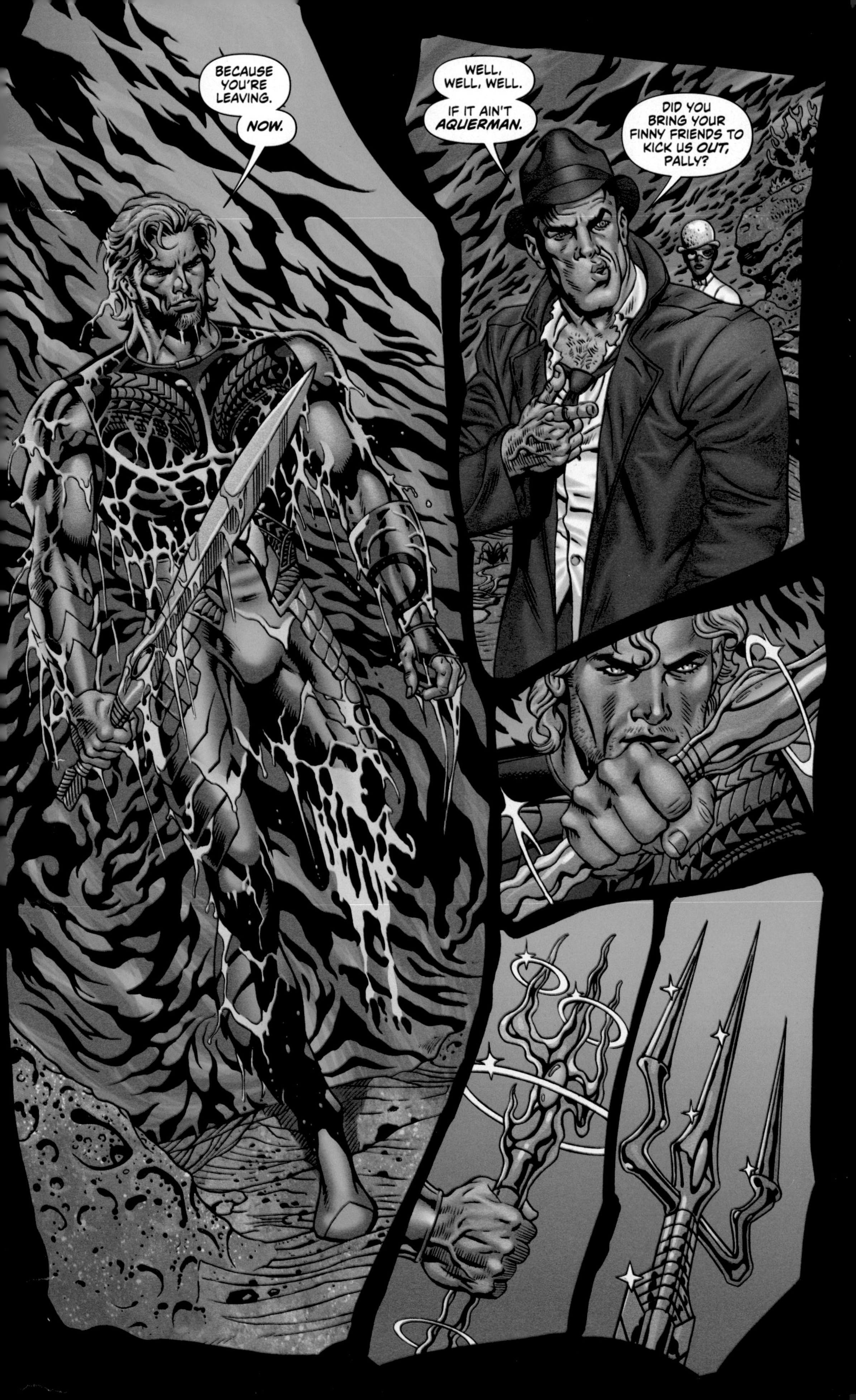
BECAUSE YOU'RE LEAVING.
NOW.
WELL, WELL, WELL.
IF IT AIN'T AQUERMAN.
DID YOU BRING YOUR FINNY FRIENDS TO KICK US OUT, PALLY?

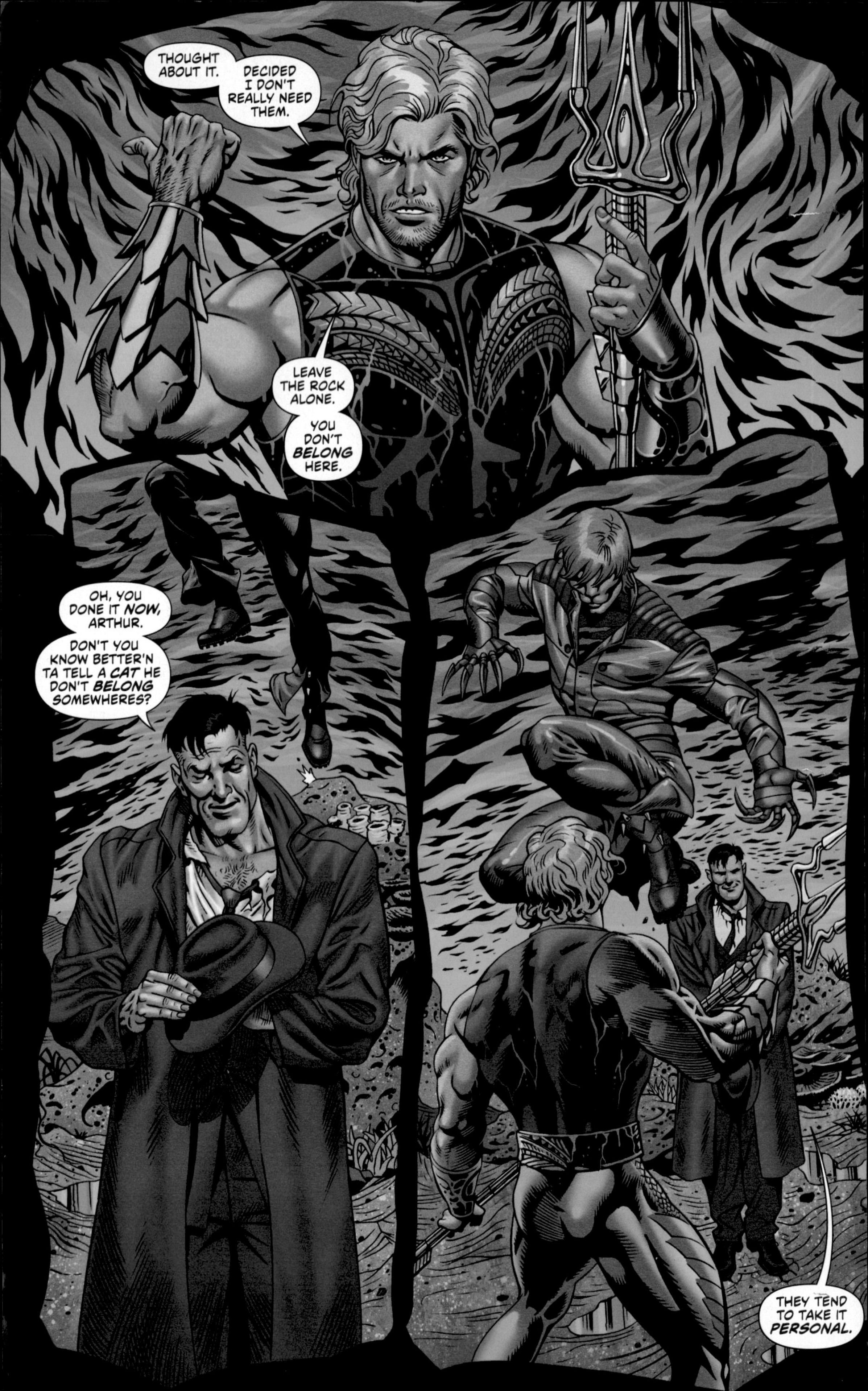
THOUGHT ABOUT IT.
DECIDED I DON'T REALLY NEED THEM.
LEAVE THE ROCK ALONE.
YOU DON'T *BELONG* HERE.
OH, YOU DONE IT *NOW,* ARTHUR.
DON'T YOU KNOW BETTER'N TA TELL A *CAT* HE DON'T *BELONG* SOMEWHERES?
THEY TEND TO TAKE IT *PERSONAL.*

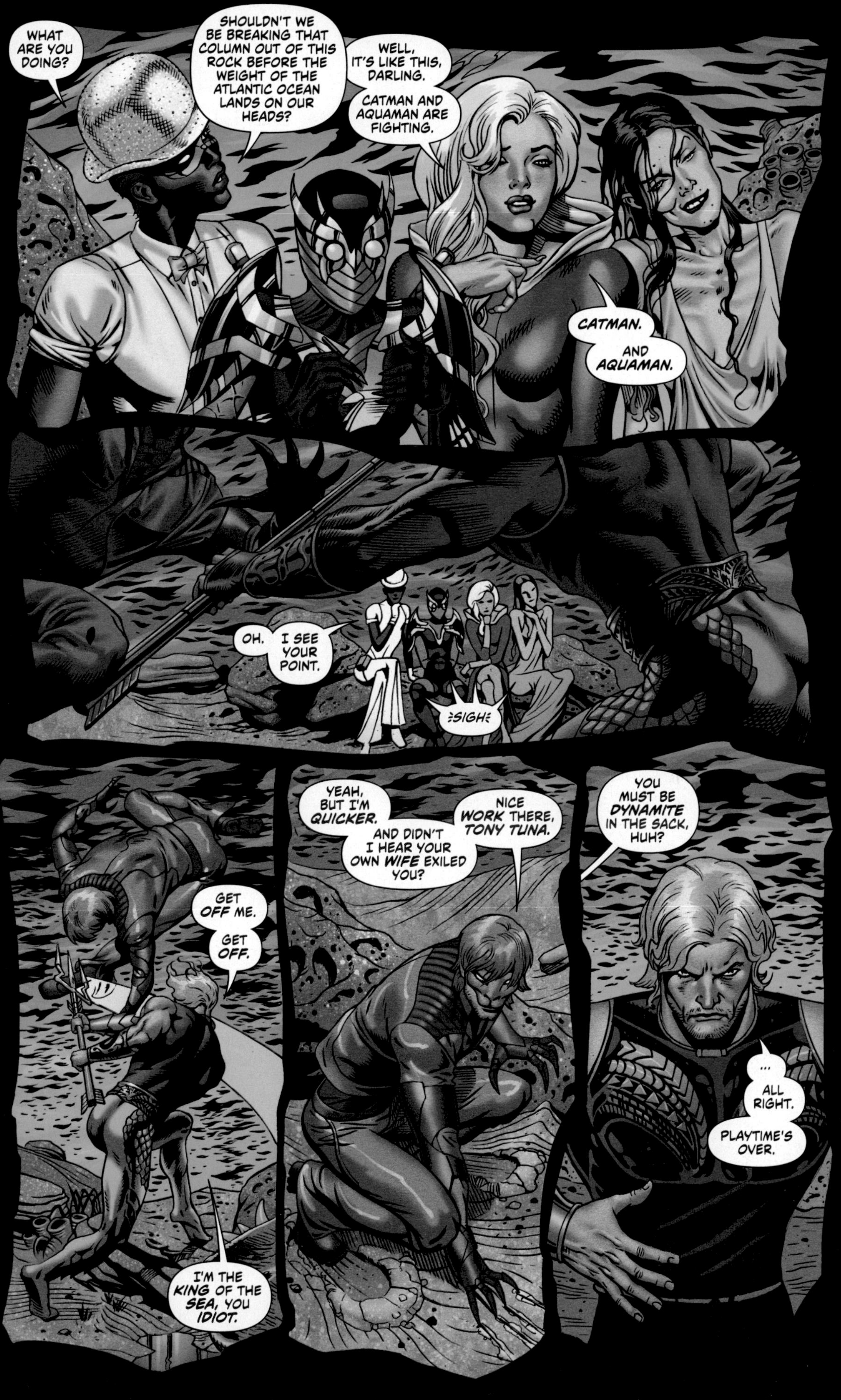
WHAT ARE YOU DOING?
SHOULDN'T WE BE BREAKING THAT COLUMN OUT OF THIS ROCK BEFORE THE WEIGHT OF THE ATLANTIC OCEAN LANDS ON OUR HEADS?
WELL, IT'S LIKE THIS, DARLING.
CATMAN AND AQUAMAN ARE FIGHTING.
CATMAN.
AND AQUAMAN.
OH. I SEE YOUR POINT.
SIGH
GET OFF ME.
GET OFF.
I'M THE KING OF THE SEA, YOU IDIOT.
YEAH, BUT I'M QUICKER.
AND DIDN'T I HEAR YOUR OWN WIFE EXILED YOU?
NICE WORK THERE, TONY TUNA.
YOU MUST BE DYNAMITE IN THE SACK, HUH?
... ALL RIGHT.
PLAYTIME'S OVER.

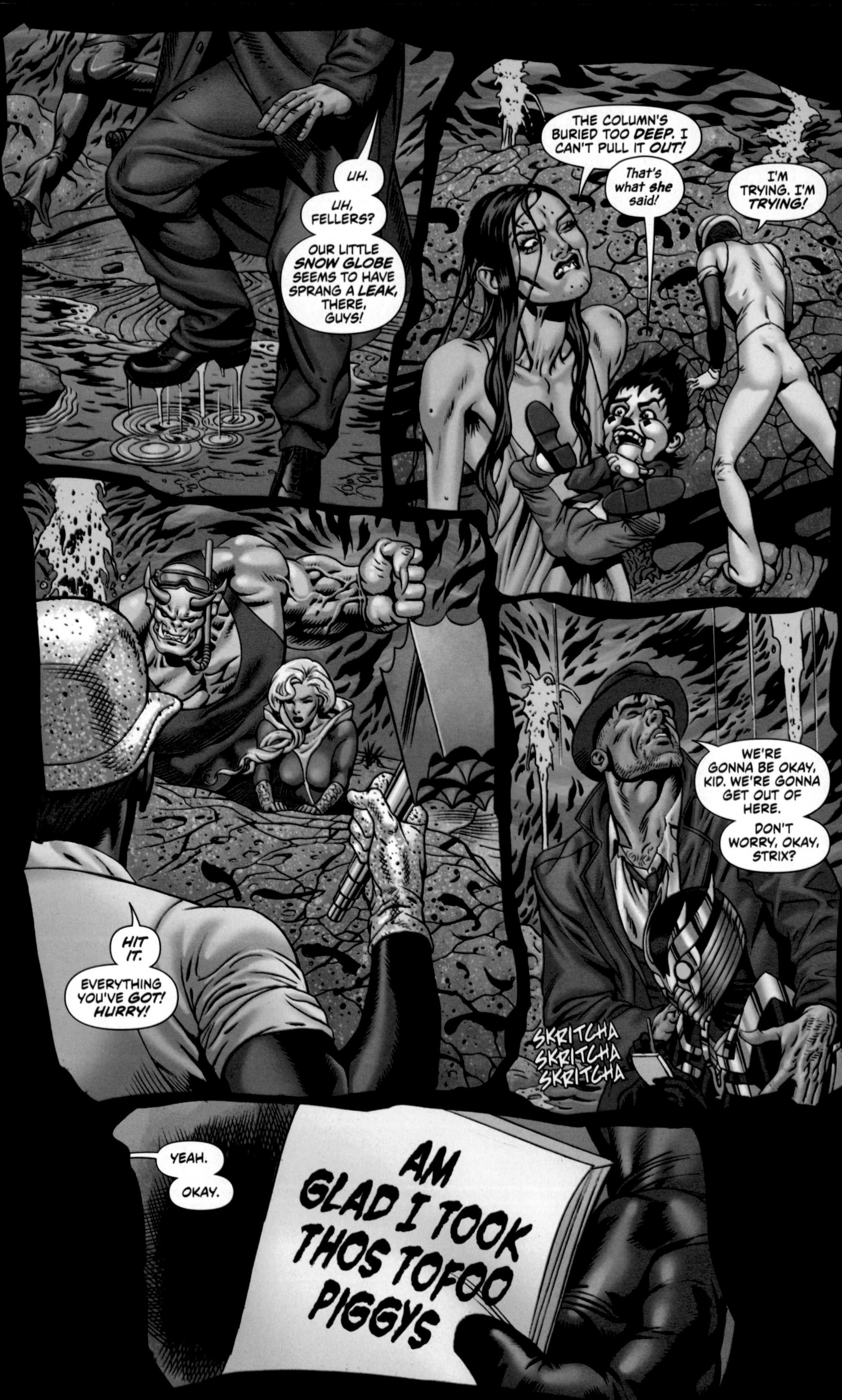
UH.
UH, FELLERS?
OUR LITTLE SNOW GLOBE SEEMS TO HAVE SPRANG A LEAK, THERE, GUYS!
THE COLUMN'S BURIED TOO DEEP. I CAN'T PULL IT OUT!
That's what she said!
I'M TRYING. I'M TRYING!
HIT IT.
EVERYTHING YOU'VE GOT! HURRY!
WE'RE GONNA BE OKAY, KID. WE'RE GONNA GET OUT OF HERE.
DON'T WORRY, OKAY, STRIX?
SKRITCHA SKRITCHA SKRITCHA
YEAH.
OKAY.
AM GLAD I TOOK THOS TOFOO PIGGYS

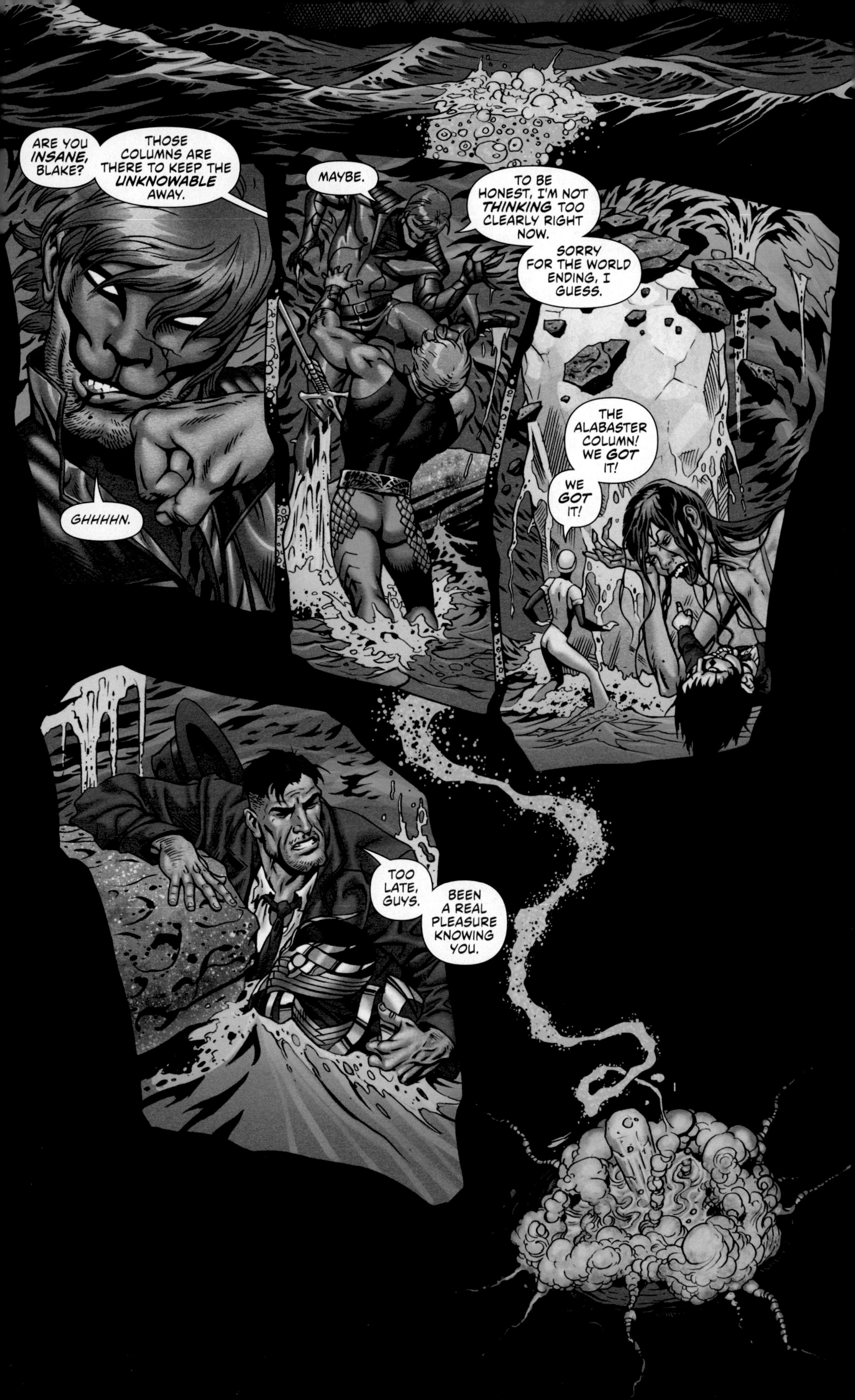
ARE YOU INSANE, BLAKE?
THOSE COLUMNS ARE THERE TO KEEP THE UNKNOWABLE AWAY.
GHHHHN.
MAYBE.
TO BE HONEST, I'M NOT THINKING TOO CLEARLY RIGHT NOW.
SORRY FOR THE WORLD ENDING, I GUESS.
THE ALABASTER COLUMN! WE GOT IT!
WE GOT IT!
TOO LATE, GUYS.
BEEN A REAL PLEASURE KNOWING YOU.

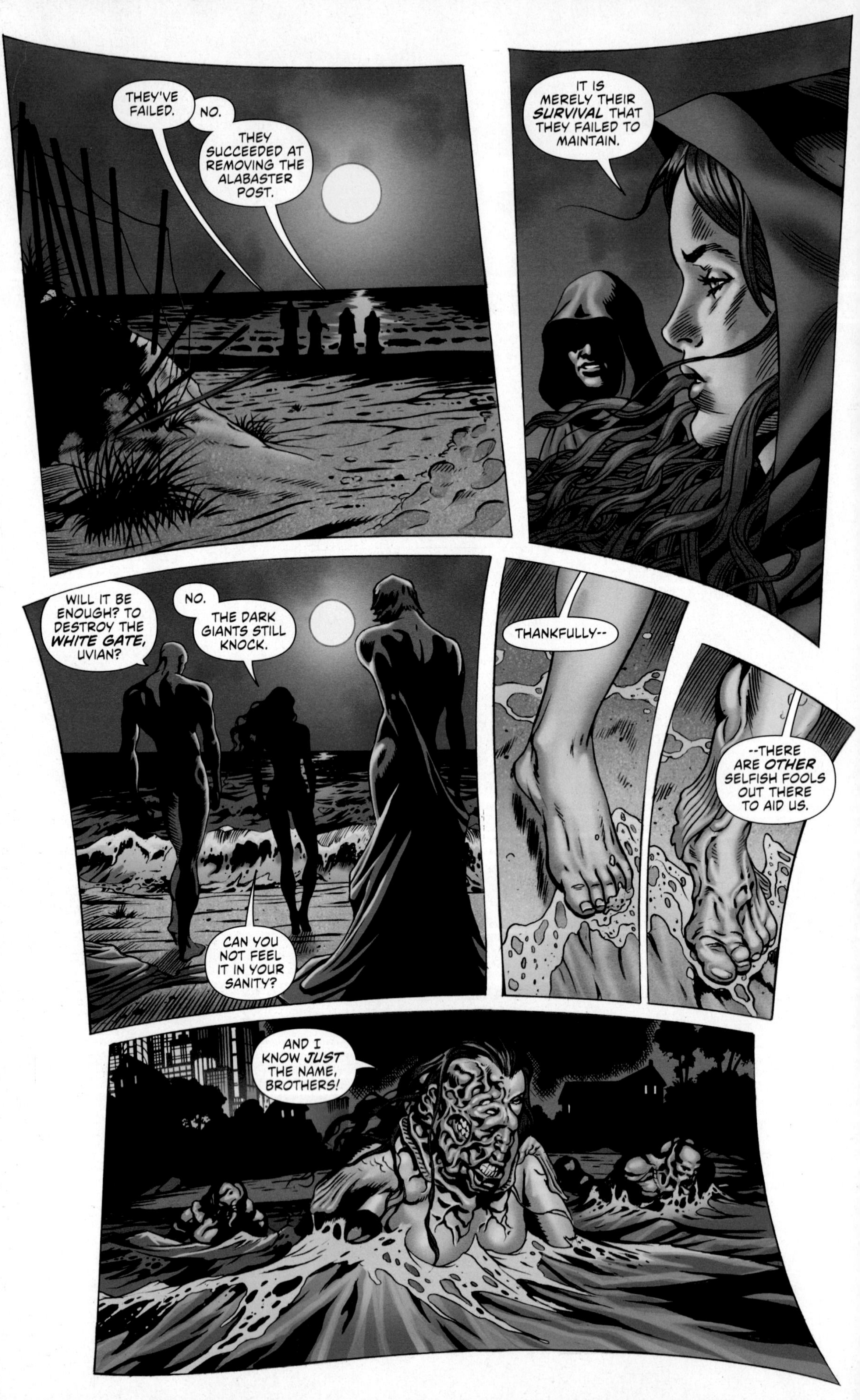
THEY'VE FAILED.
NO.
THEY SUCCEEDED AT REMOVING THE ALABASTER POST.
IT IS MERELY THEIR SURVIVAL THAT THEY FAILED TO MAINTAIN.
WILL IT BE ENOUGH? TO DESTROY THE WHITE GATE, UVIAN?
NO.
THE DARK GIANTS STILL KNOCK.
CAN YOU NOT FEEL IT IN YOUR SANITY?
THANKFULLY--
--THERE ARE OTHER SELFISH FOOLS OUT THERE TO AID US.
AND I KNOW JUST THE NAME, BROTHERS!

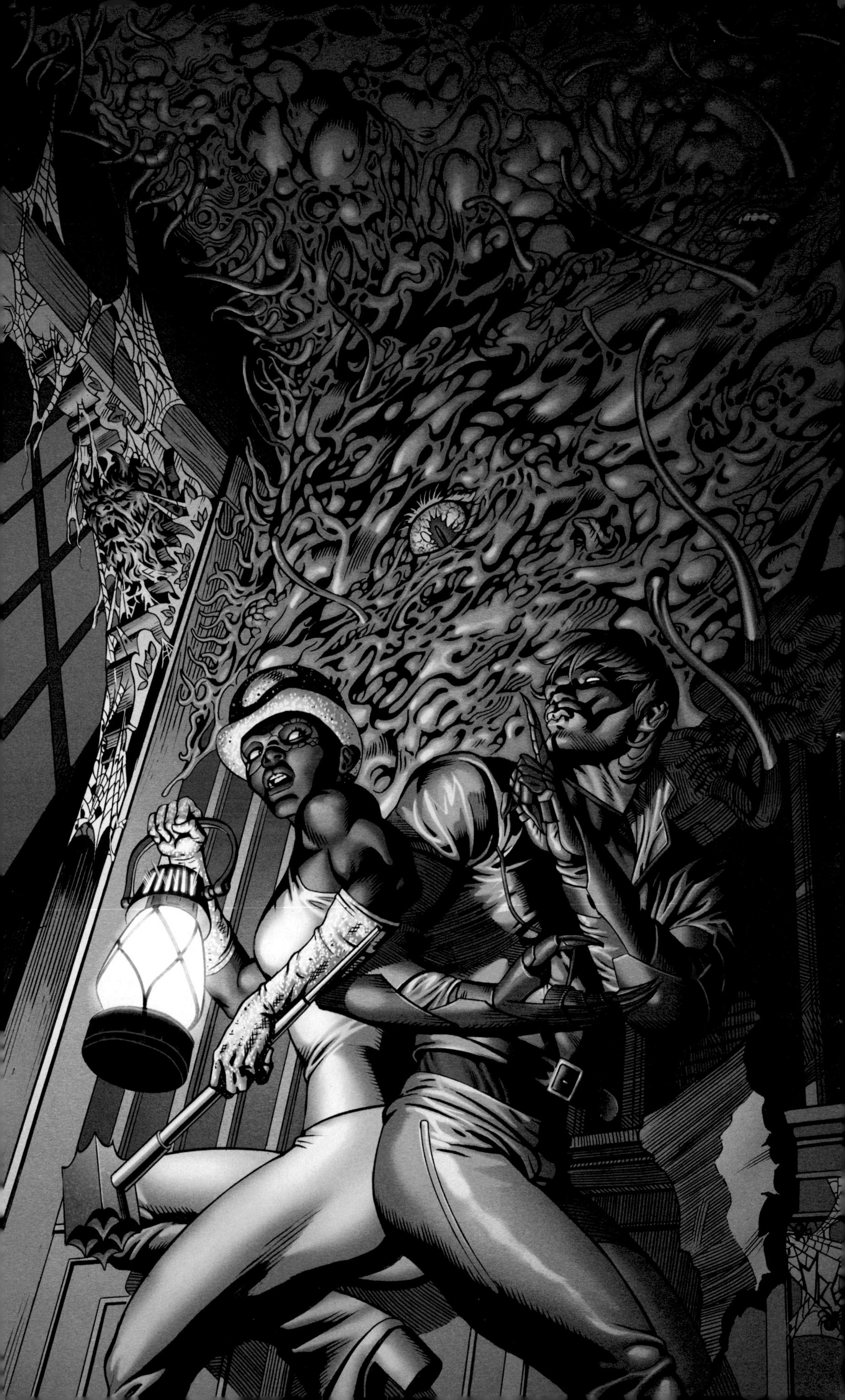

THE WHITE GATE, THE BLACK SUN

GAIL SIMONE writer **TOM DERENICK** artist **JASON WRIGHT** colorist **TRAVIS LANHAM** letterer
cover by **DALE EAGLESHAM & JASON WRIGHT**

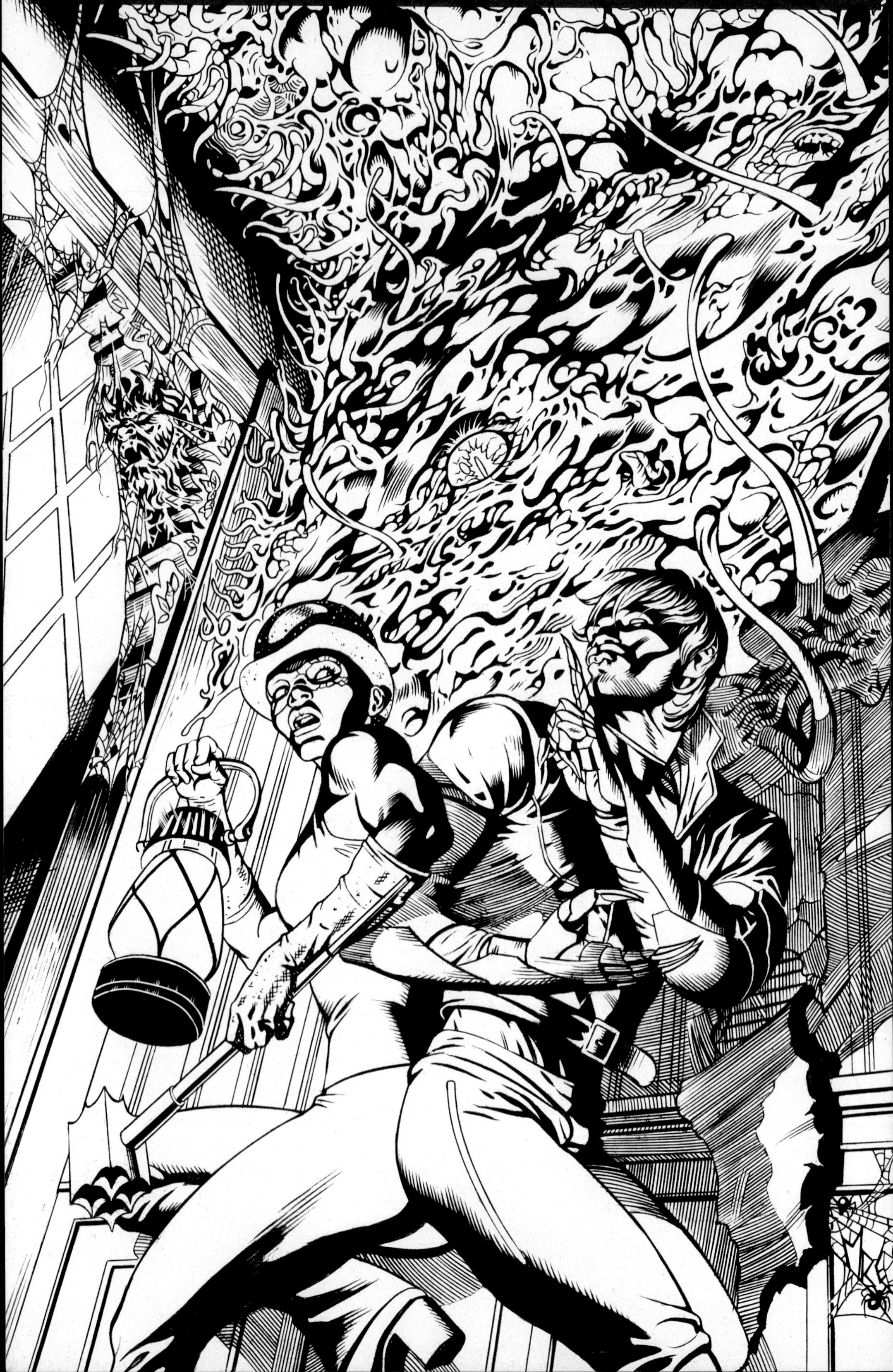

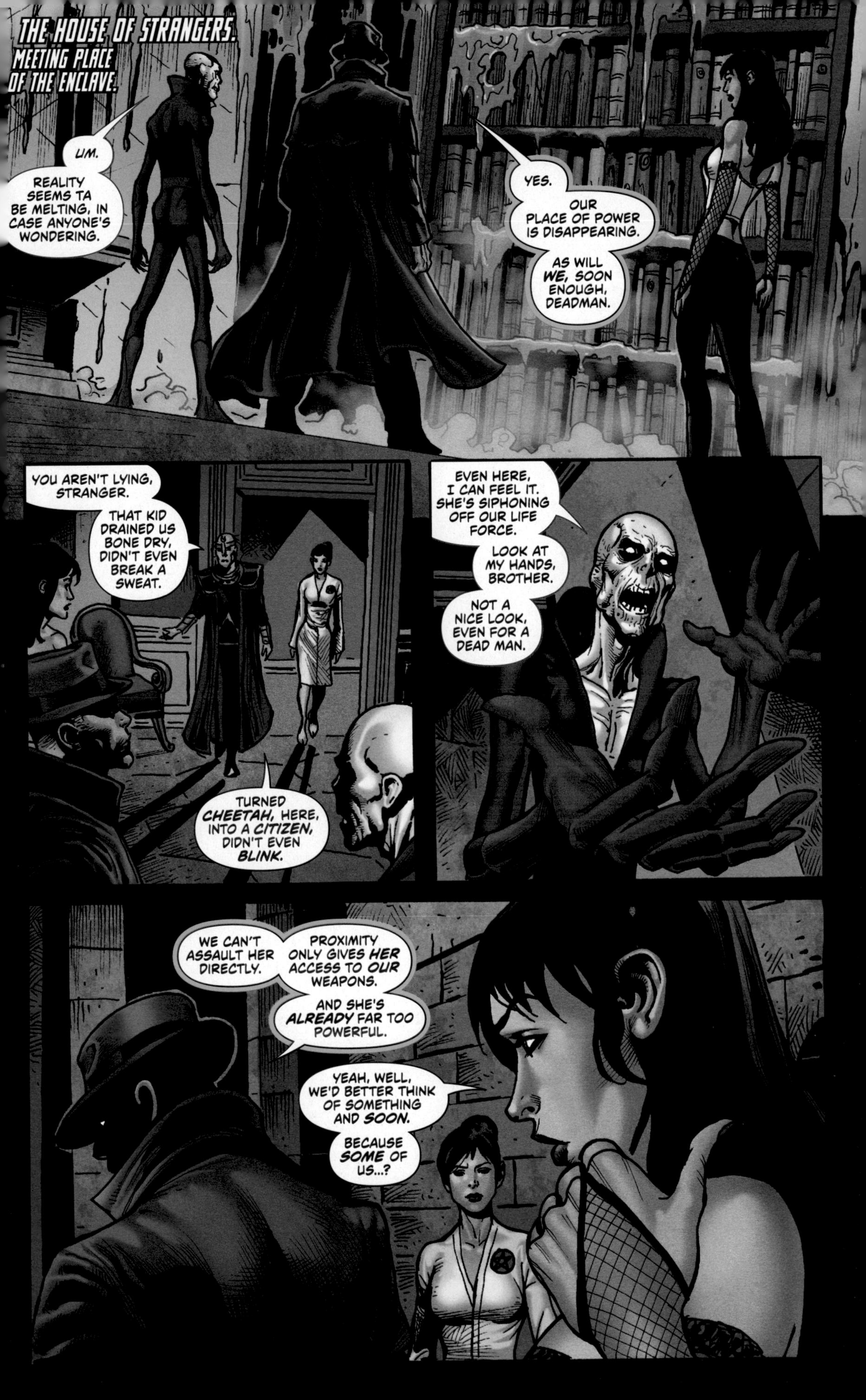

THE HOUSE OF STRANGERS.
MEETING PLACE OF THE ENCLAVE.
UM.
REALITY SEEMS TA BE MELTING, IN CASE ANYONE'S WONDERING.
YES.
OUR PLACE OF POWER IS DISAPPEARING.
AS WILL WE, SOON ENOUGH, DEADMAN.
YOU AREN'T LYING, STRANGER.
THAT KID DRAINED US BONE DRY, DIDN'T EVEN BREAK A SWEAT.
TURNED CHEETAH, HERE, INTO A CITIZEN, DIDN'T EVEN BLINK.
EVEN HERE, I CAN FEEL IT. SHE'S SIPHONING OFF OUR LIFE FORCE.
LOOK AT MY HANDS, BROTHER.
NOT A NICE LOOK, EVEN FOR A DEAD MAN.
WE CAN'T ASSAULT HER DIRECTLY.
PROXIMITY ONLY GIVES HER ACCESS TO OUR WEAPONS.
AND SHE'S ALREADY FAR TOO POWERFUL.
YEAH, WELL, WE'D BETTER THINK OF SOMETHING AND SOON.
BECAUSE SOME OF US...?

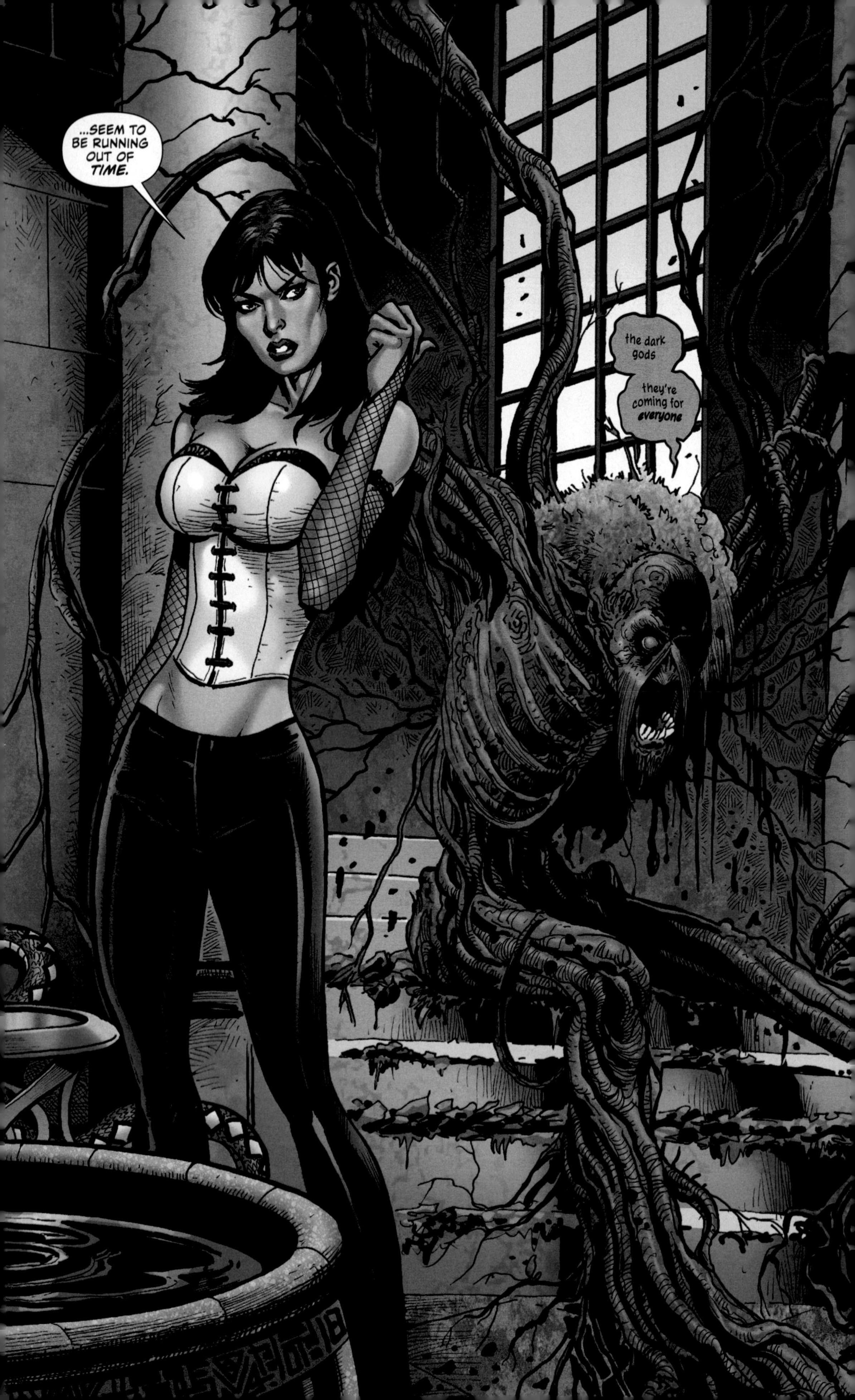
...SEEM TO BE RUNNING OUT OF TIME.
the dark gods
they're coming for everyone

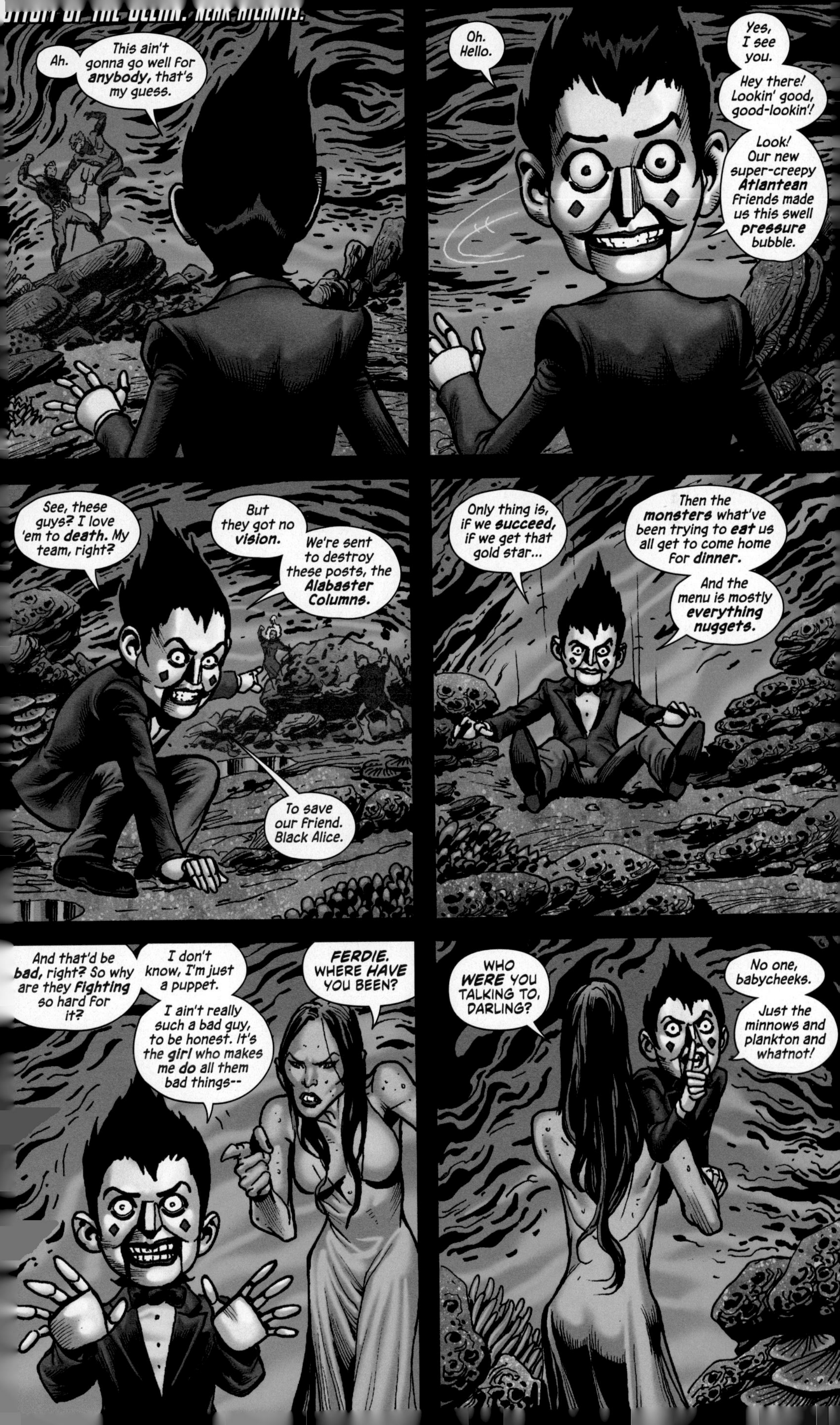
Ah.
This ain't gonna go well for anybody, that's my guess.
Oh. Hello.
Yes, I see you.
Hey there! Lookin' good, good-lookin'!
Look! Our new super-creepy Atlantean friends made us this swell pressure bubble.
See, these guys? I love 'em to death. My team, right?
But they got no vision.
We're sent to destroy these posts, the Alabaster Columns.
To save our friend. Black Alice.
Only thing is, if we succeed, if we get that gold star...
Then the monsters what've been trying to eat us all get to come home for dinner.
And the menu is mostly everything nuggets.
And that'd be bad, right? So why are they fighting so hard for it?
I don't know, I'm just a puppet.
I ain't really such a bad guy, to be honest. It's the girl who makes me do all them bad things--
FERDIE. WHERE HAVE YOU BEEN?
WHO WERE YOU TALKING TO, DARLING?
No one, babycheeks.
Just the minnows and plankton and whatnot!

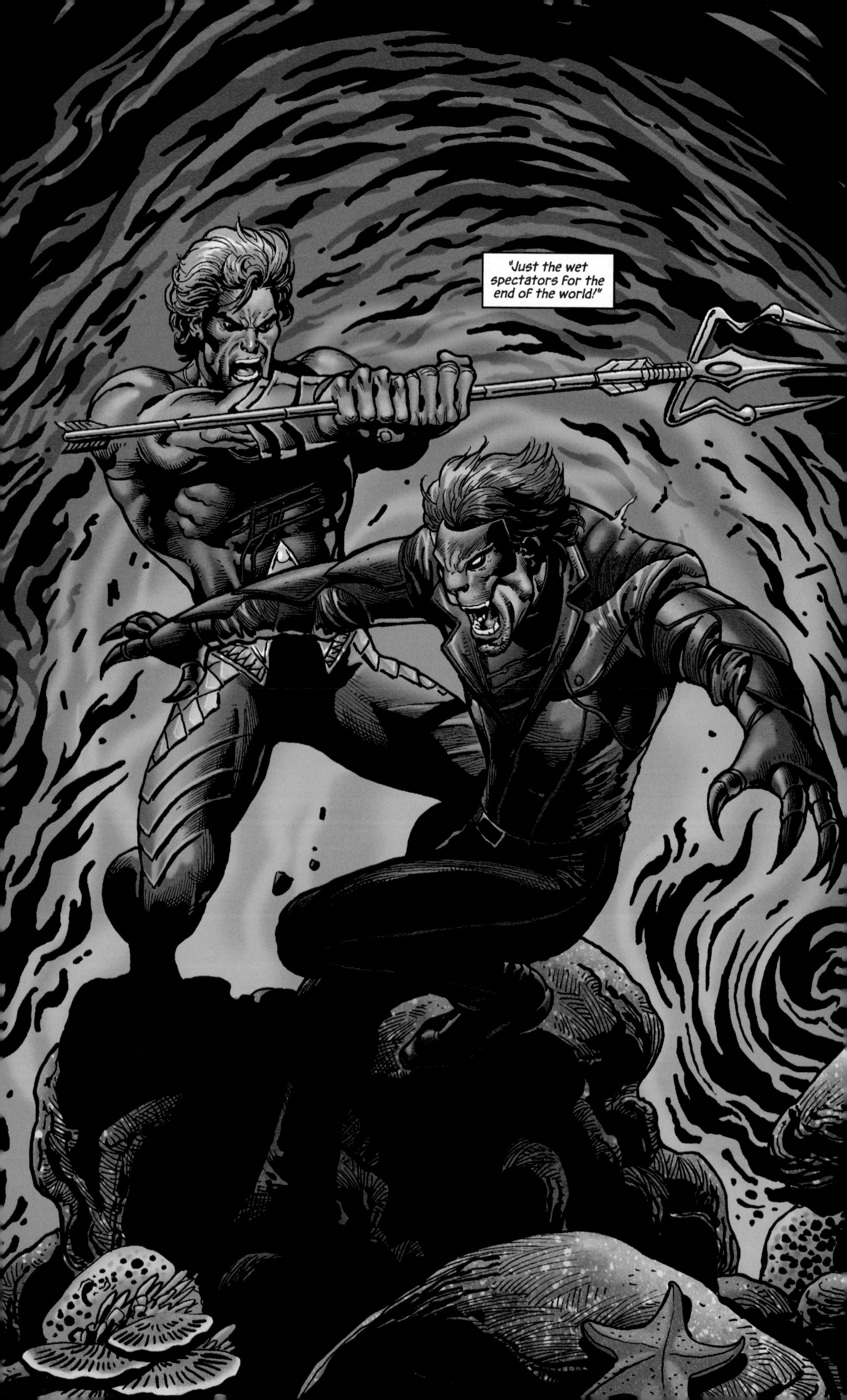
"Just the wet spectators for the end of the world!"

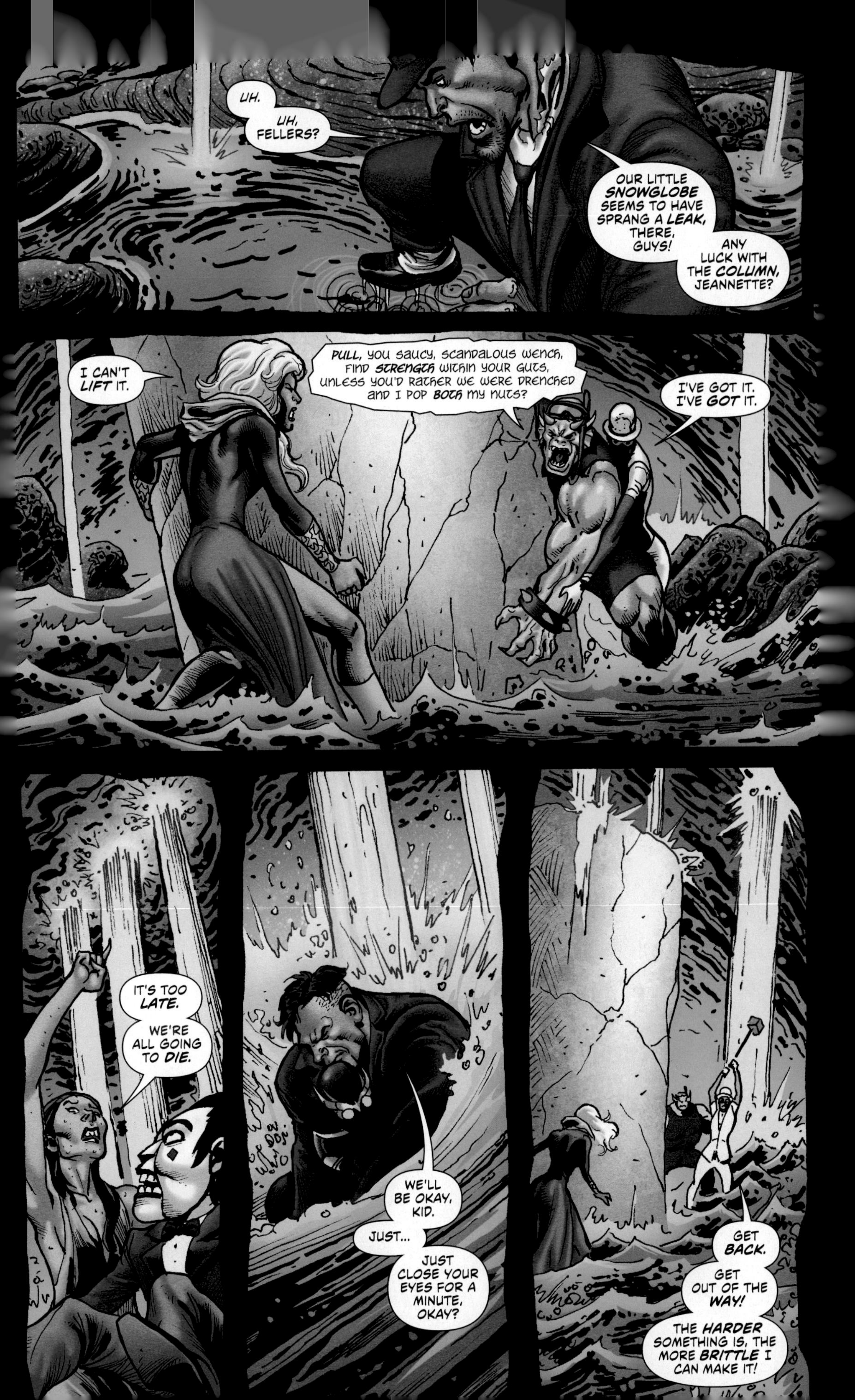
UH.
UH, FELLERS?
OUR LITTLE SNOWGLOBE SEEMS TO HAVE SPRANG A LEAK, THERE, GUYS!
ANY LUCK WITH THE COLUMN, JEANNETTE?
I CAN'T LIFT IT.
PULL, YOU SAUCY, SCANDALOUS WENCH, FIND STRENGTH WITHIN YOUR GUTS, UNLESS YOU'D RATHER WE WERE DRENCHED AND I POP BOTH MY NUTS?
I'VE GOT IT. I'VE GOT IT.
IT'S TOO LATE.
WE'RE ALL GOING TO DIE.
WE'LL BE OKAY, KID.
JUST...
JUST CLOSE YOUR EYES FOR A MINUTE, OKAY?
GET BACK.
GET OUT OF THE WAY!
THE HARDER SOMETHING IS, THE MORE BRITTLE I CAN MAKE IT!

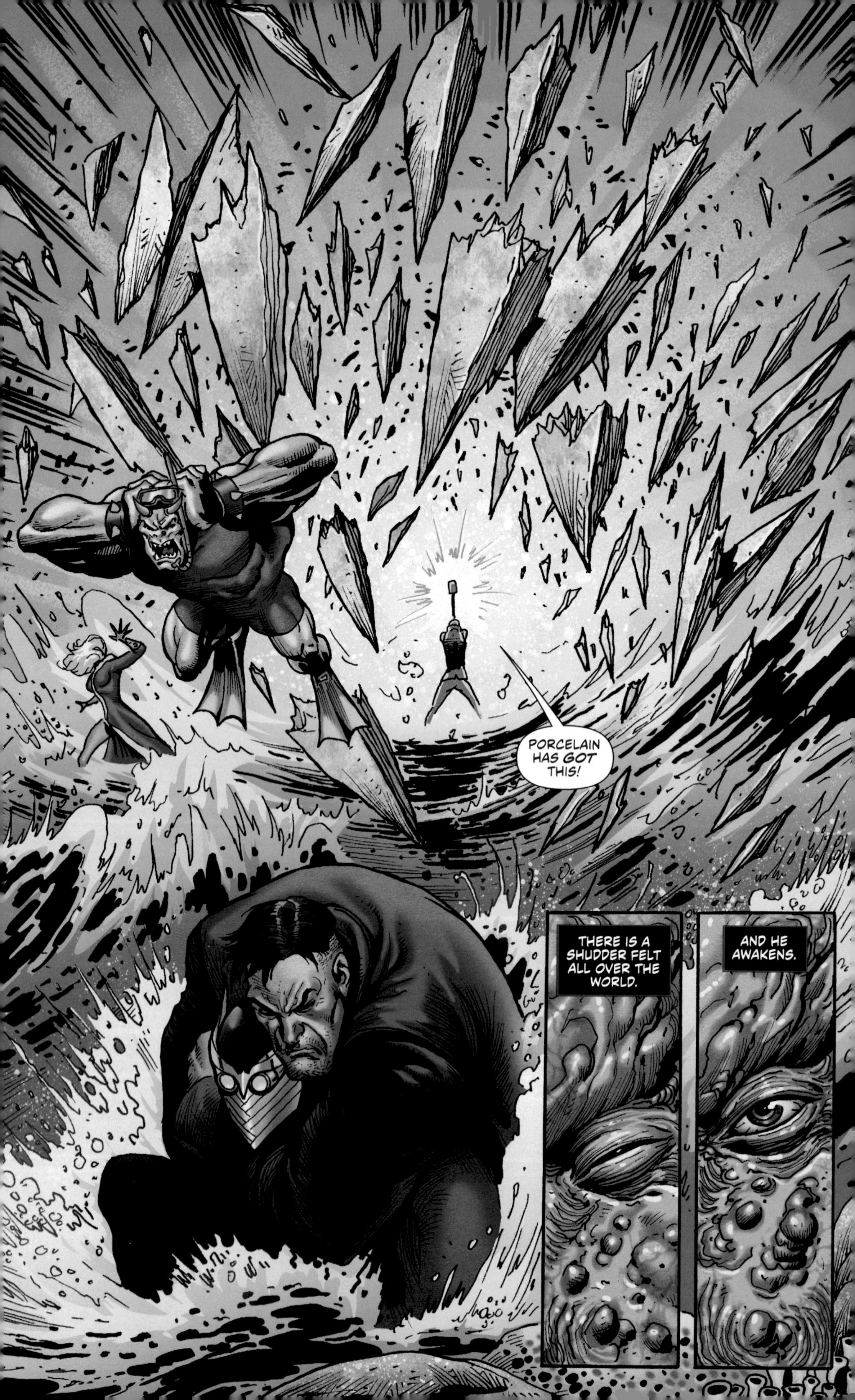
PORCELAIN HAS GOT THIS!
THERE IS A SHUDDER FELT ALL OVER THE WORLD.
AND HE AWAKENS.

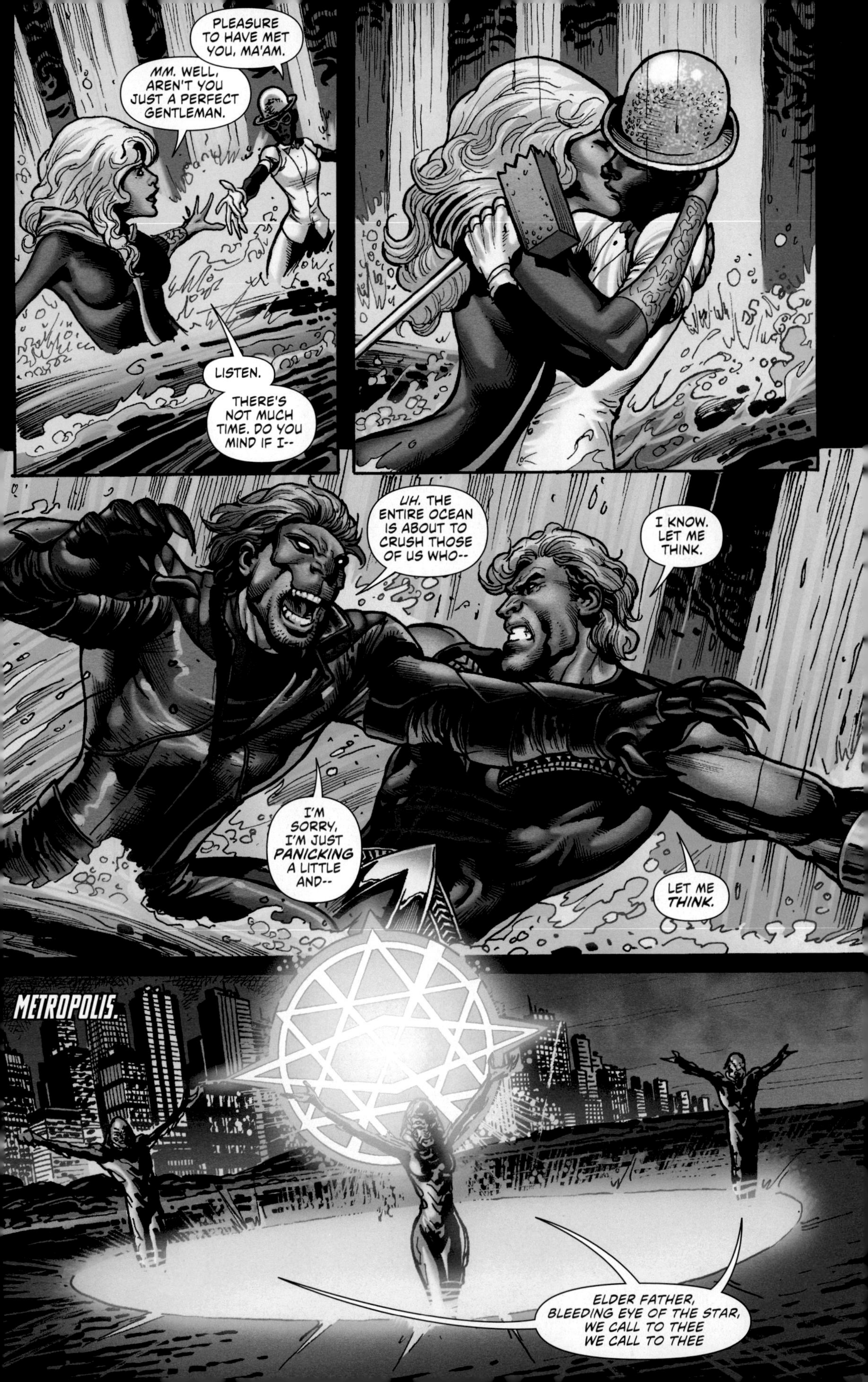
PLEASURE TO HAVE MET YOU, MA'AM.
MM. WELL, AREN'T YOU JUST A PERFECT GENTLEMAN.
LISTEN.
THERE'S NOT MUCH TIME. DO YOU MIND IF I--
UH. THE ENTIRE OCEAN IS ABOUT TO CRUSH THOSE OF US WHO--
I KNOW. LET ME THINK.
I'M SORRY, I'M JUST PANICKING A LITTLE AND--
LET ME THINK.
METROPOLIS.
ELDER FATHER, BLEEDING EYE OF THE STAR, WE CALL TO THEE WE CALL TO THEE

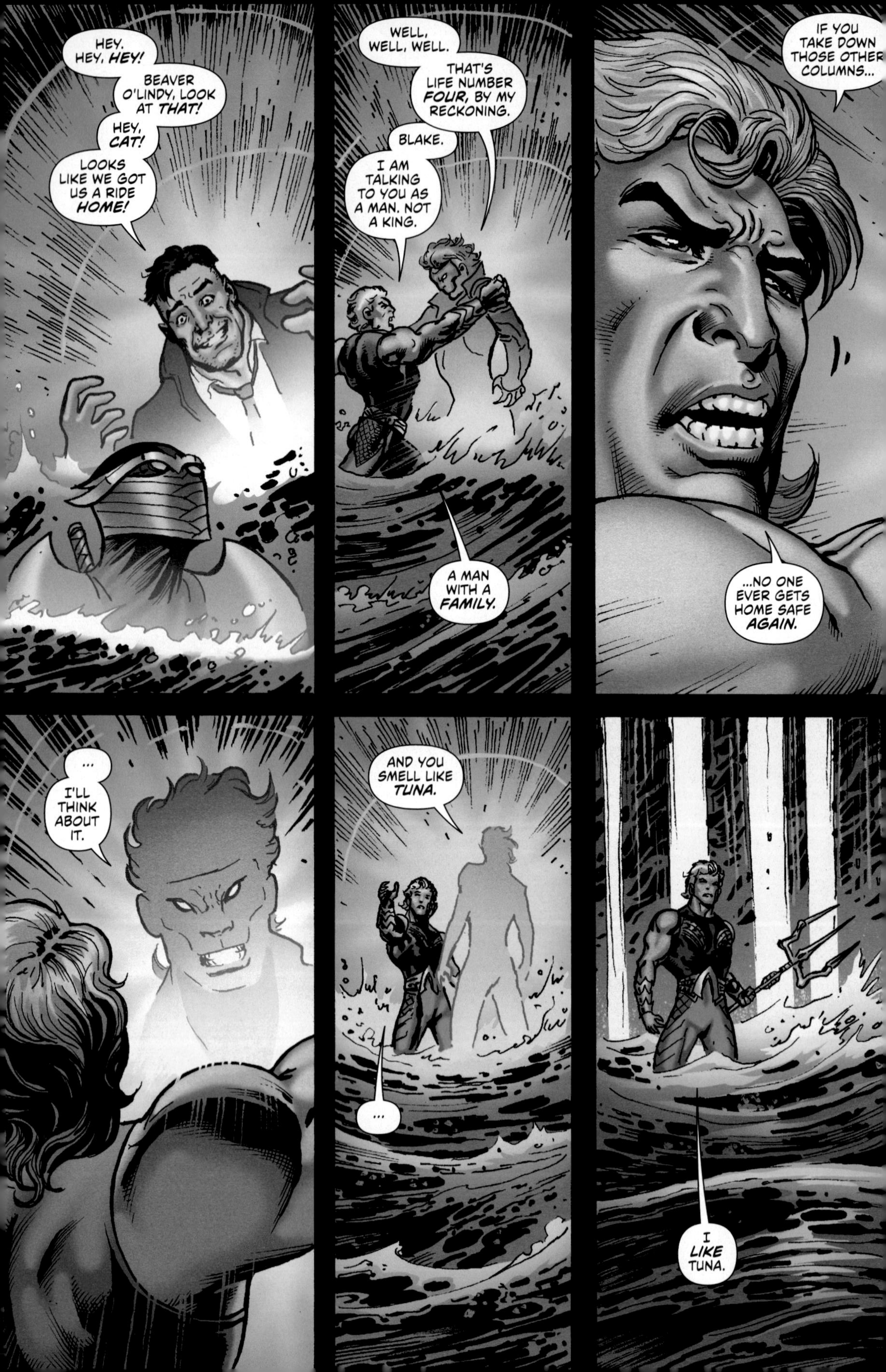
HEY. HEY, HEY!
BEAVER O'LINDY, LOOK AT THAT!
HEY, CAT!
LOOKS LIKE WE GOT US A RIDE HOME!
WELL, WELL, WELL.
THAT'S LIFE NUMBER FOUR, BY MY RECKONING.
BLAKE.
I AM TALKING TO YOU AS A MAN. NOT A KING.
A MAN WITH A FAMILY.
IF YOU TAKE DOWN THOSE OTHER COLUMNS...
...NO ONE EVER GETS HOME SAFE AGAIN.
...
I'LL THINK ABOUT IT.
AND YOU SMELL LIKE TUNA.
...
I LIKE TUNA.

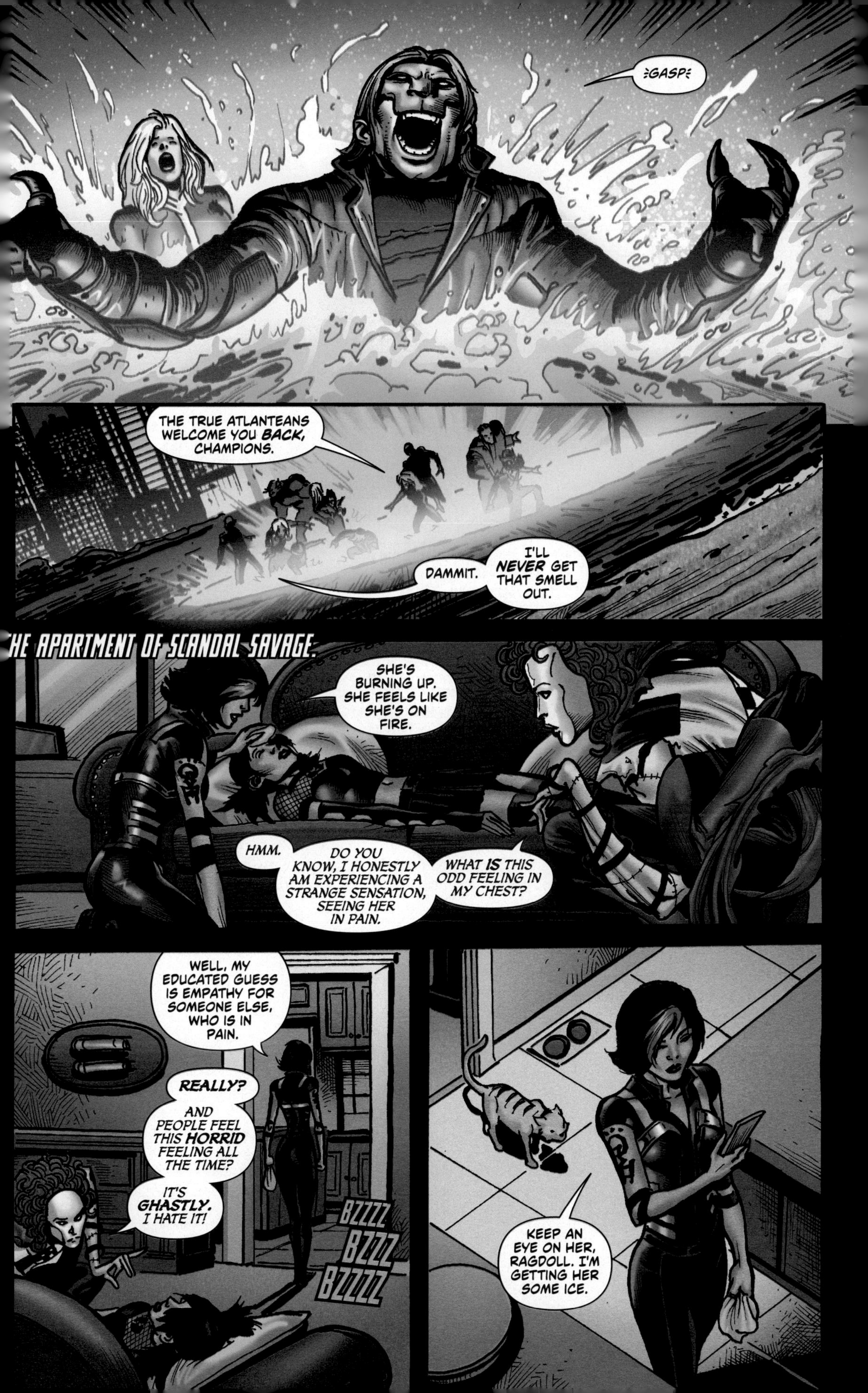
:GASP:
THE TRUE ATLANTEANS WELCOME YOU BACK, CHAMPIONS.
DAMMIT.
I'LL NEVER GET THAT SMELL OUT.
HE APARTMENT OF SCANDAL SAVAGE.
SHE'S BURNING UP. SHE FEELS LIKE SHE'S ON FIRE.
HMM.
DO YOU KNOW, I HONESTLY AM EXPERIENCING A STRANGE SENSATION, SEEING HER IN PAIN.
WHAT IS THIS ODD FEELING IN MY CHEST?
WELL, MY EDUCATED GUESS IS EMPATHY FOR SOMEONE ELSE, WHO IS IN PAIN.
REALLY?
AND PEOPLE FEEL THIS HORRID FEELING ALL THE TIME?
IT'S GHASTLY. I HATE IT!
BZZZZ
BZZZ
BZZZZ
KEEP AN EYE ON HER, RAGDOLL. I'M GETTING HER SOME ICE.

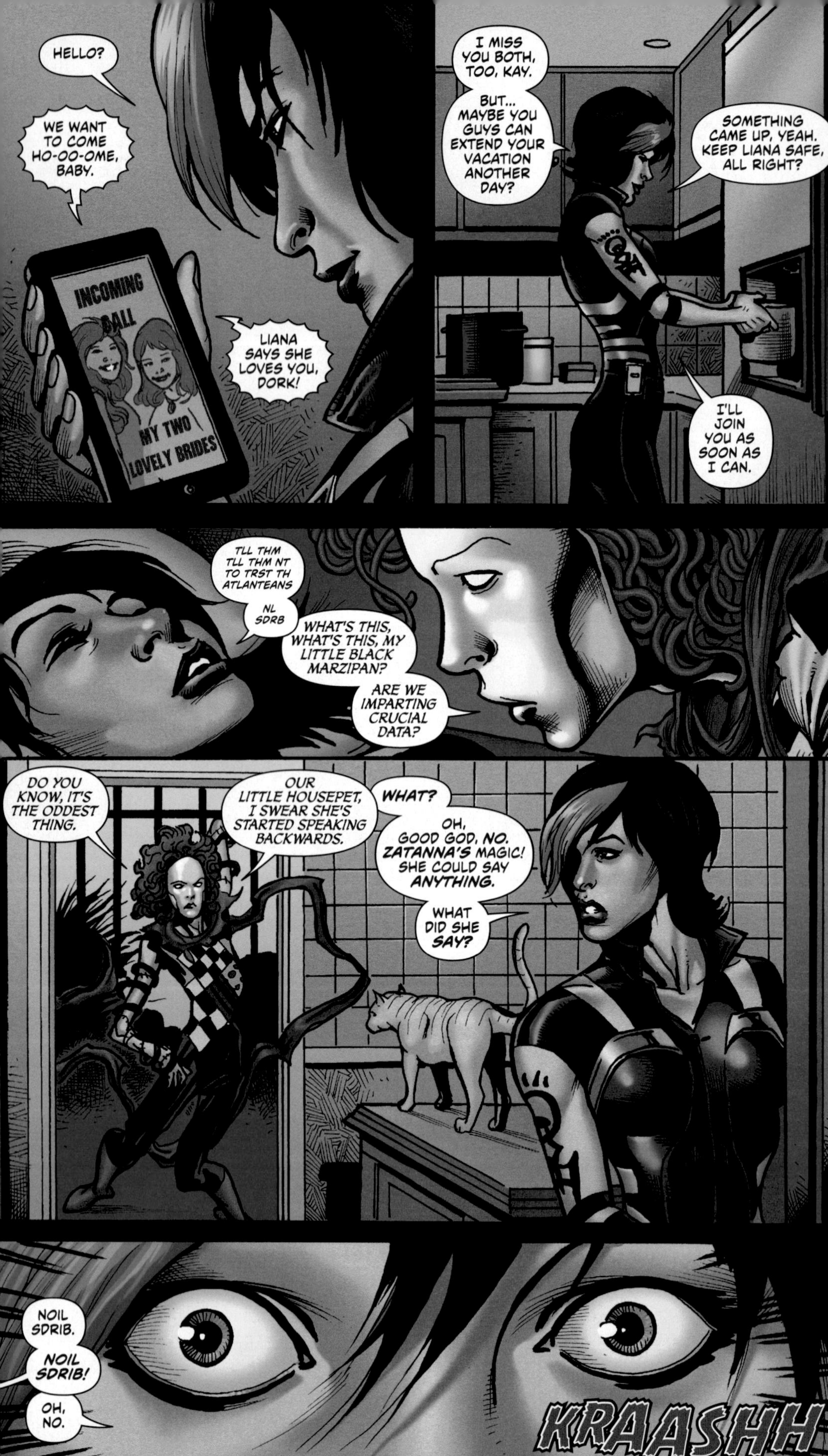
HELLO?
WE WANT TO COME HO-OO-OME, BABY.
INCOMING CALL
MY TWO LOVELY BRIDES
LIANA SAYS SHE LOVES YOU, DORK!
I MISS YOU BOTH, TOO, KAY.
BUT... MAYBE YOU GUYS CAN EXTEND YOUR VACATION ANOTHER DAY?
SOMETHING CAME UP, YEAH. KEEP LIANA SAFE, ALL RIGHT?
I'LL JOIN YOU AS SOON AS I CAN.
TLL THM TLL THM NT TO TRST TH ATLANTEANS
NL SDRB
WHAT'S THIS, WHAT'S THIS, MY LITTLE BLACK MARZIPAN?
ARE WE IMPARTING CRUCIAL DATA?
DO YOU KNOW, IT'S THE ODDEST THING.
OUR LITTLE HOUSEPET, I SWEAR SHE'S STARTED SPEAKING BACKWARDS.
WHAT?
OH, GOOD GOD, NO. ZATANNA'S MAGIC! SHE COULD SAY ANYTHING.
WHAT DID SHE SAY?
NOIL SDRIB.
NOIL SDRIB!
OH, NO.
KRAASHH

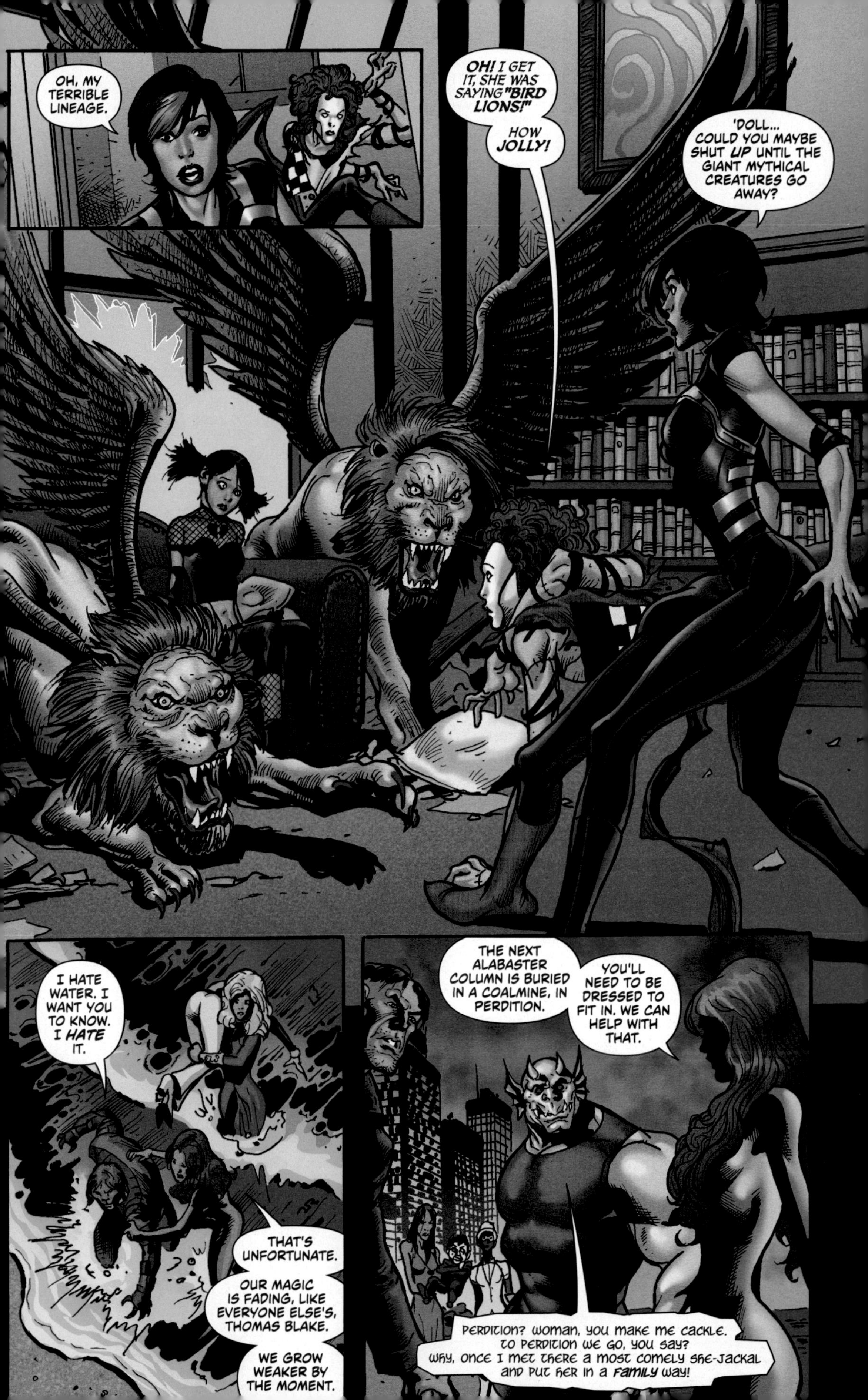
OH, MY TERRIBLE LINEAGE.
OH! I GET IT, SHE WAS SAYING "BIRD LIONS!"
HOW JOLLY!
'DOLL... COULD YOU MAYBE SHUT UP UNTIL THE GIANT MYTHICAL CREATURES GO AWAY?
I HATE WATER. I WANT YOU TO KNOW. I HATE IT.
THAT'S UNFORTUNATE.
OUR MAGIC IS FADING, LIKE EVERYONE ELSE'S, THOMAS BLAKE.
WE GROW WEAKER BY THE MOMENT.
THE NEXT ALABASTER COLUMN IS BURIED IN A COALMINE, IN PERDITION.
YOU'LL NEED TO BE DRESSED TO FIT IN. WE CAN HELP WITH THAT.
PERDITION? WOMAN, YOU MAKE ME CACKLE.
TO PERDITION WE GO, YOU SAY?
WHY, ONCE I MET THERE A MOST COMELY SHE-JACKAL
AND PUT HER IN A FAMILY WAY!

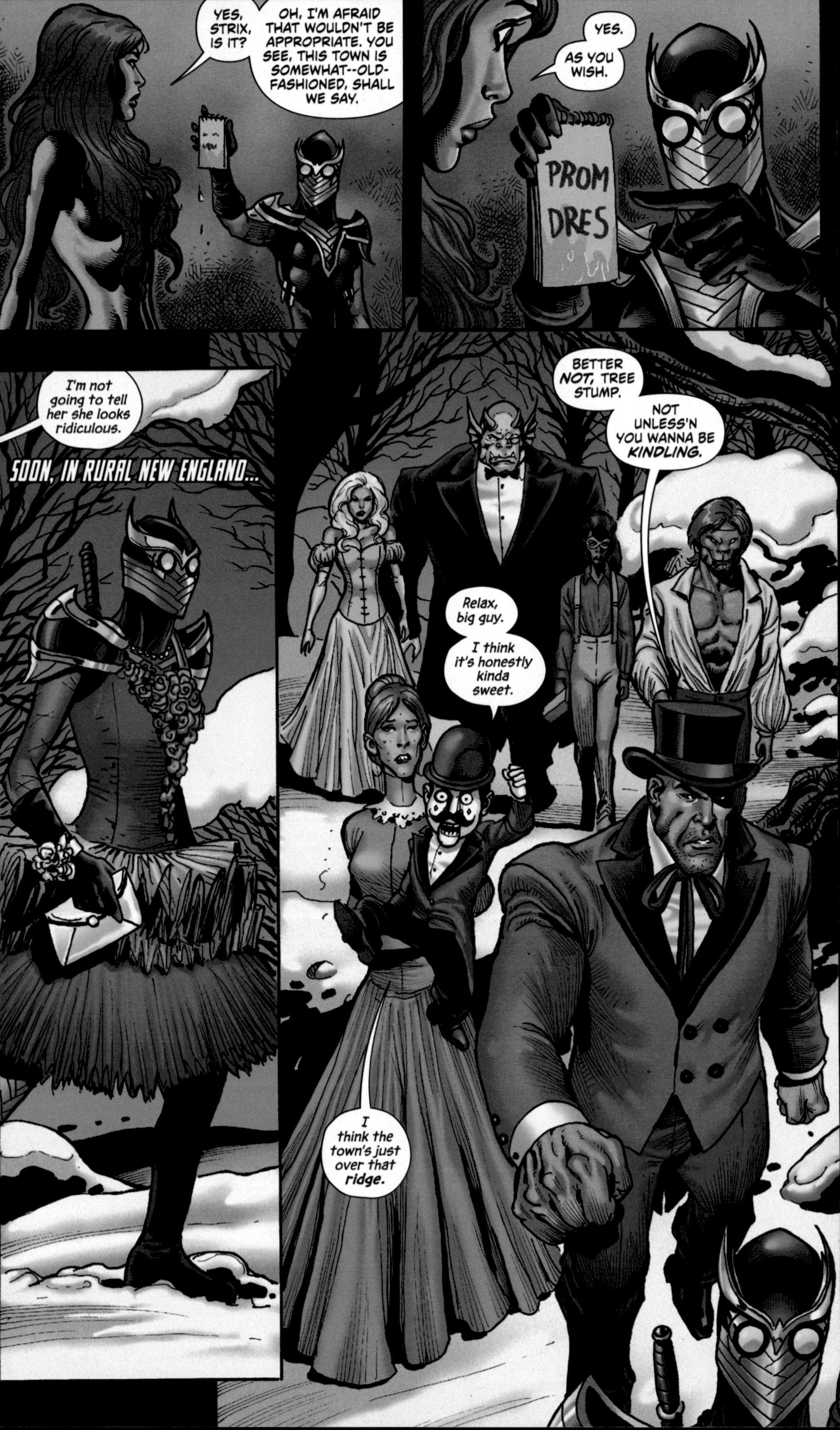
YES, STRIX, IS IT?
OH, I'M AFRAID THAT WOULDN'T BE APPROPRIATE. YOU SEE, THIS TOWN IS SOMEWHAT--OLD-FASHIONED, SHALL WE SAY.
YES.
AS YOU WISH.
PROM DRES
I'm not going to tell her she looks ridiculous.
SOON, IN RURAL NEW ENGLAND...
BETTER NOT, TREE STUMP.
NOT UNLESS'N YOU WANNA BE KINDLING.
Relax, big guy.
I think it's honestly kinda sweet.
I think the town's just over that ridge.

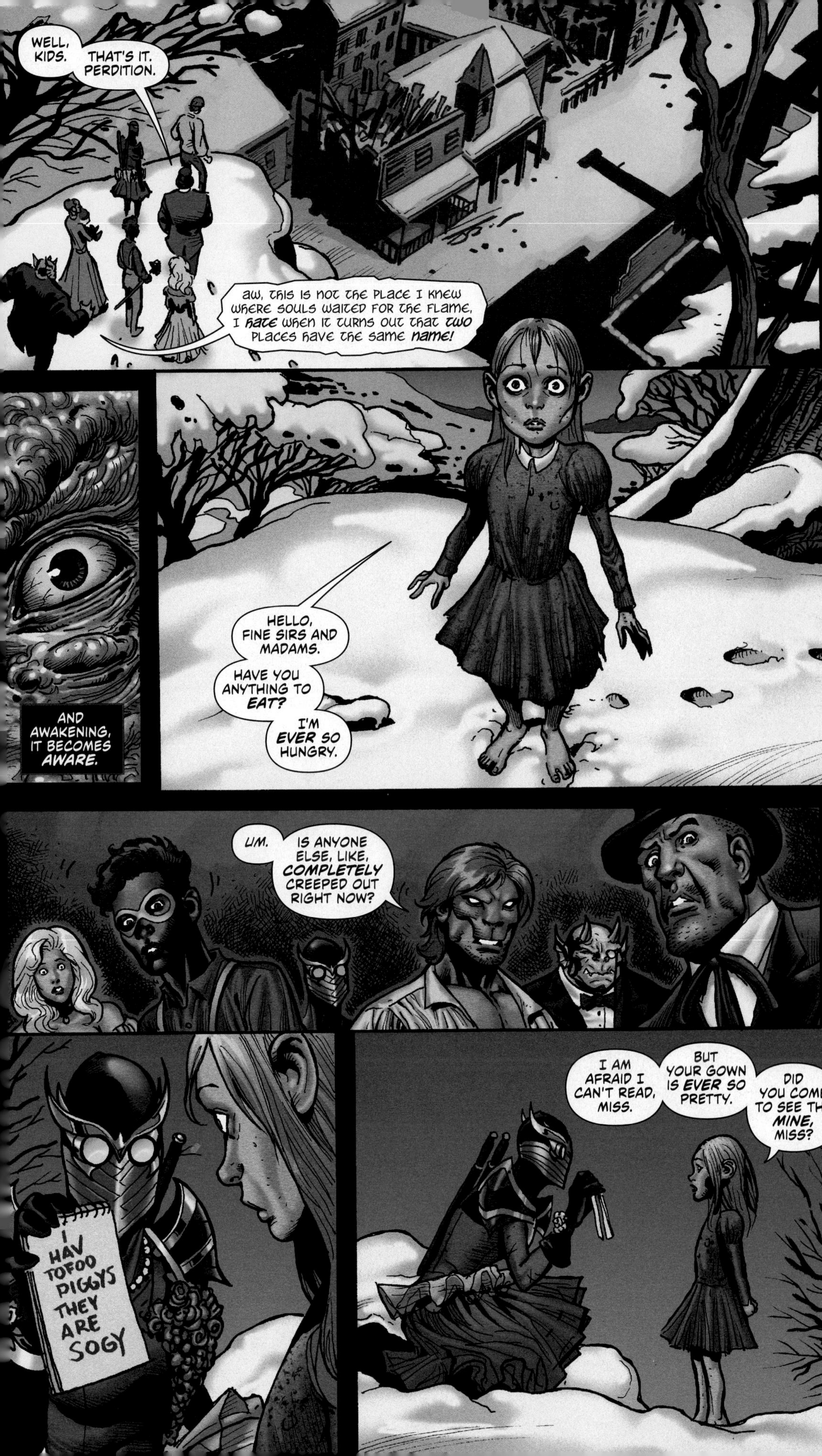
WELL, KIDS.
THAT'S IT. PERDITION.
AW, THIS IS NOT THE PLACE I KNEW WHERE SOULS WAITED FOR THE FLAME, I HATE WHEN IT TURNS OUT THAT TWO PLACES HAVE THE SAME NAME!
AND AWAKENING, IT BECOMES AWARE.
HELLO, FINE SIRS AND MADAMS.
HAVE YOU ANYTHING TO EAT?
I'M EVER SO HUNGRY.
UM.
IS ANYONE ELSE, LIKE, COMPLETELY CREEPED OUT RIGHT NOW?
I HAV TOFOO DIGGYS THEY ARE SOGY
I AM AFRAID I CAN'T READ, MISS.
BUT YOUR GOWN IS EVER SO PRETTY.
DID YOU COME TO SEE THE MINE, MISS?

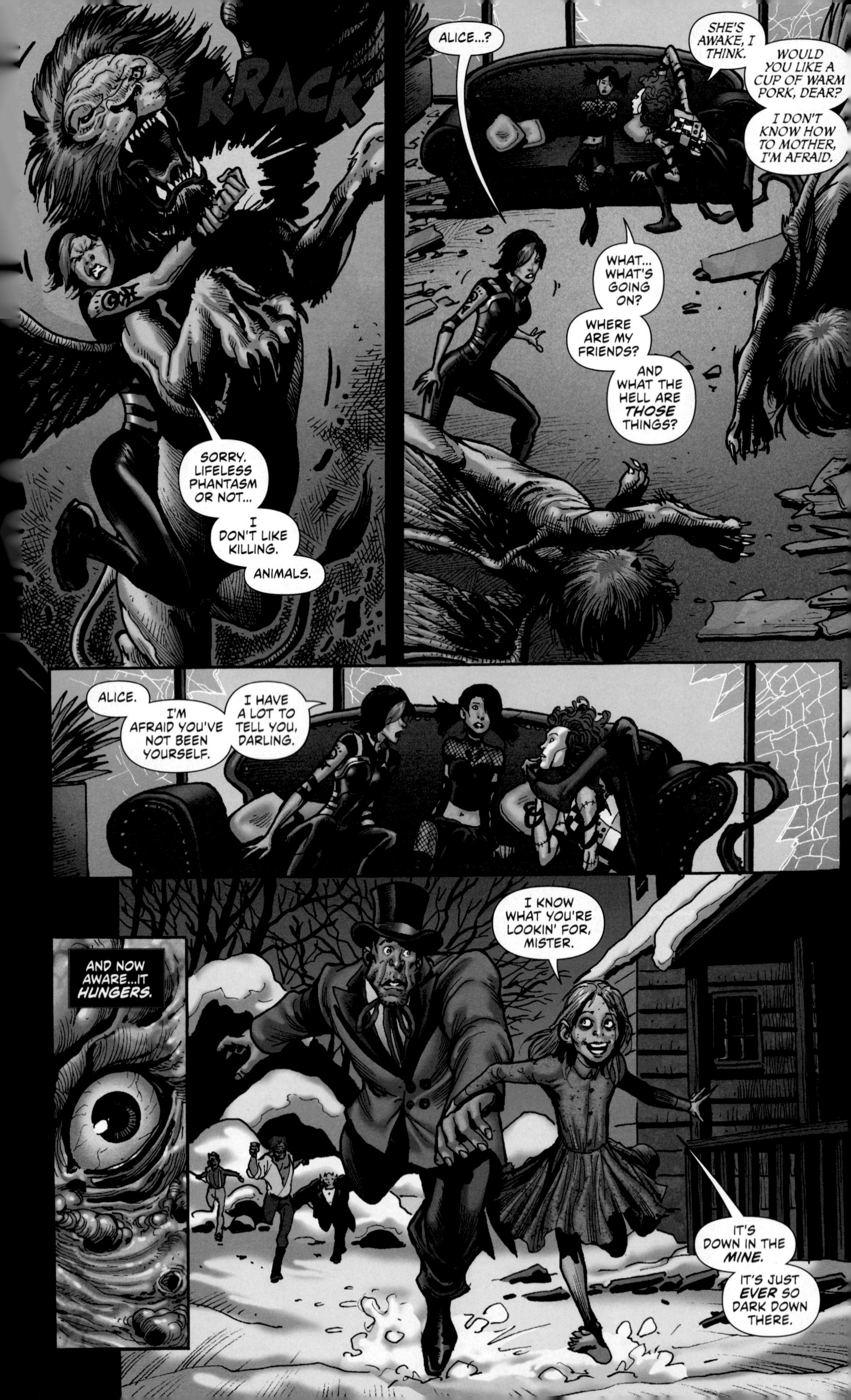
KRACK
SORRY. LIFELESS PHANTASM OR NOT...
I DON'T LIKE KILLING.
ANIMALS.
ALICE...?
SHE'S AWAKE, I THINK.
WOULD YOU LIKE A CUP OF WARM PORK, DEAR?
I DON'T KNOW HOW TO MOTHER, I'M AFRAID.
WHAT... WHAT'S GOING ON?
WHERE ARE MY FRIENDS?
AND WHAT THE HELL ARE THOSE THINGS?
ALICE.
I'M AFRAID YOU'VE NOT BEEN YOURSELF.
I HAVE A LOT TO TELL YOU, DARLING.
AND NOW AWARE...IT HUNGERS.
I KNOW WHAT YOU'RE LOOKIN' FOR, MISTER.
IT'S DOWN IN THE MINE.
IT'S JUST EVER SO DARK DOWN THERE.

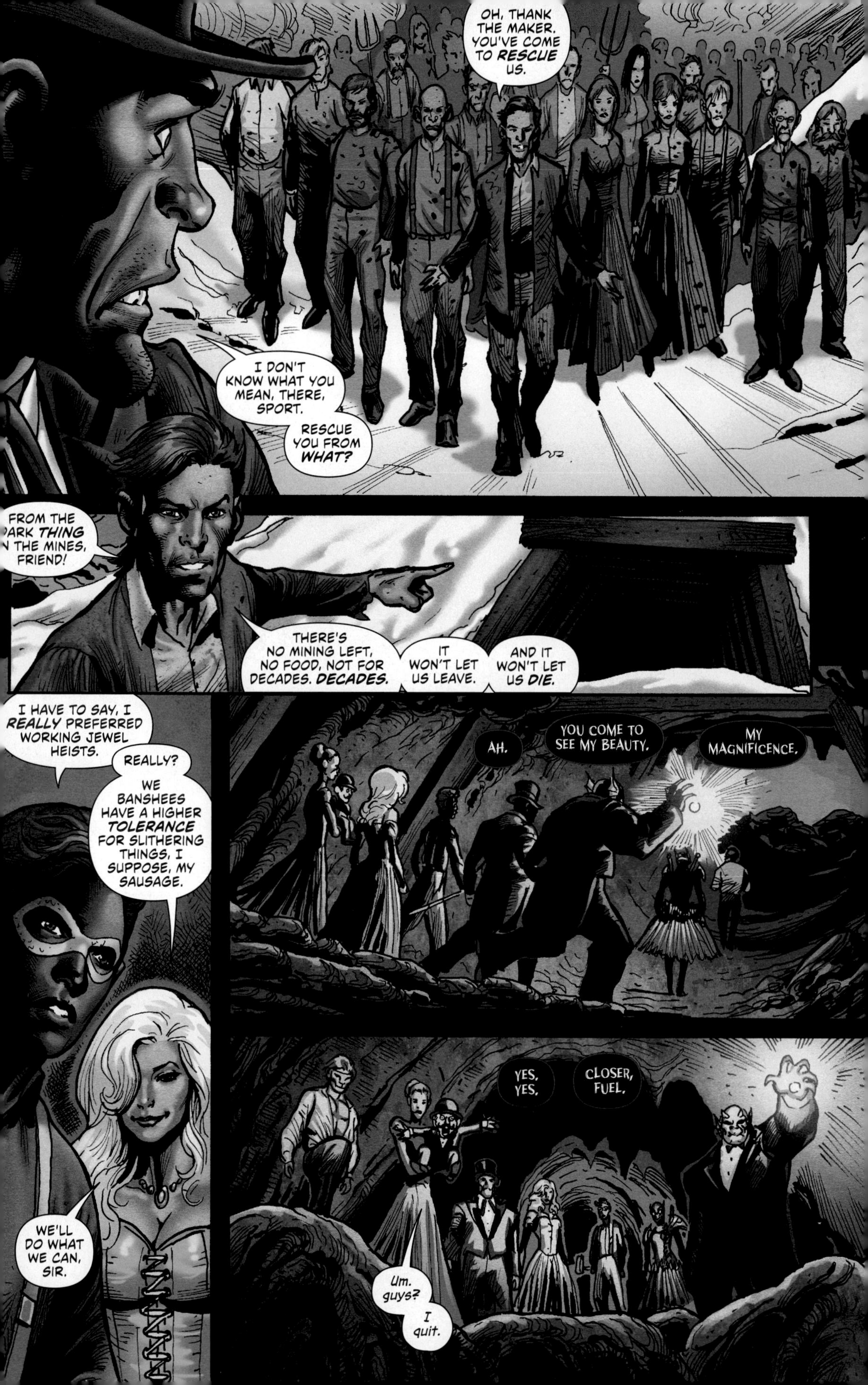
OH, THANK THE MAKER. YOU'VE COME TO RESCUE US.
I DON'T KNOW WHAT YOU MEAN, THERE, SPORT.
RESCUE YOU FROM WHAT?
FROM THE DARK THING IN THE MINES, FRIEND!
THERE'S NO MINING LEFT, NO FOOD, NOT FOR DECADES. DECADES.
IT WON'T LET US LEAVE.
AND IT WON'T LET US DIE.
I HAVE TO SAY, I REALLY PREFERRED WORKING JEWEL HEISTS.
REALLY?
WE BANSHEES HAVE A HIGHER TOLERANCE FOR SLITHERING THINGS, I SUPPOSE, MY SAUSAGE.
WE'LL DO WHAT WE CAN, SIR.
AH.
YOU COME TO SEE MY BEAUTY.
MY MAGNIFICENCE.
YES, YES.
CLOSER, FUEL.
Um. guys?
I quit.

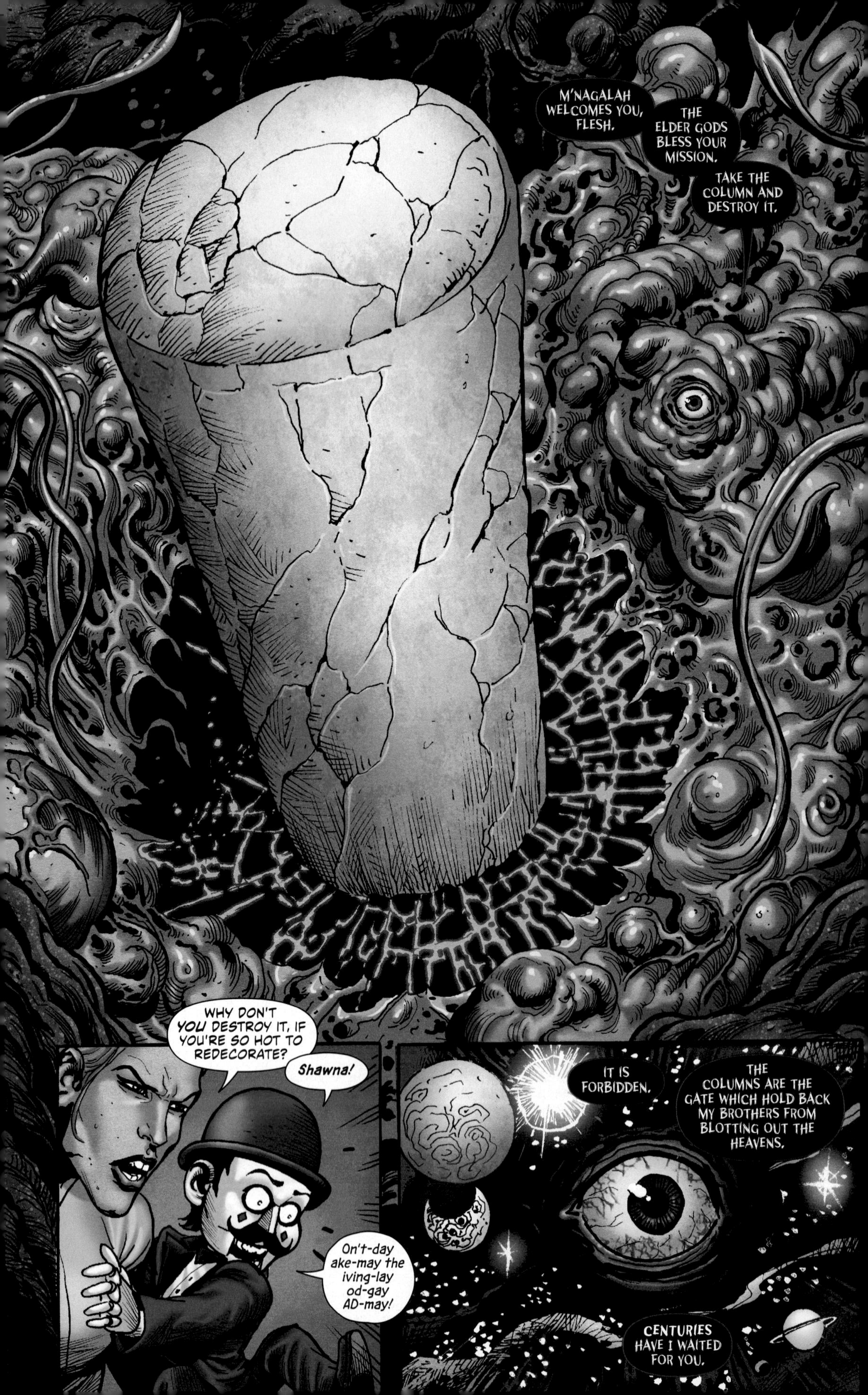
M'NAGALAH WELCOMES YOU, FLESH.
THE ELDER GODS BLESS YOUR MISSION.
TAKE THE COLUMN AND DESTROY IT.
WHY DON'T YOU DESTROY IT, IF YOU'RE SO HOT TO REDECORATE?
Shawna!
On't-day ake-may the iving-lay od-gay AD-may!
IT IS FORBIDDEN.
THE COLUMNS ARE THE GATE WHICH HOLD BACK MY BROTHERS FROM BLOTTING OUT THE HEAVENS.
CENTURIES HAVE I WAITED FOR YOU.

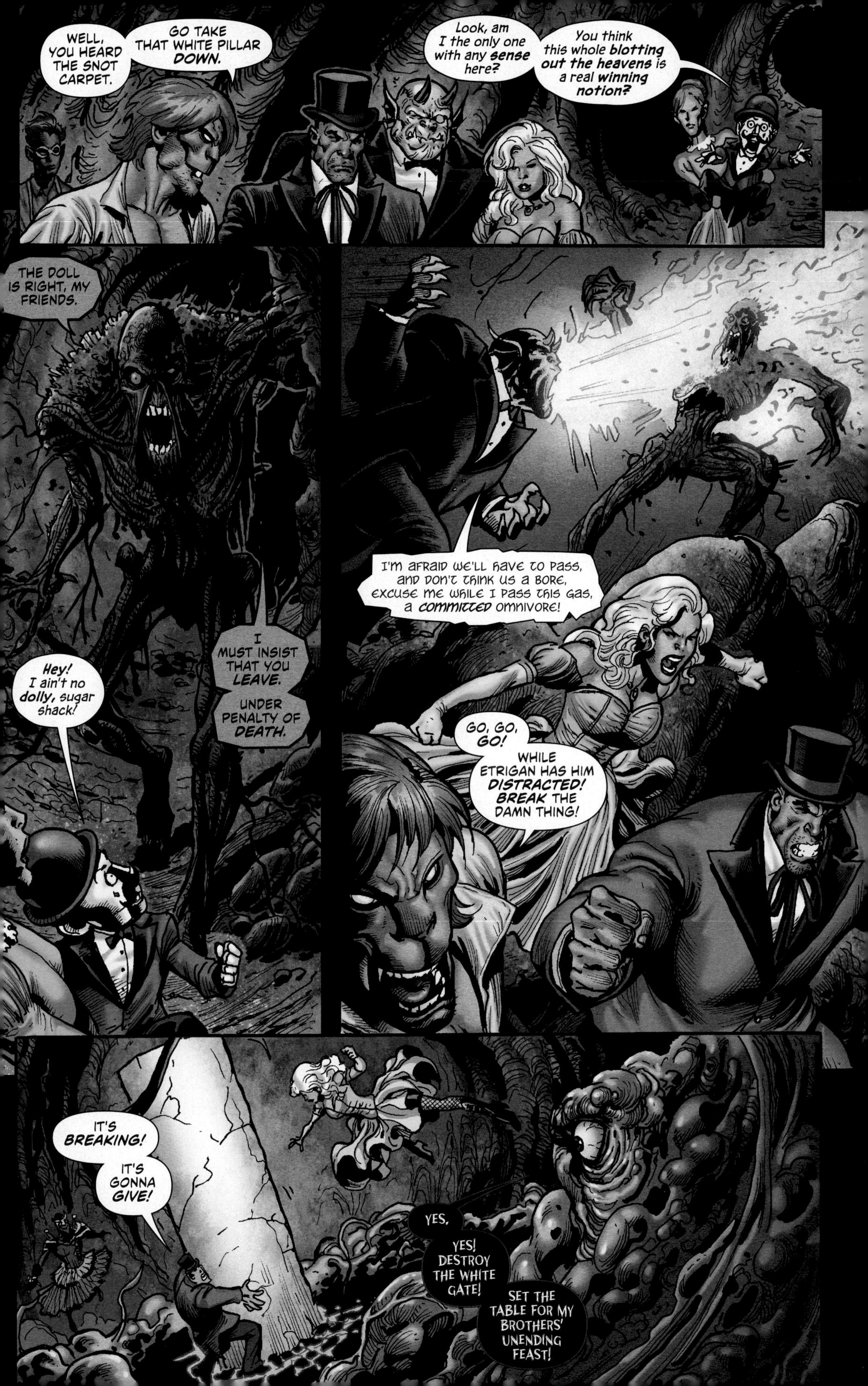
WELL, YOU HEARD THE SNOT CARPET.
GO TAKE THAT WHITE PILLAR DOWN.
Look, am I the only one with any sense here?
You think this whole blotting out the heavens is a real winning notion?
THE DOLL IS RIGHT, MY FRIENDS.
I MUST INSIST THAT YOU LEAVE.
UNDER PENALTY OF DEATH.
Hey! I ain't no dolly, sugar shack!
I'M AFRAID WE'LL HAVE TO PASS, AND DON'T THINK US A BORE, EXCUSE ME WHILE I PASS THIS GAS, A COMMITTED OMNIVORE!
GO, GO, GO!
WHILE ETRIGAN HAS HIM DISTRACTED! BREAK THE DAMN THING!
IT'S BREAKING!
IT'S GONNA GIVE!
YES.
YES! DESTROY THE WHITE GATE!
SET THE TABLE FOR MY BROTHERS' UNENDING FEAST!

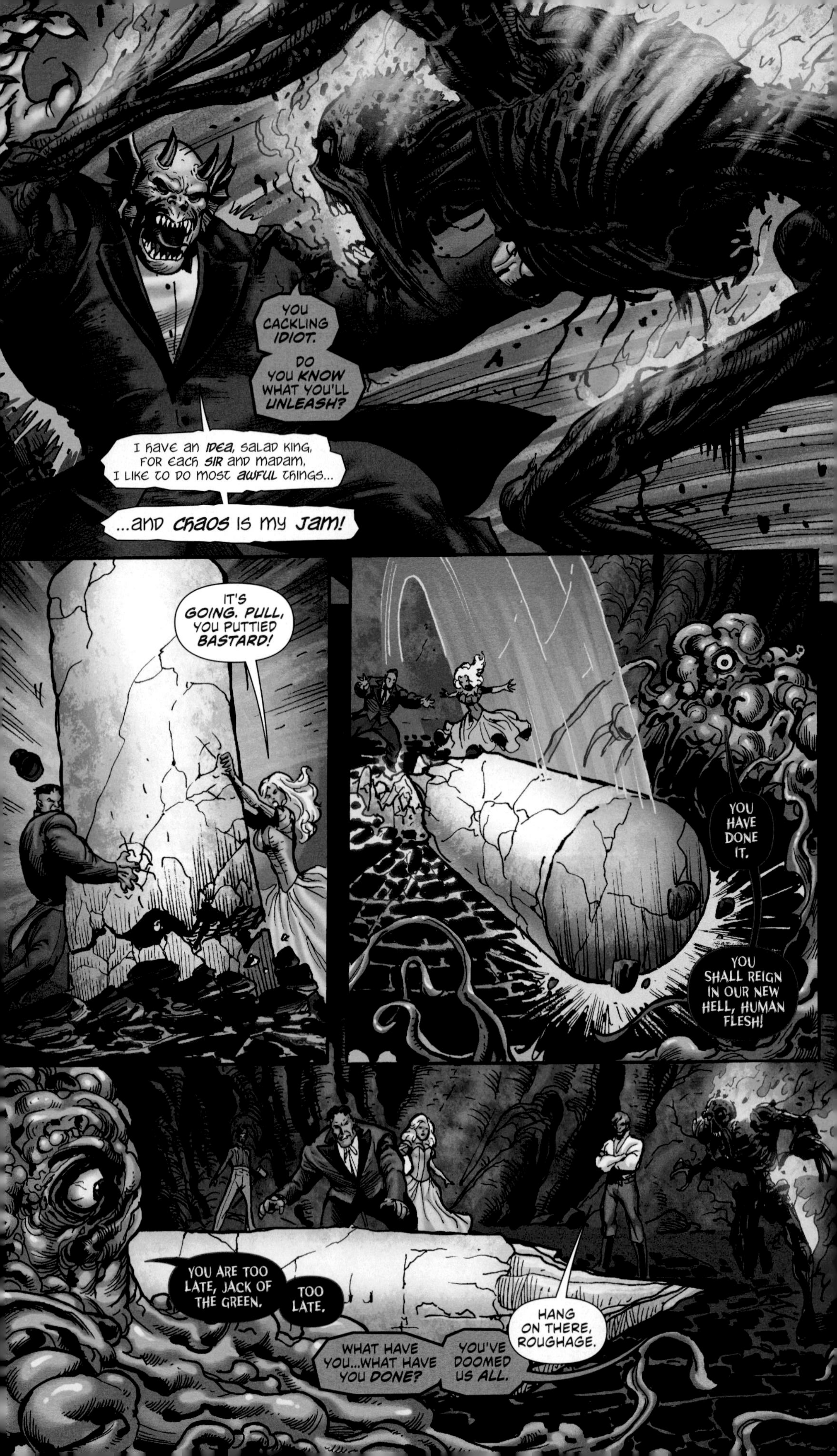
YOU CACKLING IDIOT.
DO YOU KNOW WHAT YOU'LL UNLEASH?
I HAVE AN IDEA, SALAD KING, FOR EACH SIR AND MADAM, I LIKE TO DO MOST AWFUL THINGS...
...AND CHAOS IS MY JAM!
IT'S GOING. PULL, YOU PUTTIED BASTARD!
YOU HAVE DONE IT.
YOU SHALL REIGN IN OUR NEW HELL, HUMAN FLESH!
YOU ARE TOO LATE, JACK OF THE GREEN.
TOO LATE.
HANG ON THERE, ROUGHAGE.
WHAT HAVE YOU...WHAT HAVE YOU DONE?
YOU'VE DOOMED US ALL.

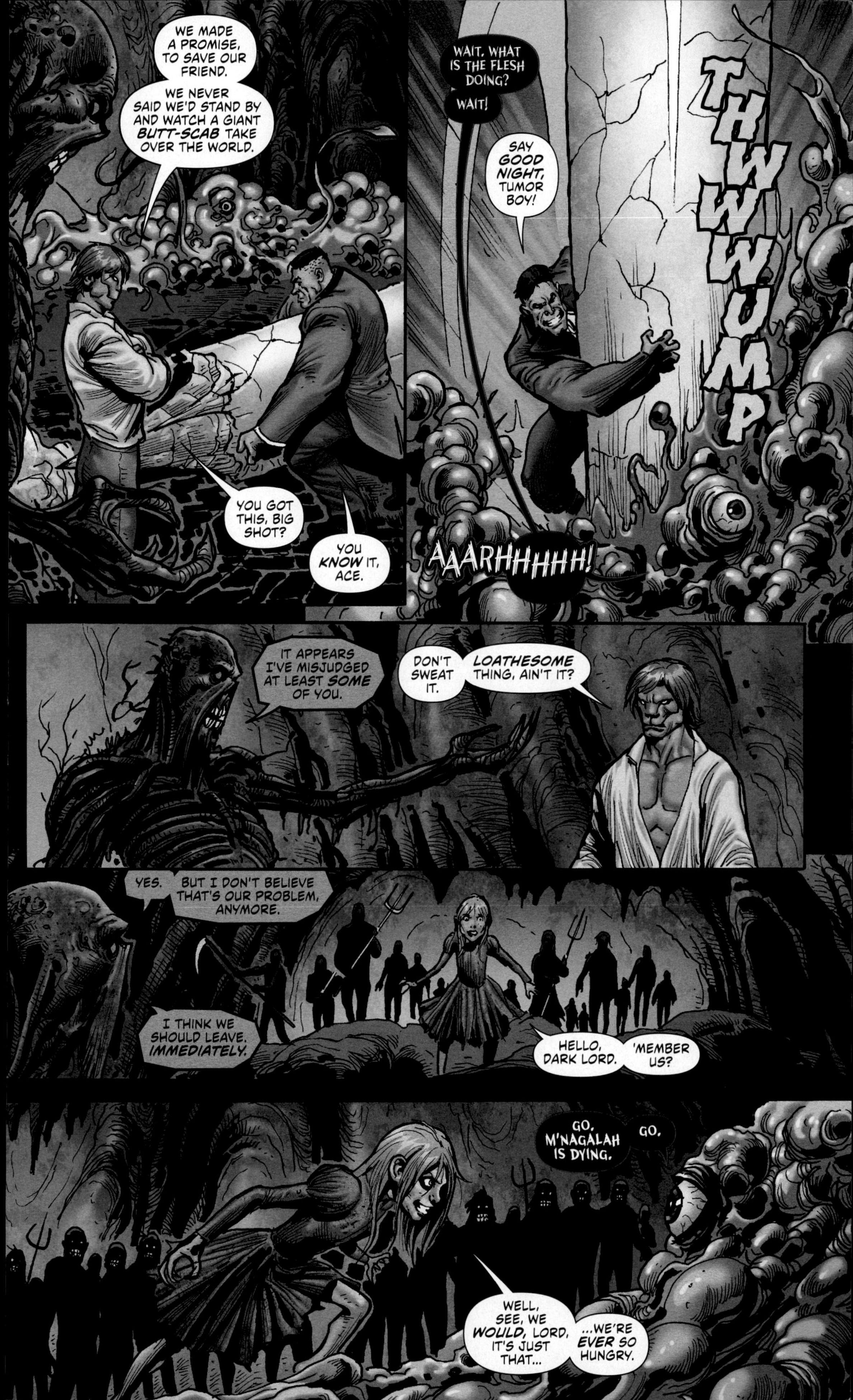
WE MADE A PROMISE, TO SAVE OUR FRIEND.
WE NEVER SAID WE'D STAND BY AND WATCH A GIANT BUTT-SCAB TAKE OVER THE WORLD.
YOU GOT THIS, BIG SHOT?
YOU KNOW IT, ACE.
WAIT. WHAT IS THE FLESH DOING?
WAIT!
SAY GOOD NIGHT, TUMOR BOY!
THWWWUMP
AAARHHHHH!
IT APPEARS I'VE MISJUDGED AT LEAST SOME OF YOU.
DON'T SWEAT IT.
LOATHESOME THING, AIN'T IT?
YES.
BUT I DON'T BELIEVE THAT'S OUR PROBLEM, ANYMORE.
I THINK WE SHOULD LEAVE. IMMEDIATELY.
HELLO, DARK LORD.
'MEMBER US?
GO. M'NAGALAH IS DYING.
GO.
WELL, SEE, WE WOULD, LORD, IT'S JUST THAT...
...WE'RE EVER SO HUNGRY.

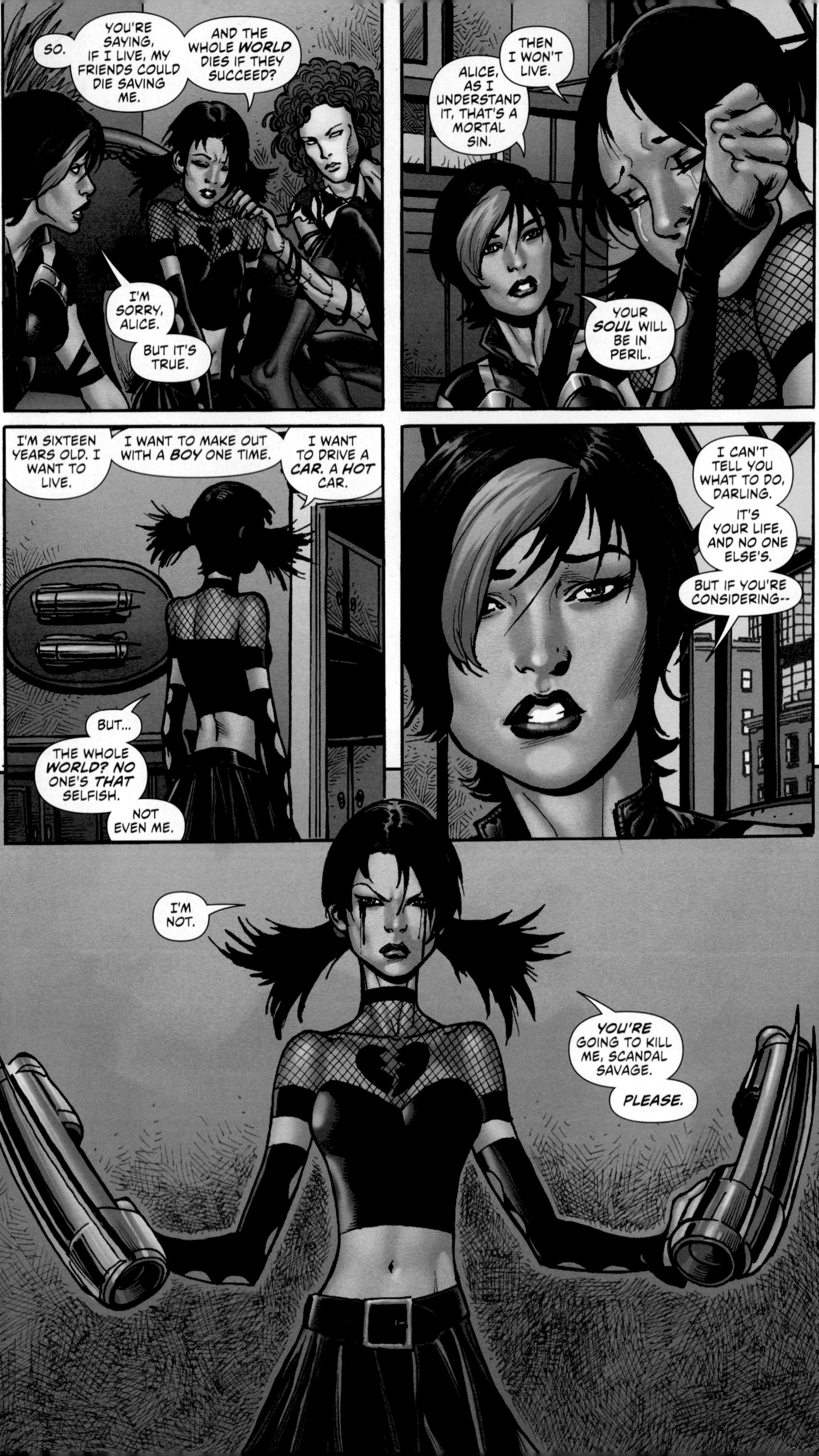
SO.
YOU'RE SAYING, IF I LIVE, MY FRIENDS COULD DIE SAVING ME.
AND THE WHOLE WORLD DIES IF THEY SUCCEED?
I'M SORRY, ALICE.
BUT IT'S TRUE.
THEN I WON'T LIVE.
ALICE, AS I UNDERSTAND IT, THAT'S A MORTAL SIN.
YOUR SOUL WILL BE IN PERIL.
I'M SIXTEEN YEARS OLD. I WANT TO LIVE.
I WANT TO MAKE OUT WITH A BOY ONE TIME.
I WANT TO DRIVE A CAR. A HOT CAR.
BUT...
THE WHOLE WORLD? NO ONE'S THAT SELFISH.
NOT EVEN ME.
I CAN'T TELL YOU WHAT TO DO, DARLING.
IT'S YOUR LIFE, AND NO ONE ELSE'S.
BUT IF YOU'RE CONSIDERING--
I'M NOT.
YOU'RE GOING TO KILL ME, SCANDAL SAVAGE.
PLEASE.

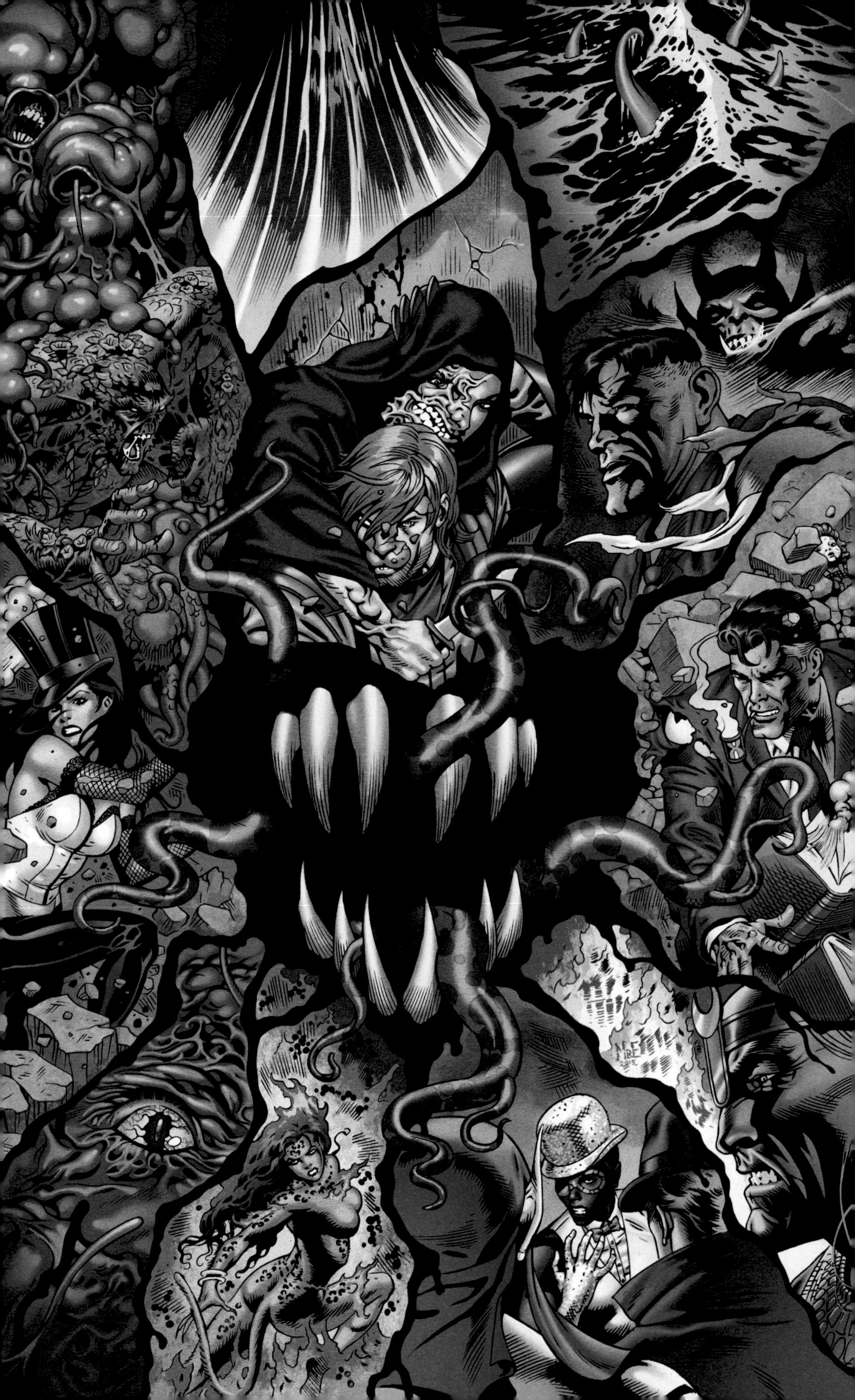

cover by DALE EAGLESHAM & JASON WRIGHT

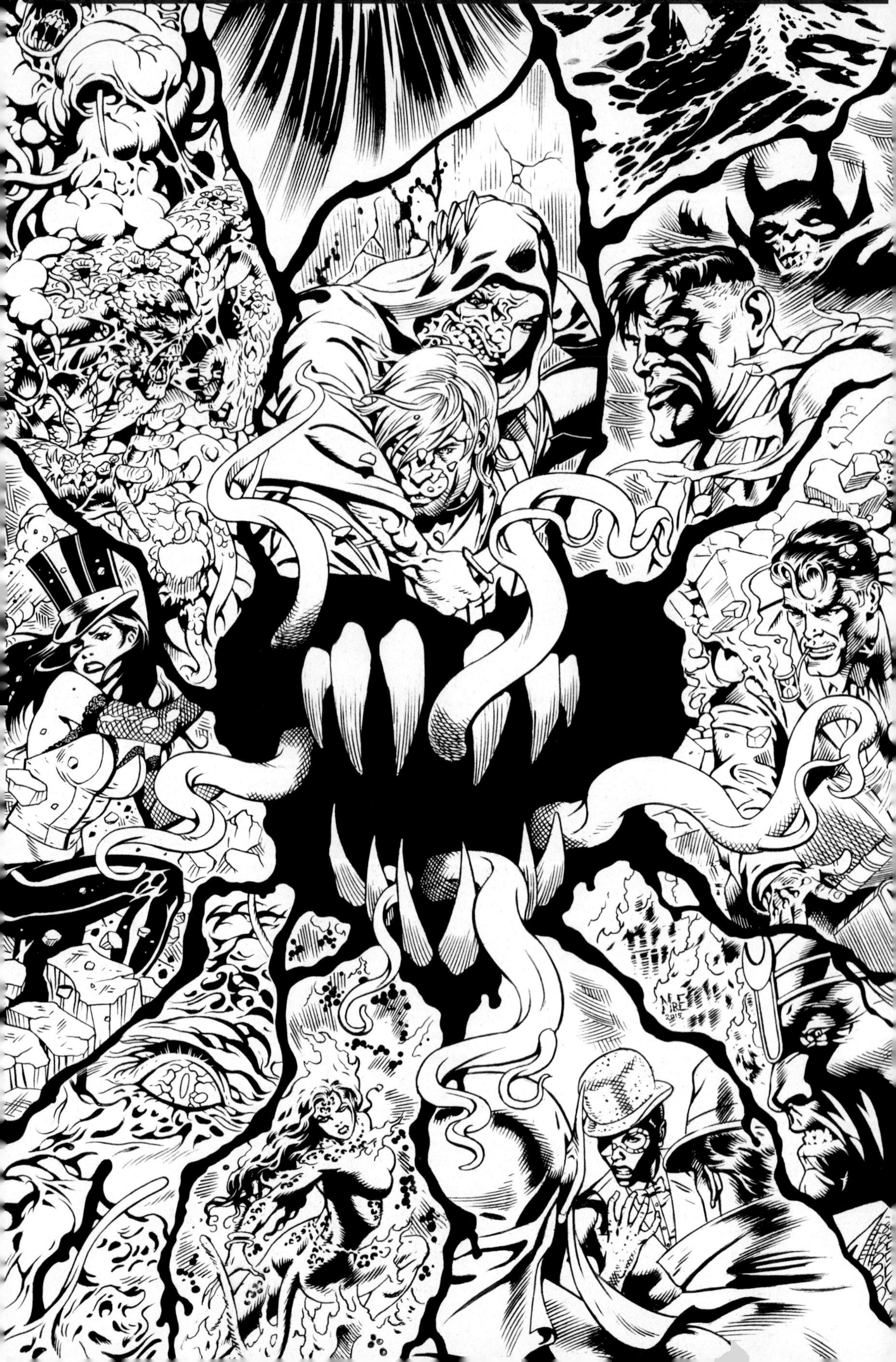

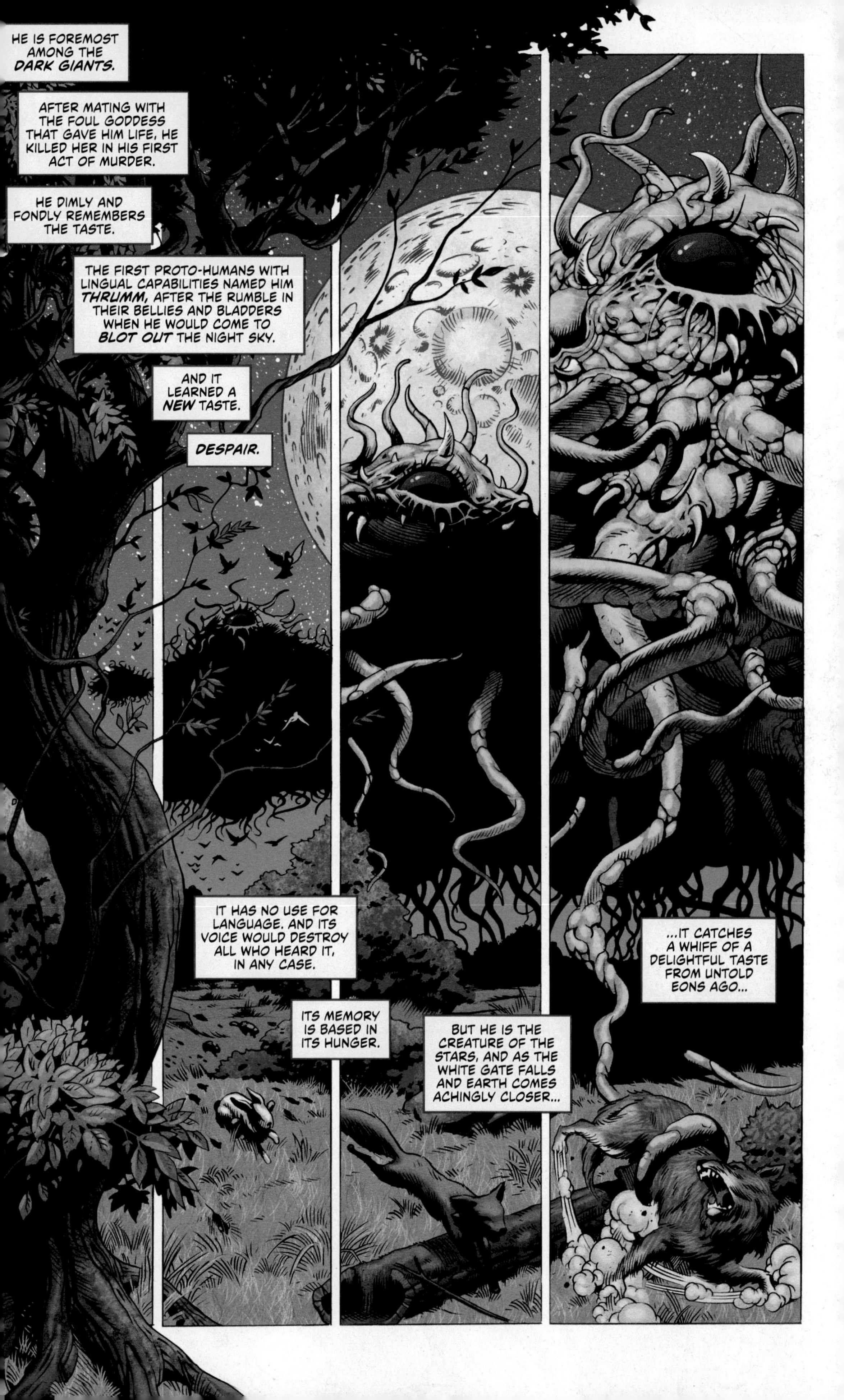
HE IS FOREMOST AMONG THE DARK GIANTS.
AFTER MATING WITH THE FOUL GODDESS THAT GAVE HIM LIFE, HE KILLED HER IN HIS FIRST ACT OF MURDER.
HE DIMLY AND FONDLY REMEMBERS THE TASTE.
THE FIRST PROTO-HUMANS WITH LINGUAL CAPABILITIES NAMED HIM THRUMM, AFTER THE RUMBLE IN THEIR BELLIES AND BLADDERS WHEN HE WOULD COME TO BLOT OUT THE NIGHT SKY.
AND IT LEARNED A NEW TASTE.
DESPAIR.
IT HAS NO USE FOR LANGUAGE. AND ITS VOICE WOULD DESTROY ALL WHO HEARD IT, IN ANY CASE.
ITS MEMORY IS BASED IN ITS HUNGER.
BUT HE IS THE CREATURE OF THE STARS, AND AS THE WHITE GATE FALLS AND EARTH COMES ACHINGLY CLOSER...
...IT CATCHES A WHIFF OF A DELIGHTFUL TASTE FROM UNTOLD EONS AGO...

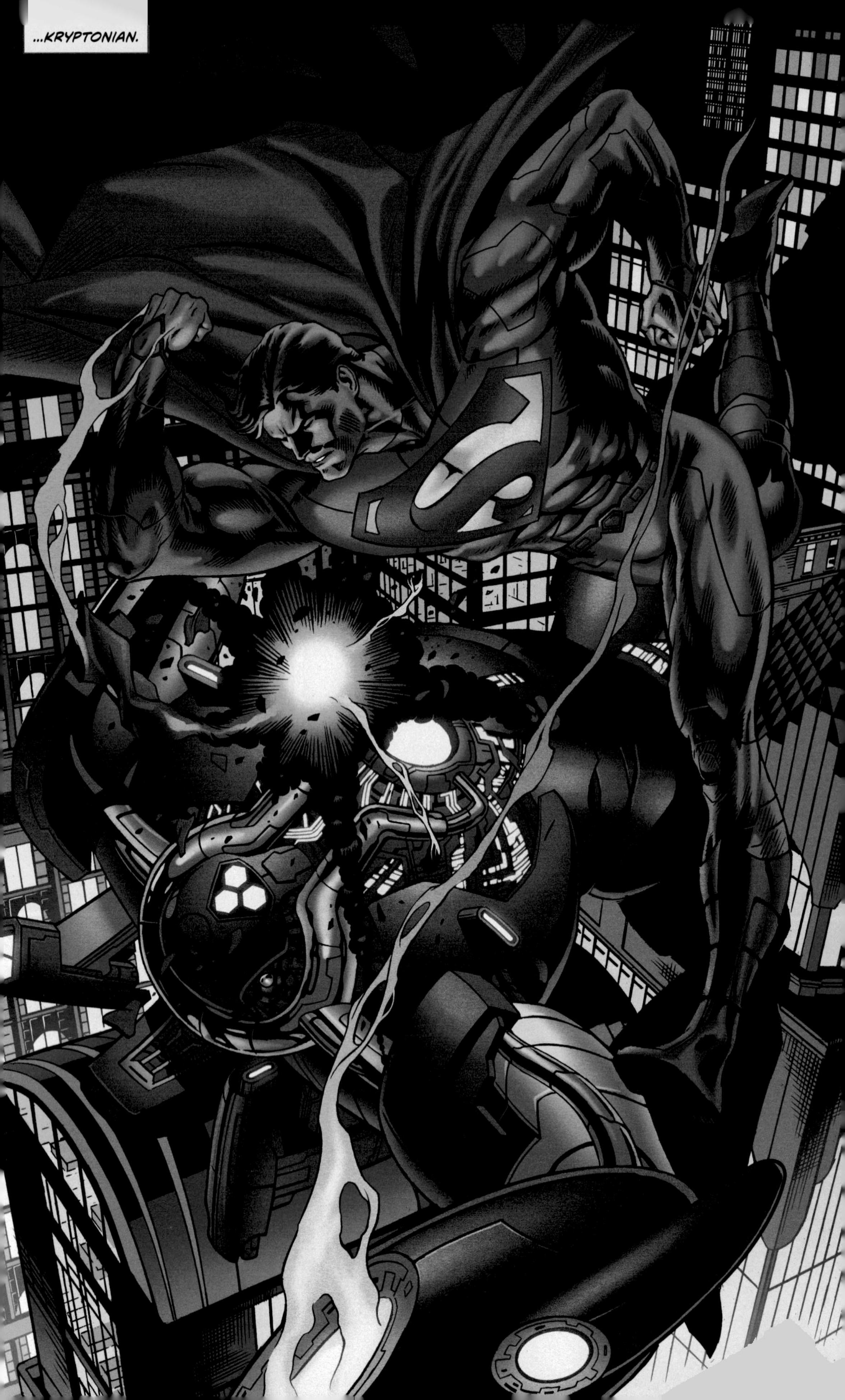
...KRYPTONIAN.

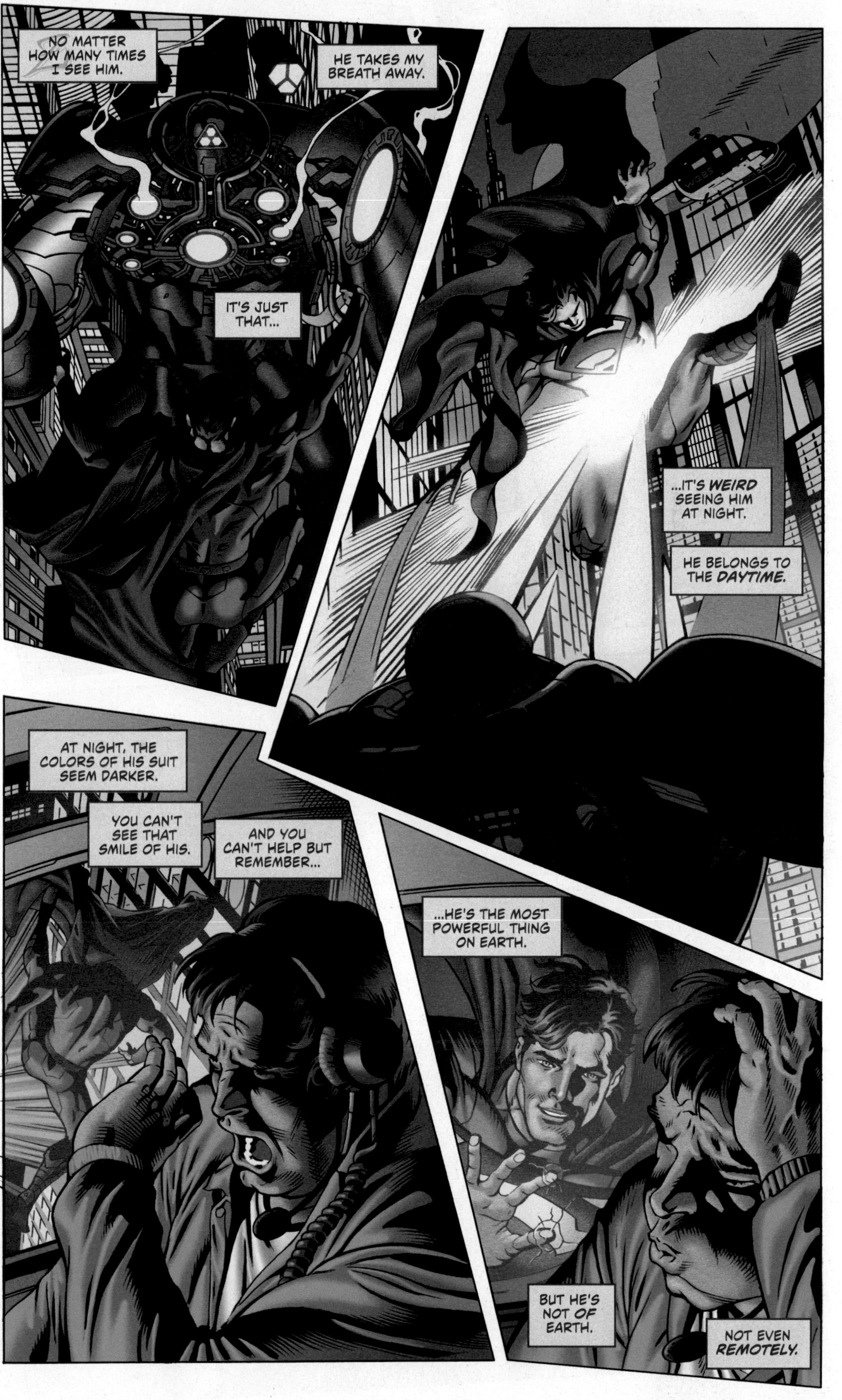
NO MATTER HOW MANY TIMES I SEE HIM.
HE TAKES MY BREATH AWAY.
IT'S JUST THAT...
...IT'S *WEIRD* SEEING HIM AT NIGHT.
HE BELONGS TO THE *DAYTIME.*
AT NIGHT, THE COLORS OF HIS SUIT SEEM DARKER.
YOU CAN'T SEE THAT SMILE OF HIS.
AND YOU CAN'T HELP BUT REMEMBER...
...HE'S THE MOST POWERFUL THING ON EARTH.
BUT HE'S NOT OF EARTH.
NOT EVEN *REMOTELY.*

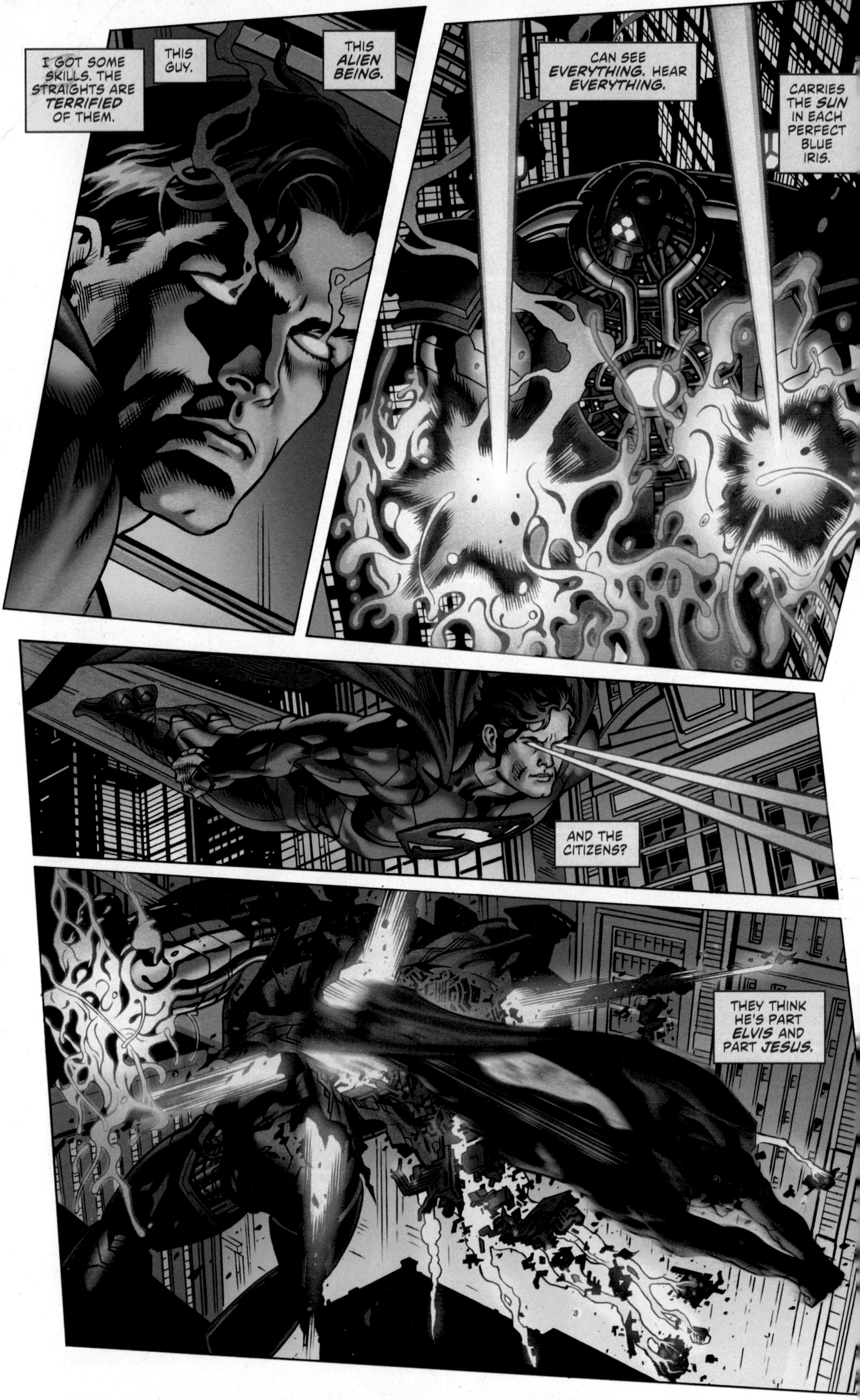
I GOT SOME SKILLS. THE STRAIGHTS ARE TERRIFIED OF THEM.
THIS GUY.
THIS ALIEN BEING.
CAN SEE EVERYTHING. HEAR EVERYTHING.
CARRIES THE SUN IN EACH PERFECT BLUE IRIS.
AND THE CITIZENS?
THEY THINK HE'S PART ELVIS AND PART JESUS.

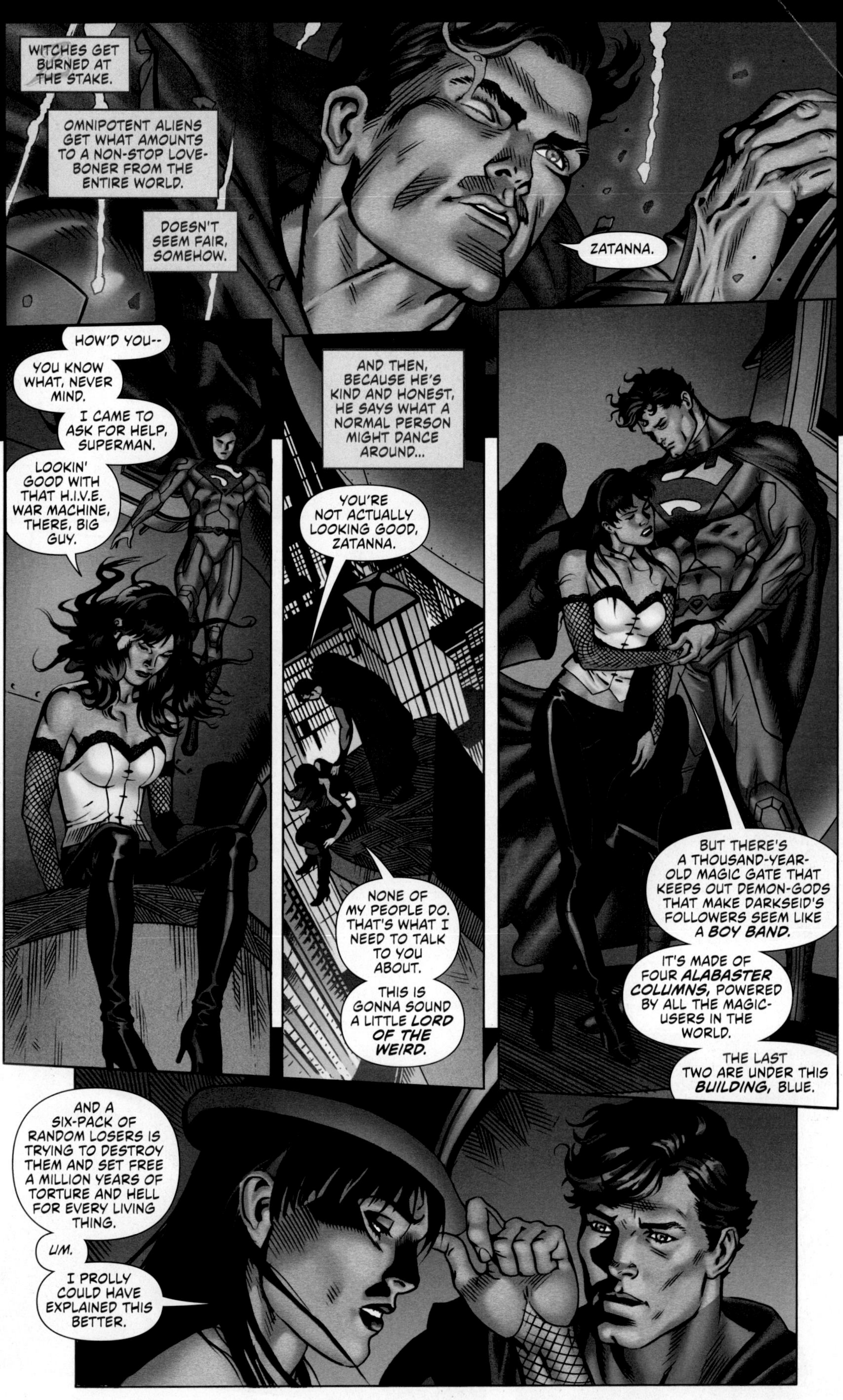
WITCHES GET BURNED AT THE STAKE.
OMNIPOTENT ALIENS GET WHAT AMOUNTS TO A NON-STOP LOVE-BONER FROM THE ENTIRE WORLD.
DOESN'T SEEM FAIR, SOMEHOW.
ZATANNA.
HOW'D YOU--
YOU KNOW WHAT, NEVER MIND.
I CAME TO ASK FOR HELP, SUPERMAN.
LOOKIN' GOOD WITH THAT H.I.V.E. WAR MACHINE, THERE, BIG GUY.
AND THEN, BECAUSE HE'S KIND AND HONEST, HE SAYS WHAT A NORMAL PERSON MIGHT DANCE AROUND...
YOU'RE NOT ACTUALLY LOOKING GOOD, ZATANNA.
NONE OF MY PEOPLE DO. THAT'S WHAT I NEED TO TALK TO YOU ABOUT.
THIS IS GONNA SOUND A LITTLE LORD OF THE WEIRD.
BUT THERE'S A THOUSAND-YEAR-OLD MAGIC GATE THAT KEEPS OUT DEMON-GODS THAT MAKE DARKSEID'S FOLLOWERS SEEM LIKE A BOY BAND.
IT'S MADE OF FOUR ALABASTER COLUMNS, POWERED BY ALL THE MAGIC-USERS IN THE WORLD.
THE LAST TWO ARE UNDER THIS BUILDING, BLUE.
AND A SIX-PACK OF RANDOM LOSERS IS TRYING TO DESTROY THEM AND SET FREE A MILLION YEARS OF TORTURE AND HELL FOR EVERY LIVING THING.
UM.
I PROLLY COULD HAVE EXPLAINED THIS BETTER.

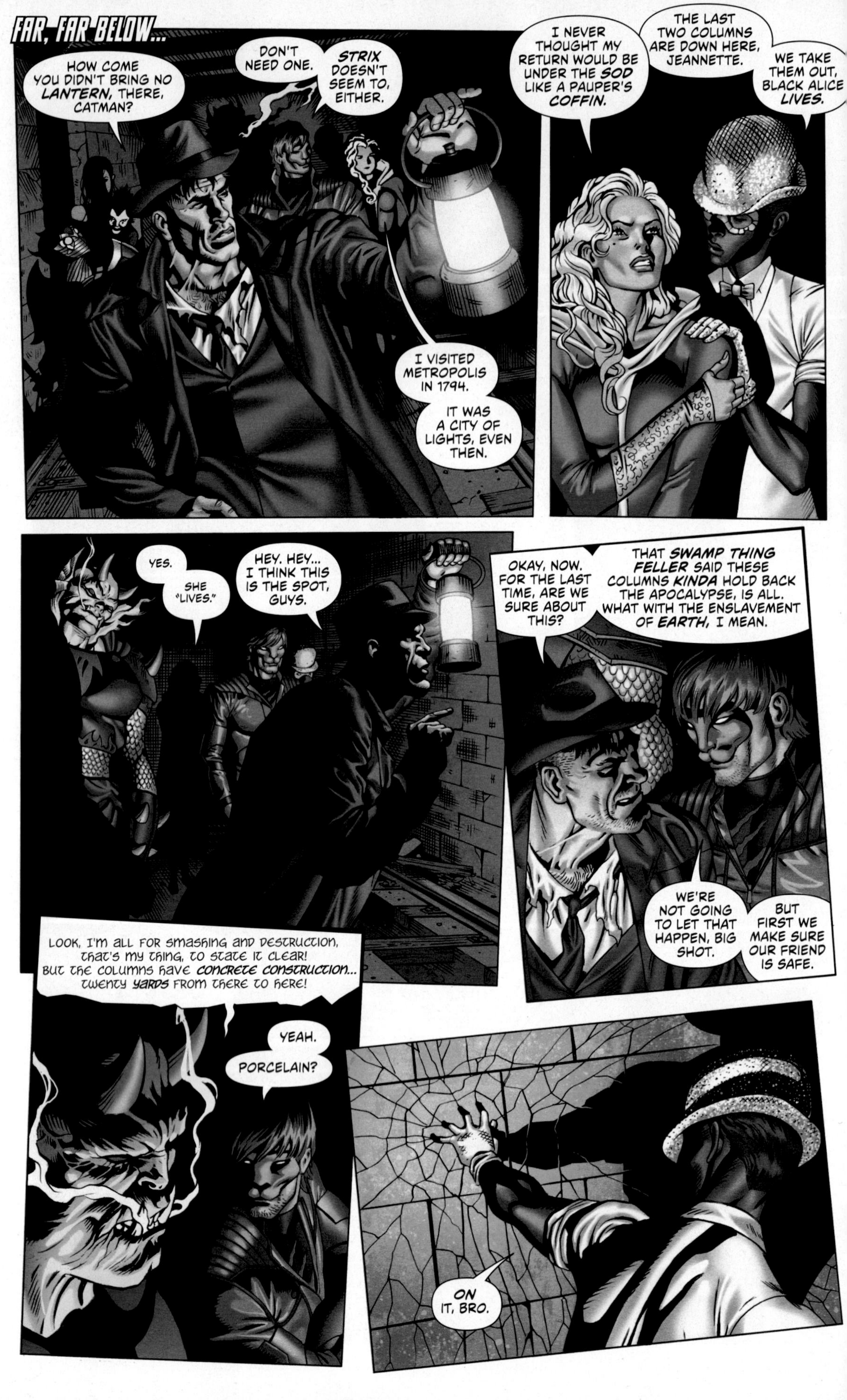
FAR, FAR BELOW...
HOW COME YOU DIDN'T BRING NO LANTERN, THERE, CATMAN?
DON'T NEED ONE.
STRIX DOESN'T SEEM TO, EITHER.
I VISITED METROPOLIS IN 1794.
IT WAS A CITY OF LIGHTS, EVEN THEN.
I NEVER THOUGHT MY RETURN WOULD BE UNDER THE SOD LIKE A PAUPER'S COFFIN.
THE LAST TWO COLUMNS ARE DOWN HERE, JEANNETTE.
WE TAKE THEM OUT, BLACK ALICE LIVES.
YES.
SHE "LIVES."
HEY. HEY... I THINK THIS IS THE SPOT, GUYS.
OKAY, NOW. FOR THE LAST TIME, ARE WE SURE ABOUT THIS?
THAT SWAMP THING FELLER SAID THESE COLUMNS KINDA HOLD BACK THE APOCALYPSE, IS ALL. WHAT WITH THE ENSLAVEMENT OF EARTH, I MEAN.
WE'RE NOT GOING TO LET THAT HAPPEN, BIG SHOT.
BUT FIRST WE MAKE SURE OUR FRIEND IS SAFE.
LOOK, I'M ALL FOR SMASHING AND DESTRUCTION, THAT'S MY THING, TO STATE IT CLEAR! BUT THE COLUMNS HAVE CONCRETE CONSTRUCTION... TWENTY YARDS FROM THERE TO HERE!
YEAH.
PORCELAIN?
ON IT, BRO.

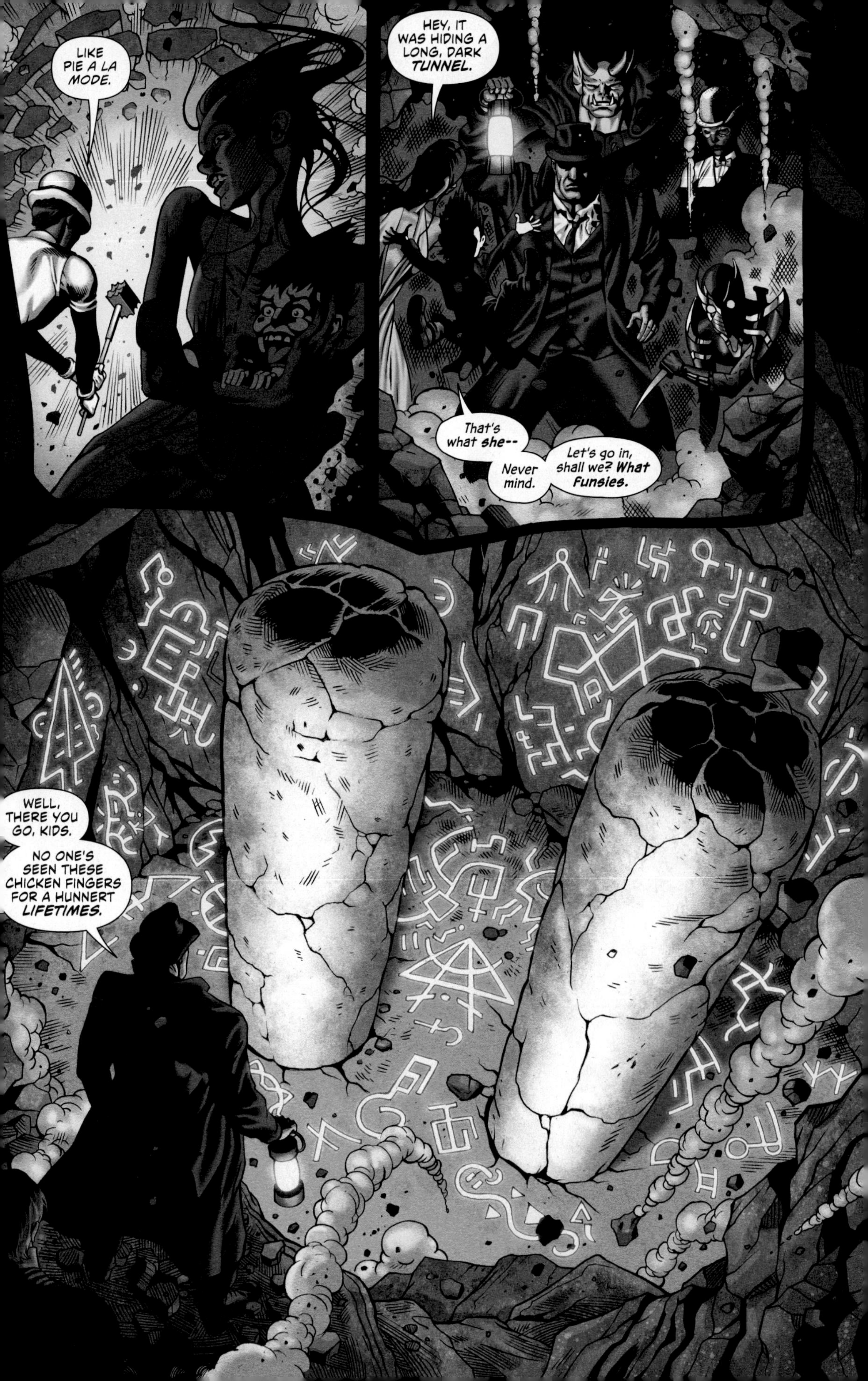
LIKE PIE A LA MODE.
HEY, IT WAS HIDING A LONG, DARK TUNNEL.
That's what she--
Never mind.
Let's go in, shall we? What Funsies.
WELL, THERE YOU GO, KIDS.
NO ONE'S SEEN THESE CHICKEN FINGERS FOR A HUNNERT LIFETIMES.

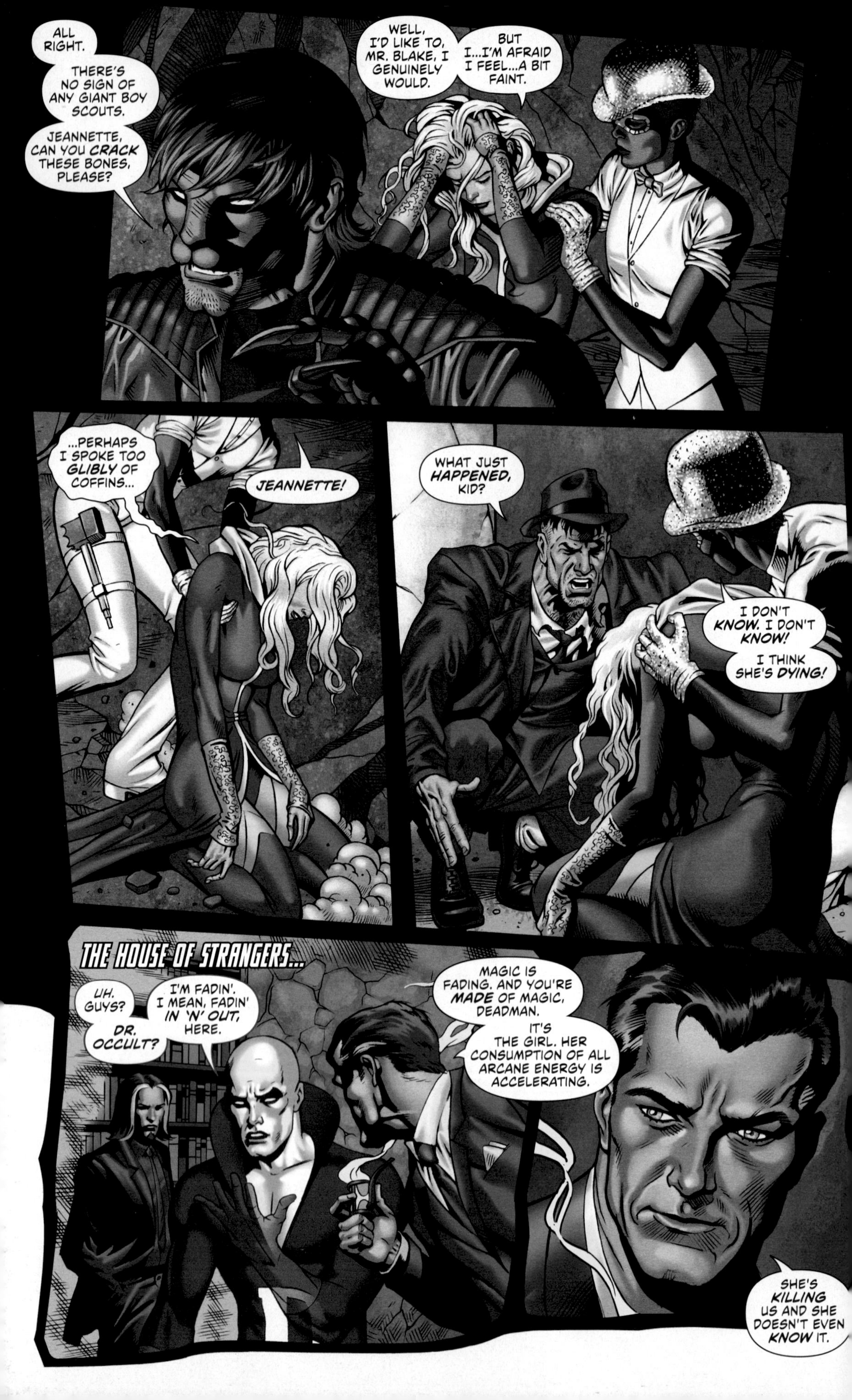
ALL RIGHT.
THERE'S NO SIGN OF ANY GIANT BOY SCOUTS.
JEANNETTE, CAN YOU CRACK THESE BONES, PLEASE?
WELL, I'D LIKE TO, MR. BLAKE, I GENUINELY WOULD.
BUT I...I'M AFRAID I FEEL...A BIT FAINT.
...PERHAPS I SPOKE TOO GLIBLY OF COFFINS...
JEANNETTE!
WHAT JUST HAPPENED, KID?
I DON'T KNOW. I DON'T KNOW!
I THINK SHE'S DYING!
THE HOUSE OF STRANGERS...
UH. GUYS?
DR. OCCULT?
I'M FADIN'. I MEAN, FADIN' IN 'N' OUT, HERE.
MAGIC IS FADING. AND YOU'RE MADE OF MAGIC, DEADMAN.
IT'S THE GIRL. HER CONSUMPTION OF ALL ARCANE ENERGY IS ACCELERATING.
SHE'S KILLING US AND SHE DOESN'T EVEN KNOW IT.

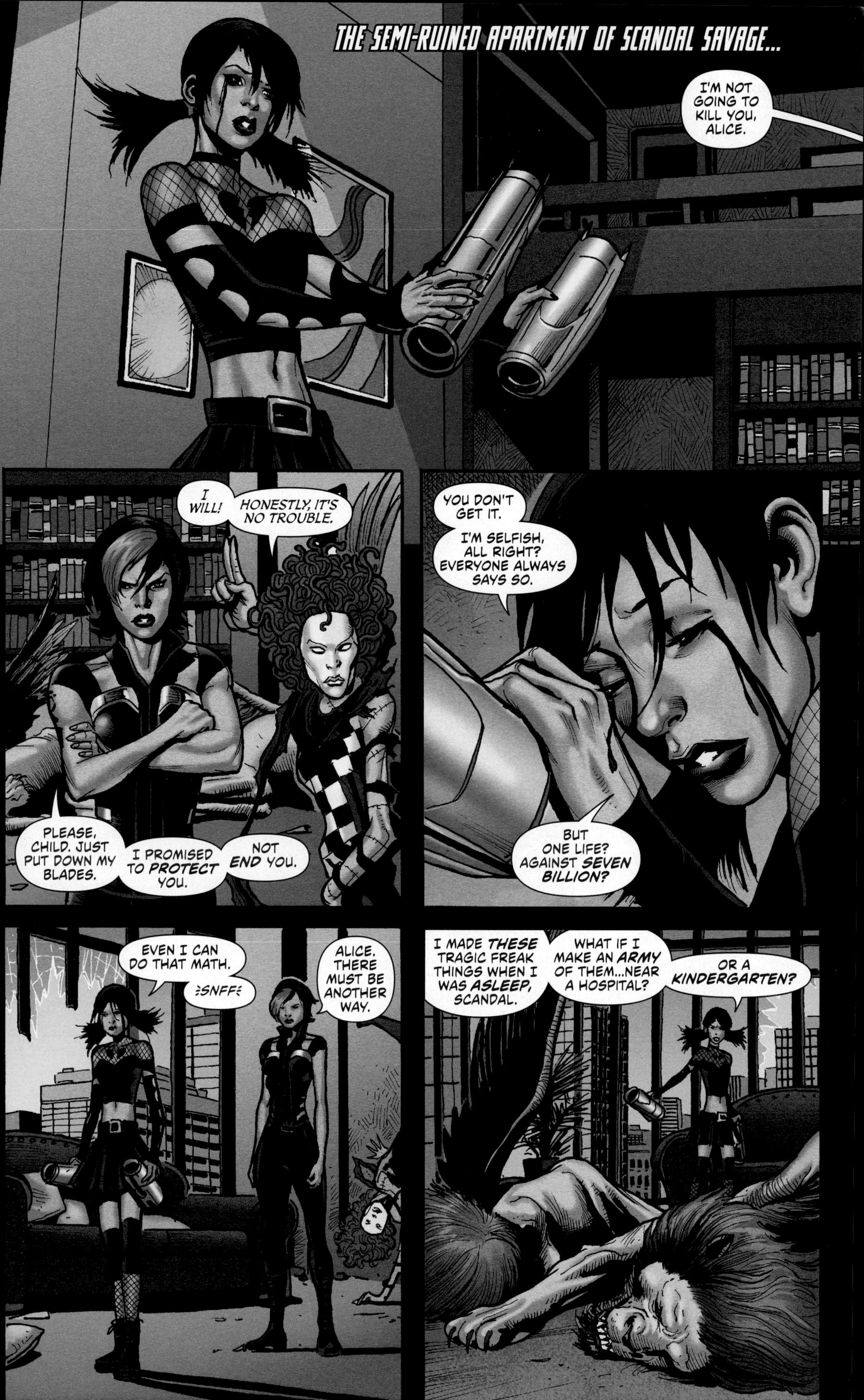
THE SEMI-RUINED APARTMENT OF SCANDAL SAVAGE...
I'M NOT GOING TO KILL YOU, ALICE.
I WILL!
HONESTLY, IT'S NO TROUBLE.
PLEASE, CHILD. JUST PUT DOWN MY BLADES.
I PROMISED TO PROTECT YOU.
NOT END YOU.
YOU DON'T GET IT.
I'M SELFISH, ALL RIGHT? EVERYONE ALWAYS SAYS SO.
BUT ONE LIFE? AGAINST SEVEN BILLION?
EVEN I CAN DO THAT MATH.
SNFF
ALICE. THERE MUST BE ANOTHER WAY.
I MADE THESE TRAGIC FREAK THINGS WHEN I WAS ASLEEP, SCANDAL.
WHAT IF I MAKE AN ARMY OF THEM...NEAR A HOSPITAL?
OR A KINDERGARTEN?

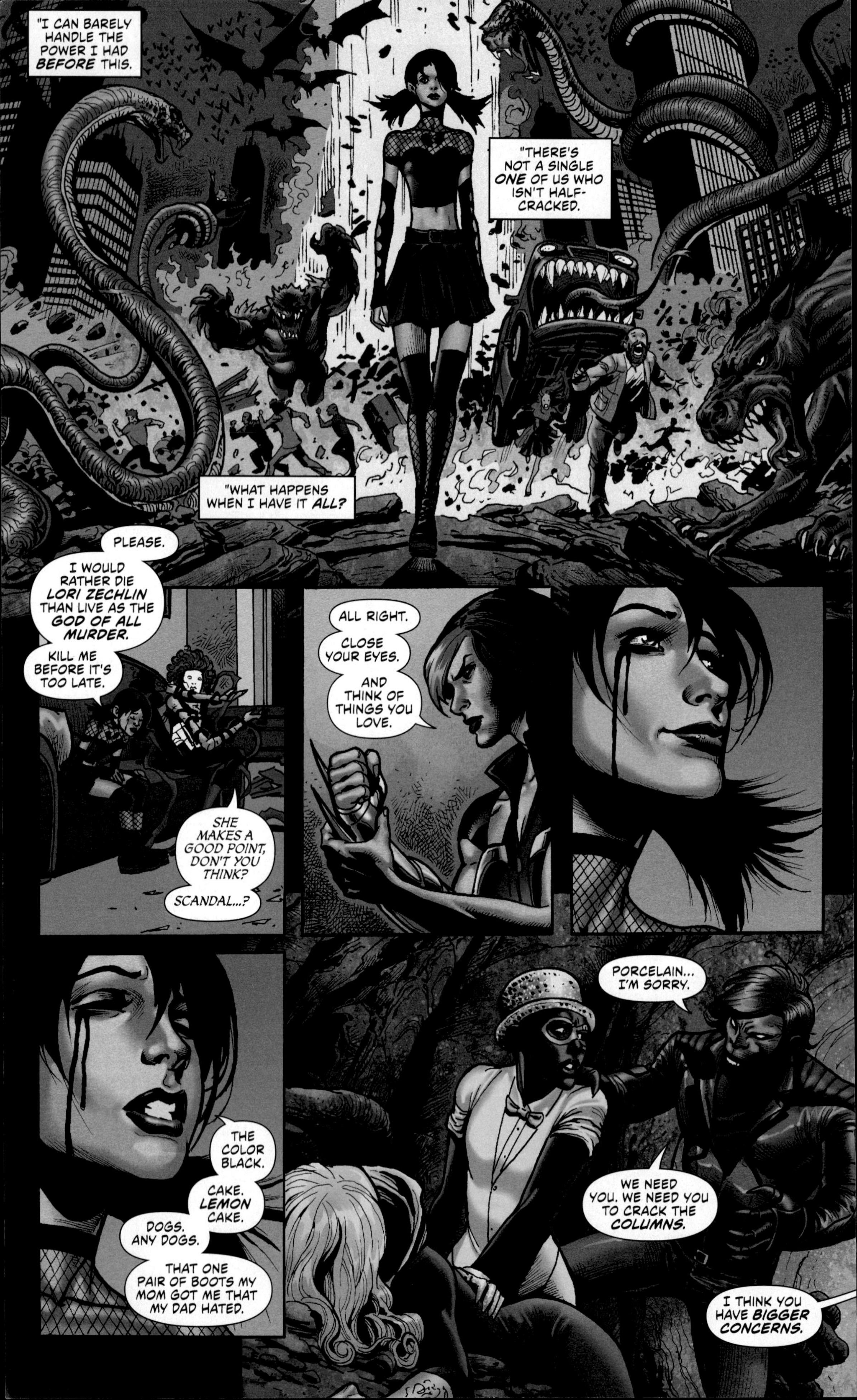
"I CAN BARELY HANDLE THE POWER I HAD BEFORE THIS.
"THERE'S NOT A SINGLE ONE OF US WHO ISN'T HALF-CRACKED.
"WHAT HAPPENS WHEN I HAVE IT ALL?
PLEASE.
I WOULD RATHER DIE LORI ZECHLIN THAN LIVE AS THE GOD OF ALL MURDER.
KILL ME BEFORE IT'S TOO LATE.
SHE MAKES A GOOD POINT, DON'T YOU THINK?
SCANDAL...?
ALL RIGHT.
CLOSE YOUR EYES.
AND THINK OF THINGS YOU LOVE.
THE COLOR BLACK.
CAKE. LEMON CAKE.
DOGS. ANY DOGS.
THAT ONE PAIR OF BOOTS MY MOM GOT ME THAT MY DAD HATED.
PORCELAIN... I'M SORRY.
WE NEED YOU. WE NEED YOU TO CRACK THE COLUMNS.
I THINK YOU HAVE BIGGER CONCERNS.

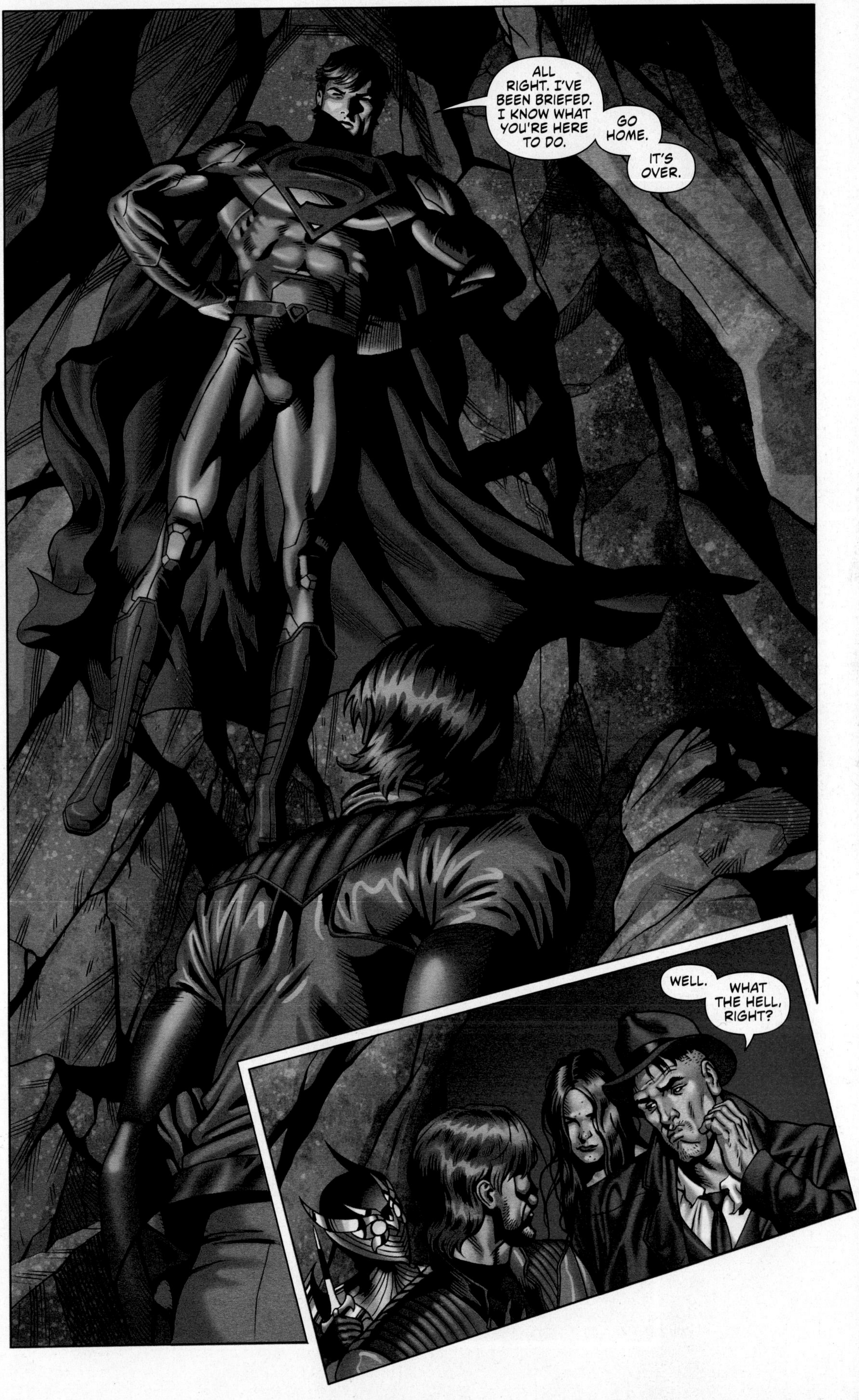
ALL RIGHT. I'VE BEEN BRIEFED. I KNOW WHAT YOU'RE HERE TO DO.
GO HOME.
IT'S OVER.
WELL.
WHAT THE HELL, RIGHT?

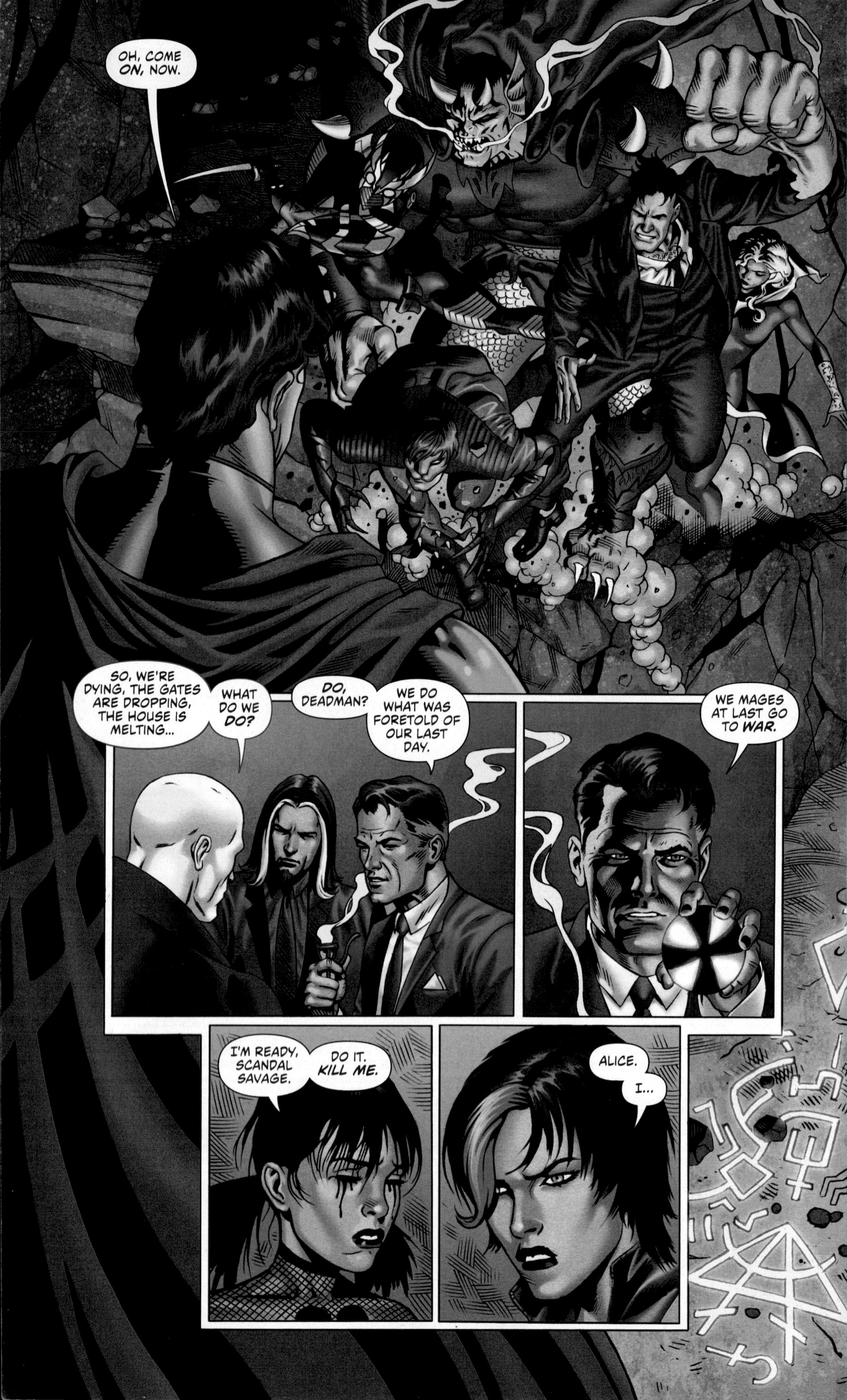
OH, COME ON, NOW.
SO, WE'RE DYING, THE GATES ARE DROPPING, THE HOUSE IS MELTING...
WHAT DO WE DO?
DO, DEADMAN?
WE DO WHAT WAS FORETOLD OF OUR LAST DAY.
WE MAGES AT LAST GO TO WAR.
I'M READY, SCANDAL SAVAGE.
DO IT. KILL ME.
ALICE.
I...

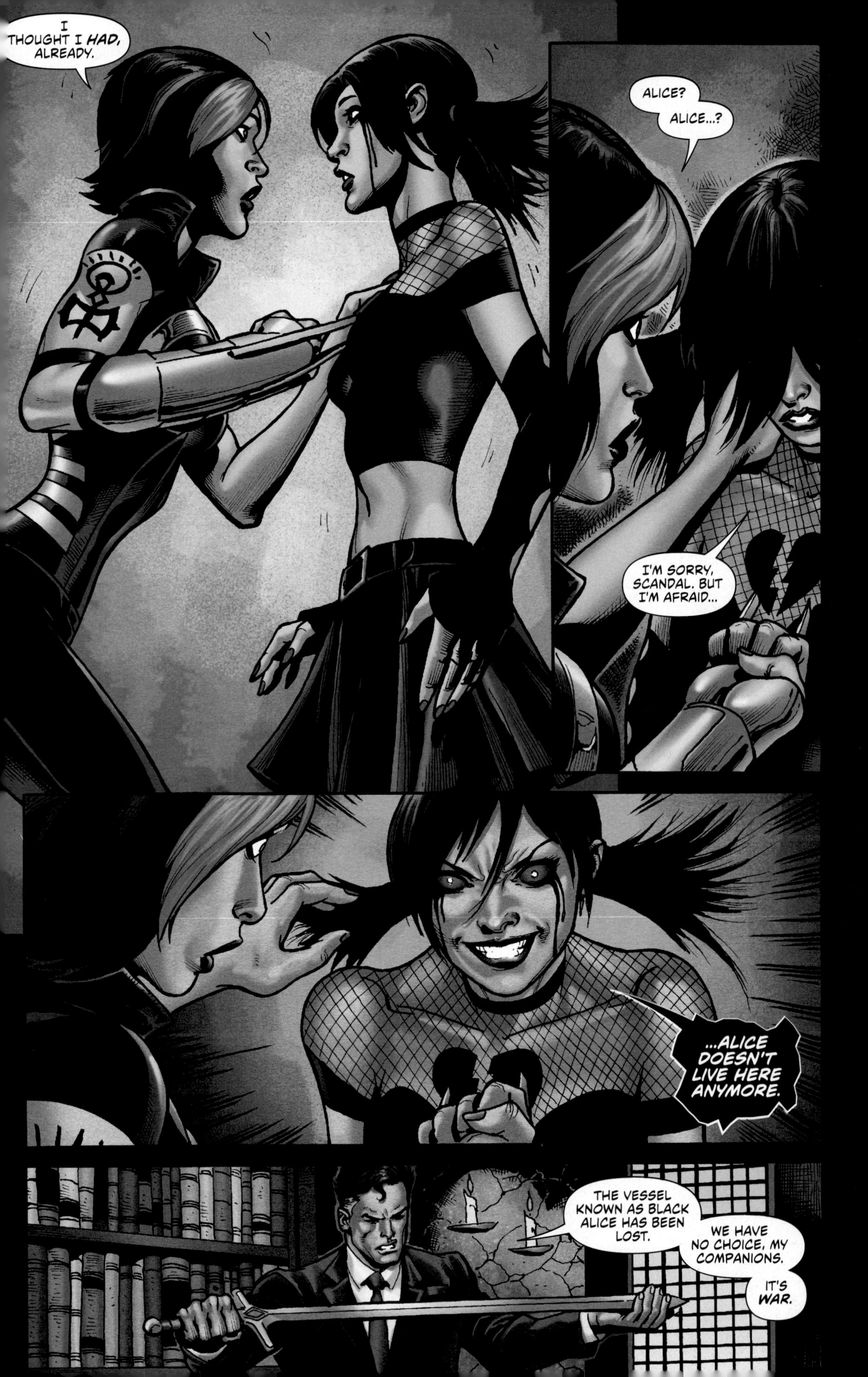
I THOUGHT I *HAD*, ALREADY.
ALICE?
ALICE...?
I'M SORRY, SCANDAL. BUT I'M AFRAID...
...ALICE DOESN'T LIVE HERE ANYMORE.
THE VESSEL KNOWN AS BLACK ALICE HAS BEEN LOST.
WE HAVE NO CHOICE, MY COMPANIONS.
IT'S *WAR*.

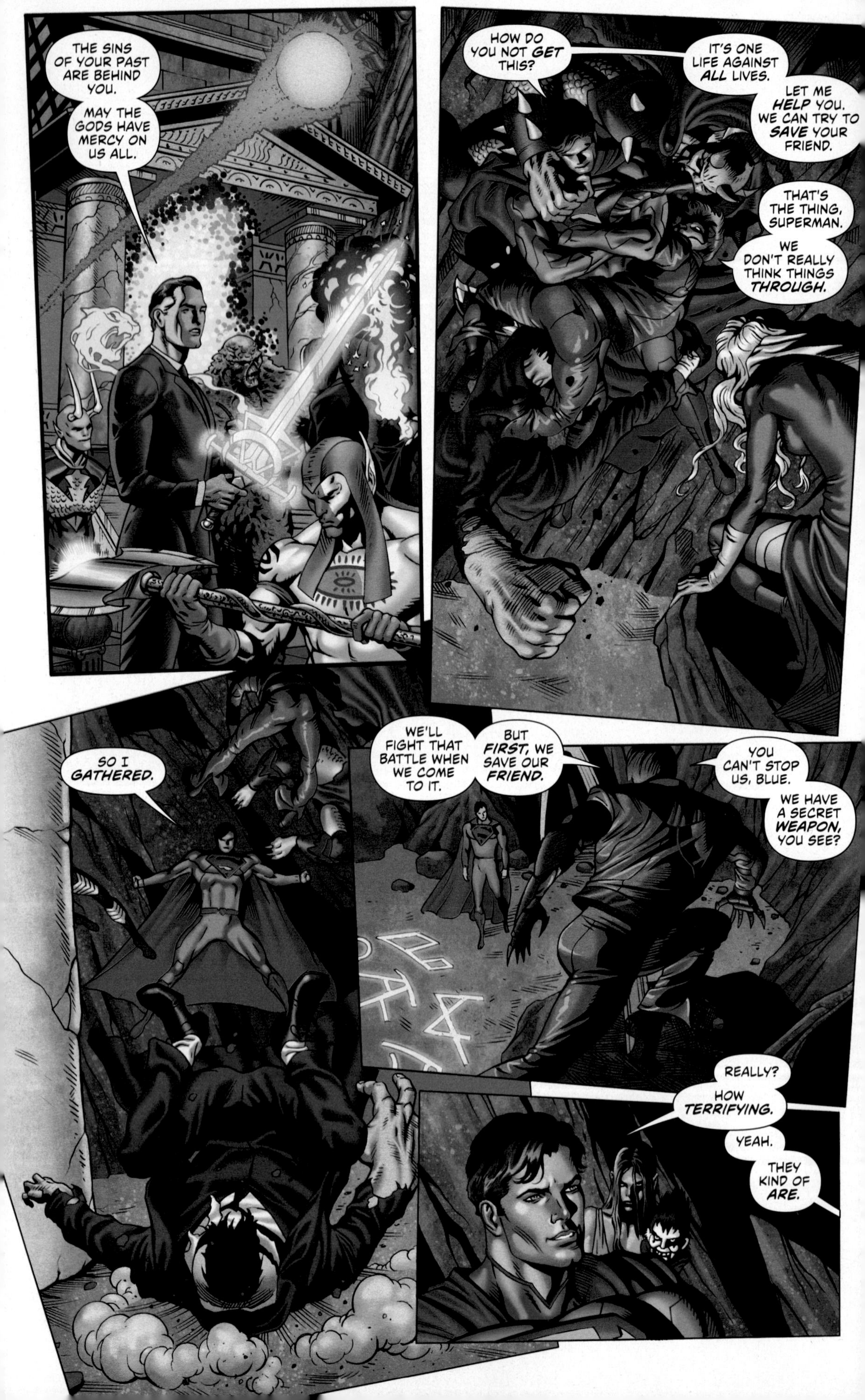
THE SINS OF YOUR PAST ARE BEHIND YOU.
MAY THE GODS HAVE MERCY ON US ALL.
HOW DO YOU NOT GET THIS?
IT'S ONE LIFE AGAINST ALL LIVES.
LET ME HELP YOU. WE CAN TRY TO SAVE YOUR FRIEND.
THAT'S THE THING, SUPERMAN.
WE DON'T REALLY THINK THINGS THROUGH.
SO I GATHERED.
WE'LL FIGHT THAT BATTLE WHEN WE COME TO IT.
BUT FIRST, WE SAVE OUR FRIEND.
YOU CAN'T STOP US, BLUE.
WE HAVE A SECRET WEAPON, YOU SEE?
REALLY?
HOW TERRIFYING.
YEAH.
THEY KIND OF ARE.

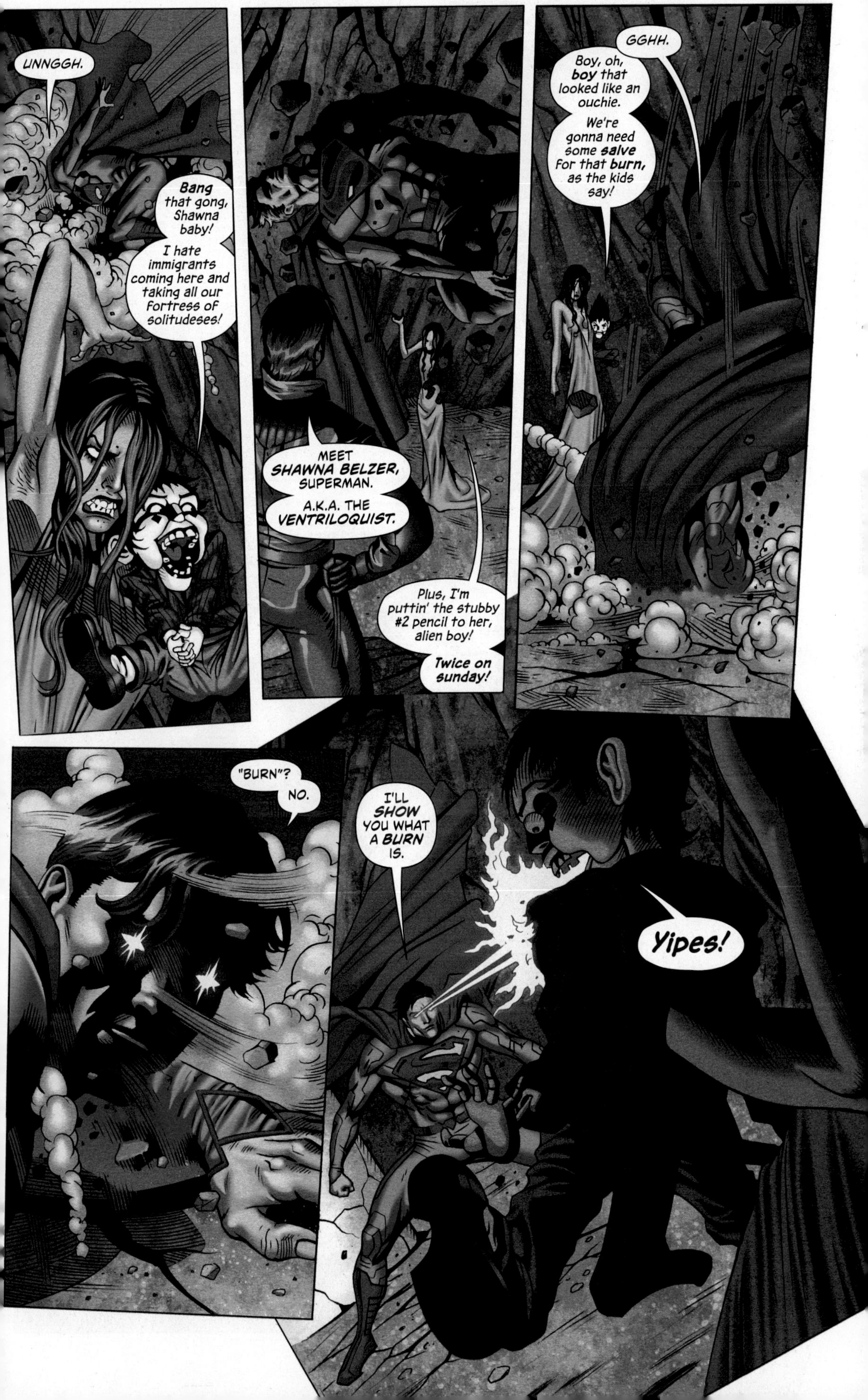
UNNGGH.
Bang that gong, Shawna baby!
I hate immigrants coming here and taking all our fortress of solitudeses!
MEET SHAWNA BELZER, SUPERMAN.
A.K.A. THE VENTRILOQUIST.
Plus, I'm puttin' the stubby #2 pencil to her, alien boy!
Twice on sunday!
GGHH.
Boy, oh, boy that looked like an ouchie.
We're gonna need some salve for that burn, as the kids say!
"BURN"?
NO.
I'LL SHOW YOU WHAT A BURN IS.
Yipes!

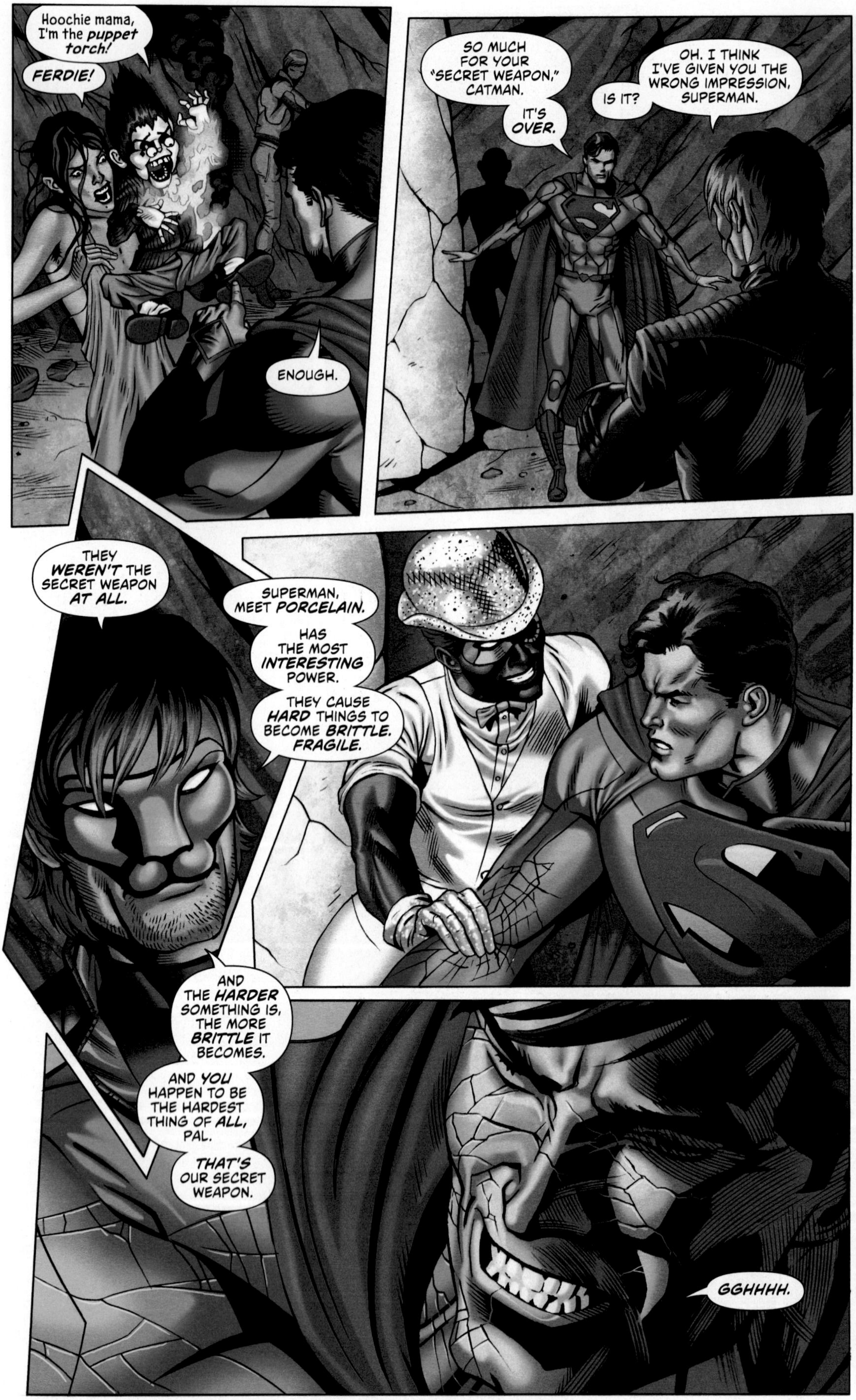
Hoochie mama, I'm the *puppet torch!*
FERDIE!
ENOUGH.
SO MUCH FOR YOUR "SECRET WEAPON," CATMAN.
IT'S *OVER.*
IS IT?
OH. I THINK I'VE GIVEN YOU THE WRONG IMPRESSION, SUPERMAN.
THEY *WEREN'T* THE SECRET WEAPON *AT ALL.*
SUPERMAN, MEET *PORCELAIN.*
HAS THE MOST *INTERESTING* POWER.
THEY CAUSE *HARD* THINGS TO BECOME *BRITTLE. FRAGILE.*
AND THE *HARDER* SOMETHING IS, THE MORE *BRITTLE* IT BECOMES.
AND *YOU* HAPPEN TO BE THE HARDEST THING OF *ALL,* PAL.
THAT'S OUR SECRET WEAPON.
GGHHHH.

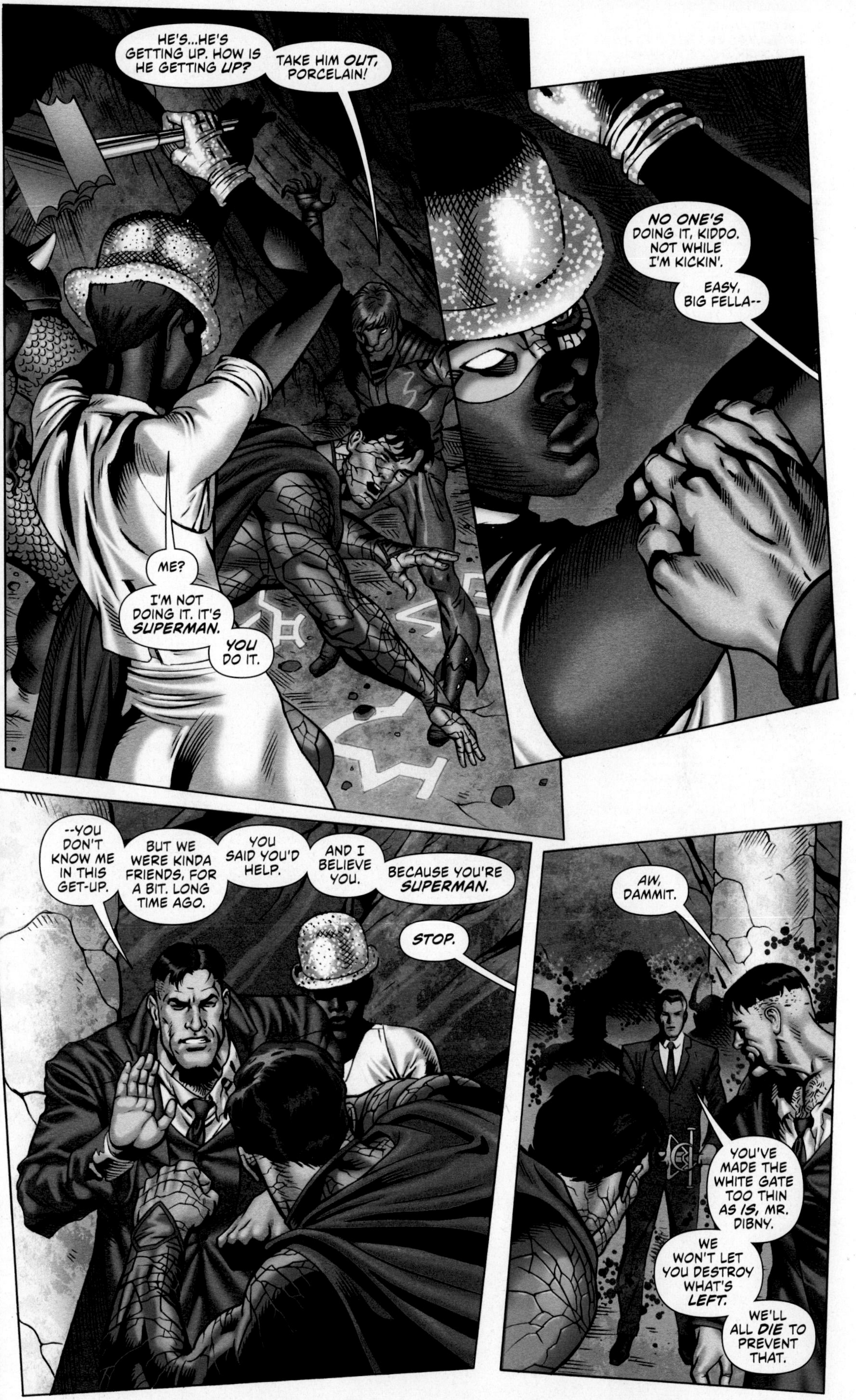
HE'S...HE'S GETTING UP. HOW IS HE GETTING UP?
TAKE HIM OUT, PORCELAIN!
ME?
I'M NOT DOING IT. IT'S SUPERMAN.
YOU DO IT.
NO ONE'S DOING IT, KIDDO. NOT WHILE I'M KICKIN'.
EASY, BIG FELLA--
--YOU DON'T KNOW ME IN THIS GET-UP.
BUT WE WERE KINDA FRIENDS, FOR A BIT. LONG TIME AGO.
YOU SAID YOU'D HELP.
AND I BELIEVE YOU.
BECAUSE YOU'RE SUPERMAN.
STOP.
AW, DAMMIT.
YOU'VE MADE THE WHITE GATE TOO THIN AS IS, MR. DIBNY.
WE WON'T LET YOU DESTROY WHAT'S LEFT.
WE'LL ALL DIE TO PREVENT THAT.

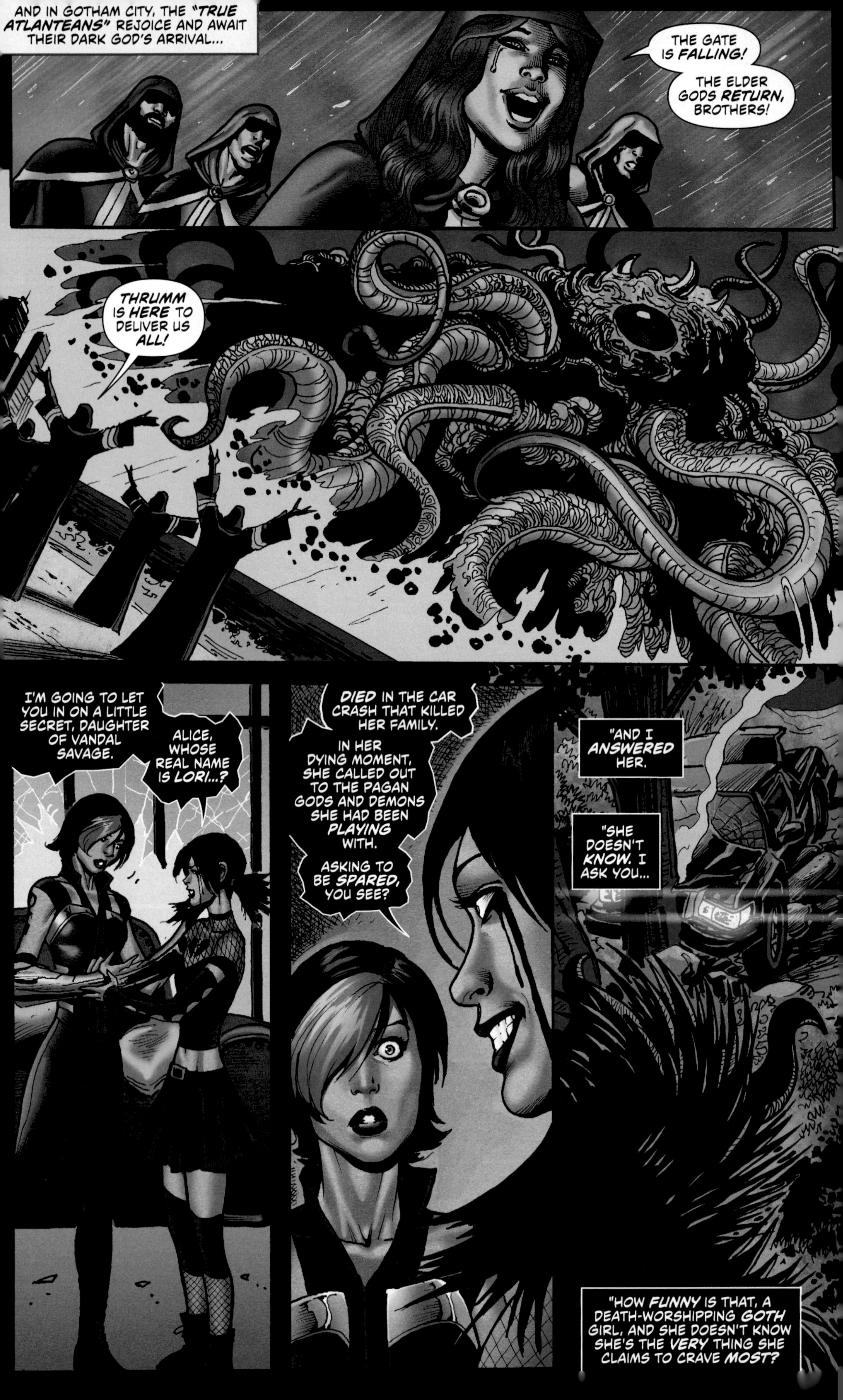
AND IN GOTHAM CITY, THE "TRUE ATLANTEANS" REJOICE AND AWAIT THEIR DARK GOD'S ARRIVAL...
THE GATE IS FALLING!
THE ELDER GODS RETURN, BROTHERS!
THRUMM IS HERE TO DELIVER US ALL!
I'M GOING TO LET YOU IN ON A LITTLE SECRET, DAUGHTER OF VANDAL SAVAGE.
ALICE, WHOSE REAL NAME IS LORI...?
DIED IN THE CAR CRASH THAT KILLED HER FAMILY.
IN HER DYING MOMENT, SHE CALLED OUT TO THE PAGAN GODS AND DEMONS SHE HAD BEEN PLAYING WITH.
ASKING TO BE SPARED, YOU SEE?
"AND I ANSWERED HER.
"SHE DOESN'T KNOW. I ASK YOU...
"HOW FUNNY IS THAT, A DEATH-WORSHIPPING GOTH GIRL, AND SHE DOESN'T KNOW SHE'S THE VERY THING SHE CLAIMS TO CRAVE MOST?

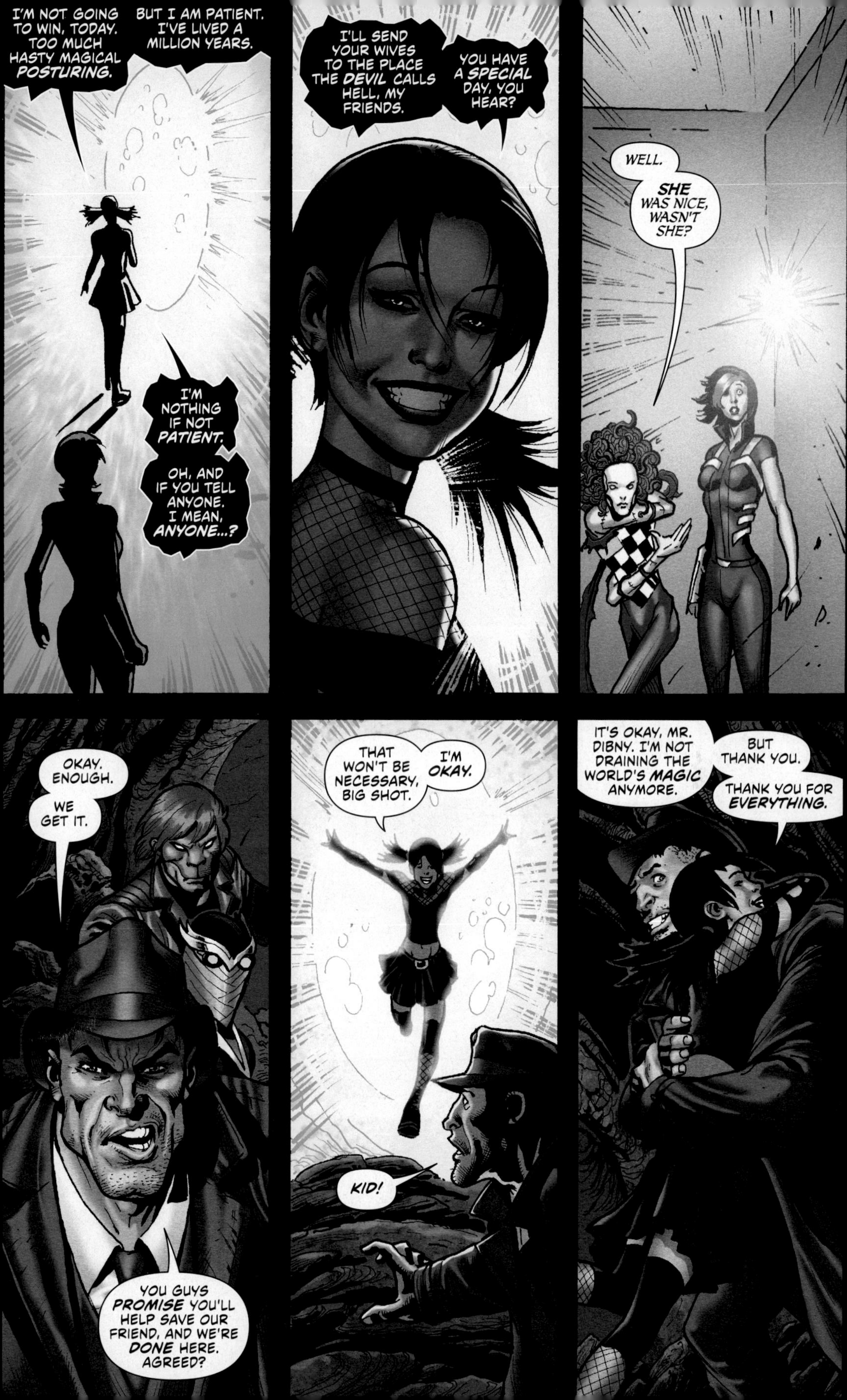
I'M NOT GOING TO WIN, TODAY. TOO MUCH HASTY MAGICAL POSTURING.
BUT I AM PATIENT. I'VE LIVED A MILLION YEARS.
I'M NOTHING IF NOT PATIENT.
OH, AND IF YOU TELL ANYONE. I MEAN, ANYONE...?
I'LL SEND YOUR WIVES TO THE PLACE THE DEVIL CALLS HELL, MY FRIENDS.
YOU HAVE A SPECIAL DAY, YOU HEAR?
WELL.
SHE WAS NICE, WASN'T SHE?
OKAY. ENOUGH.
WE GET IT.
YOU GUYS PROMISE YOU'LL HELP SAVE OUR FRIEND, AND WE'RE DONE HERE. AGREED?
THAT WON'T BE NECESSARY, BIG SHOT.
I'M OKAY.
KID!
IT'S OKAY, MR. DIBNY. I'M NOT DRAINING THE WORLD'S MAGIC ANYMORE.
BUT THANK YOU.
THANK YOU FOR EVERYTHING.

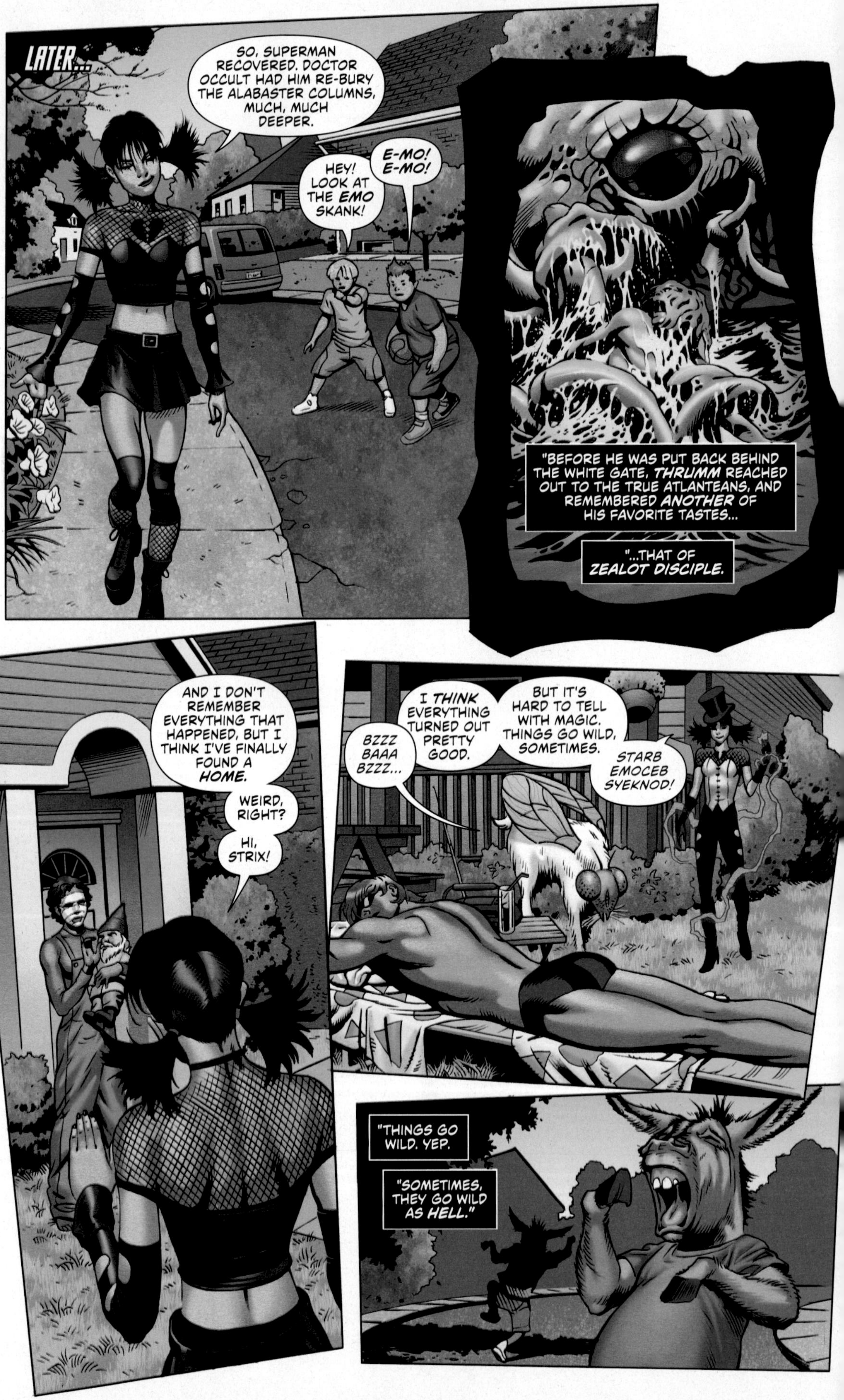
LATER...
SO, SUPERMAN RECOVERED. DOCTOR OCCULT HAD HIM RE-BURY THE ALABASTER COLUMNS, MUCH, MUCH DEEPER.
HEY! LOOK AT THE EMO SKANK!
E-MO! E-MO!
"BEFORE HE WAS PUT BACK BEHIND THE WHITE GATE, THRUMM REACHED OUT TO THE TRUE ATLANTEANS, AND REMEMBERED ANOTHER OF HIS FAVORITE TASTES...
"...THAT OF ZEALOT DISCIPLE.
AND I DON'T REMEMBER EVERYTHING THAT HAPPENED, BUT I THINK I'VE FINALLY FOUND A HOME.
WEIRD, RIGHT?
HI, STRIX!
BZZZ BAAA BZZZ...
I THINK EVERYTHING TURNED OUT PRETTY GOOD.
BUT IT'S HARD TO TELL WITH MAGIC. THINGS GO WILD, SOMETIMES.
STARB EMOCEB SYEKNOD!
"THINGS GO WILD. YEP.
"SOMETIMES, THEY GO WILD AS HELL."

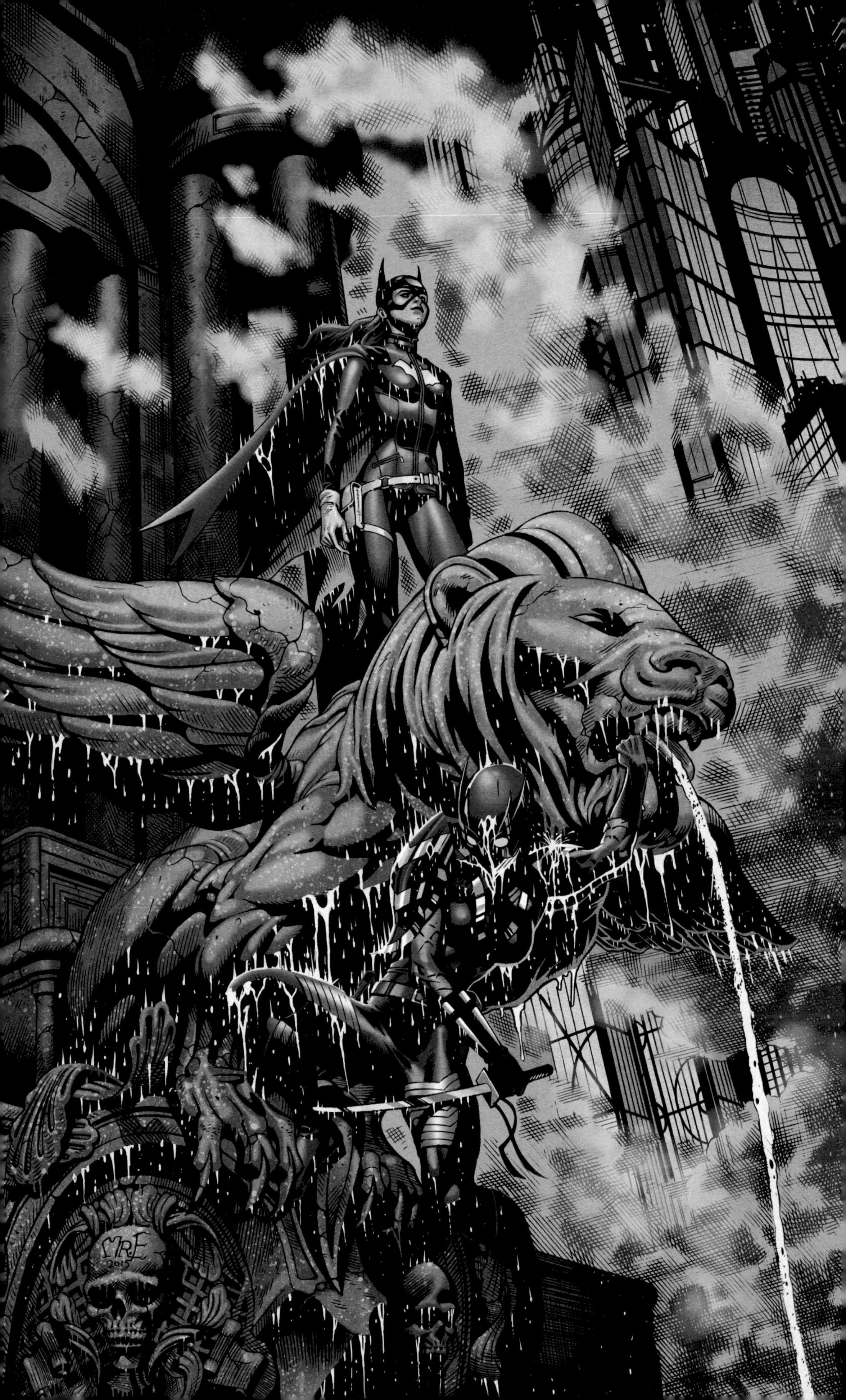

THE GAUNTLET

GAIL SIMONE writer **DALE EAGLESHAM TOM DERENICK** artists **JASON WRIGHT** colorist **TRAVIS LANHAM** letterer

cover by **DALE EAGLESHAM & JASON WRIGHT**

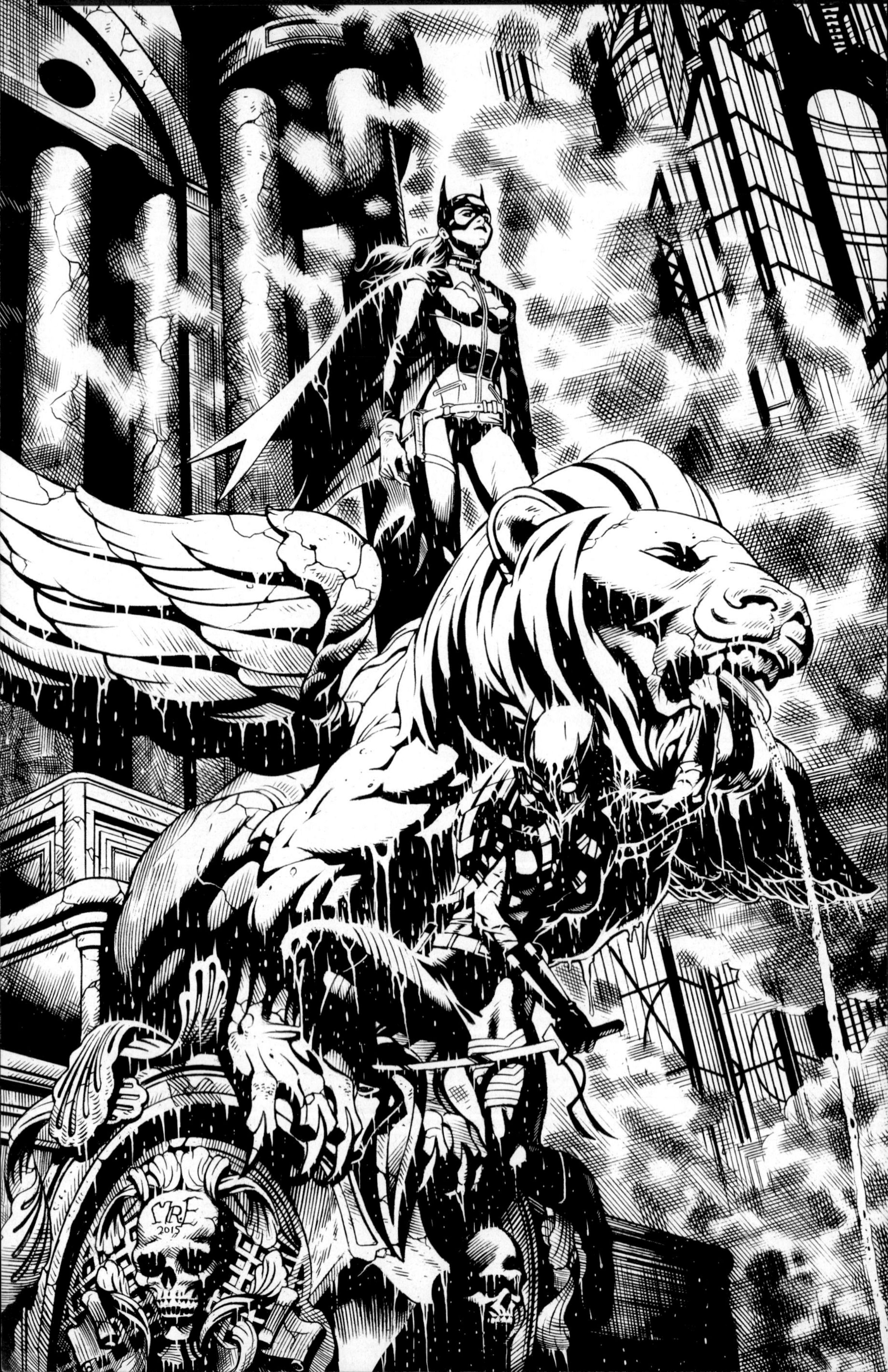

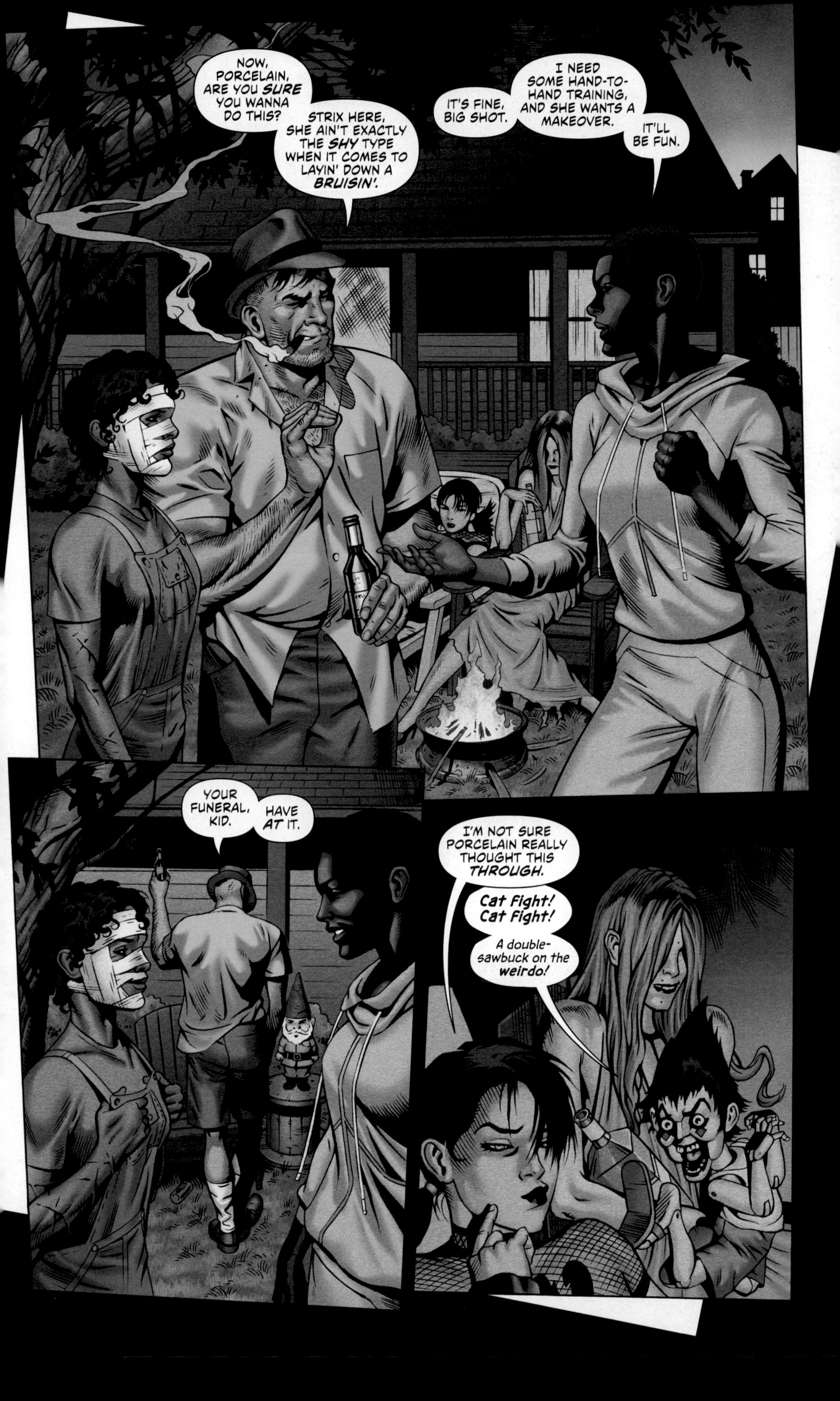
NOW, PORCELAIN, ARE YOU SURE YOU WANNA DO THIS?
STRIX HERE, SHE AIN'T EXACTLY THE SHY TYPE WHEN IT COMES TO LAYIN' DOWN A BRUISIN'.
IT'S FINE, BIG SHOT.
I NEED SOME HAND-TO-HAND TRAINING, AND SHE WANTS A MAKEOVER.
IT'LL BE FUN.
YOUR FUNERAL, KID.
HAVE AT IT.
I'M NOT SURE PORCELAIN REALLY THOUGHT THIS THROUGH.
Cat Fight! Cat Fight!
A double-sawbuck on the weirdo!

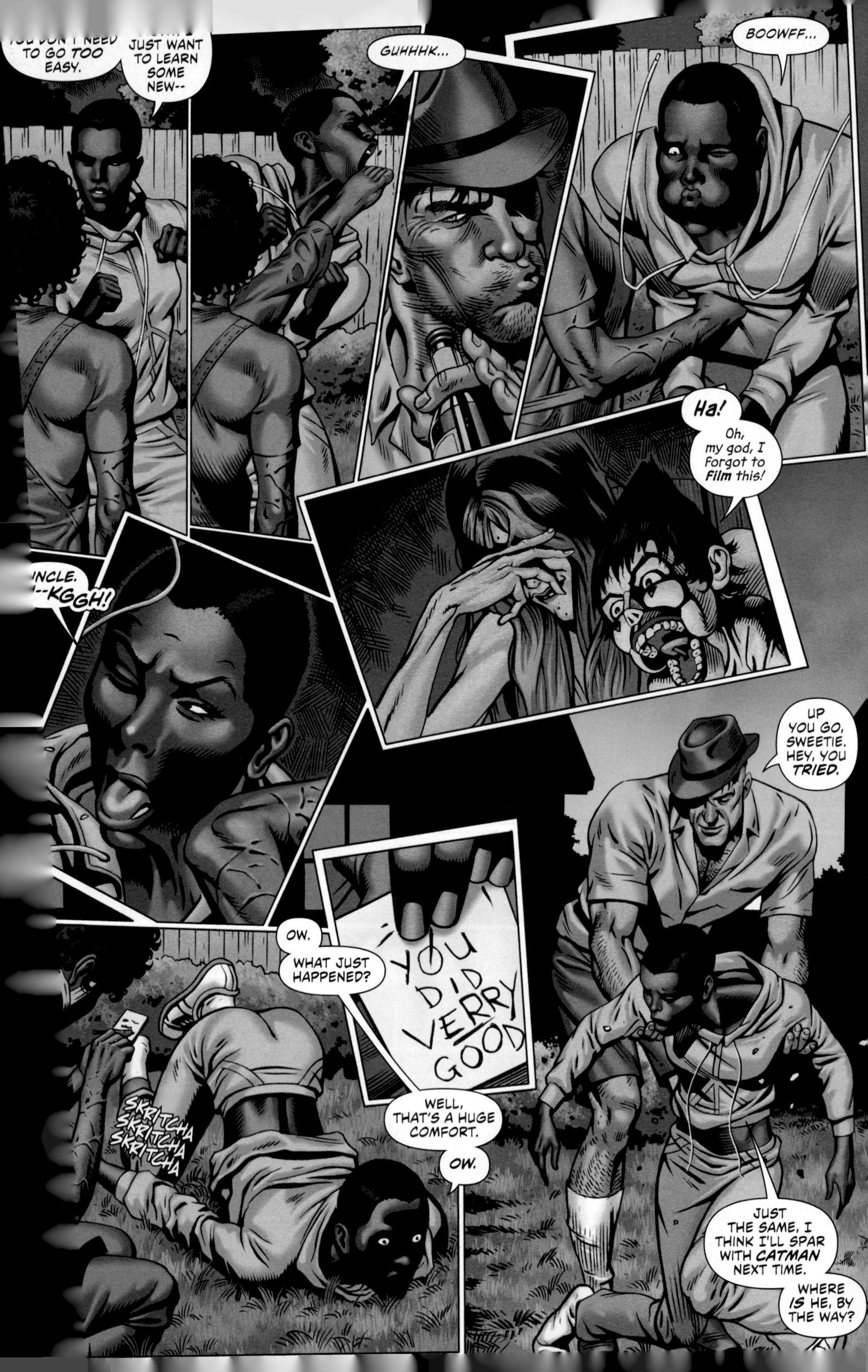
TO GO TOO EASY.
JUST WANT TO LEARN SOME NEW--
GUHHHK...
BOOWFF...
--KGGH!
Ha! Oh, my god, I forgot to Film this!
UP YOU GO, SWEETIE. HEY, YOU TRIED.
OW.
WHAT JUST HAPPENED?
YOU DID VERRY GOOD
SKRITCHA SKRITCHA SKRITCHA
WELL, THAT'S A HUGE COMFORT.
OW.
JUST THE SAME, I THINK I'LL SPAR WITH CATMAN NEXT TIME.
WHERE IS HE, BY THE WAY?

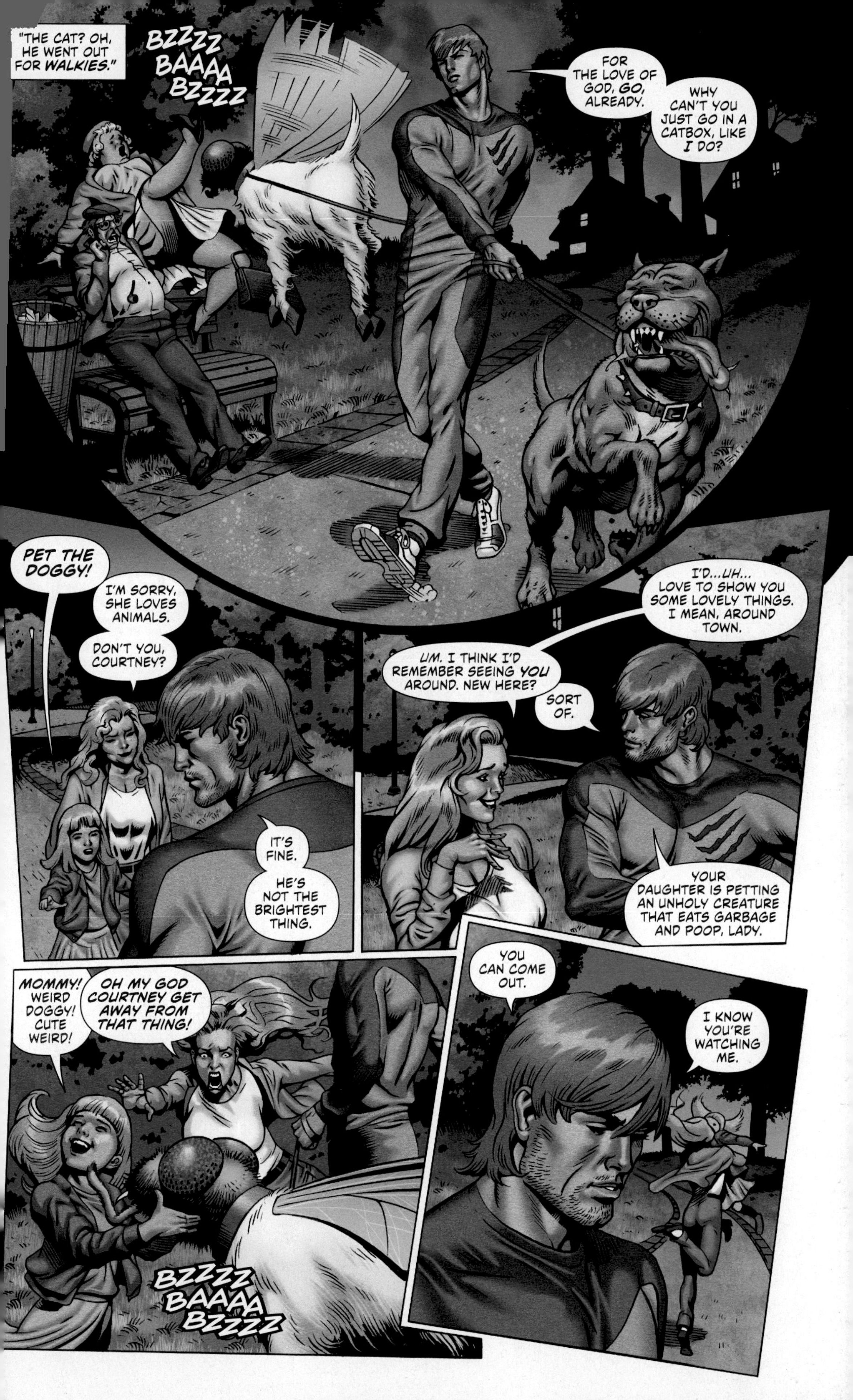

"THE CAT? OH, HE WENT OUT FOR WALKIES."
BZZZZ BAAAA BZZZZ
FOR THE LOVE OF GOD, GO, ALREADY.
WHY CAN'T YOU JUST GO IN A CATBOX, LIKE I DO?
PET THE DOGGY!
I'M SORRY, SHE LOVES ANIMALS.
DON'T YOU, COURTNEY?
IT'S FINE.
HE'S NOT THE BRIGHTEST THING.
I'D...UH... LOVE TO SHOW YOU SOME LOVELY THINGS. I MEAN, AROUND TOWN.
UM. I THINK I'D REMEMBER SEEING YOU AROUND. NEW HERE?
SORT OF.
YOUR DAUGHTER IS PETTING AN UNHOLY CREATURE THAT EATS GARBAGE AND POOP, LADY.
MOMMY! WEIRD DOGGY! CUTE WEIRD!
OH MY GOD COURTNEY GET AWAY FROM THAT THING!
BZZZZ BAAAA BZZZZ
YOU CAN COME OUT.
I KNOW YOU'RE WATCHING ME.

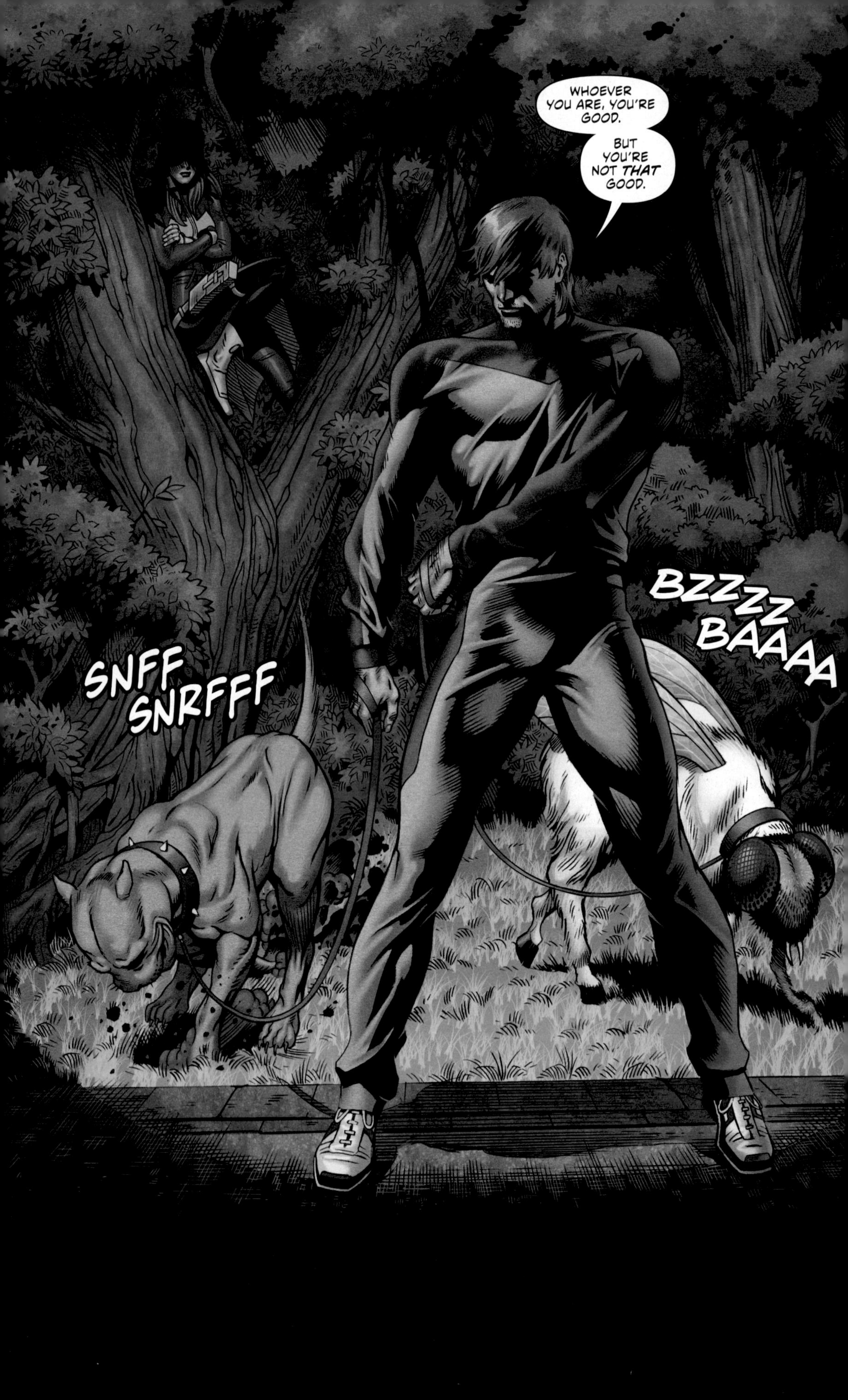
WHOEVER YOU ARE, YOU'RE GOOD.
BUT YOU'RE NOT *THAT* GOOD.
SNFF SNRFFF
BZZZZ BAAAA

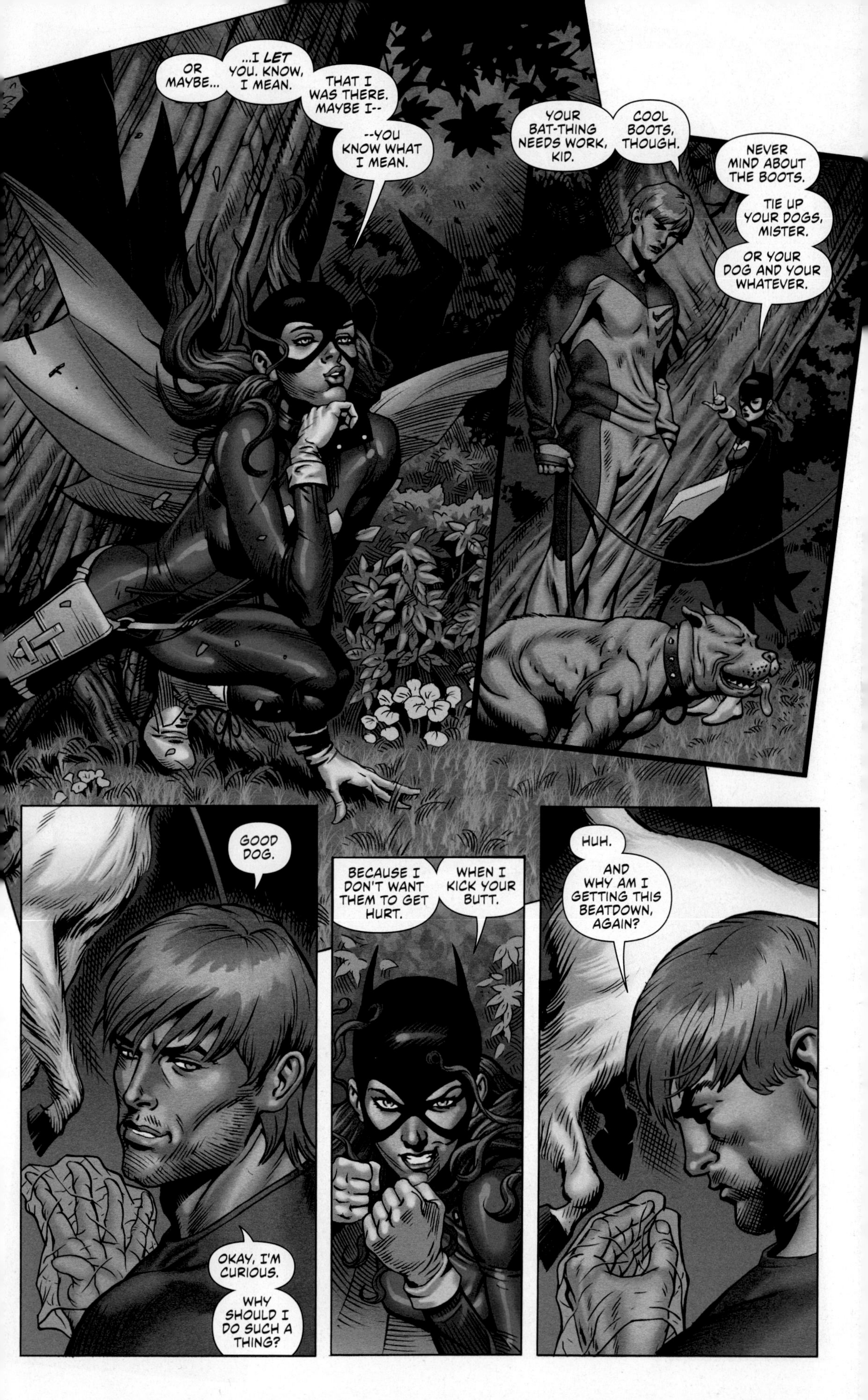
OR MAYBE...
...I LET YOU. KNOW, I MEAN.
THAT I WAS THERE. MAYBE I--
--YOU KNOW WHAT I MEAN.
YOUR BAT-THING NEEDS WORK, KID.
COOL BOOTS, THOUGH.
NEVER MIND ABOUT THE BOOTS.
TIE UP YOUR DOGS, MISTER.
OR YOUR DOG AND YOUR WHATEVER.
GOOD DOG.
OKAY, I'M CURIOUS.
WHY SHOULD I DO SUCH A THING?
BECAUSE I DON'T WANT THEM TO GET HURT.
WHEN I KICK YOUR BUTT.
HUH.
AND WHY AM I GETTING THIS BEATDOWN, AGAIN?

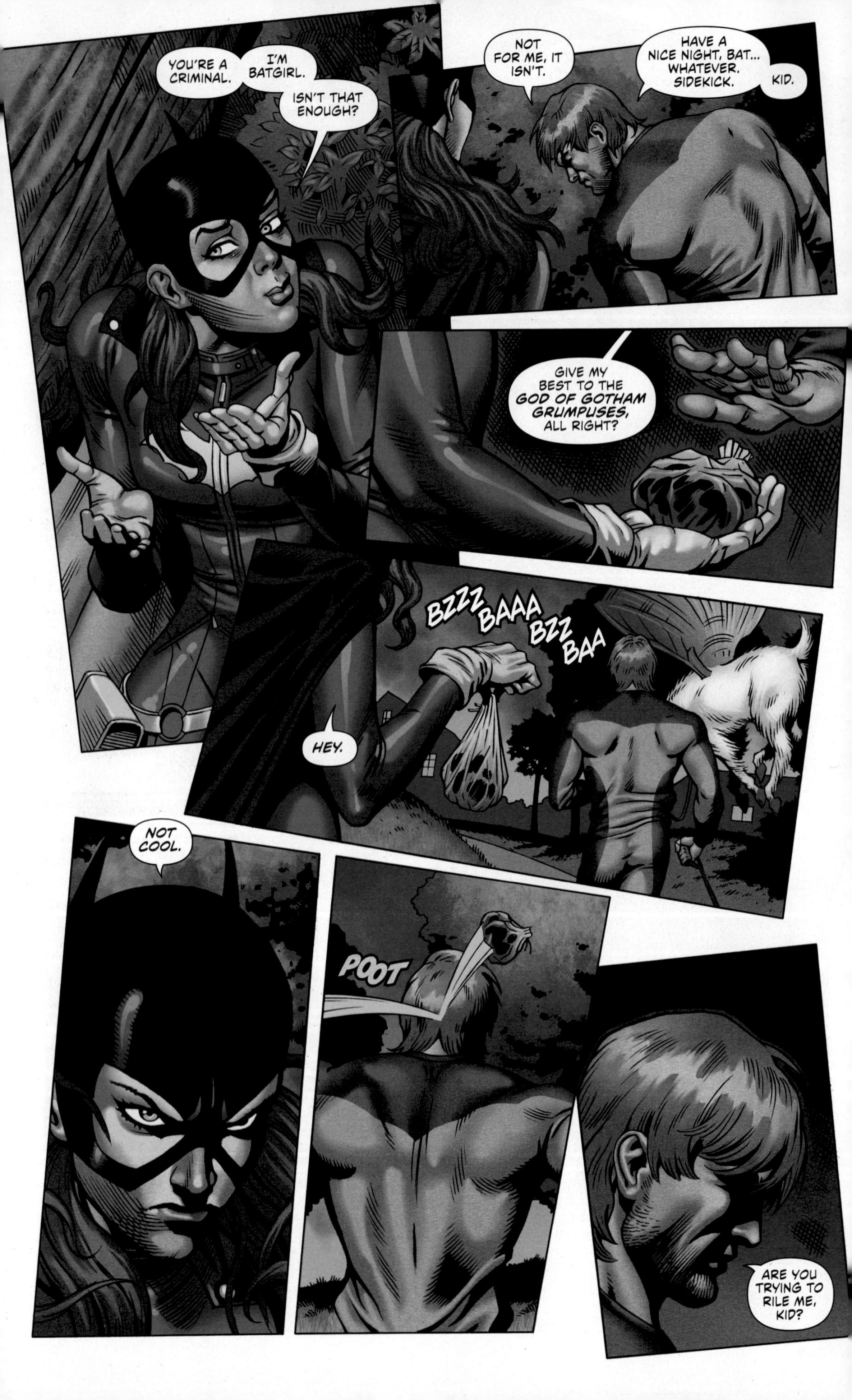

YOU'RE A CRIMINAL.
I'M BATGIRL.
ISN'T THAT ENOUGH?
NOT FOR ME, IT ISN'T.
HAVE A NICE NIGHT, BAT... WHATEVER. SIDEKICK.
KID.
GIVE MY BEST TO THE GOD OF GOTHAM GRUMPUSES, ALL RIGHT?
BZZZ BAAA BZZ BAA
HEY.
NOT COOL.
POOT
ARE YOU TRYING TO RILE ME, KID?

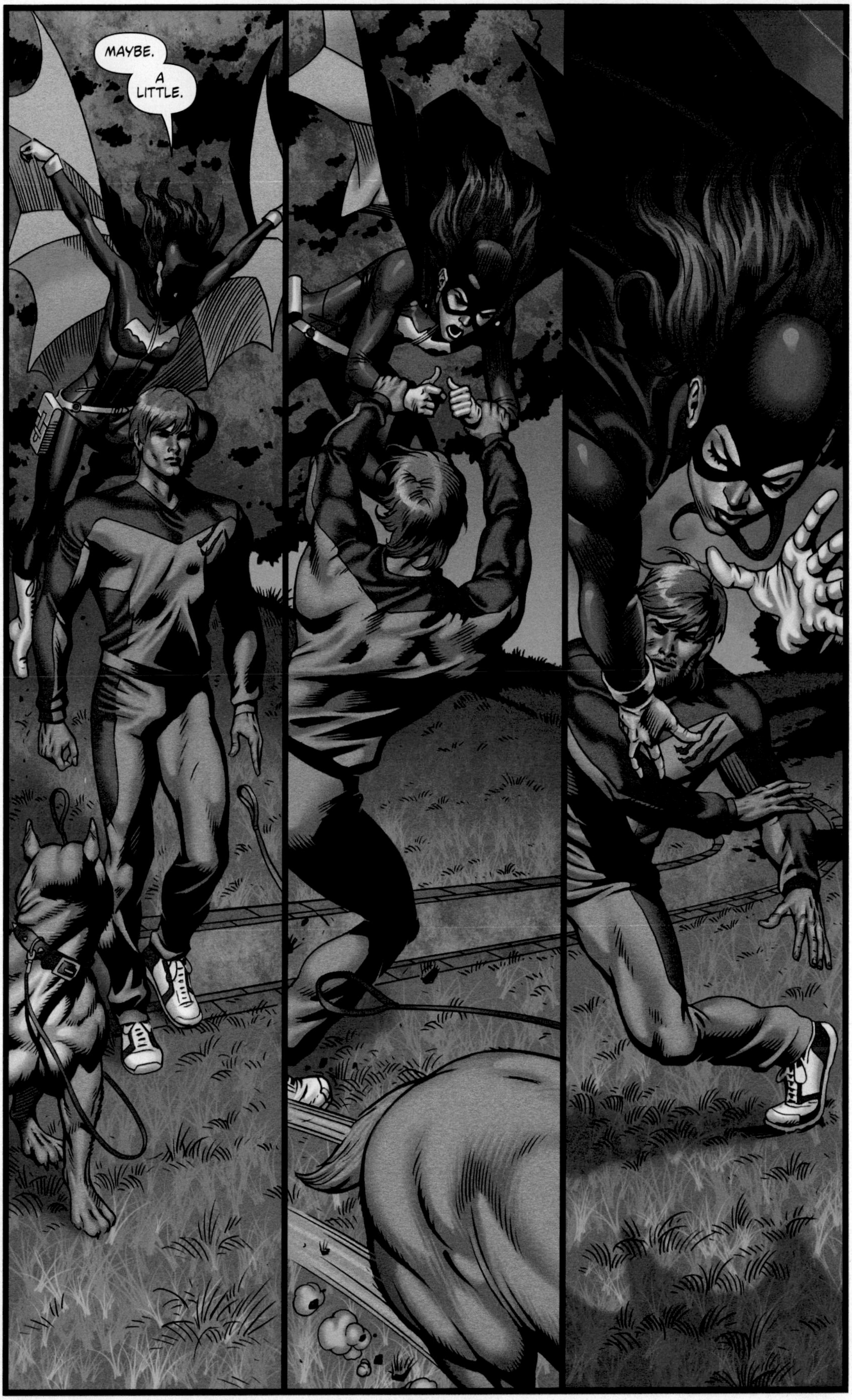
MAYBE.
A LITTLE.

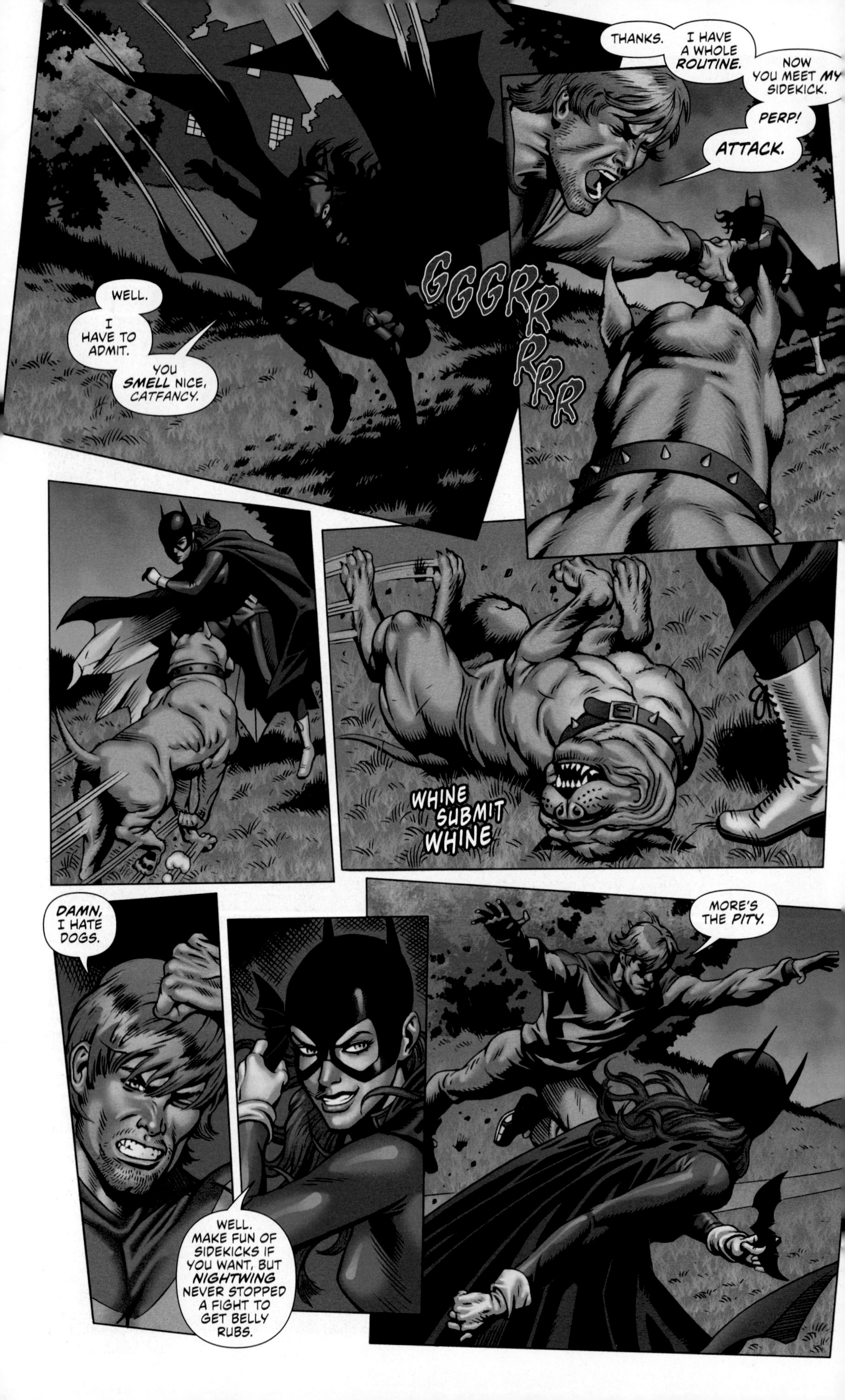

WELL.
I HAVE TO ADMIT.
YOU SMELL NICE, CATFANCY.
THANKS. I HAVE A WHOLE ROUTINE.
NOW YOU MEET MY SIDEKICK.
PERP!
ATTACK.
GGGRRRRRR
WHINE SUBMIT WHINE
DAMN, I HATE DOGS.
WELL. MAKE FUN OF SIDEKICKS IF YOU WANT, BUT NIGHTWING NEVER STOPPED A FIGHT TO GET BELLY RUBS.
MORE'S THE PITY.

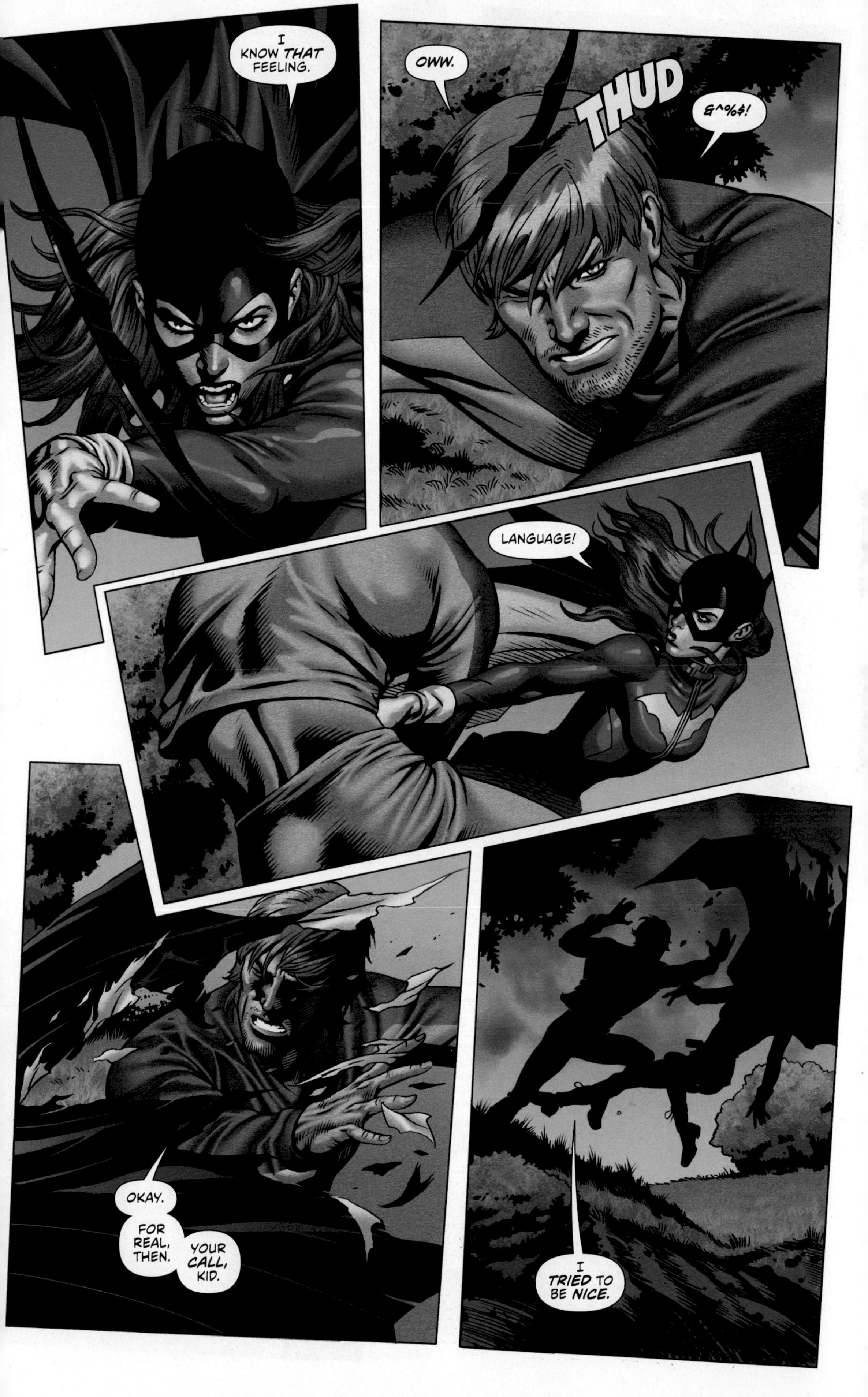
I KNOW THAT FEELING.
OWW.
THUD
&^%$!
LANGUAGE!
OKAY.
FOR REAL, THEN.
YOUR CALL, KID.
I TRIED TO BE NICE.

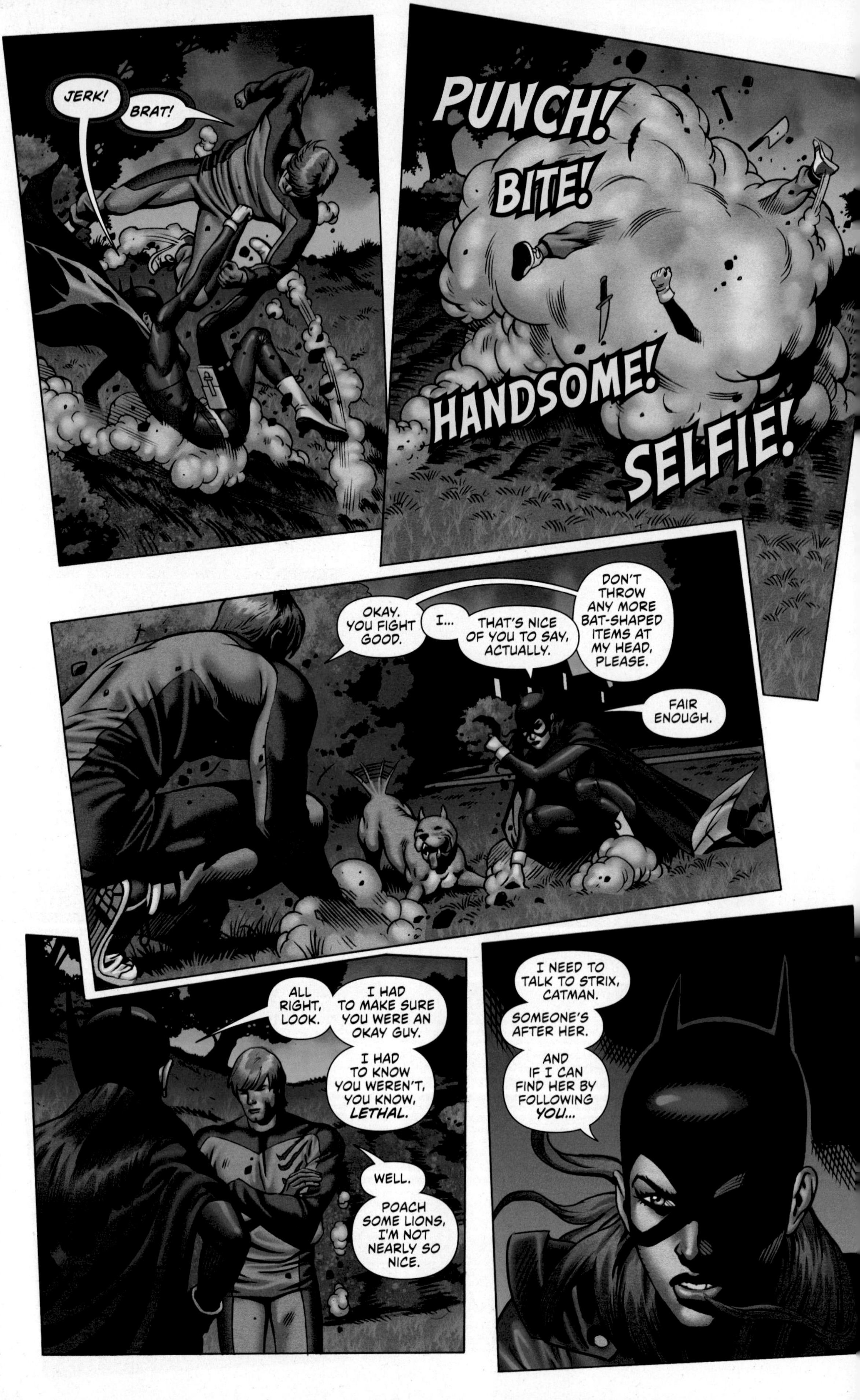
JERK!
BRAT!
PUNCH!
BITE!
HANDSOME!
SELFIE!
OKAY. YOU FIGHT GOOD.
I...
THAT'S NICE OF YOU TO SAY, ACTUALLY.
DON'T THROW ANY MORE BAT-SHAPED ITEMS AT MY HEAD, PLEASE.
FAIR ENOUGH.
ALL RIGHT, LOOK.
I HAD TO MAKE SURE YOU WERE AN OKAY GUY.
I HAD TO KNOW YOU WEREN'T, YOU KNOW, LETHAL.
WELL.
POACH SOME LIONS, I'M NOT NEARLY SO NICE.
I NEED TO TALK TO STRIX, CATMAN.
SOMEONE'S AFTER HER.
AND IF I CAN FIND HER BY FOLLOWING YOU...

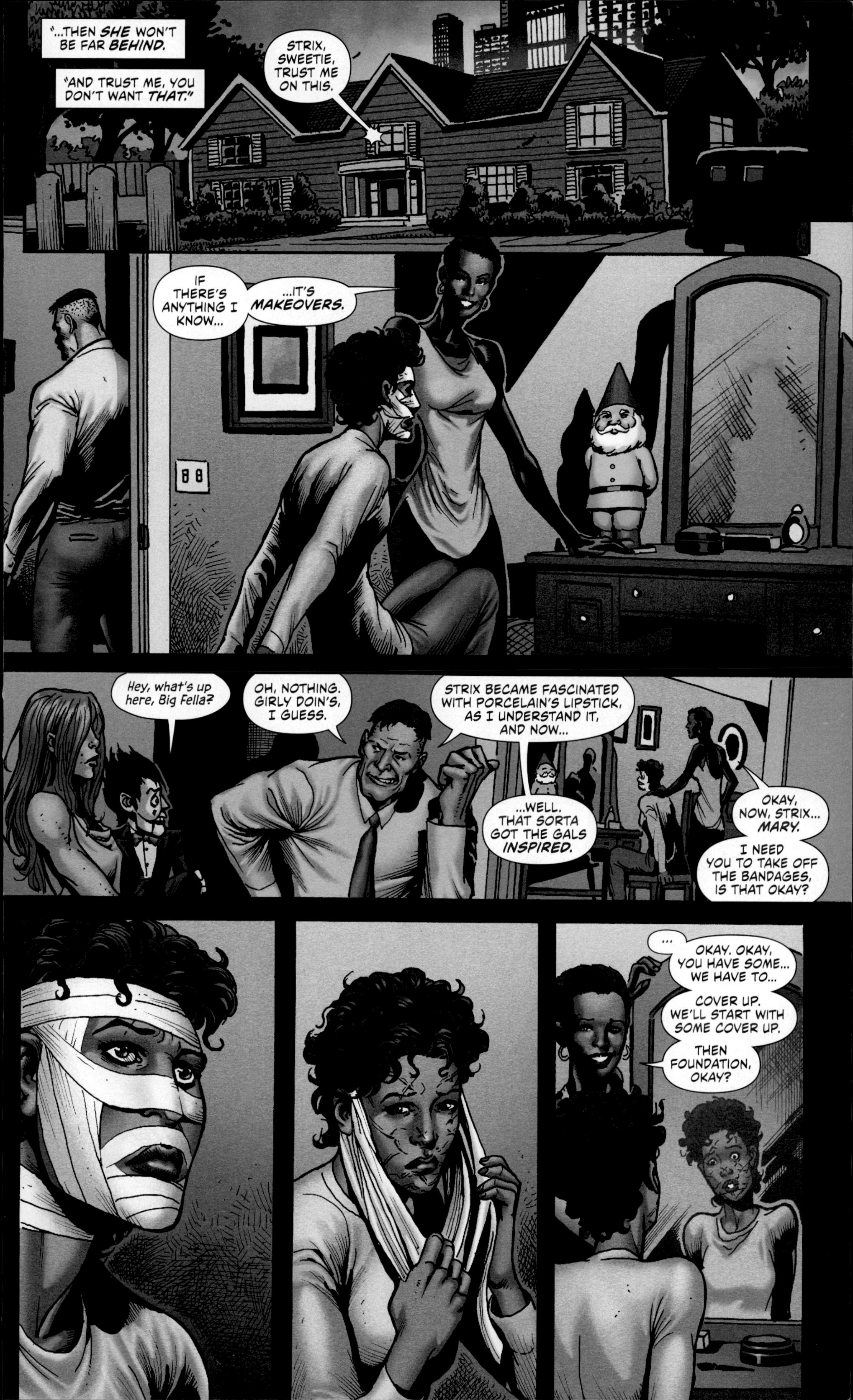
"...THEN SHE WON'T BE FAR BEHIND.
"AND TRUST ME, YOU DON'T WANT THAT."
STRIX, SWEETIE, TRUST ME ON THIS.
IF THERE'S ANYTHING I KNOW...
...IT'S MAKEOVERS.
Hey, what's up here, Big Fella?
OH, NOTHING. GIRLY DOIN'S, I GUESS.
STRIX BECAME FASCINATED WITH PORCELAIN'S LIPSTICK, AS I UNDERSTAND IT, AND NOW...
...WELL. THAT SORTA GOT THE GALS INSPIRED.
OKAY, NOW, STRIX... MARY.
I NEED YOU TO TAKE OFF THE BANDAGES, IS THAT OKAY?
...
OKAY. OKAY, YOU HAVE SOME... WE HAVE TO...
COVER UP. WE'LL START WITH SOME COVER UP.
THEN FOUNDATION, OKAY?

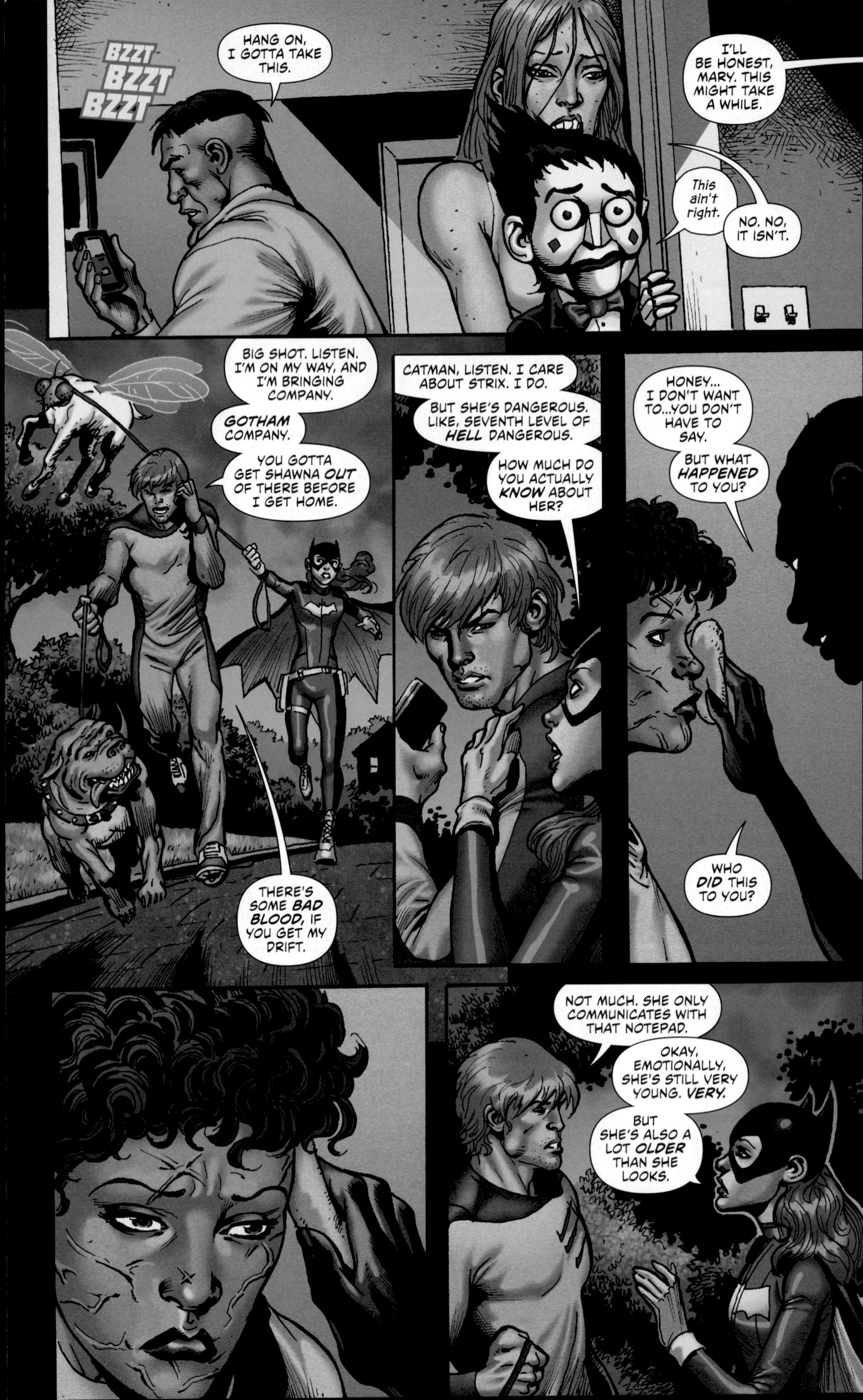
BZZT BZZT BZZT
HANG ON, I GOTTA TAKE THIS.
I'LL BE HONEST, MARY. THIS MIGHT TAKE A WHILE.
This ain't right.
NO. NO, IT ISN'T.
BIG SHOT. LISTEN. I'M ON MY WAY, AND I'M BRINGING COMPANY.
GOTHAM COMPANY.
YOU GOTTA GET SHAWNA OUT OF THERE BEFORE I GET HOME.
THERE'S SOME BAD BLOOD, IF YOU GET MY DRIFT.
CATMAN, LISTEN. I CARE ABOUT STRIX. I DO.
BUT SHE'S DANGEROUS. LIKE, SEVENTH LEVEL OF HELL DANGEROUS.
HOW MUCH DO YOU ACTUALLY KNOW ABOUT HER?
HONEY... I DON'T WANT TO...YOU DON'T HAVE TO SAY.
BUT WHAT HAPPENED TO YOU?
WHO DID THIS TO YOU?
NOT MUCH. SHE ONLY COMMUNICATES WITH THAT NOTEPAD.
OKAY, EMOTIONALLY, SHE'S STILL VERY YOUNG. VERY.
BUT SHE'S ALSO A LOT OLDER THAN SHE LOOKS.

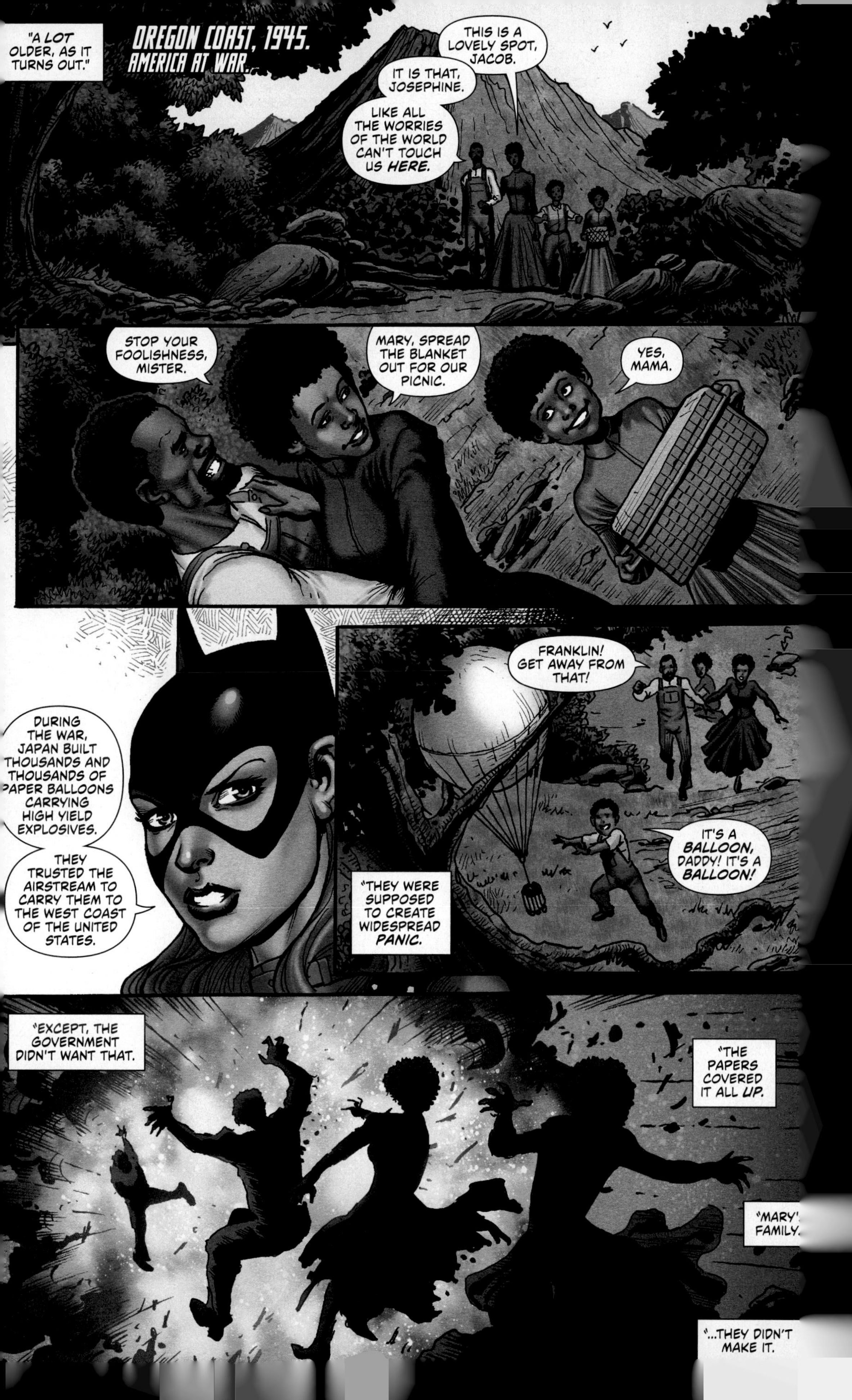
"A LOT OLDER, AS IT TURNS OUT."
OREGON COAST, 1945. AMERICA AT WAR.
THIS IS A LOVELY SPOT, JACOB.
IT IS THAT, JOSEPHINE.
LIKE ALL THE WORRIES OF THE WORLD CAN'T TOUCH US HERE.
STOP YOUR FOOLISHNESS, MISTER.
MARY, SPREAD THE BLANKET OUT FOR OUR PICNIC.
YES, MAMA.
DURING THE WAR, JAPAN BUILT THOUSANDS AND THOUSANDS OF PAPER BALLOONS CARRYING HIGH YIELD EXPLOSIVES.
THEY TRUSTED THE AIRSTREAM TO CARRY THEM TO THE WEST COAST OF THE UNITED STATES.
FRANKLIN! GET AWAY FROM THAT!
IT'S A BALLOON, DADDY! IT'S A BALLOON!
"THEY WERE SUPPOSED TO CREATE WIDESPREAD PANIC.
"EXCEPT, THE GOVERNMENT DIDN'T WANT THAT.
"THE PAPERS COVERED IT ALL UP.
"MARY'S FAMILY...
"...THEY DIDN'T MAKE IT.

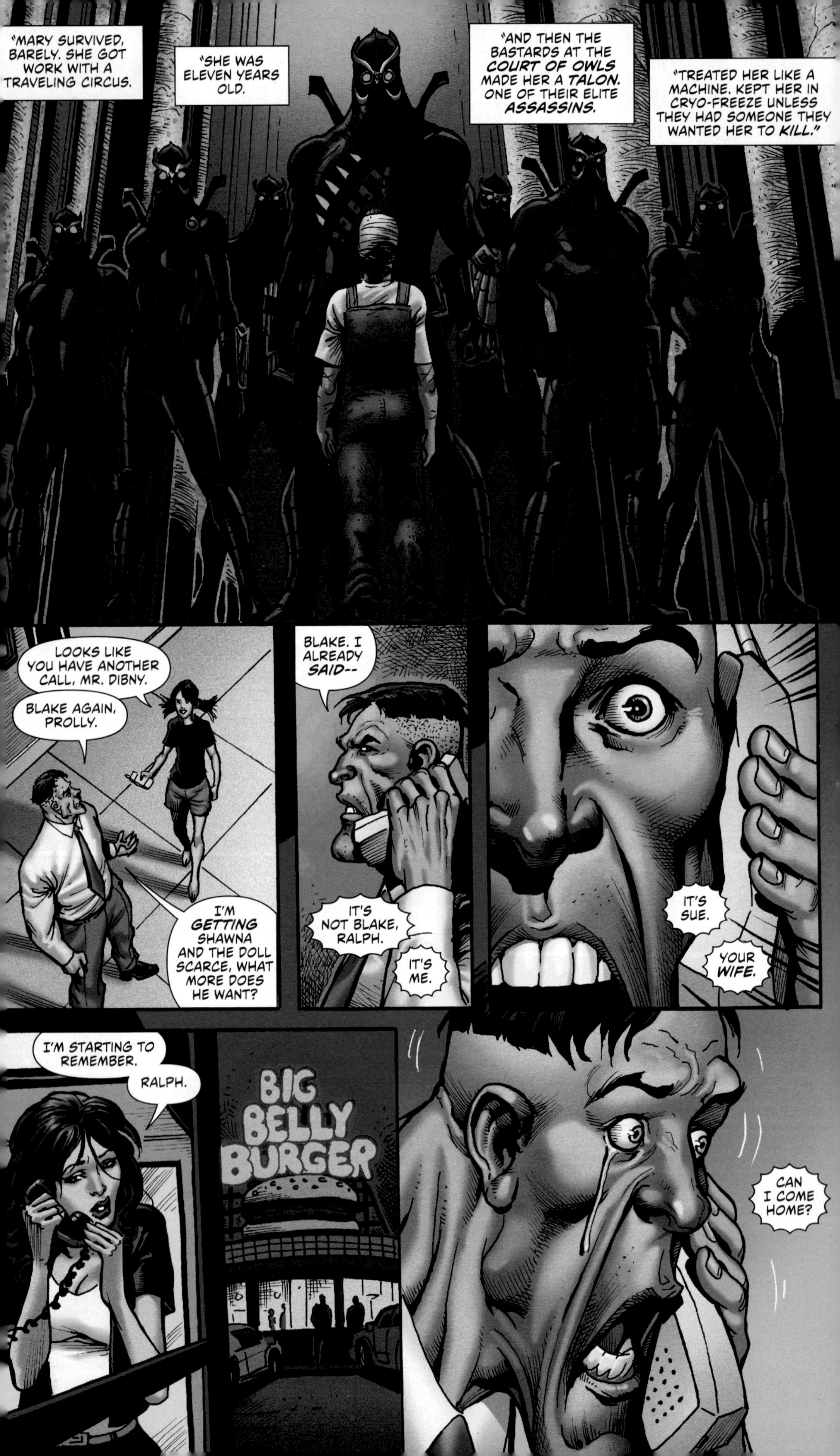
"MARY SURVIVED, BARELY. SHE GOT WORK WITH A TRAVELING CIRCUS.
"SHE WAS ELEVEN YEARS OLD.
"AND THEN THE BASTARDS AT THE COURT OF OWLS MADE HER A TALON. ONE OF THEIR ELITE ASSASSINS.
"TREATED HER LIKE A MACHINE. KEPT HER IN CRYO-FREEZE UNLESS THEY HAD SOMEONE THEY WANTED HER TO KILL."
LOOKS LIKE YOU HAVE ANOTHER CALL, MR. DIBNY.
BLAKE AGAIN, PROLLY.
I'M GETTING SHAWNA AND THE DOLL SCARCE, WHAT MORE DOES HE WANT?
BLAKE. I ALREADY SAID--
IT'S NOT BLAKE, RALPH.
IT'S ME.
IT'S SUE.
YOUR WIFE.
I'M STARTING TO REMEMBER.
RALPH.
BIG BELLY BURGER
CAN I COME HOME?

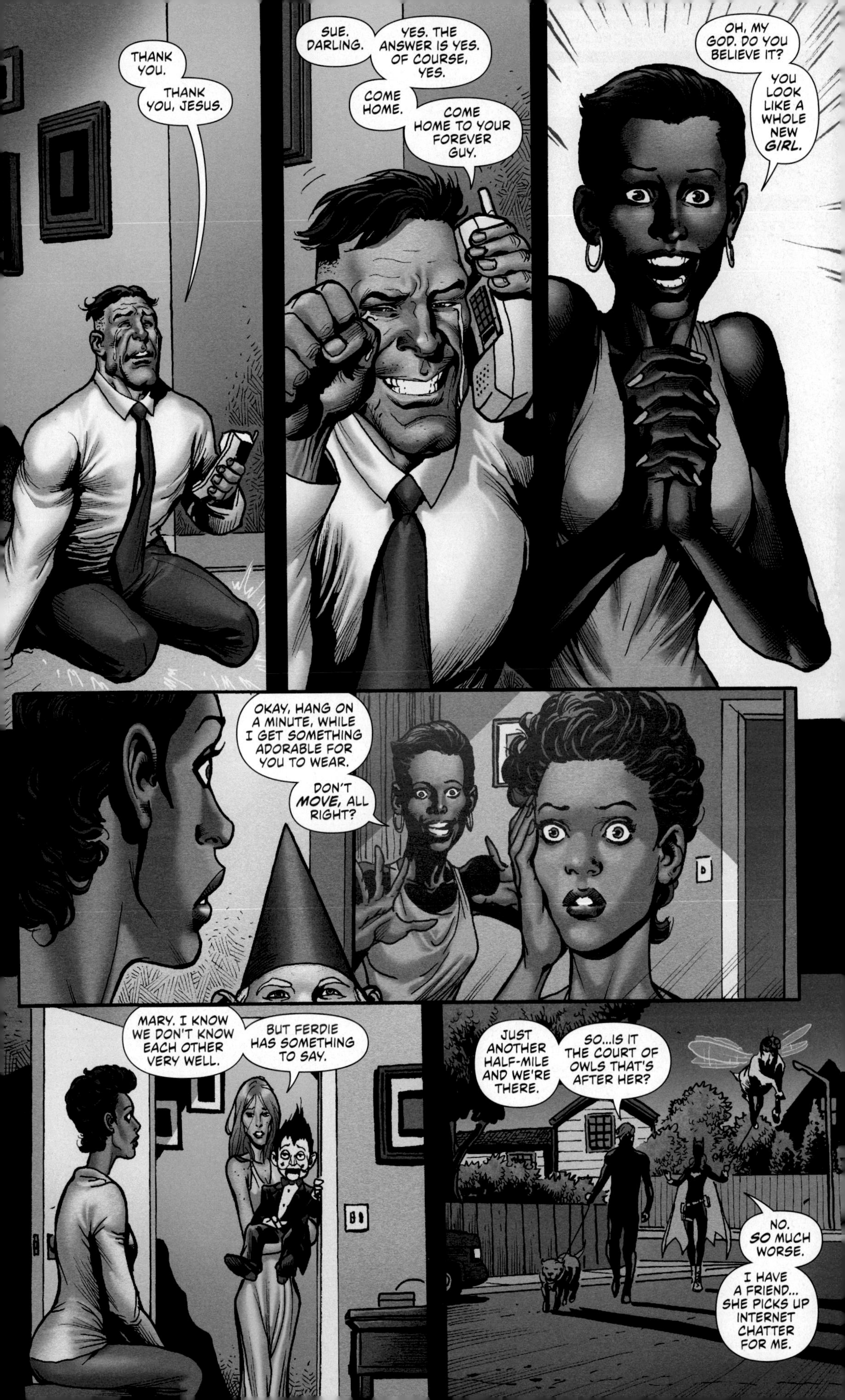
THANK YOU.
THANK YOU, JESUS.
SUE. DARLING.
YES. THE ANSWER IS YES. OF COURSE, YES.
COME HOME.
COME HOME TO YOUR FOREVER GUY.
OH, MY GOD. DO YOU BELIEVE IT?
YOU LOOK LIKE A WHOLE NEW GIRL.
OKAY, HANG ON A MINUTE, WHILE I GET SOMETHING ADORABLE FOR YOU TO WEAR.
DON'T MOVE, ALL RIGHT?
MARY. I KNOW WE DON'T KNOW EACH OTHER VERY WELL.
BUT FERDIE HAS SOMETHING TO SAY.
JUST ANOTHER HALF-MILE AND WE'RE THERE.
SO...IS IT THE COURT OF OWLS THAT'S AFTER HER?
NO. SO MUCH WORSE.
I HAVE A FRIEND... SHE PICKS UP INTERNET CHATTER FOR ME.

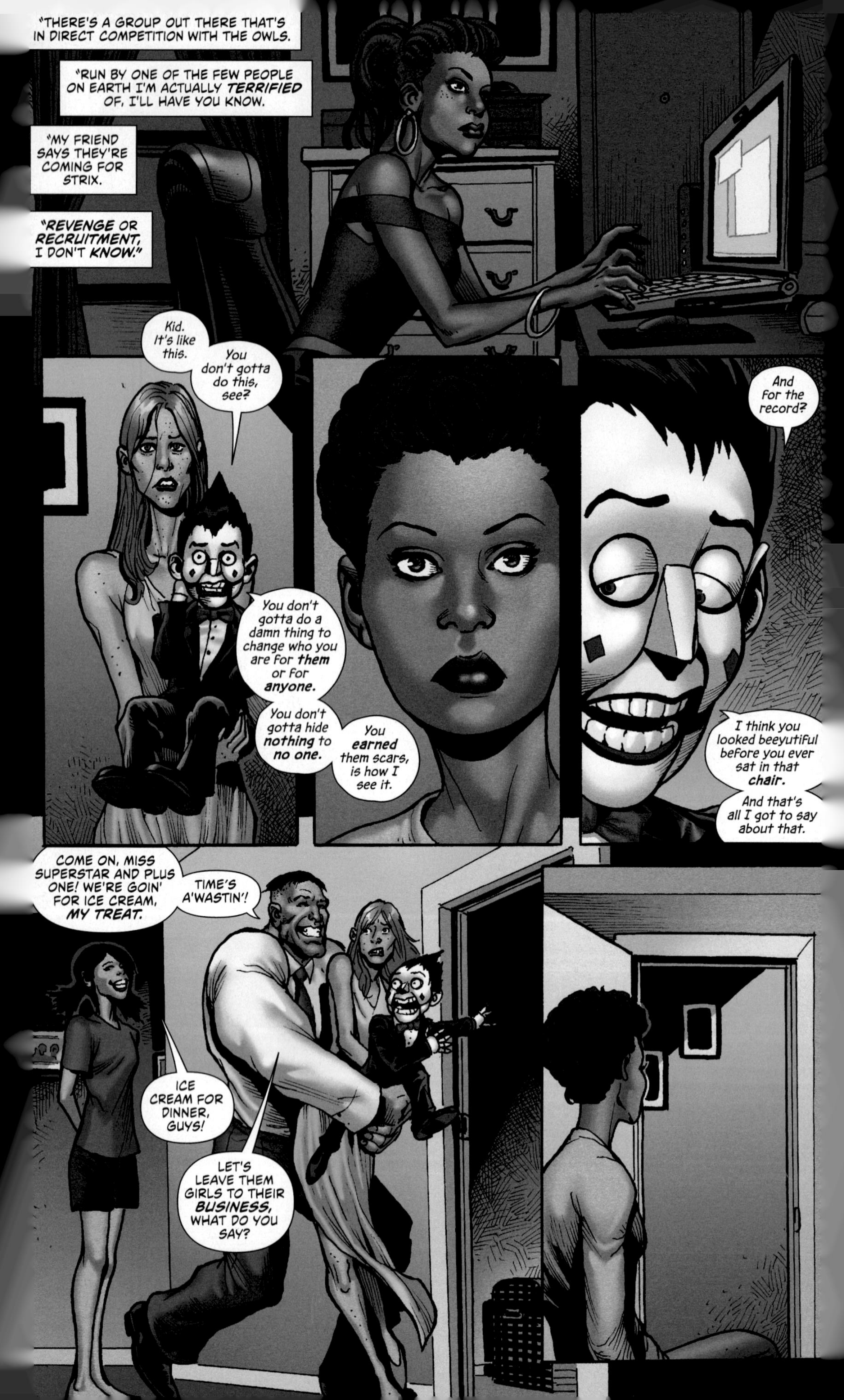
"THERE'S A GROUP OUT THERE THAT'S IN DIRECT COMPETITION WITH THE OWLS.
"RUN BY ONE OF THE FEW PEOPLE ON EARTH I'M ACTUALLY TERRIFIED OF, I'LL HAVE YOU KNOW.
"MY FRIEND SAYS THEY'RE COMING FOR STRIX.
"REVENGE OR RECRUITMENT, I DON'T KNOW."
Kid. It's like this.
You don't gotta do this, see?
You don't gotta do a damn thing to change who you are for them or for anyone.
You don't gotta hide nothing to no one.
You earned them scars, is how I see it.
And for the record?
I think you looked beeyutiful before you ever sat in that chair.
And that's all I got to say about that.
COME ON, MISS SUPERSTAR AND PLUS ONE! WE'RE GOIN' FOR ICE CREAM, MY TREAT.
TIME'S A'WASTIN'!
ICE CREAM FOR DINNER, GUYS!
LET'S LEAVE THEM GIRLS TO THEIR BUSINESS, WHAT DO YOU SAY?

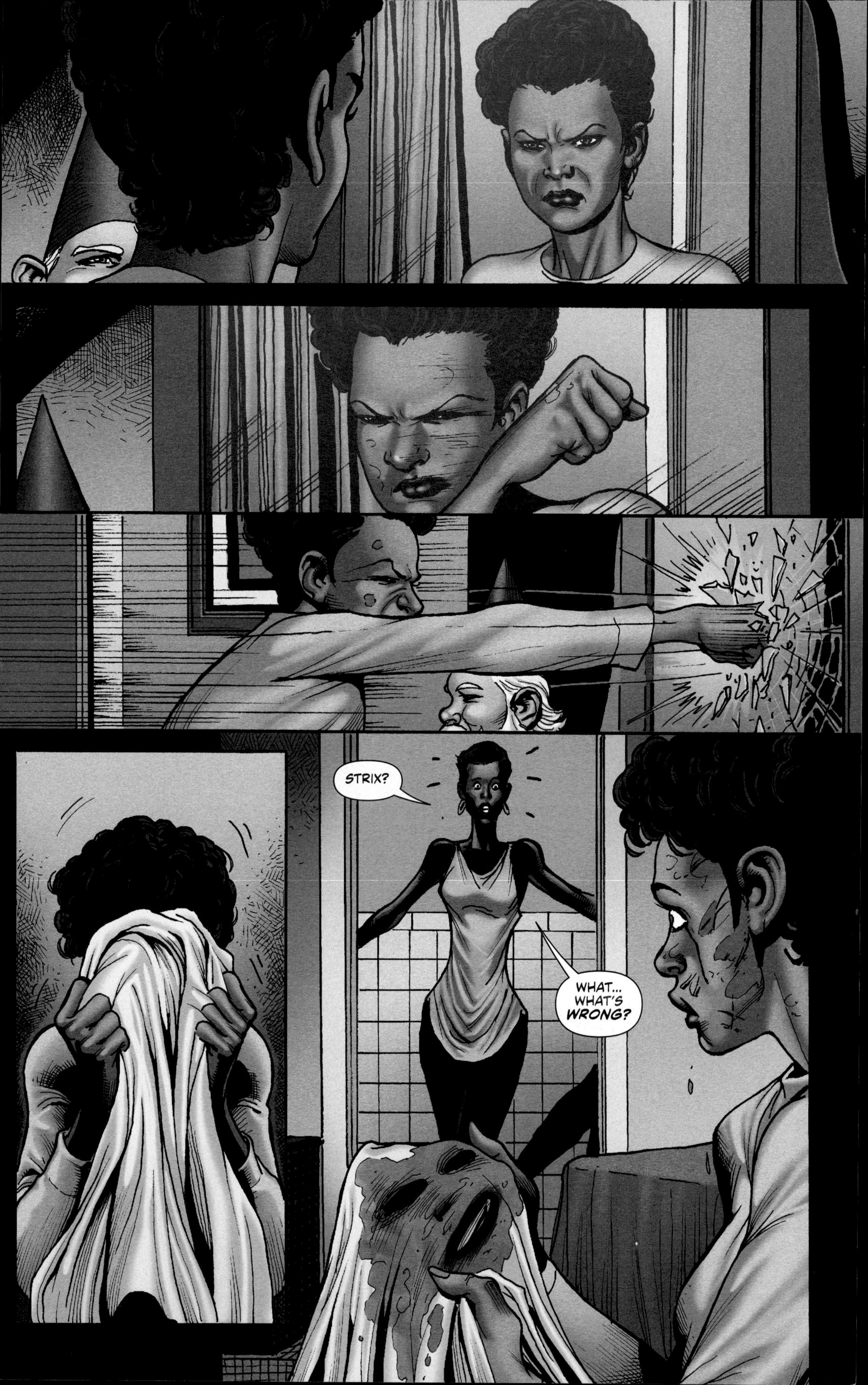
STRIX?
WHAT... WHAT'S WRONG?

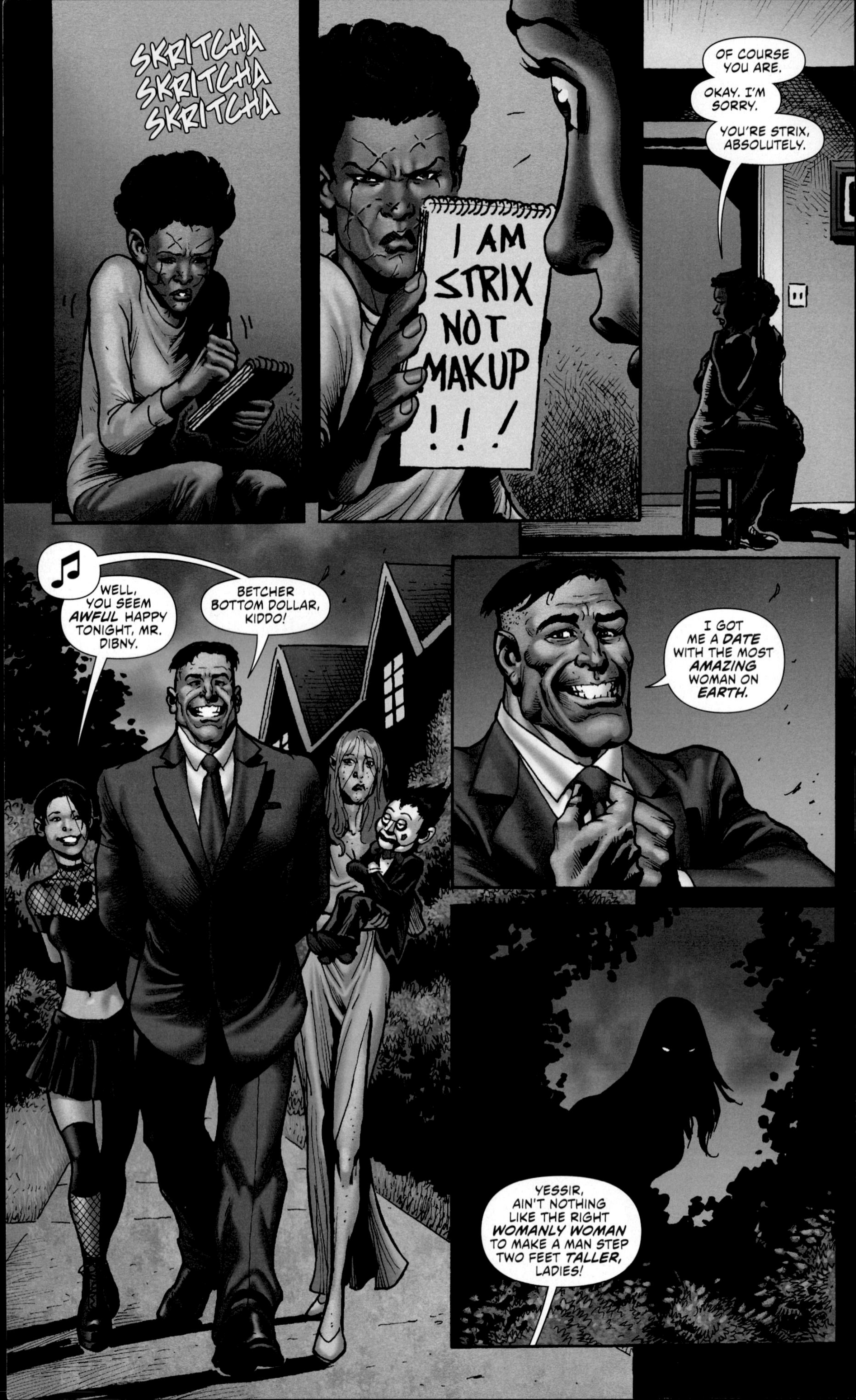
SKRITCHA SKRITCHA SKRITCHA
I AM STRIX NOT MAKUP !!!
OF COURSE YOU ARE.
OKAY. I'M SORRY.
YOU'RE STRIX, ABSOLUTELY.
♫
WELL, YOU SEEM AWFUL HAPPY TONIGHT, MR. DIBNY.
BETCHER BOTTOM DOLLAR, KIDDO!
I GOT ME A DATE WITH THE MOST AMAZING WOMAN ON EARTH.
YESSIR, AIN'T NOTHING LIKE THE RIGHT WOMANLY WOMAN TO MAKE A MAN STEP TWO FEET TALLER, LADIES!

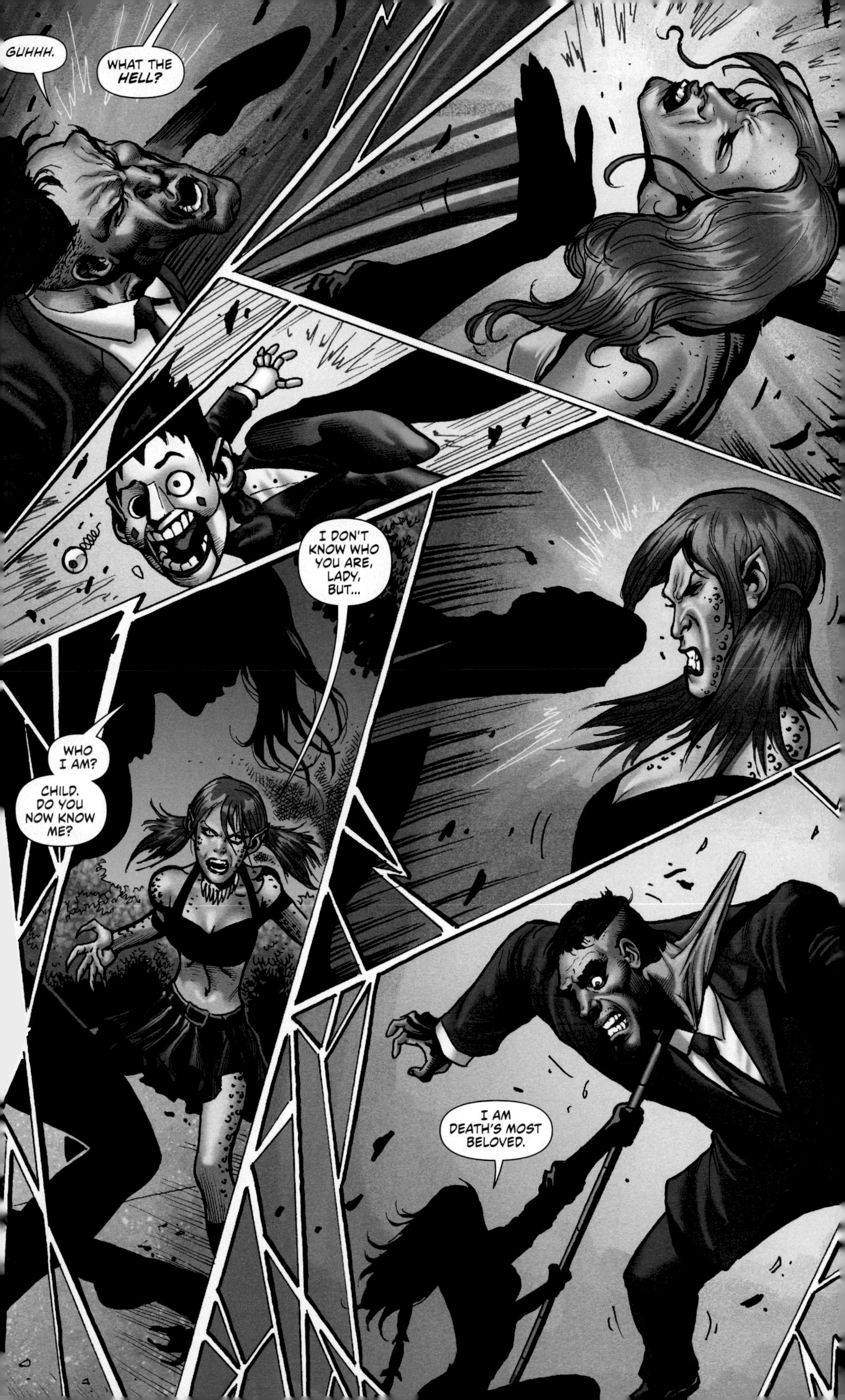
GUHHH.
WHAT THE HELL?
I DON'T KNOW WHO YOU ARE, LADY, BUT...
WHO I AM?
CHILD. DO YOU NOW KNOW ME?
I AM DEATH'S MOST BELOVED.

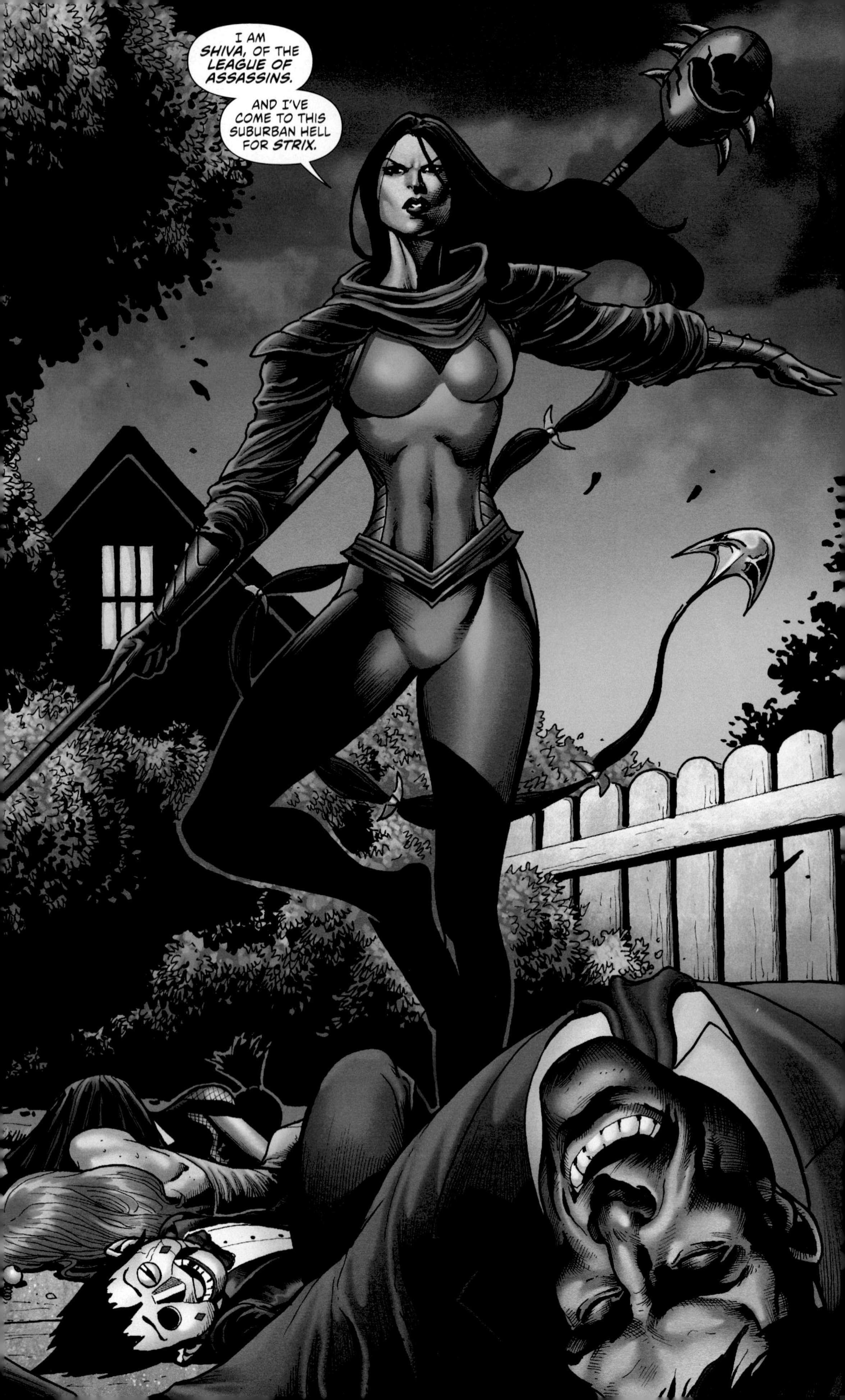
I AM SHIVA, OF THE LEAGUE OF ASSASSINS.
AND I'VE COME TO THIS SUBURBAN HELL FOR STRIX.

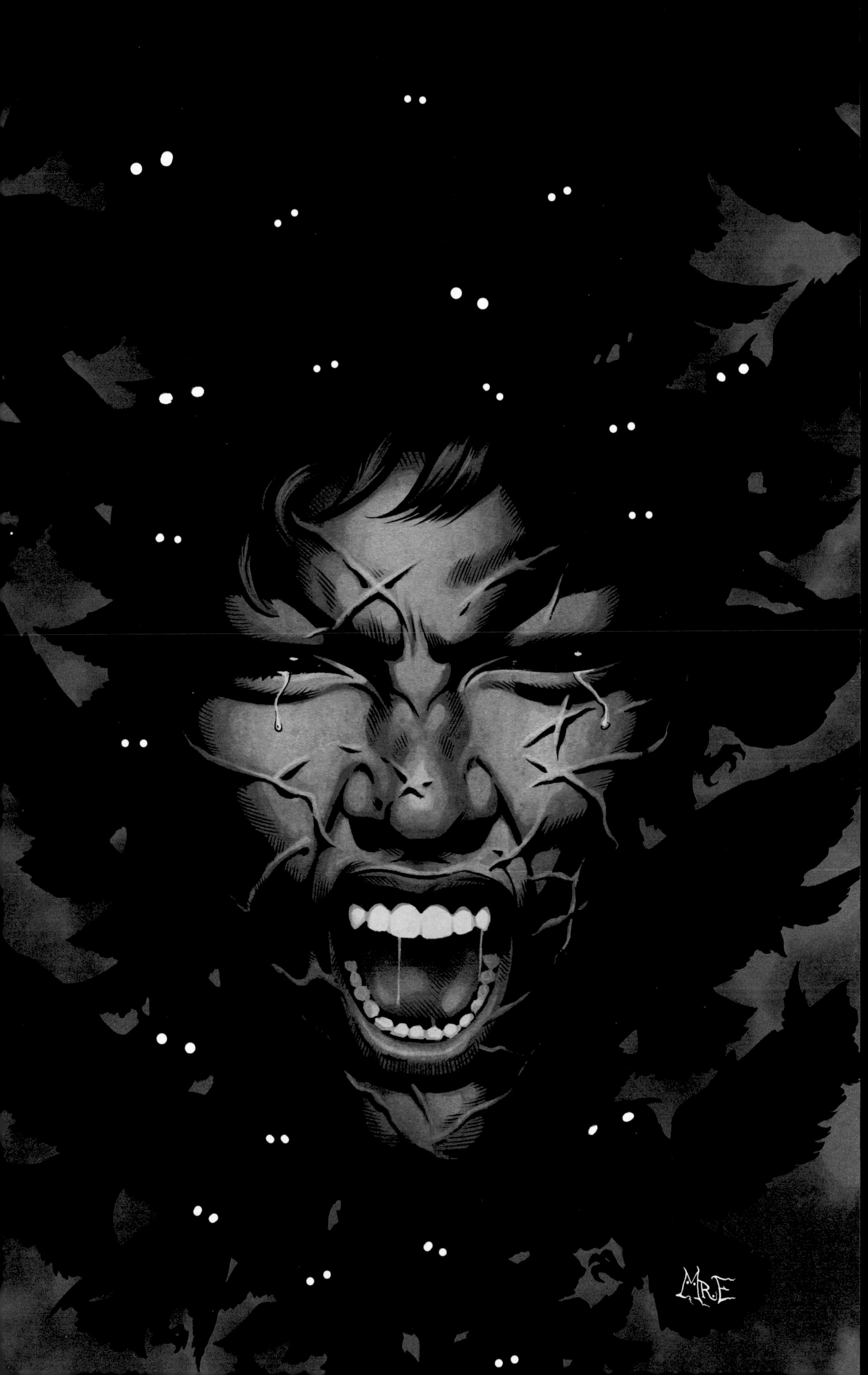

GAIL SIMONE writer DALE EAGLESHAM TOM DERENICK artists JASON WRIGHT colorist TRAVIS LANHAM letterer
cover by DALE EAGLESHAM with JASON WRIGHT

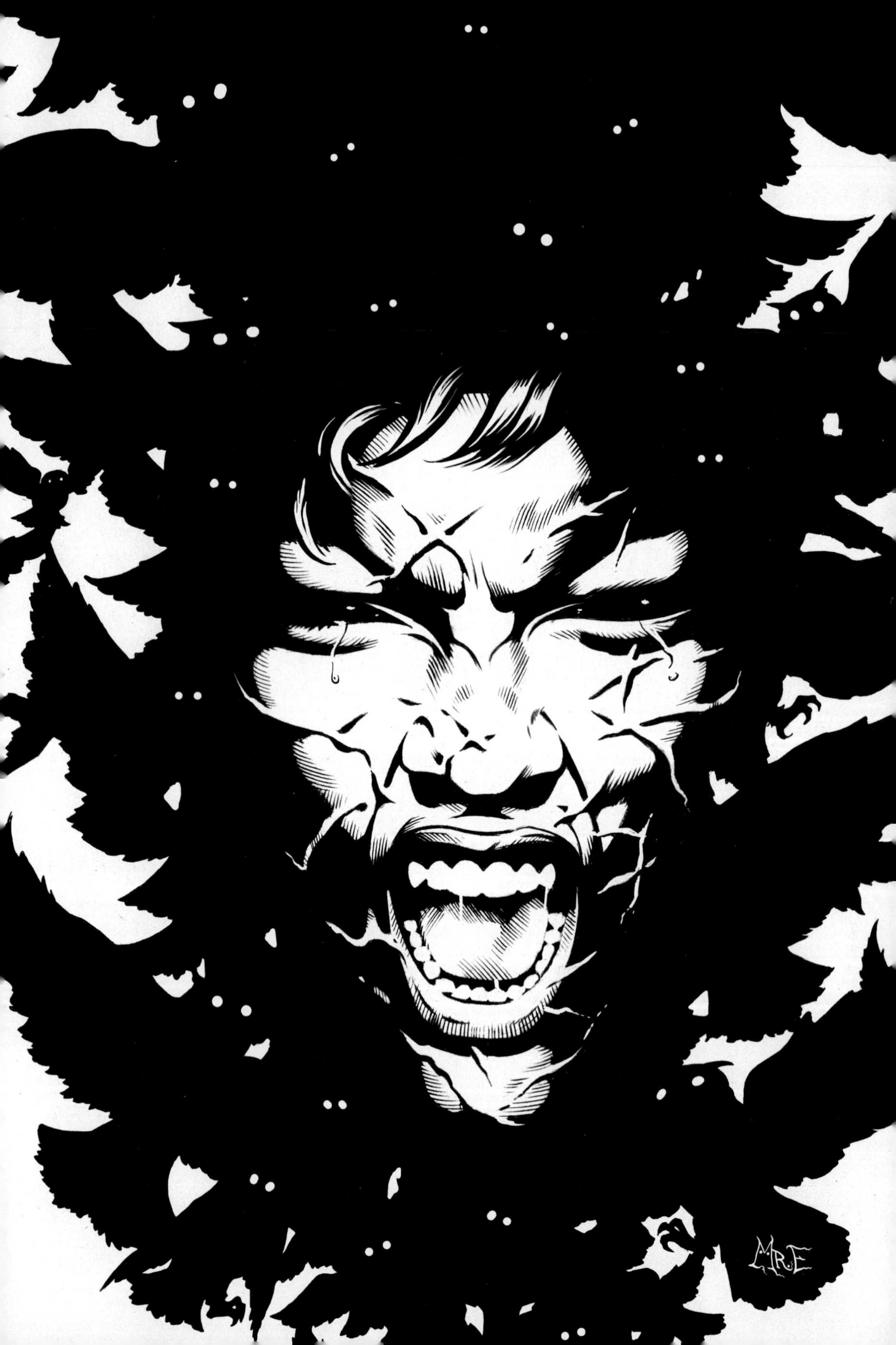

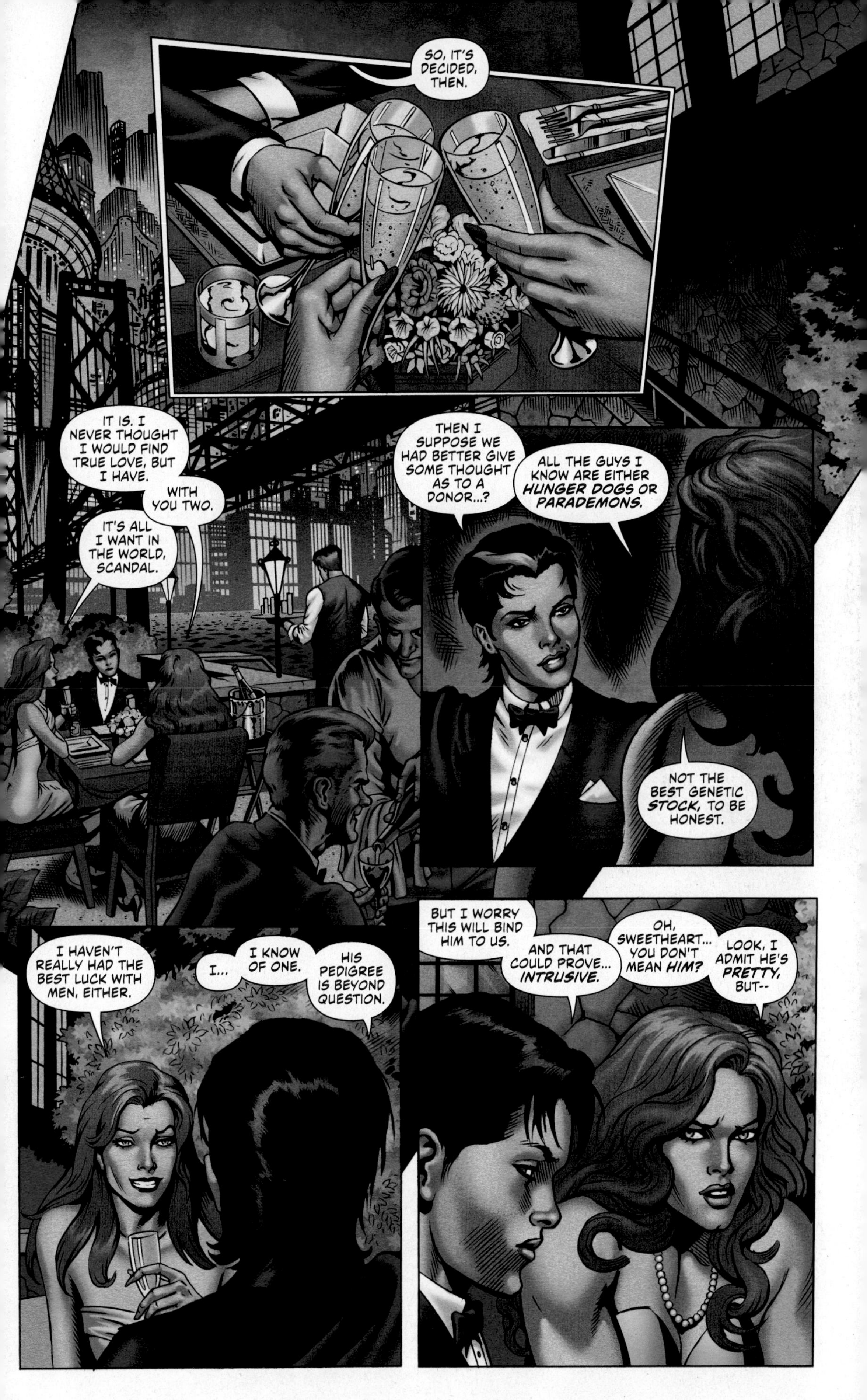
SO, IT'S DECIDED, THEN.
IT IS. I NEVER THOUGHT I WOULD FIND TRUE LOVE, BUT I HAVE.
WITH YOU TWO.
IT'S ALL I WANT IN THE WORLD, SCANDAL.
THEN I SUPPOSE WE HAD BETTER GIVE SOME THOUGHT AS TO A DONOR...?
ALL THE GUYS I KNOW ARE EITHER HUNGER DOGS OR PARADEMONS.
NOT THE BEST GENETIC STOCK, TO BE HONEST.
I HAVEN'T REALLY HAD THE BEST LUCK WITH MEN, EITHER.
I...
I KNOW OF ONE.
HIS PEDIGREE IS BEYOND QUESTION.
BUT I WORRY THIS WILL BIND HIM TO US.
AND THAT COULD PROVE... INTRUSIVE.
OH, SWEETHEART... YOU DON'T MEAN HIM?
LOOK, I ADMIT HE'S PRETTY, BUT--

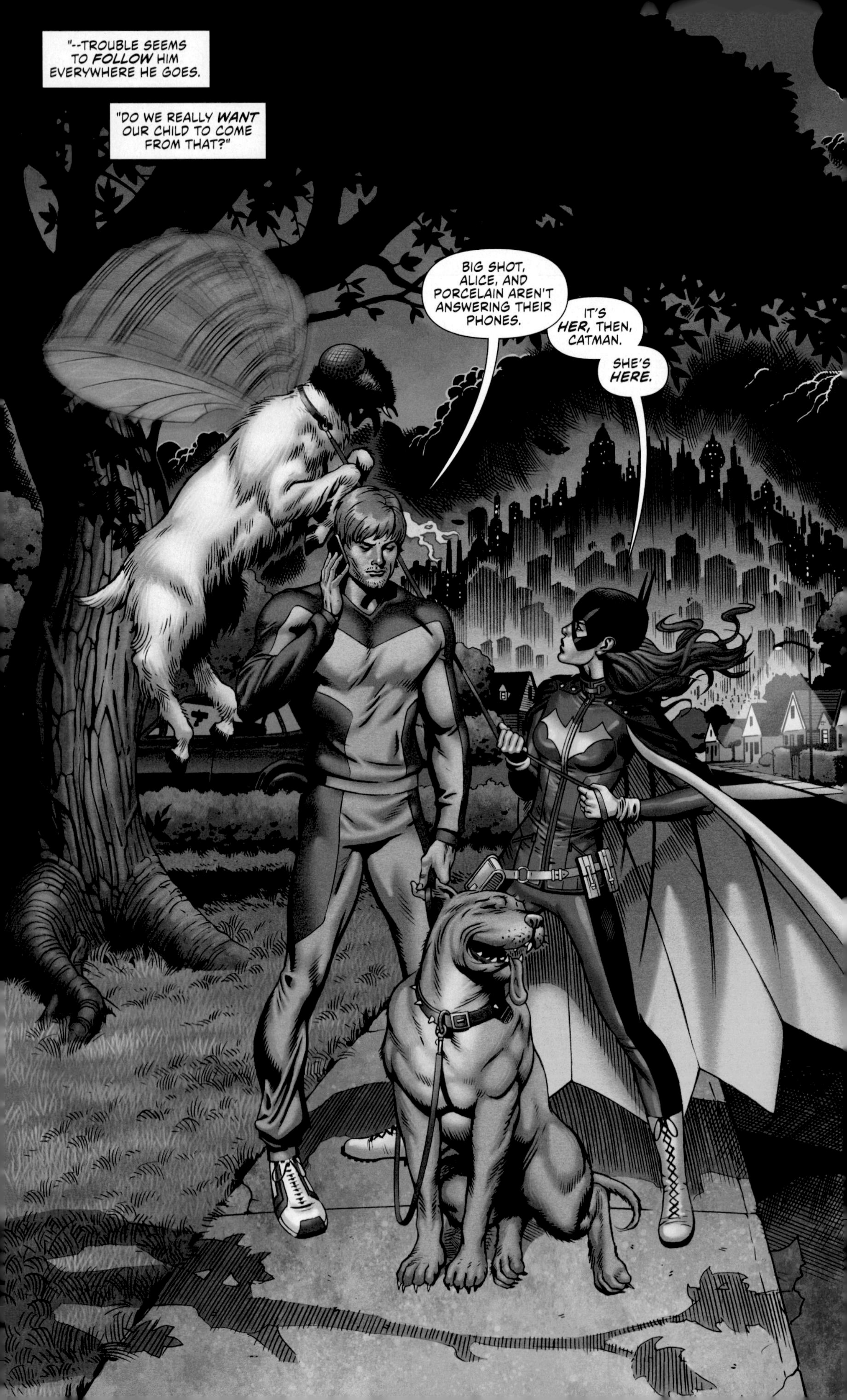
"--TROUBLE SEEMS TO FOLLOW HIM EVERYWHERE HE GOES.
"DO WE REALLY WANT OUR CHILD TO COME FROM THAT?"
BIG SHOT, ALICE, AND PORCELAIN AREN'T ANSWERING THEIR PHONES.
IT'S HER, THEN, CATMAN.
SHE'S HERE.

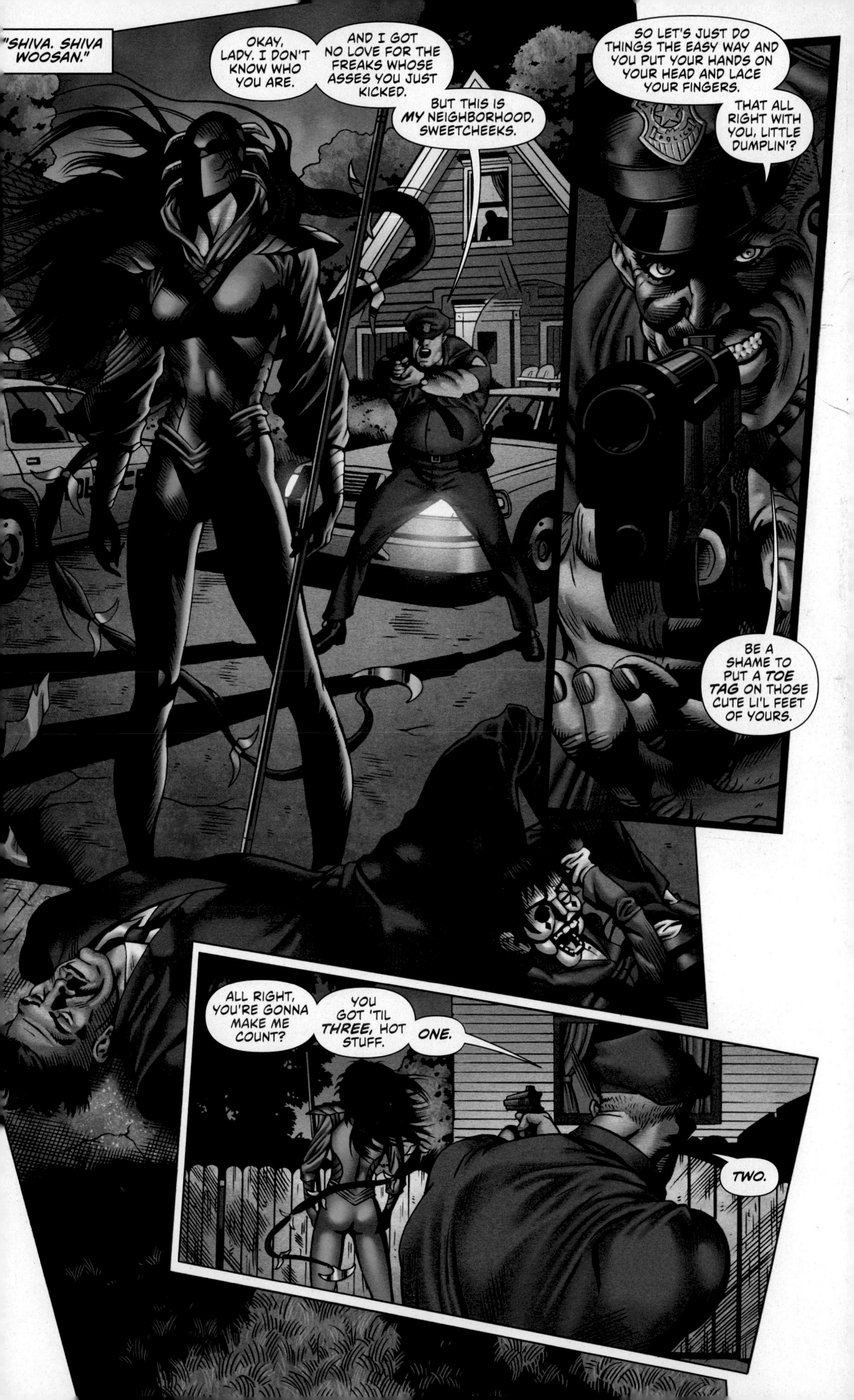
"SHIVA. SHIVA WOOSAN."
OKAY, LADY. I DON'T KNOW WHO YOU ARE.
AND I GOT NO LOVE FOR THE FREAKS WHOSE ASSES YOU JUST KICKED.
BUT THIS IS MY NEIGHBORHOOD, SWEETCHEEKS.
SO LET'S JUST DO THINGS THE EASY WAY AND YOU PUT YOUR HANDS ON YOUR HEAD AND LACE YOUR FINGERS.
THAT ALL RIGHT WITH YOU, LITTLE DUMPLIN'?
BE A SHAME TO PUT A TOE TAG ON THOSE CUTE LI'L FEET OF YOURS.
ALL RIGHT, YOU'RE GONNA MAKE ME COUNT?
YOU GOT 'TIL THREE, HOT STUFF.
ONE.
TWO.

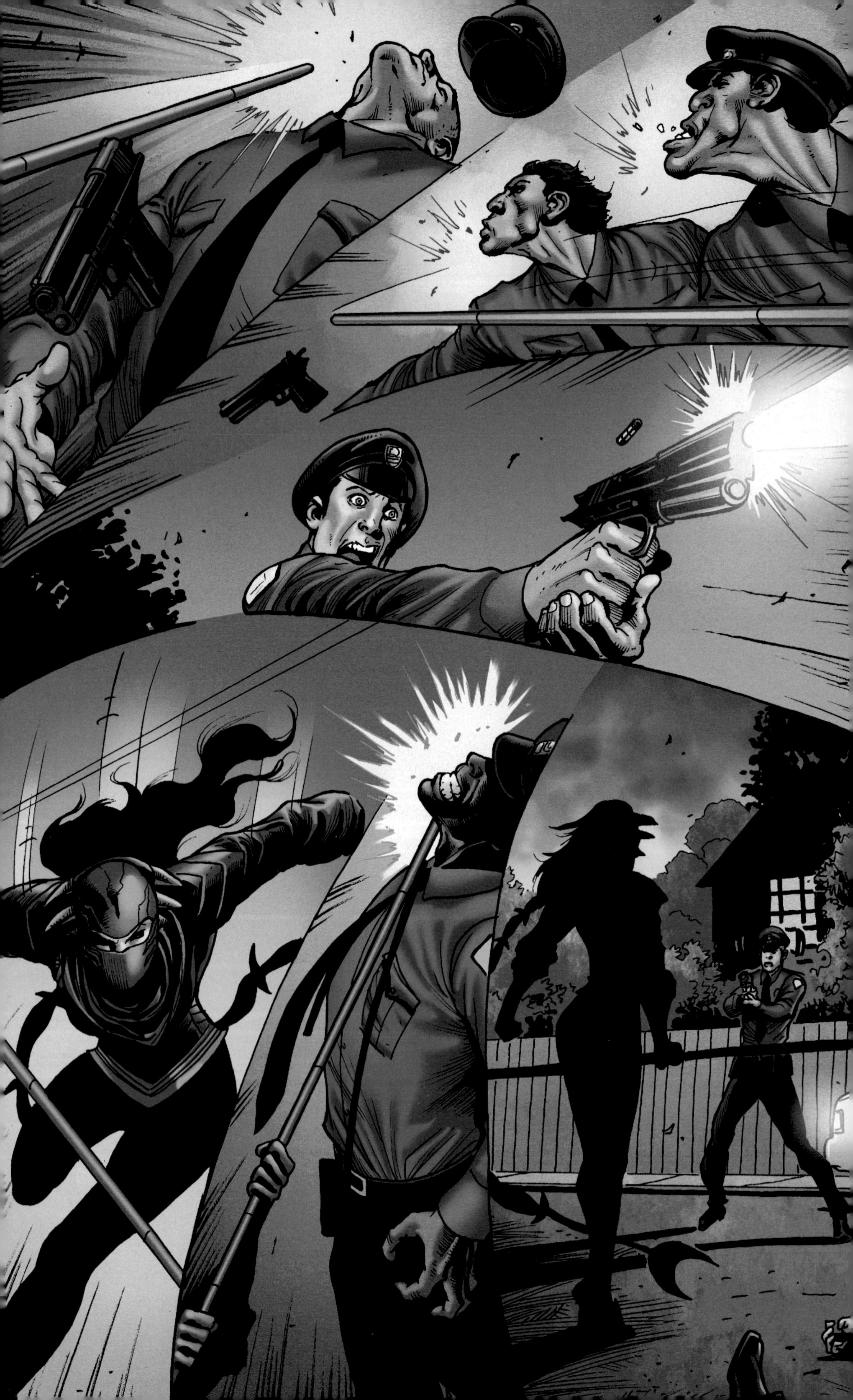

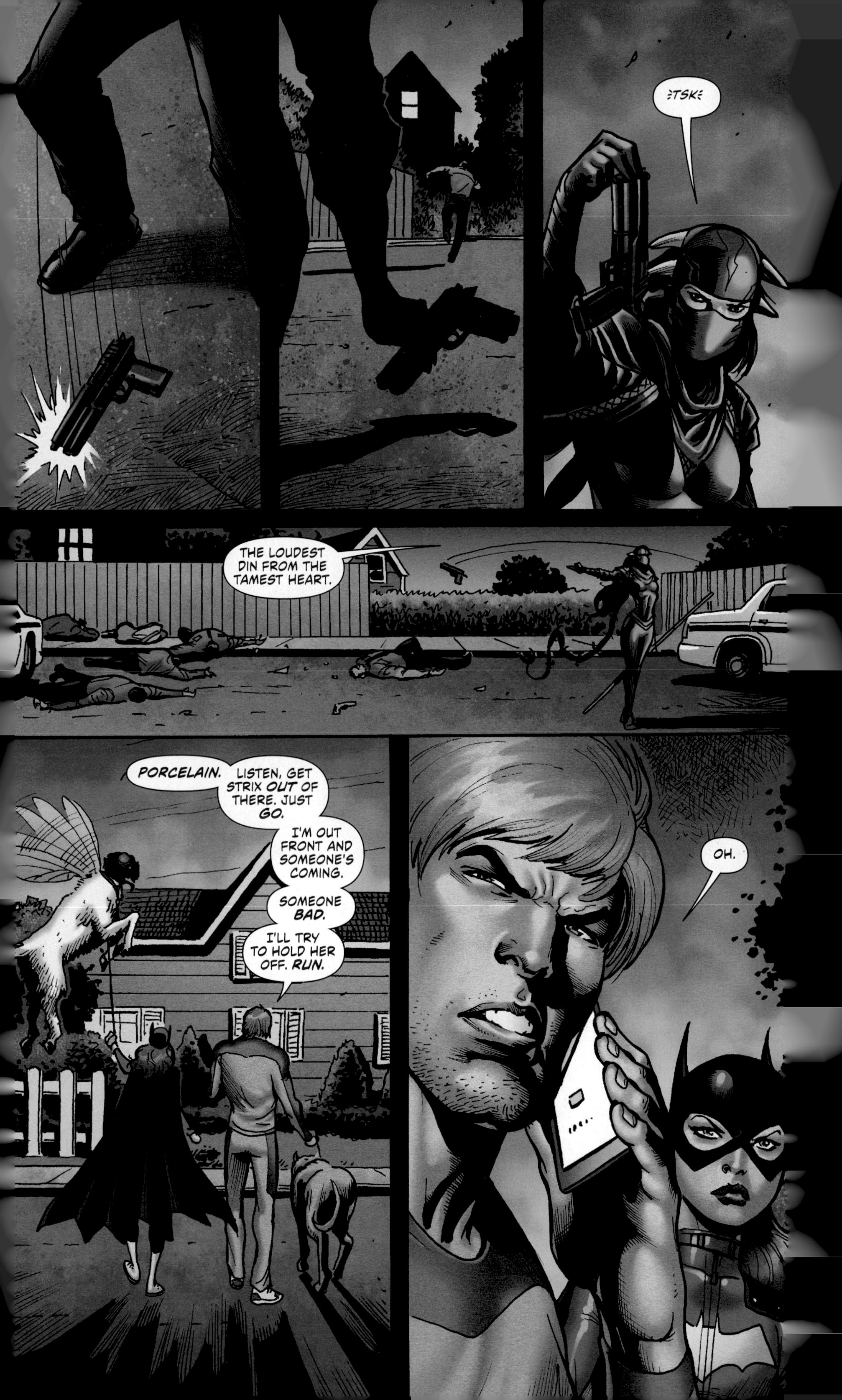
TSK
THE LOUDEST DIN FROM THE TAMEST HEART.
PORCELAIN.
LISTEN, GET STRIX OUT OF THERE. JUST GO.
I'M OUT FRONT AND SOMEONE'S COMING.
SOMEONE BAD.
I'LL TRY TO HOLD HER OFF. RUN.
OH.

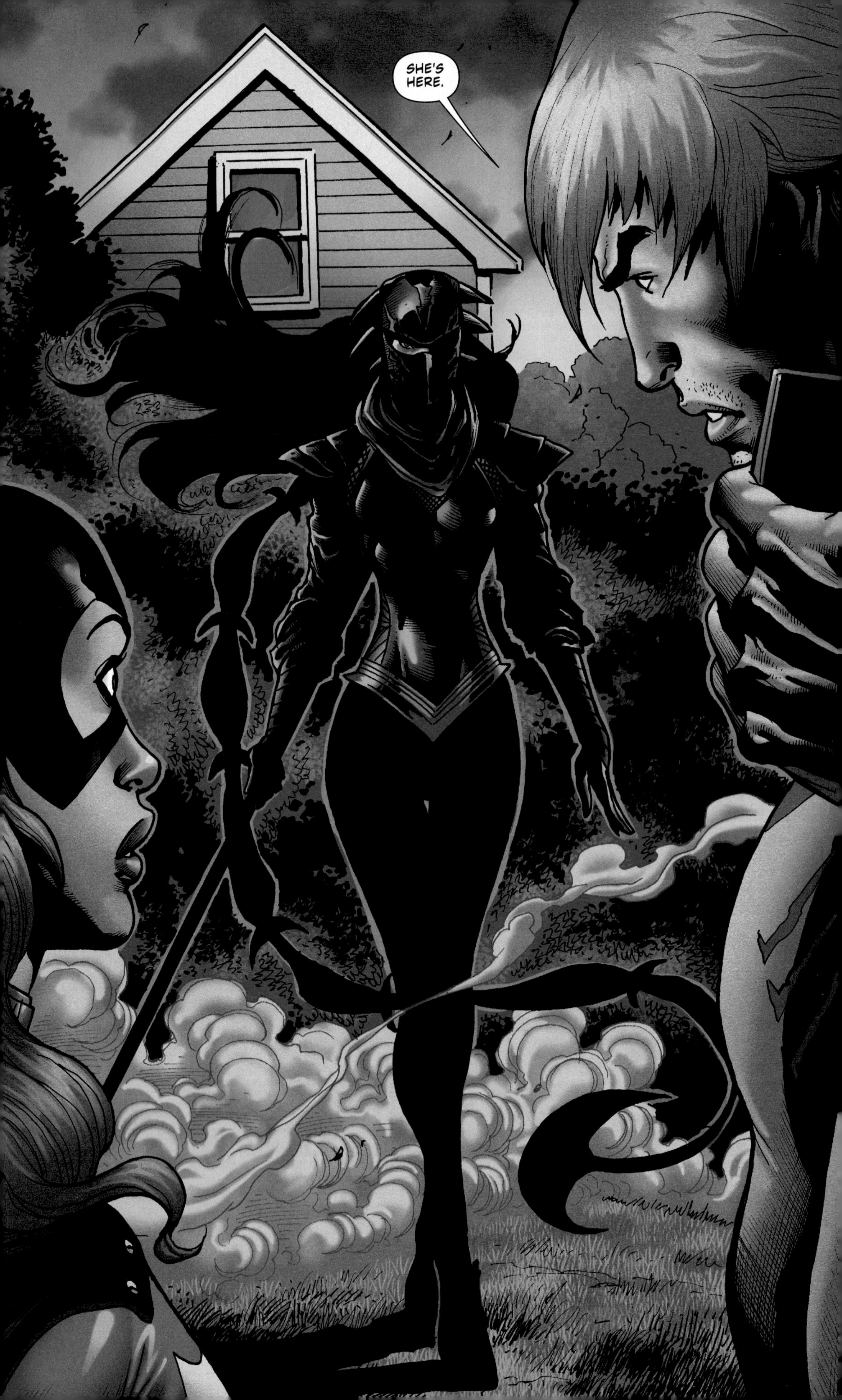
SHE'S HERE.

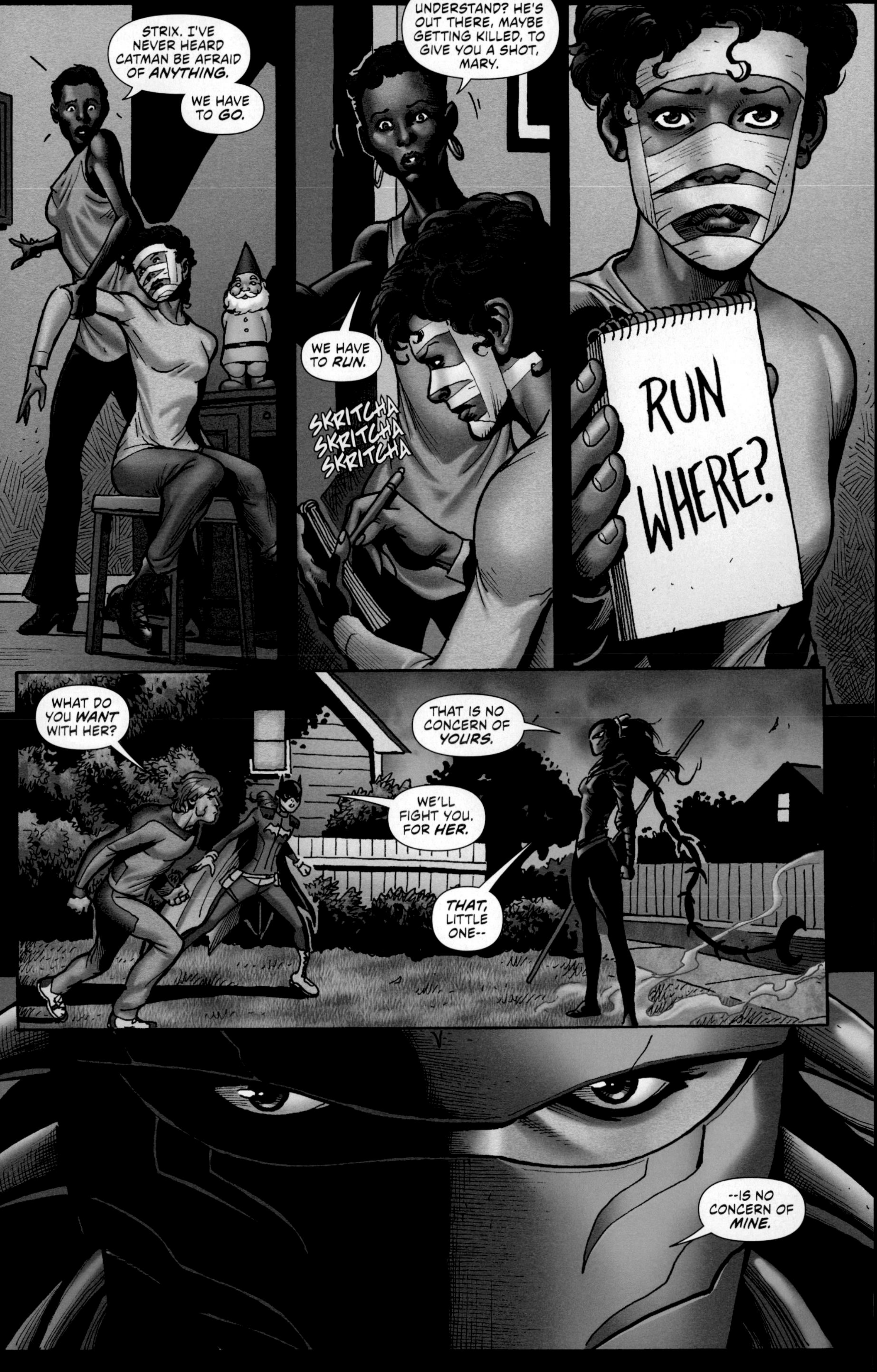
STRIX. I'VE NEVER HEARD CATMAN BE AFRAID OF ANYTHING.
WE HAVE TO GO.
DO YOU NOT UNDERSTAND? HE'S OUT THERE, MAYBE GETTING KILLED, TO GIVE YOU A SHOT, MARY.
WE HAVE TO RUN.
SKRITCHA SKRITCHA SKRITCHA
RUN WHERE?
WHAT DO YOU WANT WITH HER?
THAT IS NO CONCERN OF YOURS.
WE'LL FIGHT YOU. FOR HER.
THAT, LITTLE ONE--
--IS NO CONCERN OF MINE.

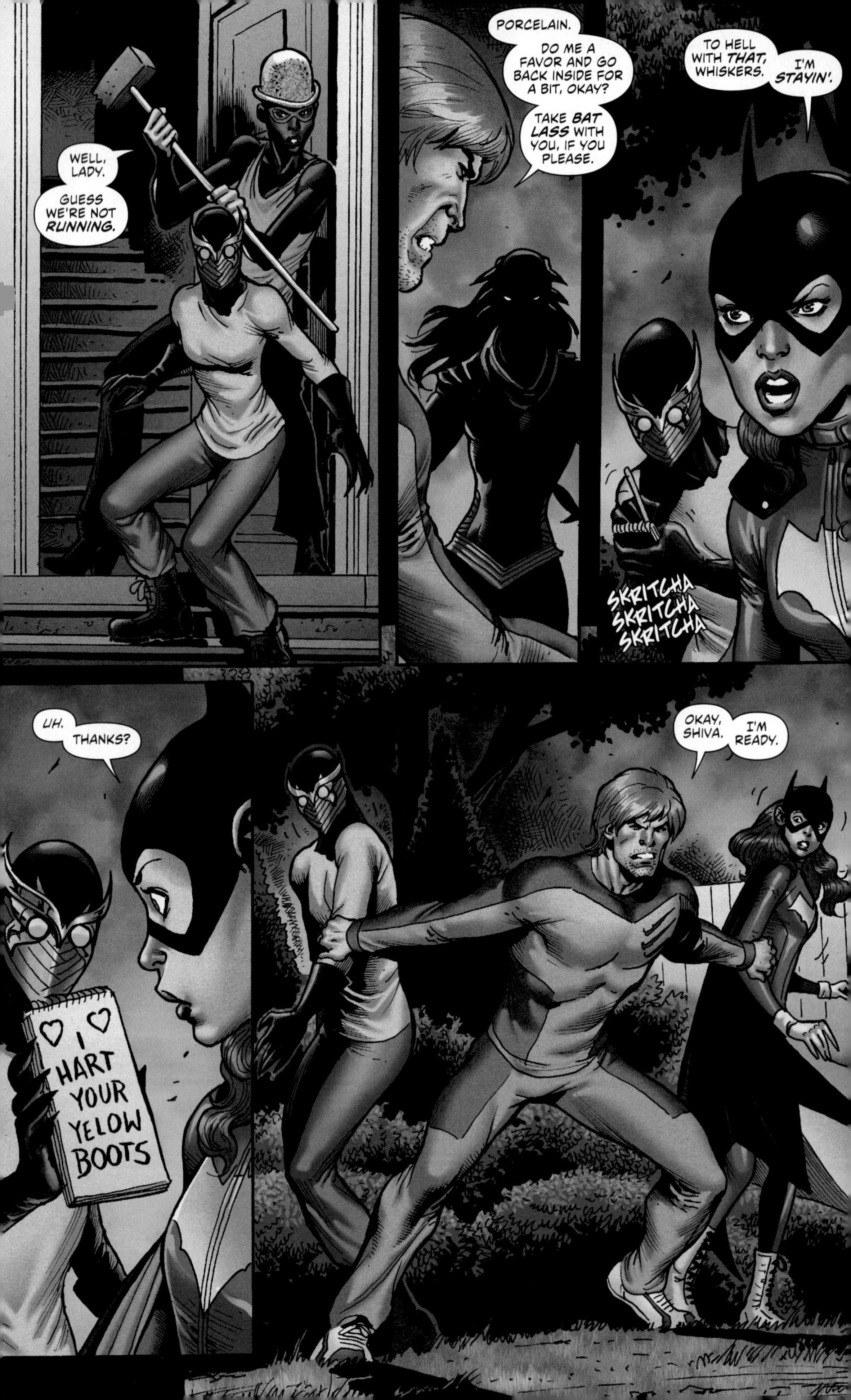
WELL, LADY.
GUESS WE'RE NOT *RUNNING*.
PORCELAIN.
DO ME A FAVOR AND GO BACK INSIDE FOR A BIT, OKAY?
TAKE **BAT LASS** WITH YOU, IF YOU PLEASE.
TO HELL WITH *THAT*, WHISKERS.
I'M *STAYIN'*.
SKRITCHA SKRITCHA SKRITCHA
UH.
THANKS?
I HART YOUR YELLOW BOOTS
OKAY, SHIVA.
I'M READY.

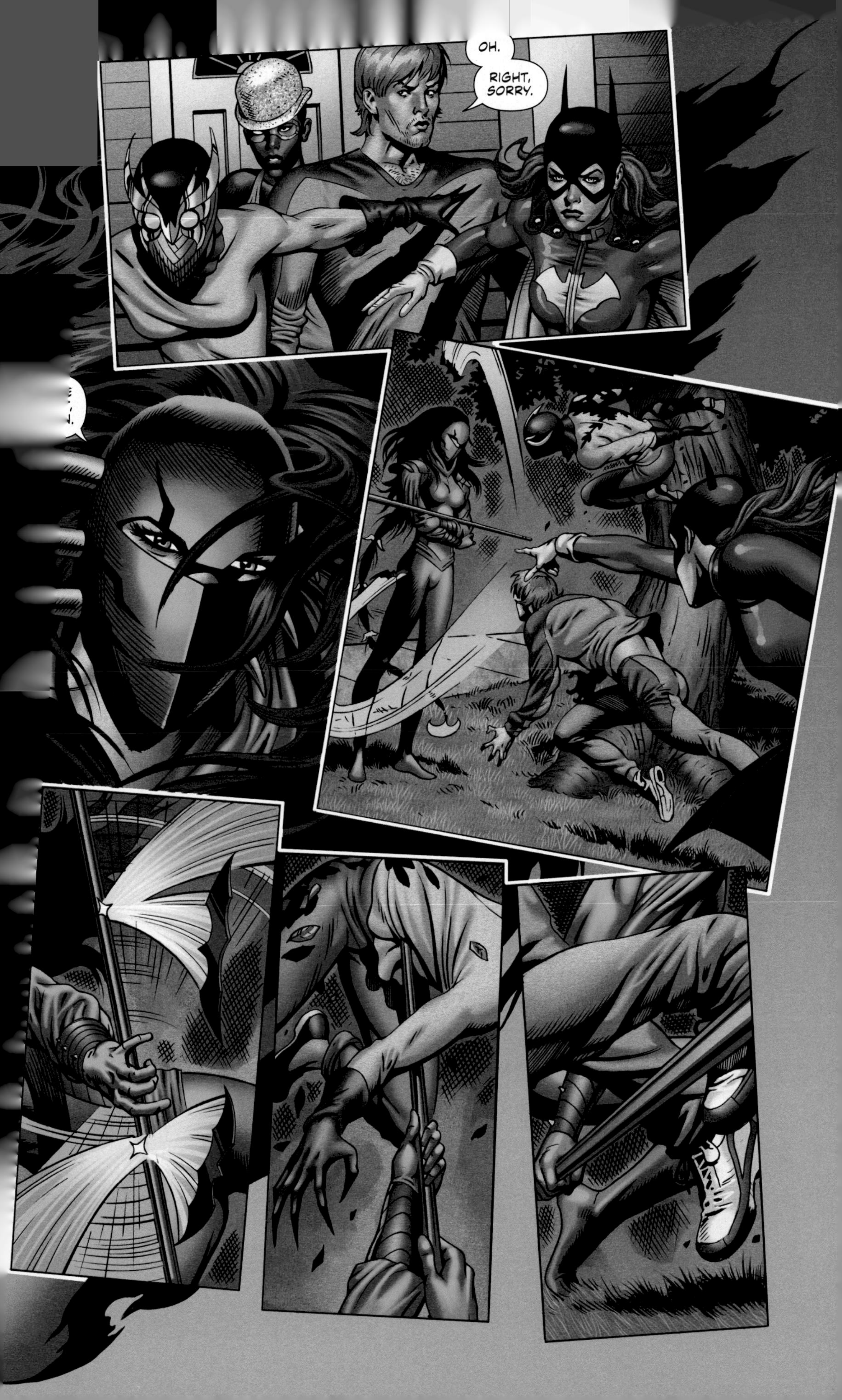
OH.
RIGHT, SORRY.

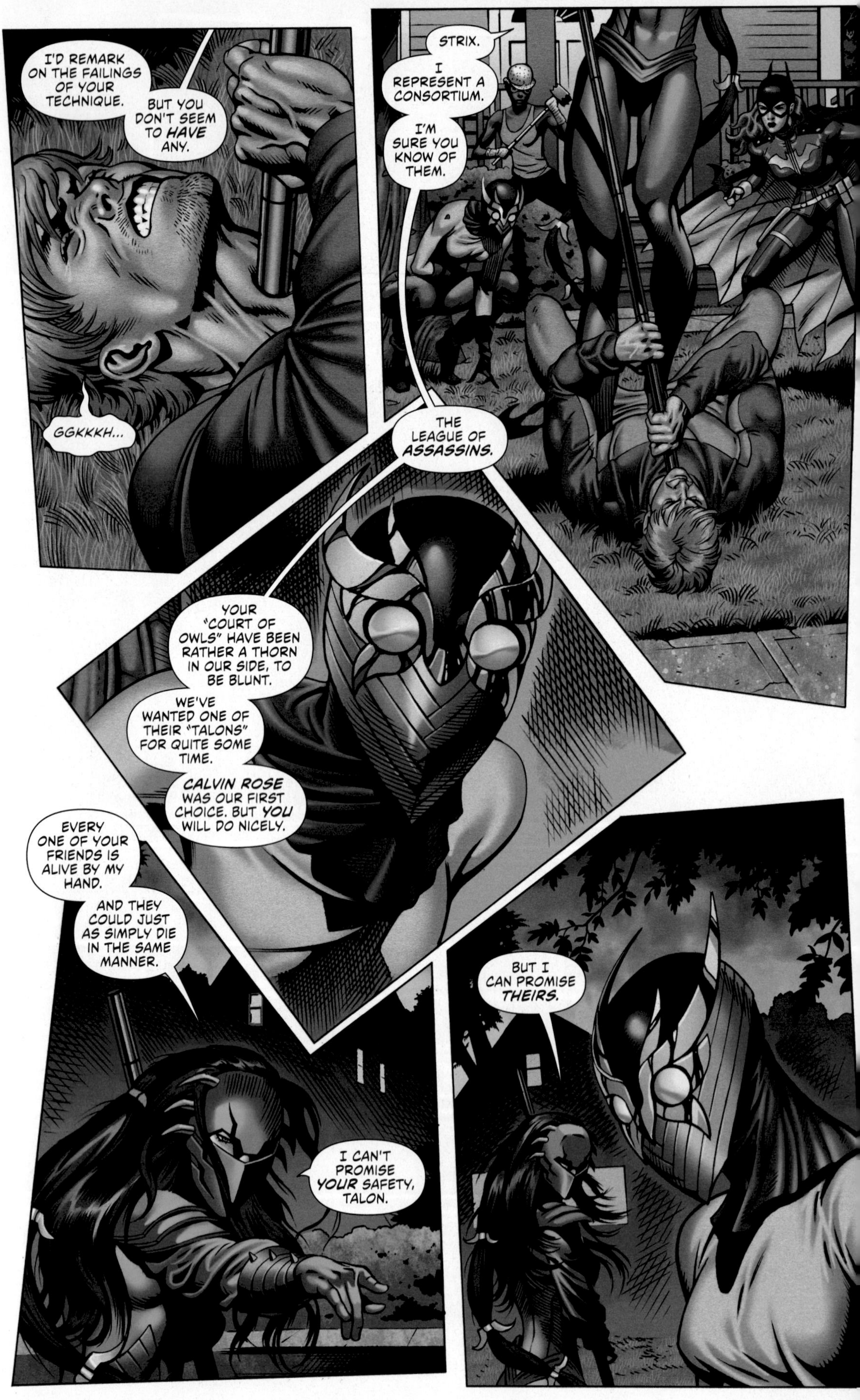

I'D REMARK ON THE FAILINGS OF YOUR TECHNIQUE.
BUT YOU DON'T SEEM TO HAVE ANY.
GGKKKH...
STRIX.
I REPRESENT A CONSORTIUM.
I'M SURE YOU KNOW OF THEM.
THE LEAGUE OF ASSASSINS.
YOUR "COURT OF OWLS" HAVE BEEN RATHER A THORN IN OUR SIDE, TO BE BLUNT.
WE'VE WANTED ONE OF THEIR "TALONS" FOR QUITE SOME TIME.
CALVIN ROSE WAS OUR FIRST CHOICE. BUT YOU WILL DO NICELY.
EVERY ONE OF YOUR FRIENDS IS ALIVE BY MY HAND.
AND THEY COULD JUST AS SIMPLY DIE IN THE SAME MANNER.
I CAN'T PROMISE YOUR SAFETY, TALON.
BUT I CAN PROMISE THEIRS.

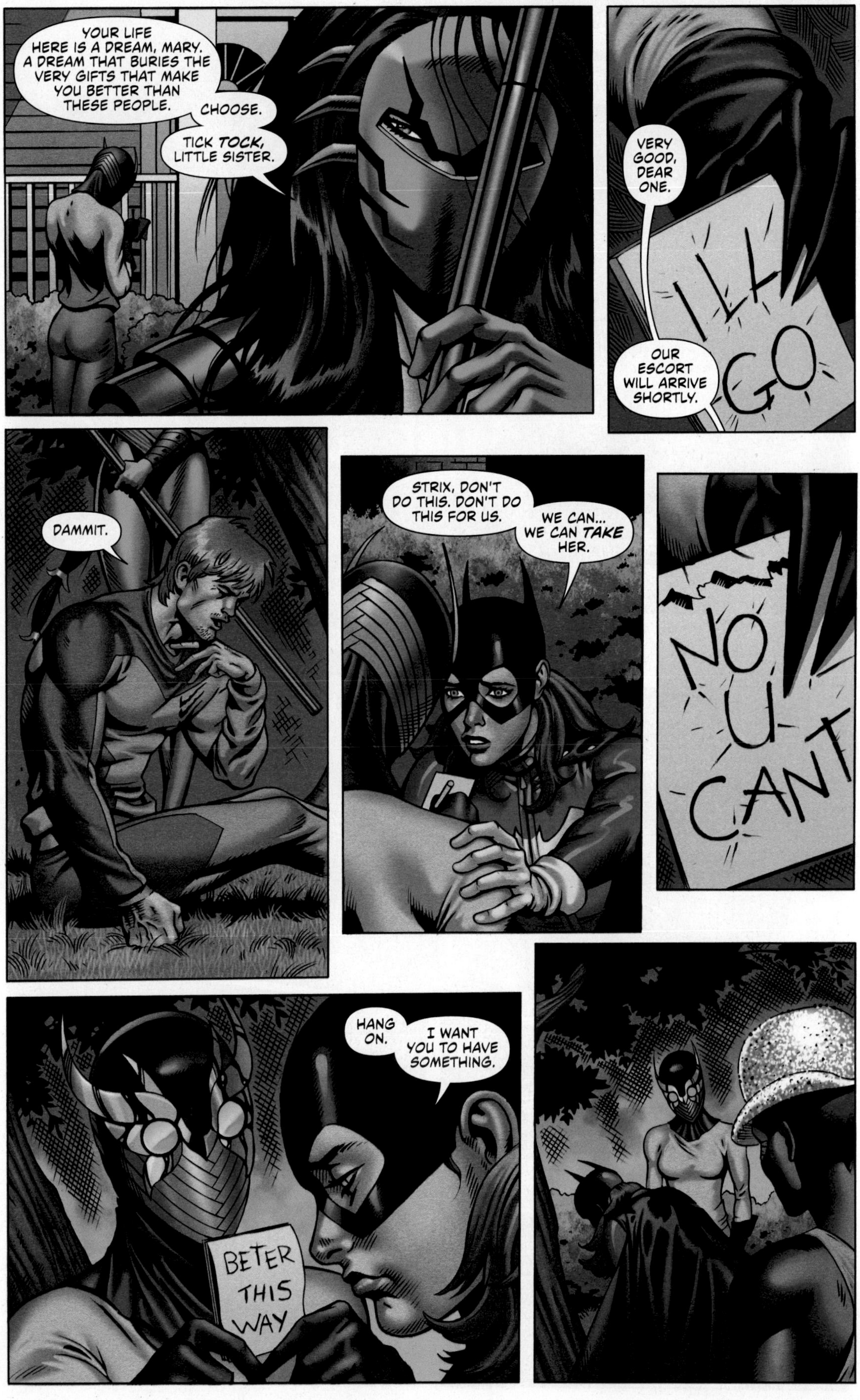
YOUR LIFE HERE IS A DREAM, MARY. A DREAM THAT BURIES THE VERY GIFTS THAT MAKE YOU BETTER THAN THESE PEOPLE.
CHOOSE.
TICK TOCK, LITTLE SISTER.
VERY GOOD, DEAR ONE.
ILL GO
OUR ESCORT WILL ARRIVE SHORTLY.
DAMMIT.
STRIX, DON'T DO THIS. DON'T DO THIS FOR US.
WE CAN... WE CAN TAKE HER.
NO U CANT
HANG ON.
I WANT YOU TO HAVE SOMETHING.
BETER THIS WAY

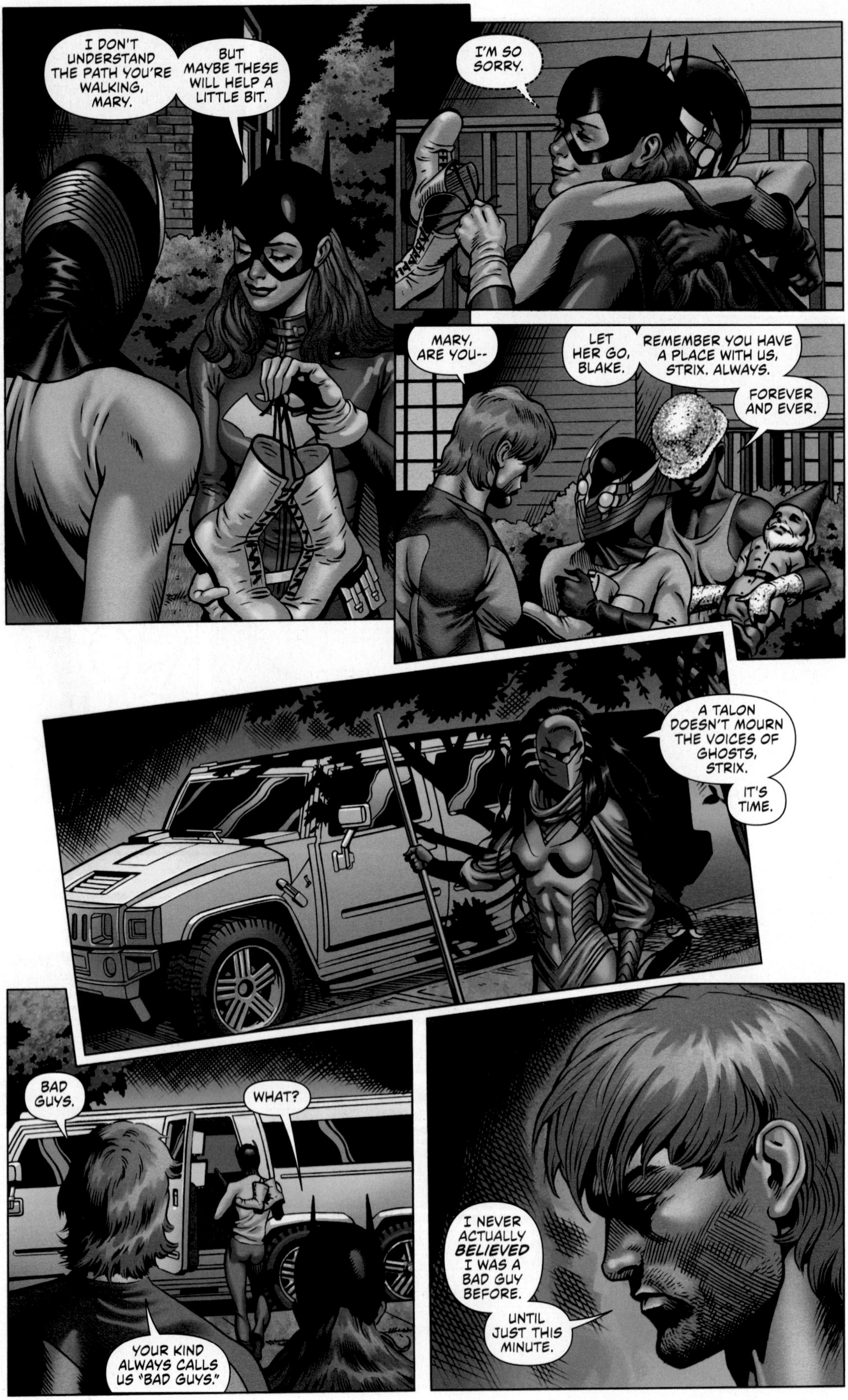
I DON'T UNDERSTAND THE PATH YOU'RE WALKING, MARY.
BUT MAYBE THESE WILL HELP A LITTLE BIT.
I'M SO SORRY.
MARY, ARE YOU--
LET HER GO, BLAKE.
REMEMBER YOU HAVE A PLACE WITH US, STRIX. ALWAYS.
FOREVER AND EVER.
A TALON DOESN'T MOURN THE VOICES OF GHOSTS, STRIX.
IT'S TIME.
BAD GUYS.
WHAT?
YOUR KIND ALWAYS CALLS US "BAD GUYS."
I NEVER ACTUALLY **BELIEVED** I WAS A BAD GUY BEFORE.
UNTIL JUST THIS MINUTE.

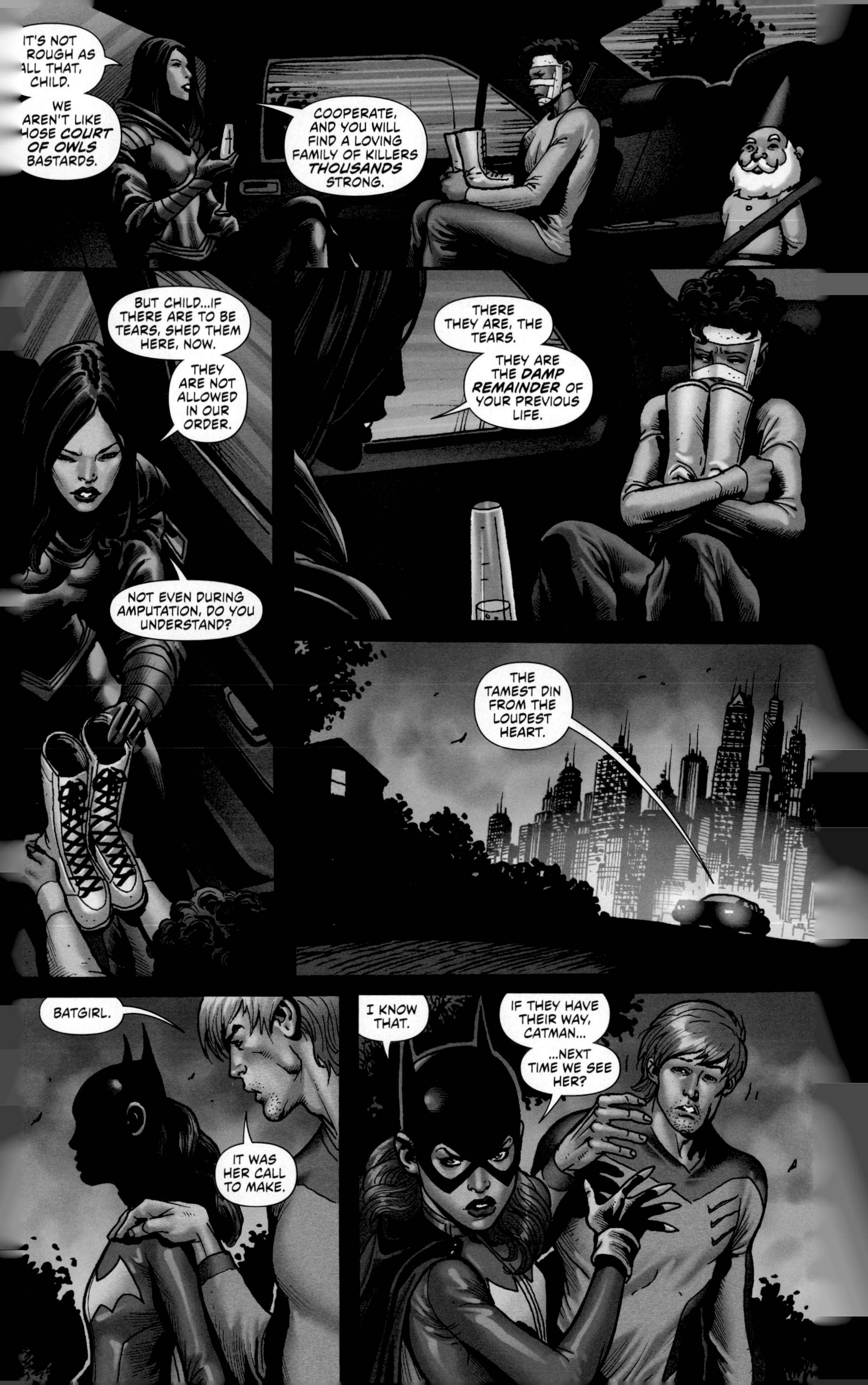

IT'S NOT ROUGH AS ALL THAT, CHILD.
WE AREN'T LIKE THOSE COURT OF OWLS BASTARDS.
COOPERATE, AND YOU WILL FIND A LOVING FAMILY OF KILLERS THOUSANDS STRONG.
BUT CHILD...IF THERE ARE TO BE TEARS, SHED THEM HERE, NOW.
THEY ARE NOT ALLOWED IN OUR ORDER.
NOT EVEN DURING AMPUTATION, DO YOU UNDERSTAND?
THERE THEY ARE, THE TEARS.
THEY ARE THE DAMP REMAINDER OF YOUR PREVIOUS LIFE.
THE TAMEST DIN FROM THE LOUDEST HEART.
BATGIRL.
IT WAS HER CALL TO MAKE.
I KNOW THAT.
IF THEY HAVE THEIR WAY, CATMAN...
...NEXT TIME WE SEE HER?

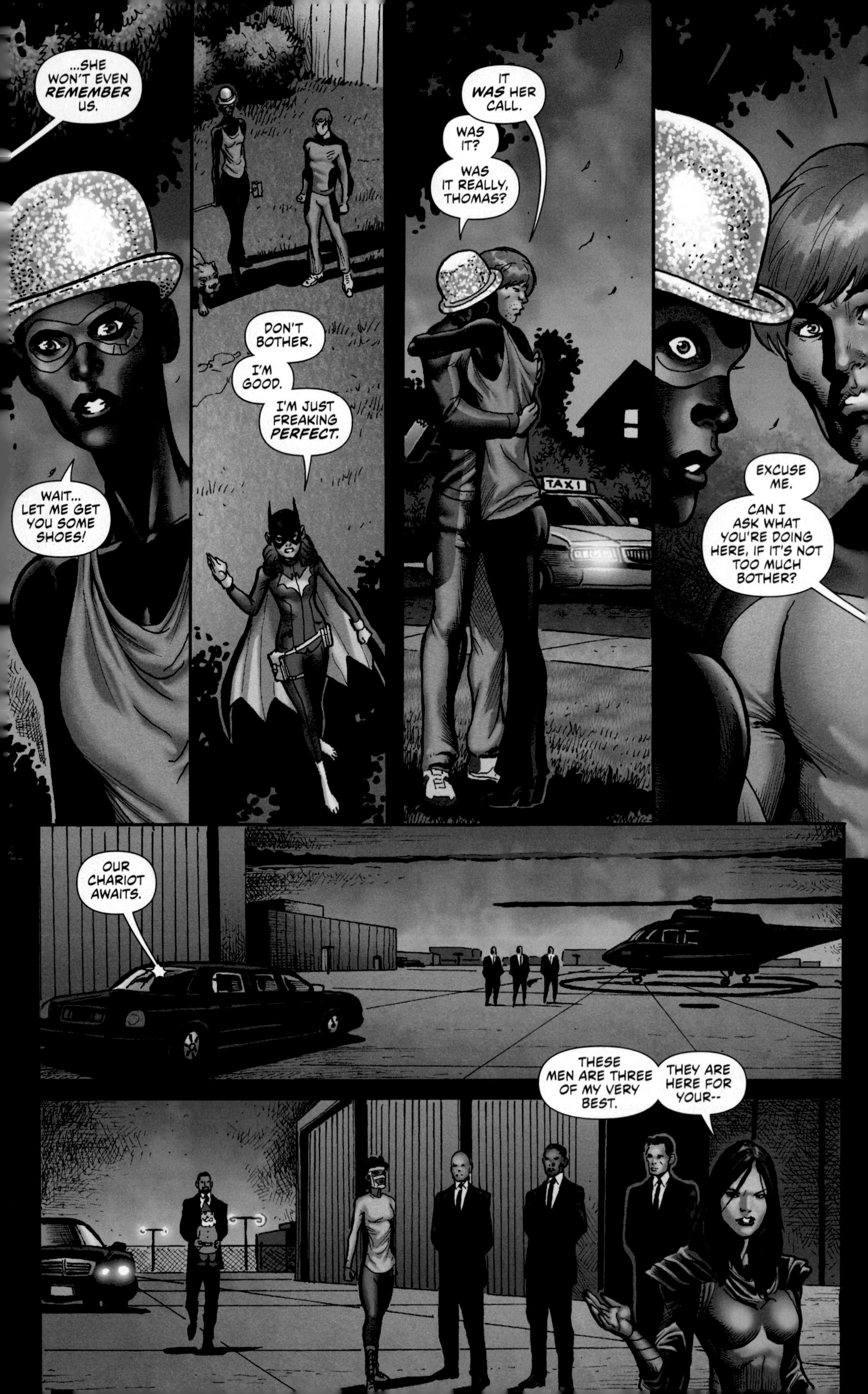
...SHE WON'T EVEN REMEMBER US.
WAIT... LET ME GET YOU SOME SHOES!
DON'T BOTHER.
I'M GOOD.
I'M JUST FREAKING PERFECT.
IT WAS HER CALL.
WAS IT?
WAS IT REALLY, THOMAS?
TAXI
EXCUSE ME.
CAN I ASK WHAT YOU'RE DOING HERE, IF IT'S NOT TOO MUCH BOTHER?
OUR CHARIOT AWAITS.
THESE MEN ARE THREE OF MY VERY BEST.
THEY ARE HERE FOR YOUR--

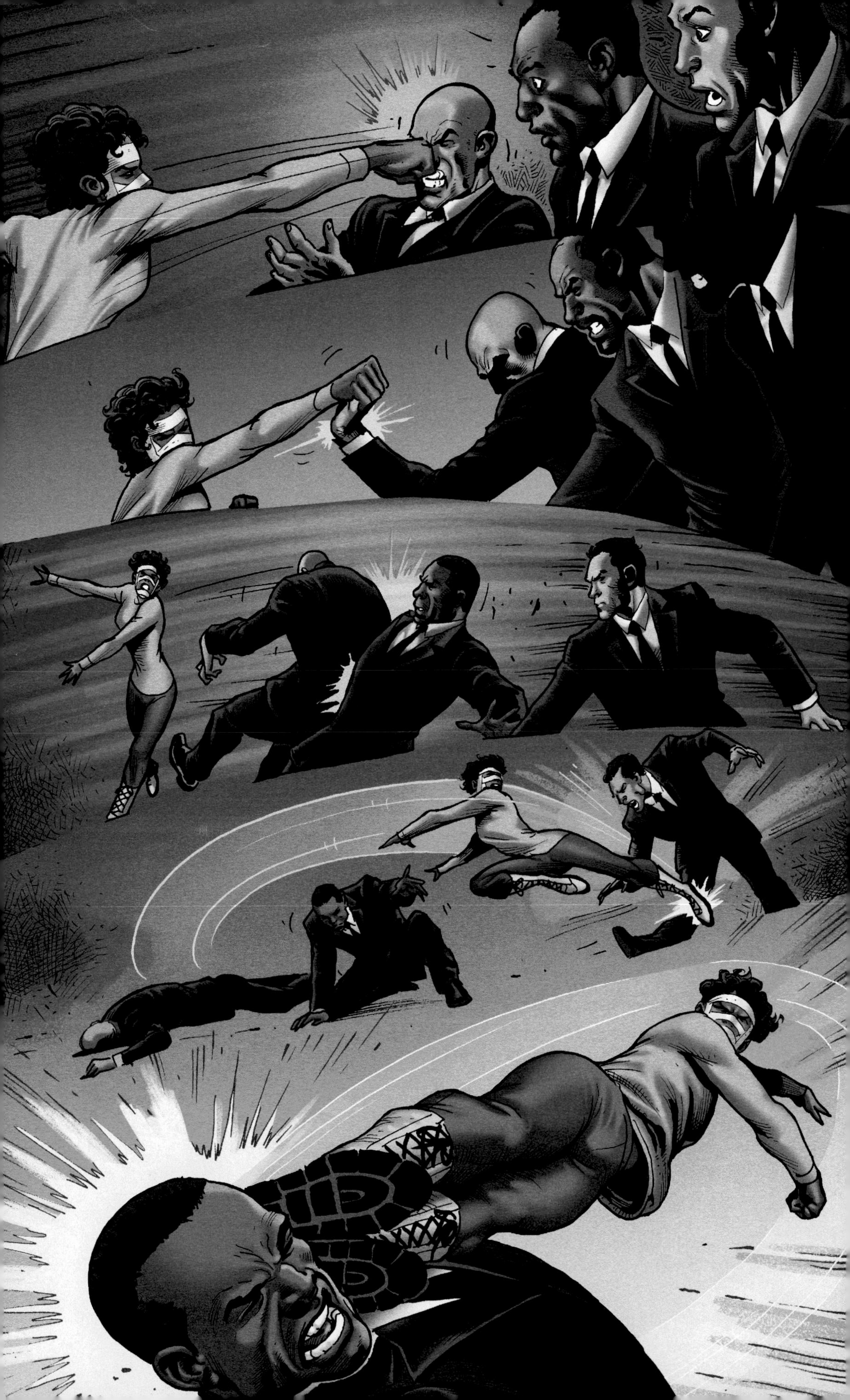

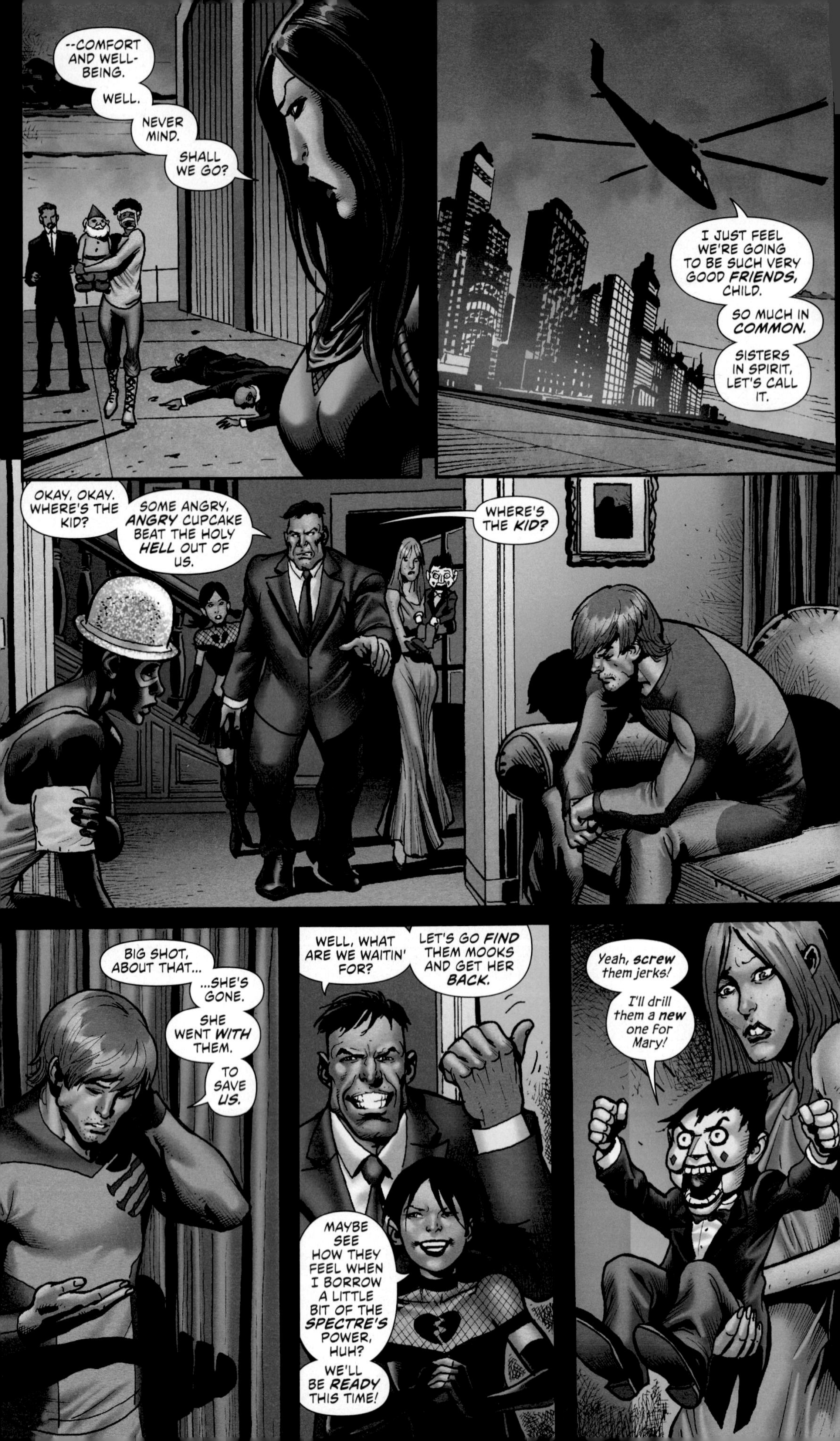
--COMFORT AND WELL-BEING.
WELL.
NEVER MIND.
SHALL WE GO?
I JUST FEEL WE'RE GOING TO BE SUCH VERY GOOD FRIENDS, CHILD.
SO MUCH IN COMMON.
SISTERS IN SPIRIT, LET'S CALL IT.
OKAY, OKAY. WHERE'S THE KID?
SOME ANGRY, ANGRY CUPCAKE BEAT THE HOLY HELL OUT OF US.
WHERE'S THE KID?
BIG SHOT, ABOUT THAT...
...SHE'S GONE.
SHE WENT WITH THEM.
TO SAVE US.
WELL, WHAT ARE WE WAITIN' FOR?
LET'S GO FIND THEM MOOKS AND GET HER BACK.
MAYBE SEE HOW THEY FEEL WHEN I BORROW A LITTLE BIT OF THE SPECTRE'S POWER, HUH?
WE'LL BE READY THIS TIME!
Yeah, screw them jerks!
I'll drill them a new one for Mary!

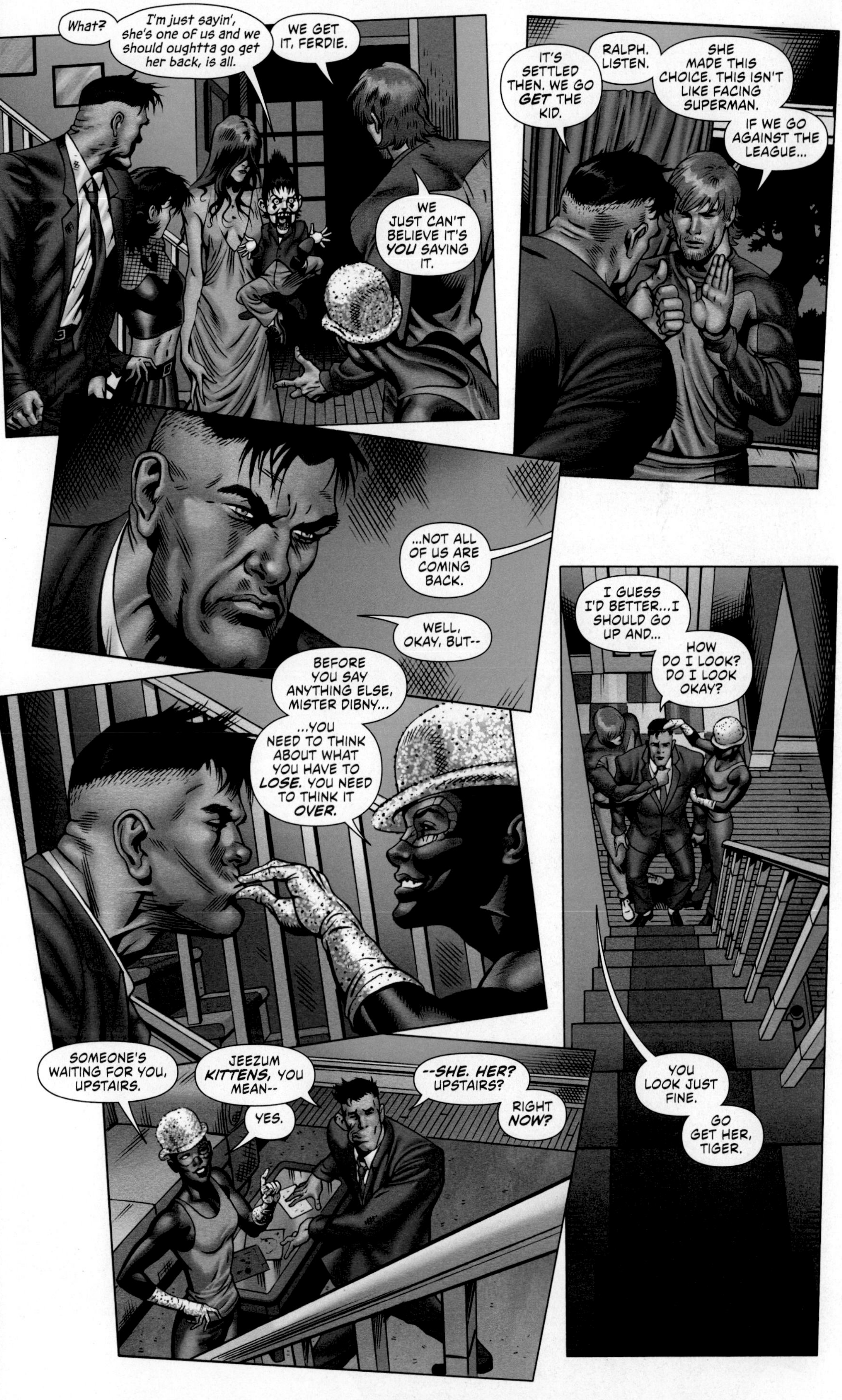
What?
I'm just sayin', she's one of us and we should oughtta go get her back, is all.
WE GET IT, FERDIE.
WE JUST CAN'T BELIEVE IT'S YOU SAYING IT.
IT'S SETTLED THEN. WE GO GET THE KID.
RALPH. LISTEN.
SHE MADE THIS CHOICE. THIS ISN'T LIKE FACING SUPERMAN.
IF WE GO AGAINST THE LEAGUE...
...NOT ALL OF US ARE COMING BACK.
WELL, OKAY, BUT--
BEFORE YOU SAY ANYTHING ELSE, MISTER DIBNY...
...YOU NEED TO THINK ABOUT WHAT YOU HAVE TO LOSE. YOU NEED TO THINK IT OVER.
SOMEONE'S WAITING FOR YOU, UPSTAIRS.
JEEZUM KITTENS, YOU MEAN--
YES.
--SHE. HER? UPSTAIRS?
RIGHT NOW?
I GUESS I'D BETTER...I SHOULD GO UP AND...
HOW DO I LOOK? DO I LOOK OKAY?
YOU LOOK JUST FINE.
GO GET HER, TIGER.

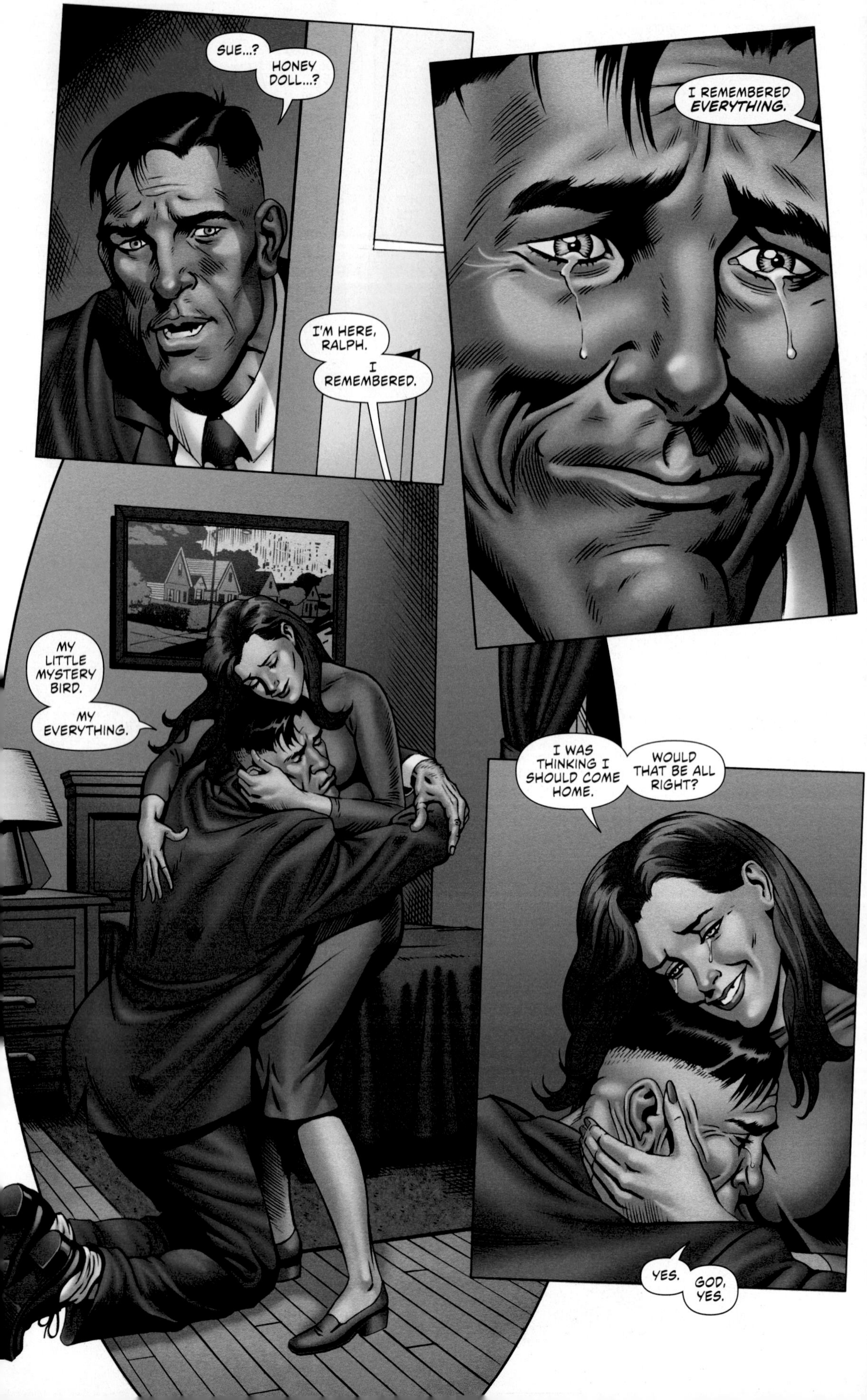
SUE...?
HONEY DOLL...?
I REMEMBERED EVERYTHING.
I'M HERE, RALPH.
I REMEMBERED.
MY LITTLE MYSTERY BIRD.
MY EVERYTHING.
I WAS THINKING I SHOULD COME HOME.
WOULD THAT BE ALL RIGHT?
YES.
GOD, YES.

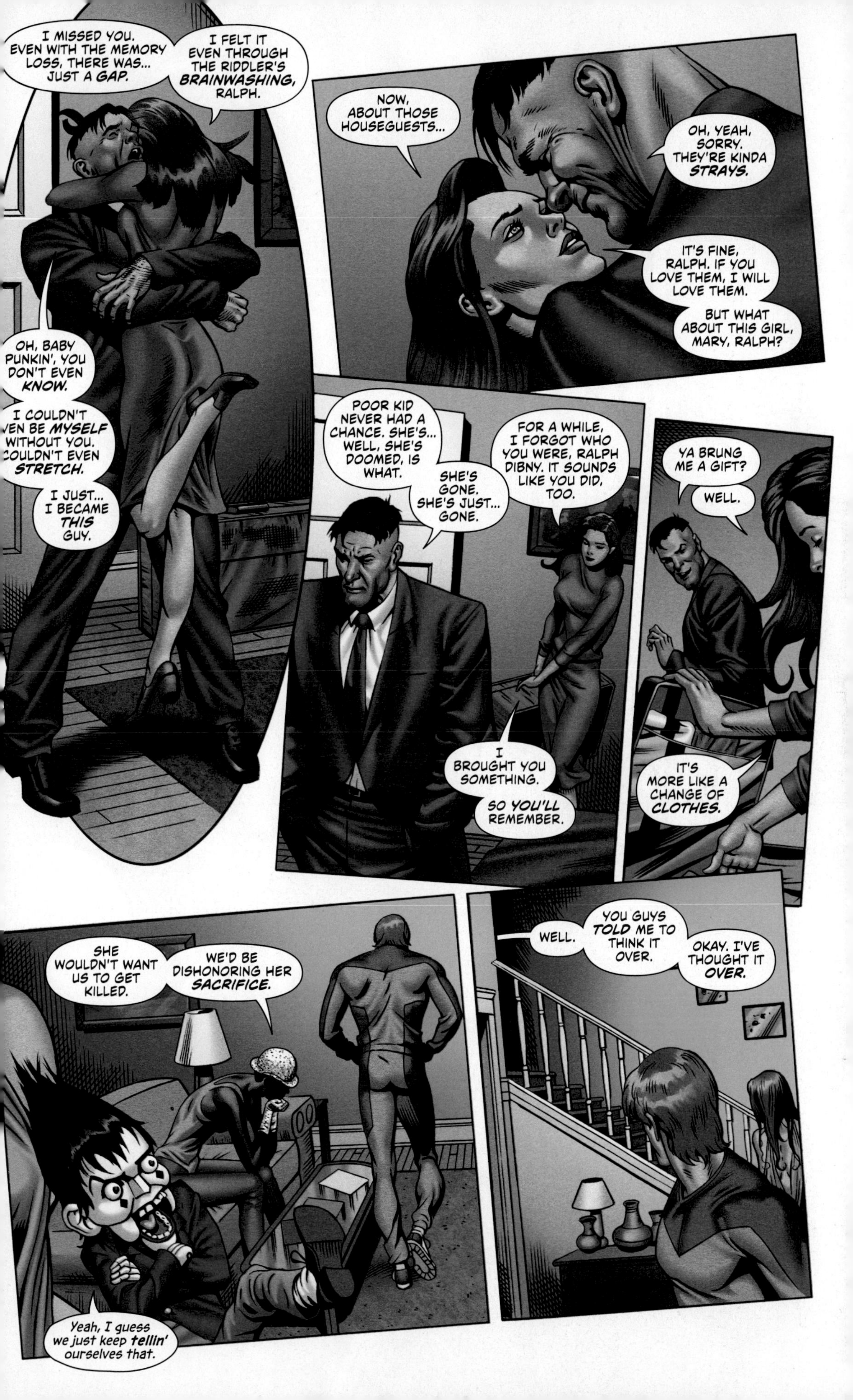
I MISSED YOU. EVEN WITH THE MEMORY LOSS, THERE WAS... JUST A GAP.
I FELT IT EVEN THROUGH THE RIDDLER'S BRAINWASHING, RALPH.
OH, BABY PUNKIN', YOU DON'T EVEN KNOW.
I COULDN'T EVEN BE MYSELF WITHOUT YOU. COULDN'T EVEN STRETCH.
I JUST... I BECAME THIS GUY.
NOW, ABOUT THOSE HOUSEGUESTS...
OH, YEAH, SORRY. THEY'RE KINDA STRAYS.
IT'S FINE, RALPH. IF YOU LOVE THEM, I WILL LOVE THEM.
BUT WHAT ABOUT THIS GIRL, MARY, RALPH?
POOR KID NEVER HAD A CHANCE. SHE'S... WELL, SHE'S DOOMED, IS WHAT.
SHE'S GONE. SHE'S JUST... GONE.
FOR A WHILE, I FORGOT WHO YOU WERE, RALPH DIBNY. IT SOUNDS LIKE YOU DID, TOO.
I BROUGHT YOU SOMETHING.
SO YOU'LL REMEMBER.
YA BRUNG ME A GIFT?
WELL.
IT'S MORE LIKE A CHANGE OF CLOTHES.
SHE WOULDN'T WANT US TO GET KILLED.
WE'D BE DISHONORING HER SACRIFICE.
Yeah, I guess we just keep tellin' ourselves that.
WELL.
YOU GUYS TOLD ME TO THINK IT OVER.
OKAY. I'VE THOUGHT IT OVER.

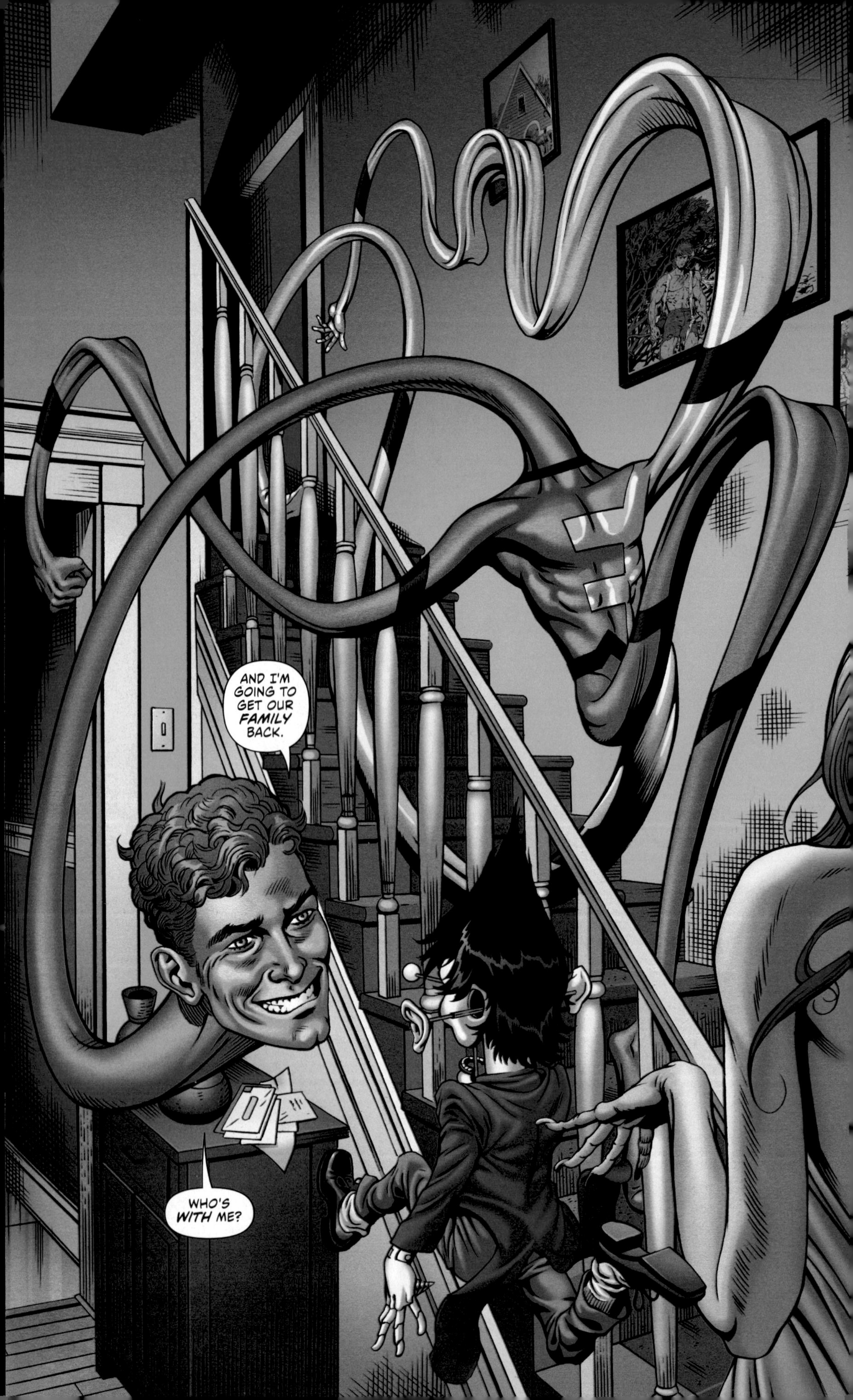
AND I'M GOING TO GET OUR FAMILY BACK.
WHO'S WITH ME?

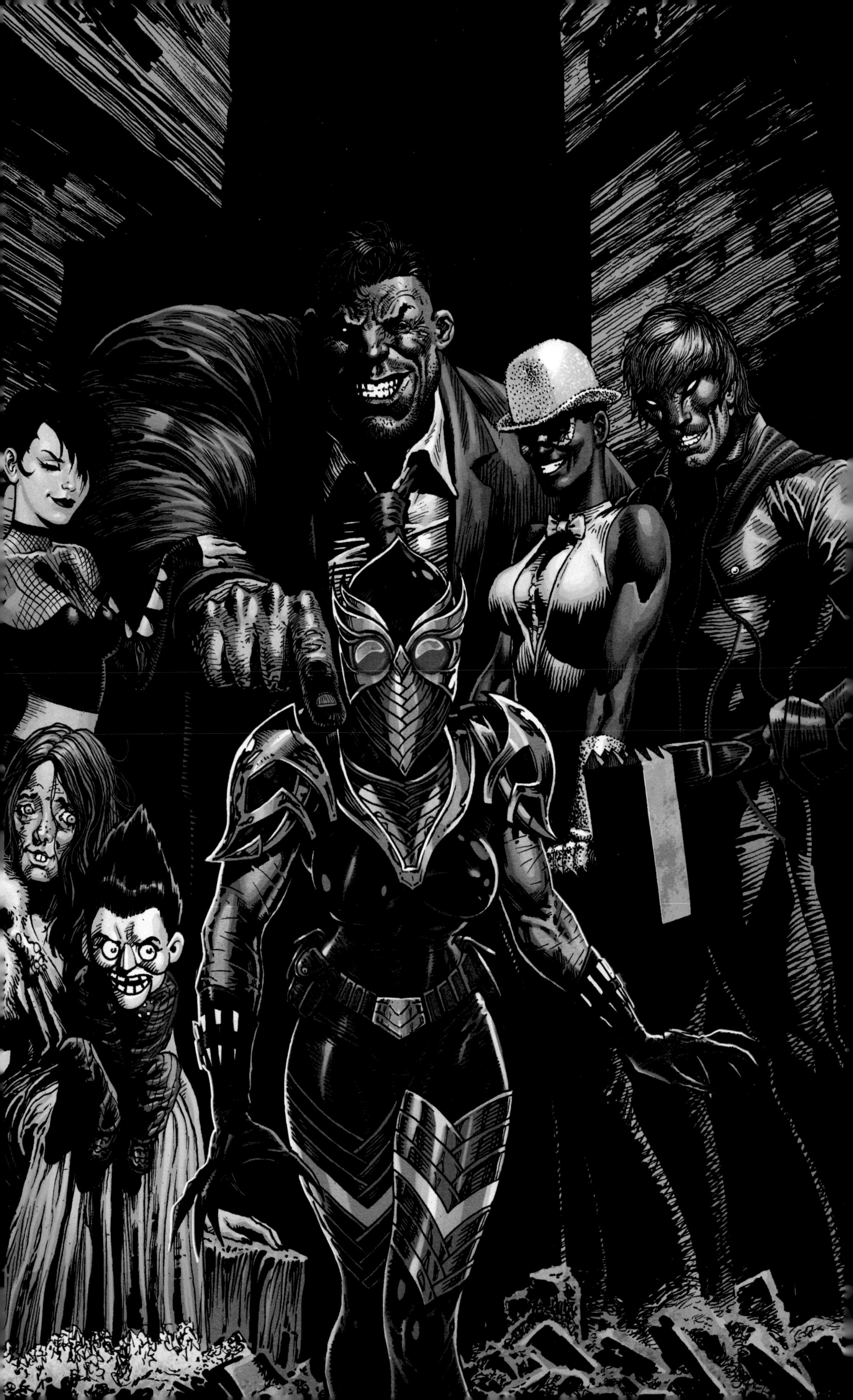

SILENT RUNNING

GAIL SIMONE writer TOM DERENICK artist JASON WRIGHT colorist TRAVIS LANHAM letterer

cover by LIAM SHARP & JASON WRIGHT

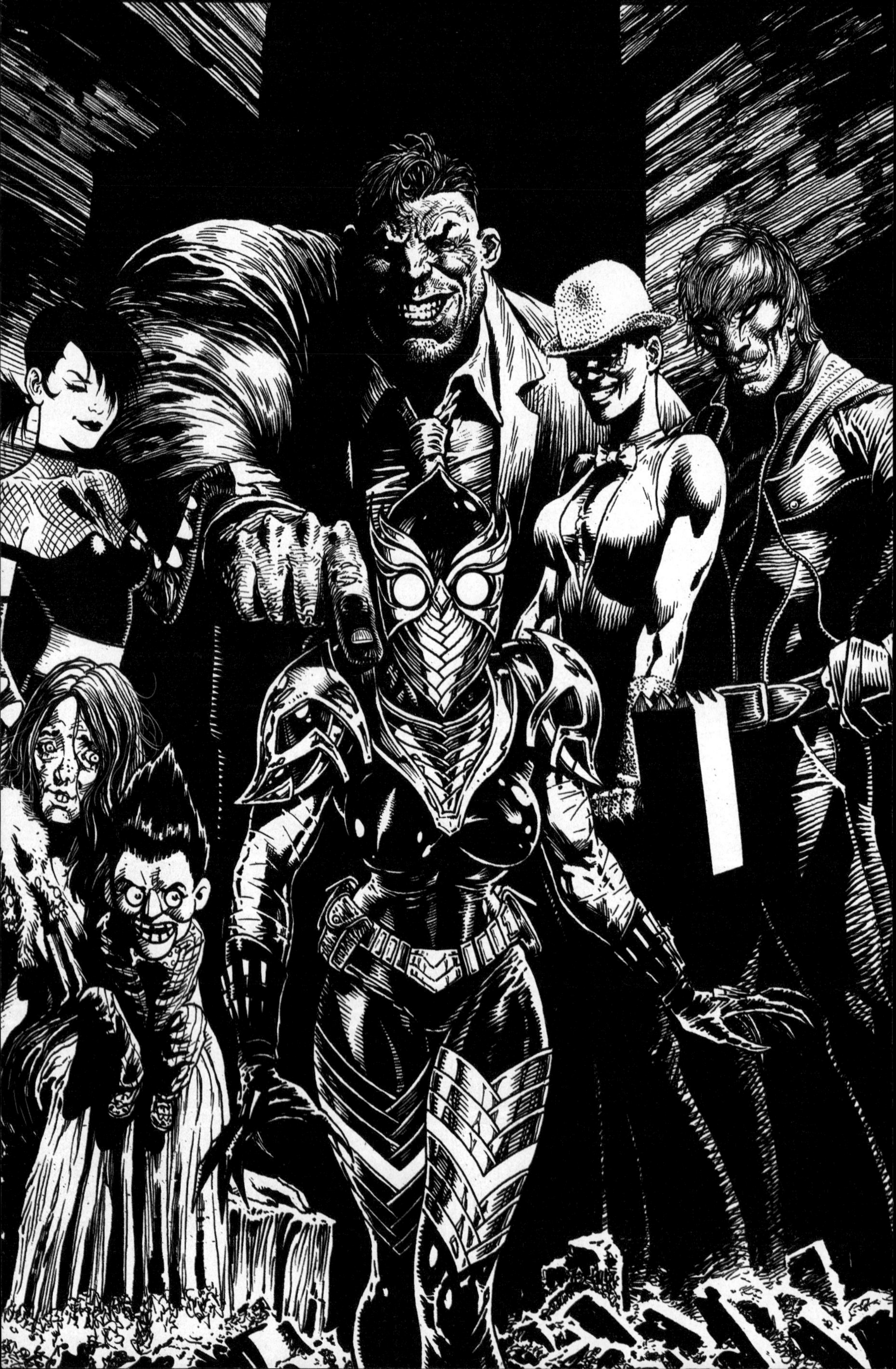

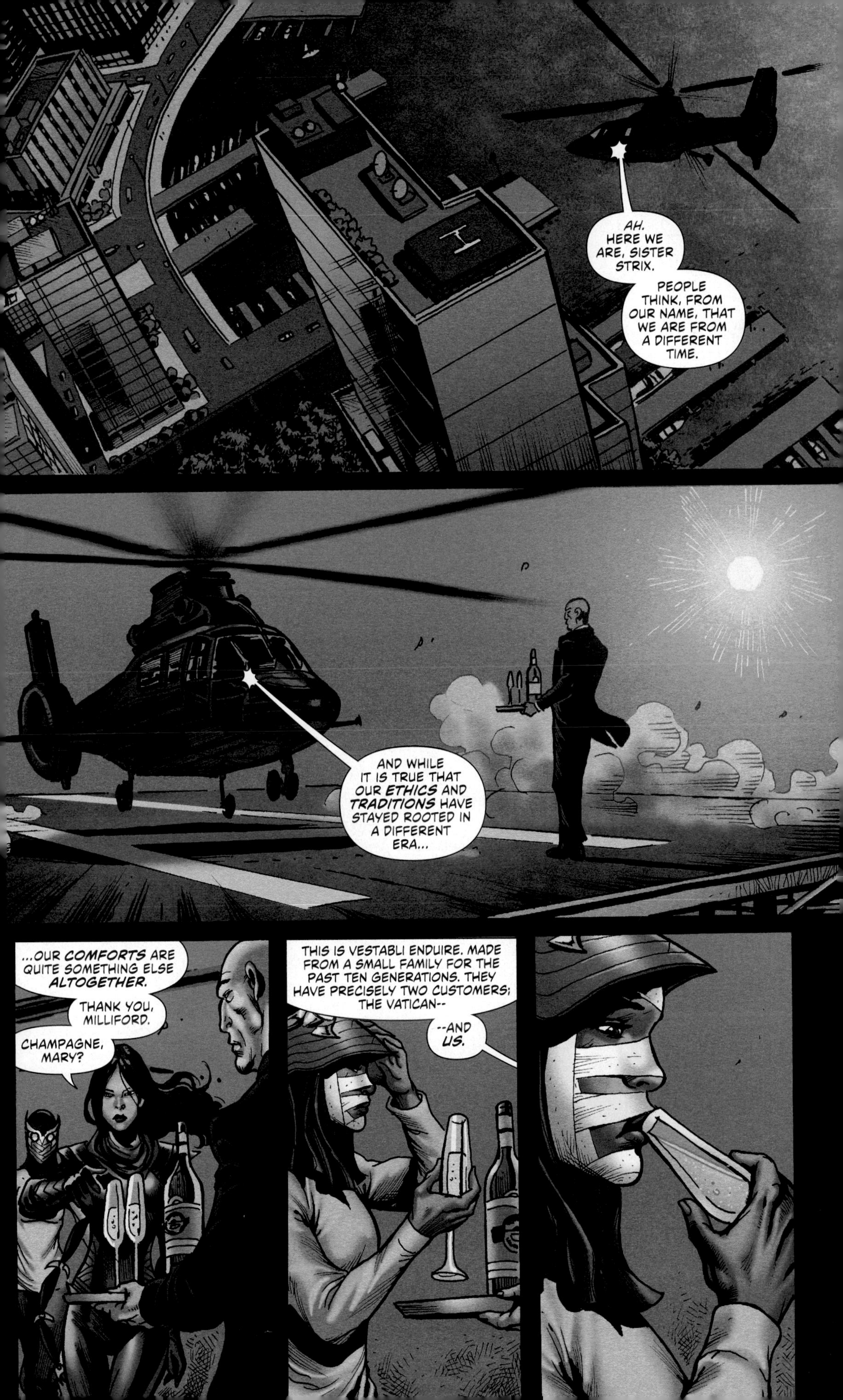

AH. HERE WE ARE, SISTER STRIX.
PEOPLE THINK, FROM OUR NAME, THAT WE ARE FROM A DIFFERENT TIME.
AND WHILE IT IS TRUE THAT OUR ETHICS AND TRADITIONS HAVE STAYED ROOTED IN A DIFFERENT ERA...
...OUR COMFORTS ARE QUITE SOMETHING ELSE ALTOGETHER.
THANK YOU, MILLIFORD.
CHAMPAGNE, MARY?
THIS IS VESTABLI ENDUIRE. MADE FROM A SMALL FAMILY FOR THE PAST TEN GENERATIONS. THEY HAVE PRECISELY TWO CUSTOMERS; THE VATICAN--
--AND US.

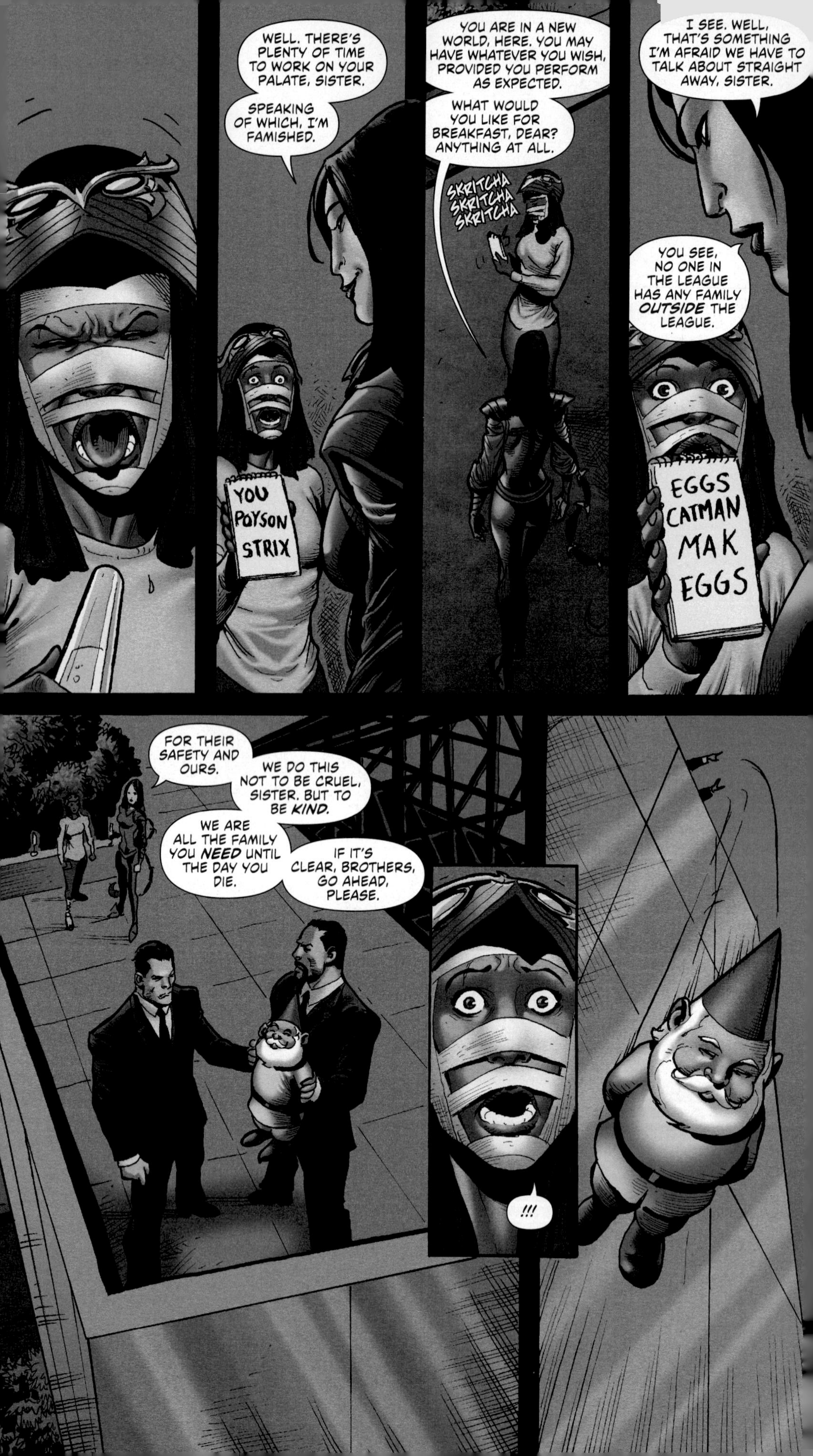
WELL. THERE'S PLENTY OF TIME TO WORK ON YOUR PALATE, SISTER.
SPEAKING OF WHICH, I'M FAMISHED.
YOU POYSON STRIX
YOU ARE IN A NEW WORLD, HERE. YOU MAY HAVE WHATEVER YOU WISH, PROVIDED YOU PERFORM AS EXPECTED.
WHAT WOULD YOU LIKE FOR BREAKFAST, DEAR? ANYTHING AT ALL.
SKRITCHA SKRITCHA SKRITCHA
I SEE. WELL, THAT'S SOMETHING I'M AFRAID WE HAVE TO TALK ABOUT STRAIGHT AWAY, SISTER.
YOU SEE, NO ONE IN THE LEAGUE HAS ANY FAMILY OUTSIDE THE LEAGUE.
EGGS CATMAN MAK EGGS
FOR THEIR SAFETY AND OURS.
WE DO THIS NOT TO BE CRUEL, SISTER. BUT TO BE KIND.
WE ARE ALL THE FAMILY YOU NEED UNTIL THE DAY YOU DIE.
IF IT'S CLEAR, BROTHERS, GO AHEAD, PLEASE.
!!!

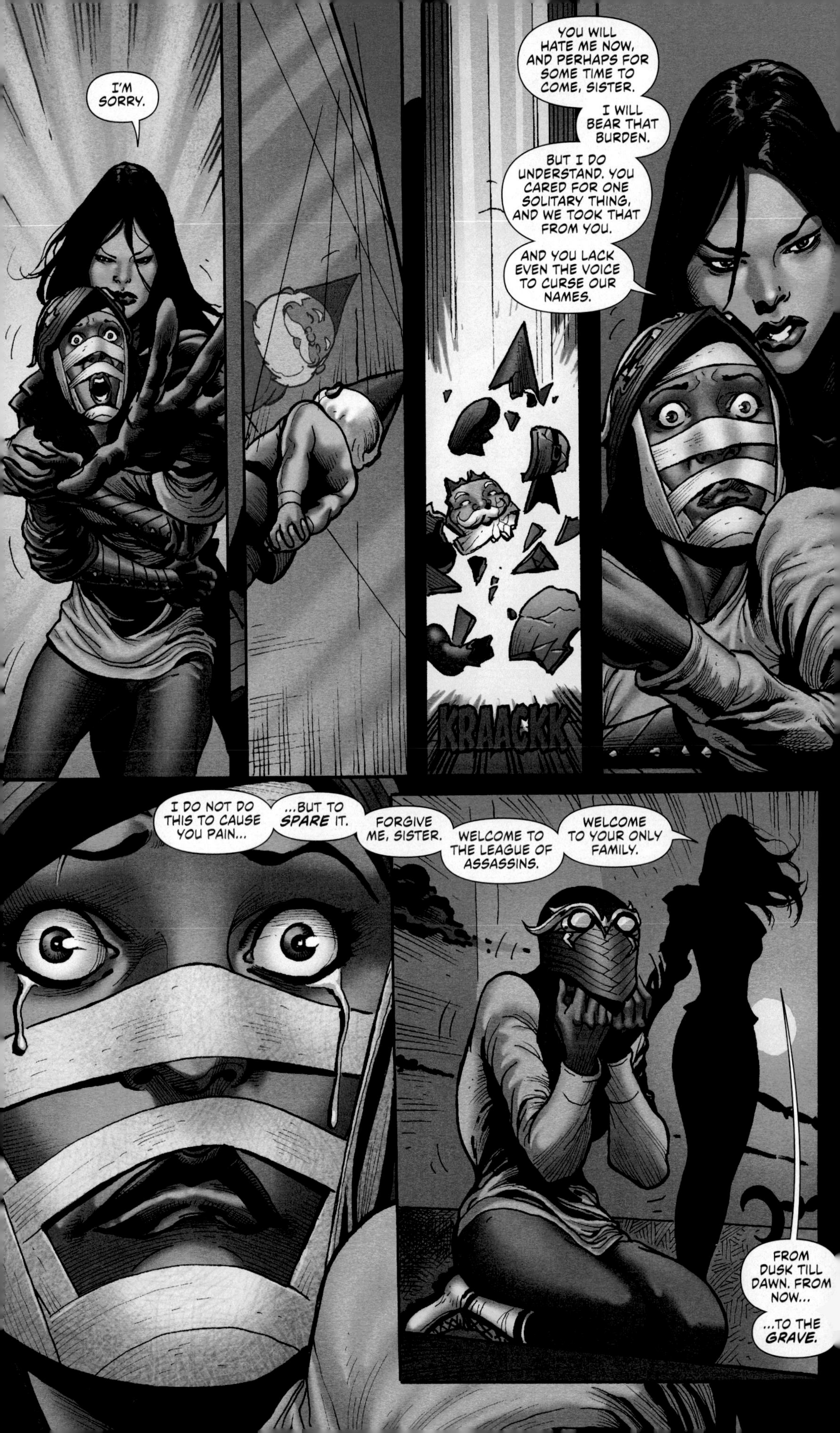
I'M SORRY.
YOU WILL HATE ME NOW, AND PERHAPS FOR SOME TIME TO COME, SISTER.
I WILL BEAR THAT BURDEN.
BUT I DO UNDERSTAND. YOU CARED FOR ONE SOLITARY THING, AND WE TOOK THAT FROM YOU.
AND YOU LACK EVEN THE VOICE TO CURSE OUR NAMES.
KRAACKK
I DO NOT DO THIS TO CAUSE YOU PAIN...
...BUT TO *SPARE* IT.
FORGIVE ME, SISTER.
WELCOME TO THE LEAGUE OF ASSASSINS.
WELCOME TO YOUR ONLY FAMILY.
FROM DUSK TILL DAWN. FROM NOW...
...TO THE *GRAVE.*

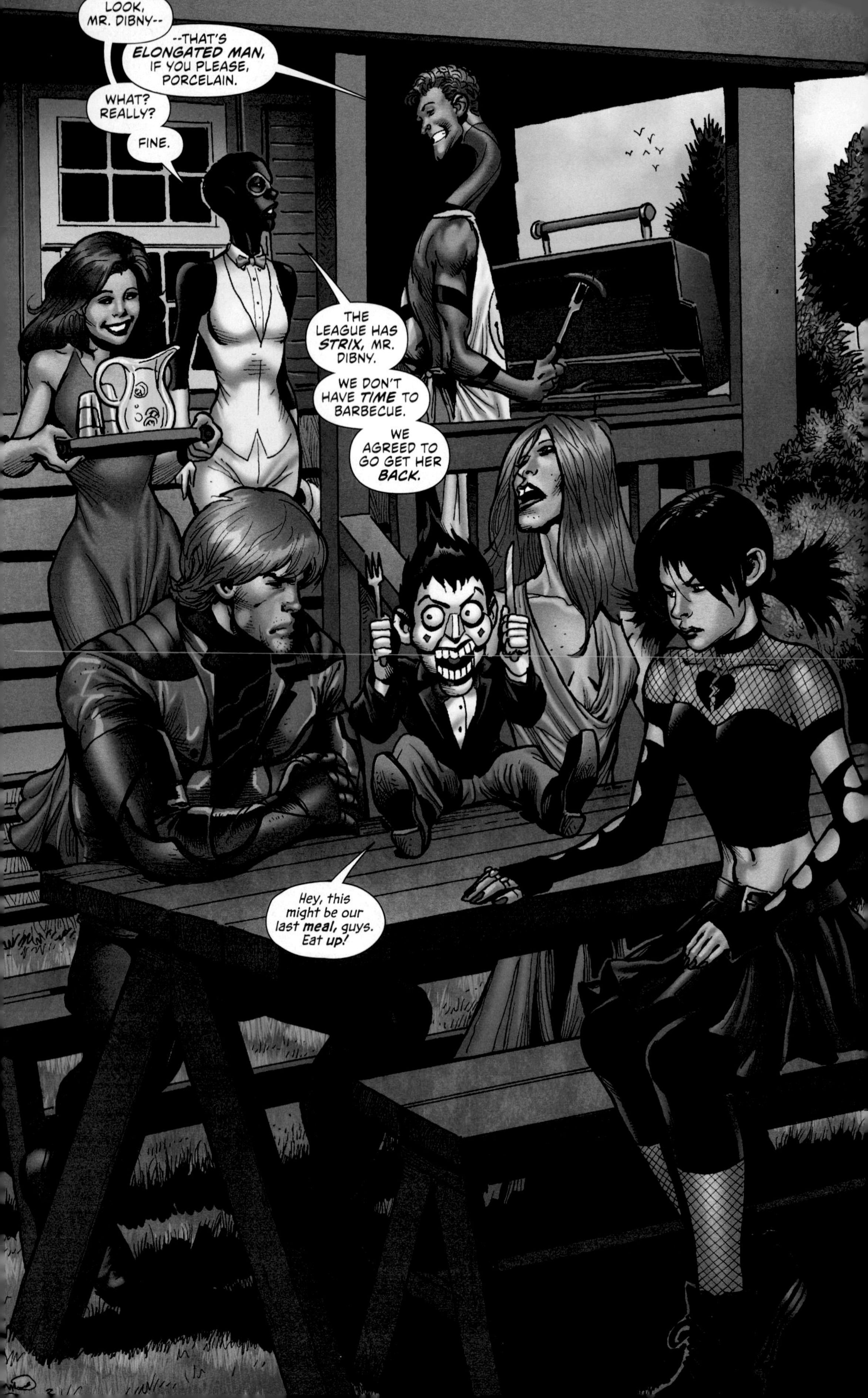
LOOK, MR. DIBNY--
--THAT'S ELONGATED MAN, IF YOU PLEASE, PORCELAIN.
WHAT? REALLY?
FINE.
THE LEAGUE HAS STRIX, MR. DIBNY.
WE DON'T HAVE TIME TO BARBECUE.
WE AGREED TO GO GET HER BACK.
Hey, this might be our last meal, guys. Eat up!

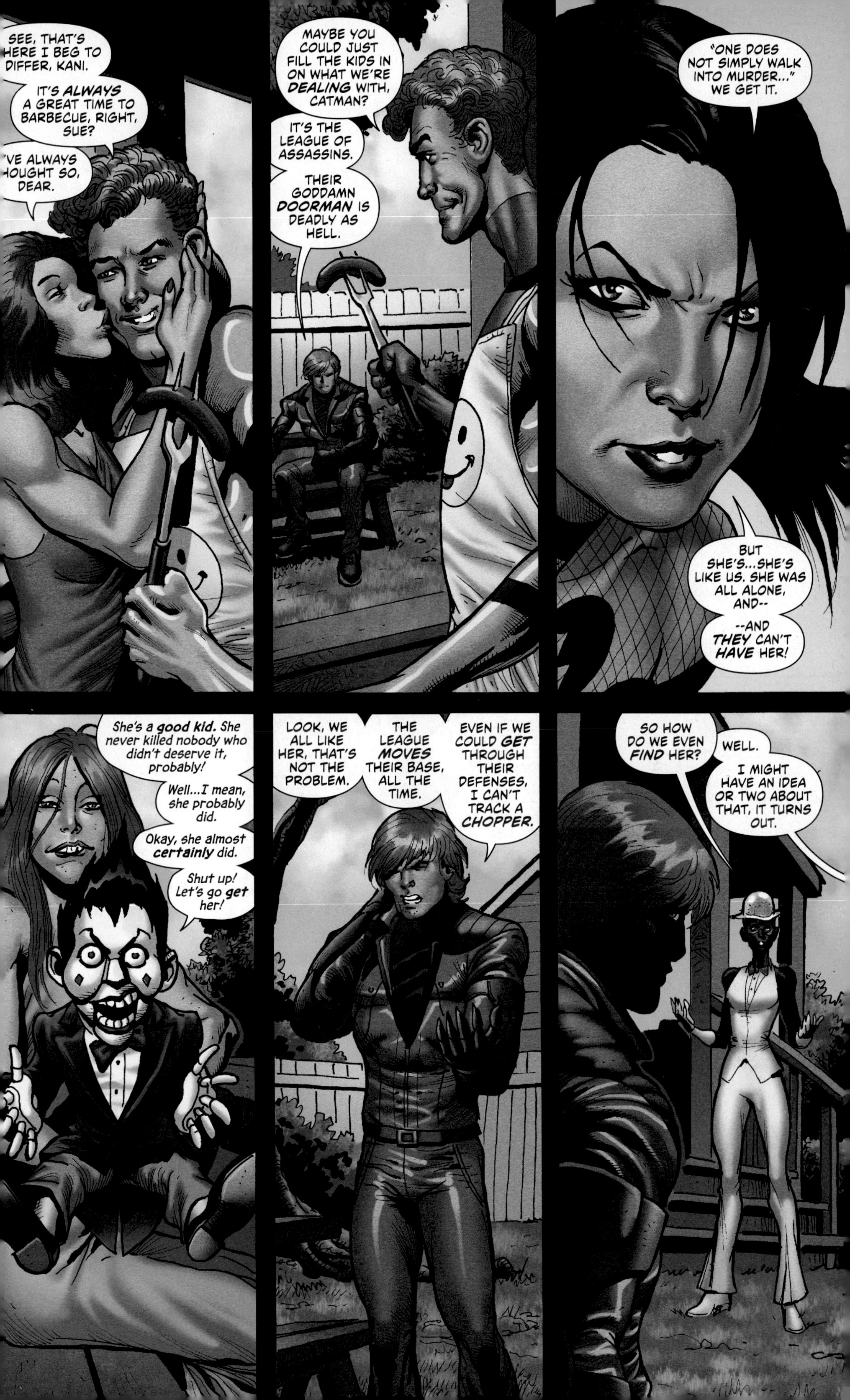

SEE, THAT'S
HERE I BEG TO DIFFER, KANI.
IT'S ALWAYS A GREAT TIME TO BARBECUE, RIGHT, SUE?
'VE ALWAYS HOUGHT SO, DEAR.
MAYBE YOU COULD JUST FILL THE KIDS IN ON WHAT WE'RE DEALING WITH, CATMAN?
IT'S THE LEAGUE OF ASSASSINS.
THEIR GODDAMN DOORMAN IS DEADLY AS HELL.
"ONE DOES NOT SIMPLY WALK INTO MURDER..." WE GET IT.
BUT SHE'S...SHE'S LIKE US. SHE WAS ALL ALONE, AND--
--AND THEY CAN'T HAVE HER!
She's a good kid. She never killed nobody who didn't deserve it, probably!
Well...I mean, she probably did.
Okay, she almost certainly did.
Shut up! Let's go get her!
LOOK, WE ALL LIKE HER, THAT'S NOT THE PROBLEM.
THE LEAGUE MOVES THEIR BASE, ALL THE TIME.
EVEN IF WE COULD GET THROUGH THEIR DEFENSES, I CAN'T TRACK A CHOPPER.
SO HOW DO WE EVEN FIND HER?
WELL.
I MIGHT HAVE AN IDEA OR TWO ABOUT THAT, IT TURNS OUT.

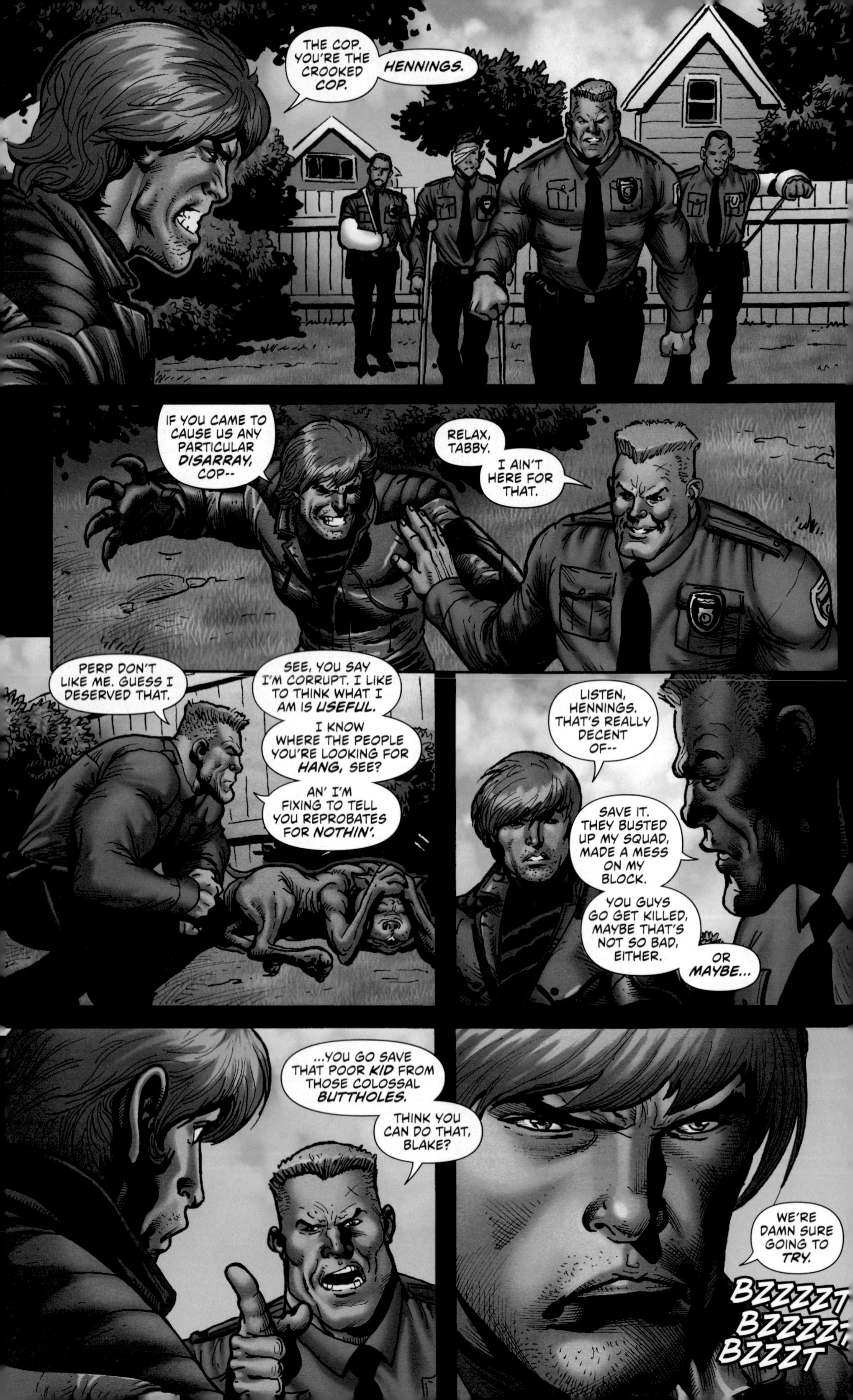
THE COP. YOU'RE THE CROOKED COP.
HENNINGS.
IF YOU CAME TO CAUSE US ANY PARTICULAR DISARRAY, COP--
RELAX, TABBY.
I AIN'T HERE FOR THAT.
PERP DON'T LIKE ME. GUESS I DESERVED THAT.
SEE, YOU SAY I'M CORRUPT. I LIKE TO THINK WHAT I AM IS USEFUL.
I KNOW WHERE THE PEOPLE YOU'RE LOOKING FOR HANG, SEE?
AN' I'M FIXING TO TELL YOU REPROBATES FOR NOTHIN'.
LISTEN, HENNINGS. THAT'S REALLY DECENT OF--
SAVE IT. THEY BUSTED UP MY SQUAD, MADE A MESS ON MY BLOCK.
YOU GUYS GO GET KILLED, MAYBE THAT'S NOT SO BAD, EITHER.
OR MAYBE...
...YOU GO SAVE THAT POOR KID FROM THOSE COLOSSAL BUTTHOLES.
THINK YOU CAN DO THAT, BLAKE?
WE'RE DAMN SURE GOING TO TRY.
BZZZZT
BZZZZT
BZZZT

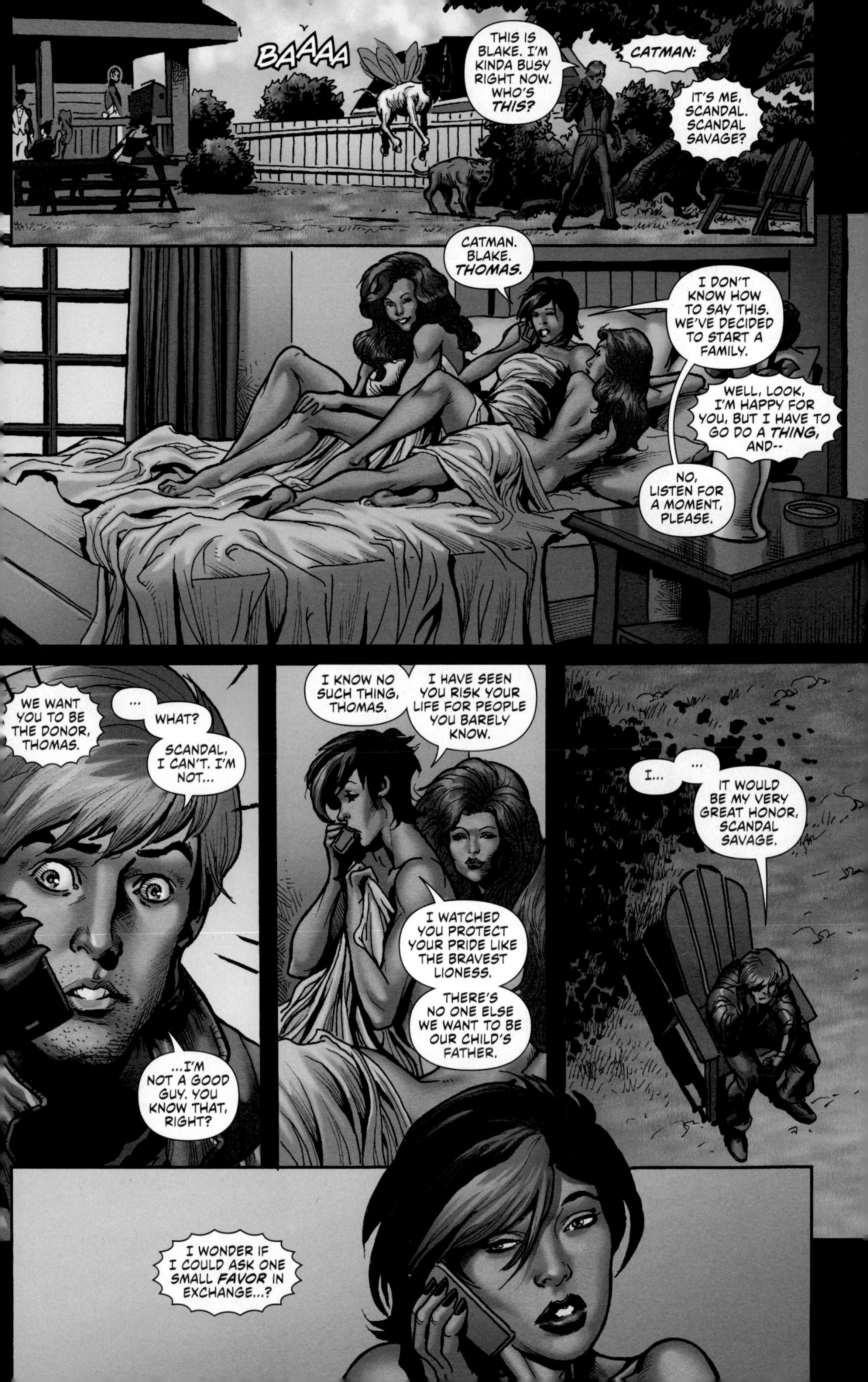
BAAAA
THIS IS BLAKE. I'M KINDA BUSY RIGHT NOW. WHO'S *THIS?*
CATMAN:
IT'S ME, SCANDAL. SCANDAL SAVAGE?
CATMAN. BLAKE. *THOMAS.*
I DON'T KNOW HOW TO SAY THIS. WE'VE DECIDED TO START A FAMILY.
WELL, LOOK, I'M HAPPY FOR YOU, BUT I HAVE TO GO DO A *THING,* AND--
NO, LISTEN FOR A MOMENT, PLEASE.
WE WANT YOU TO BE THE DONOR, THOMAS.
...
WHAT?
SCANDAL, I CAN'T. I'M NOT...
...I'M NOT A GOOD GUY. YOU KNOW THAT, RIGHT?
I KNOW NO SUCH THING, THOMAS.
I HAVE SEEN YOU RISK YOUR LIFE FOR PEOPLE YOU BARELY KNOW.
I WATCHED YOU PROTECT YOUR PRIDE LIKE THE BRAVEST LIONESS.
THERE'S NO ONE ELSE WE WANT TO BE OUR CHILD'S FATHER.
I...
...
IT WOULD BE MY VERY GREAT HONOR, SCANDAL SAVAGE.
I WONDER IF I COULD ASK ONE SMALL *FAVOR* IN EXCHANGE...?

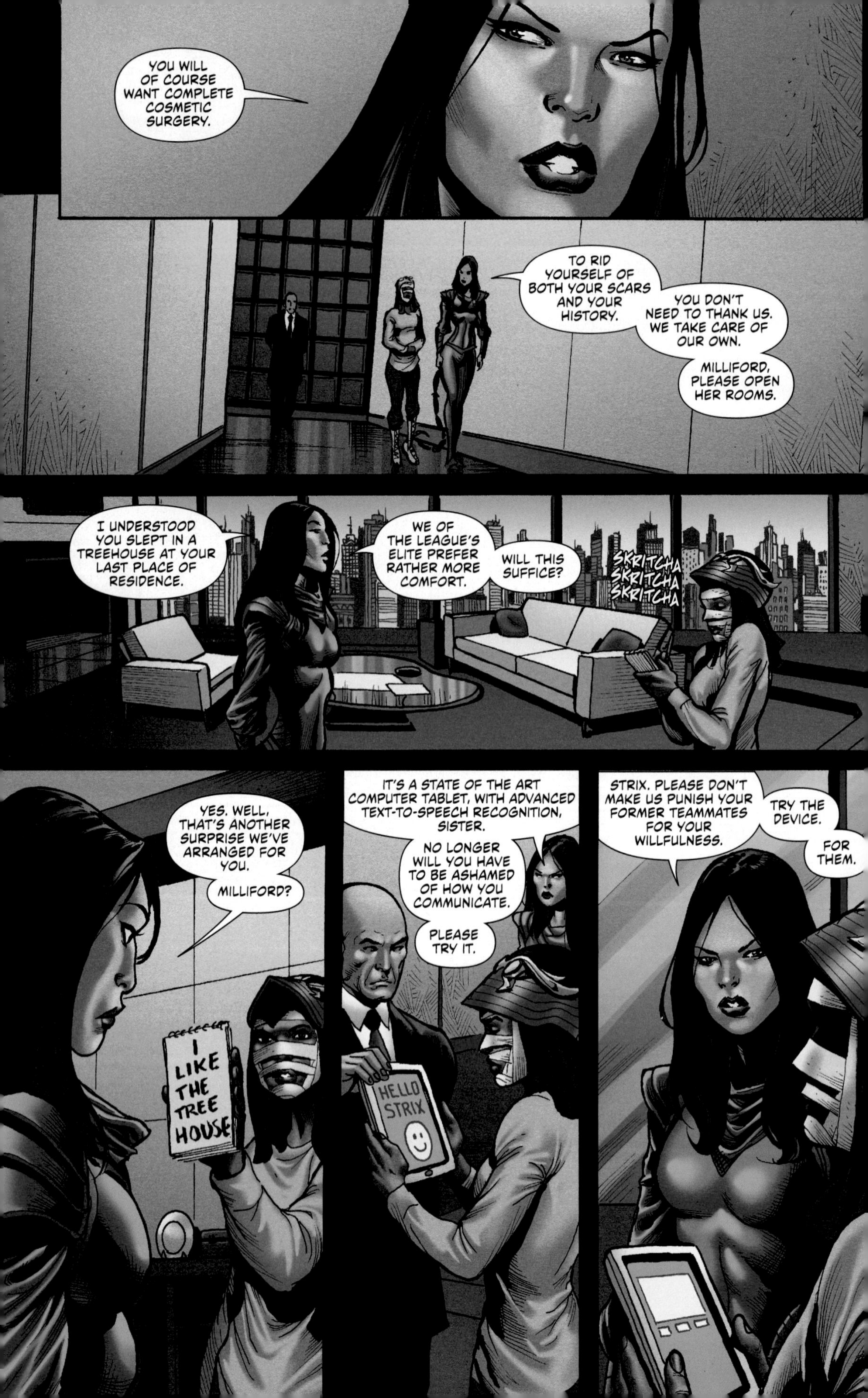
YOU WILL OF COURSE WANT COMPLETE COSMETIC SURGERY.
TO RID YOURSELF OF BOTH YOUR SCARS AND YOUR HISTORY.
YOU DON'T NEED TO THANK US. WE TAKE CARE OF OUR OWN.
MILLIFORD, PLEASE OPEN HER ROOMS.
I UNDERSTOOD YOU SLEPT IN A TREEHOUSE AT YOUR LAST PLACE OF RESIDENCE.
WE OF THE LEAGUE'S ELITE PREFER RATHER MORE COMFORT.
WILL THIS SUFFICE?
SKRITCHA SKRITCHA SKRITCHA
YES. WELL, THAT'S ANOTHER SURPRISE WE'VE ARRANGED FOR YOU.
MILLIFORD?
I LIKE THE TREE HOUSE
IT'S A STATE OF THE ART COMPUTER TABLET, WITH ADVANCED TEXT-TO-SPEECH RECOGNITION, SISTER.
NO LONGER WILL YOU HAVE TO BE ASHAMED OF HOW YOU COMMUNICATE.
PLEASE TRY IT.
HELLO STRIX
STRIX. PLEASE DON'T MAKE US PUNISH YOUR FORMER TEAMMATES FOR YOUR WILLFULNESS.
TRY THE DEVICE.
FOR THEM.

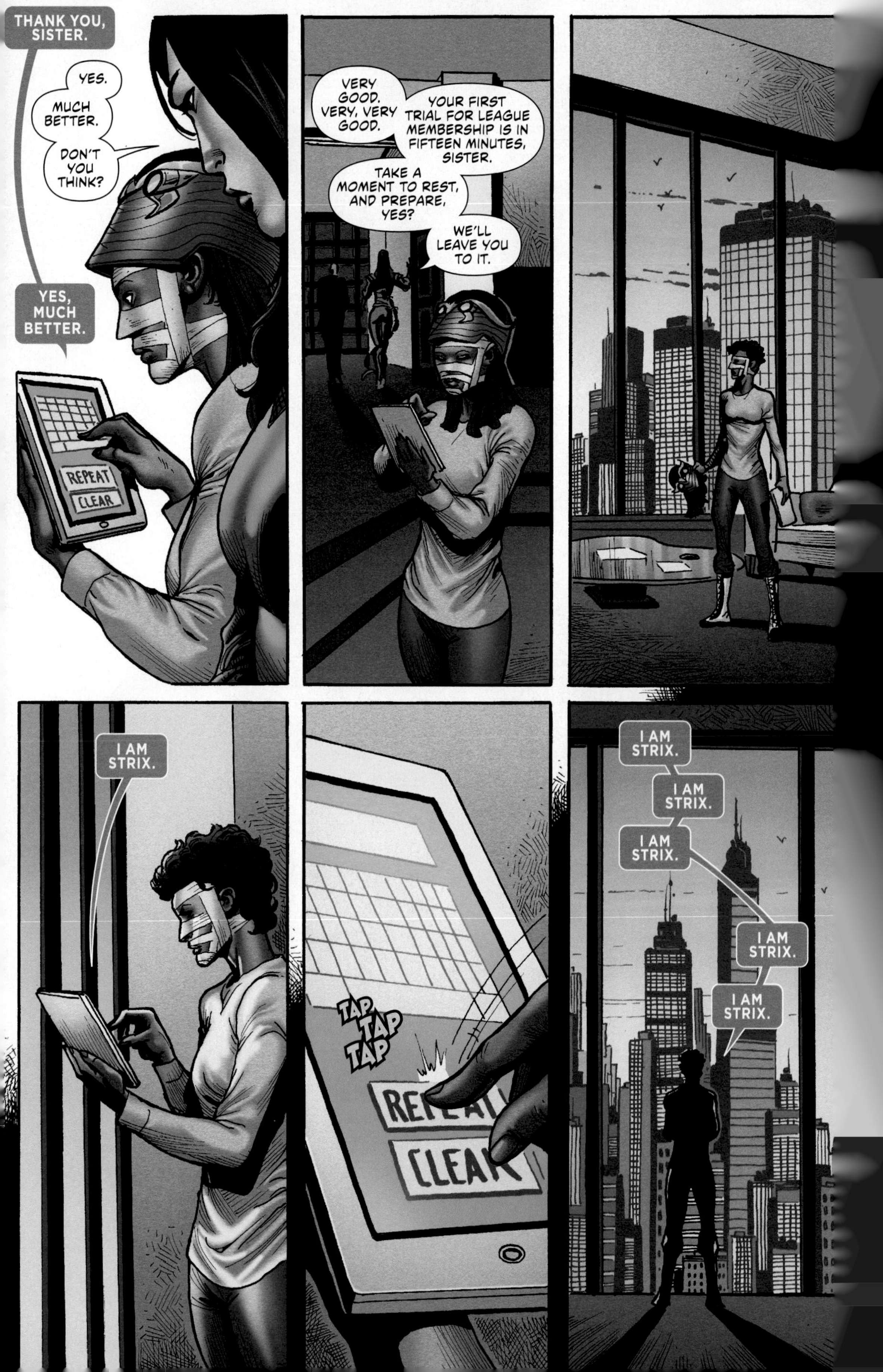
THANK YOU, SISTER.
YES.
MUCH BETTER.
DON'T YOU THINK?
YES, MUCH BETTER.
REPEAT
CLEAR
VERY GOOD. VERY, VERY GOOD.
YOUR FIRST TRIAL FOR LEAGUE MEMBERSHIP IS IN FIFTEEN MINUTES, SISTER.
TAKE A MOMENT TO REST, AND PREPARE, YES?
WE'LL LEAVE YOU TO IT.
I AM STRIX.
TAP TAP TAP
CLEAR
I AM STRIX.
I AM STRIX.
I AM STRIX.
I AM STRIX.
I AM STRIX.

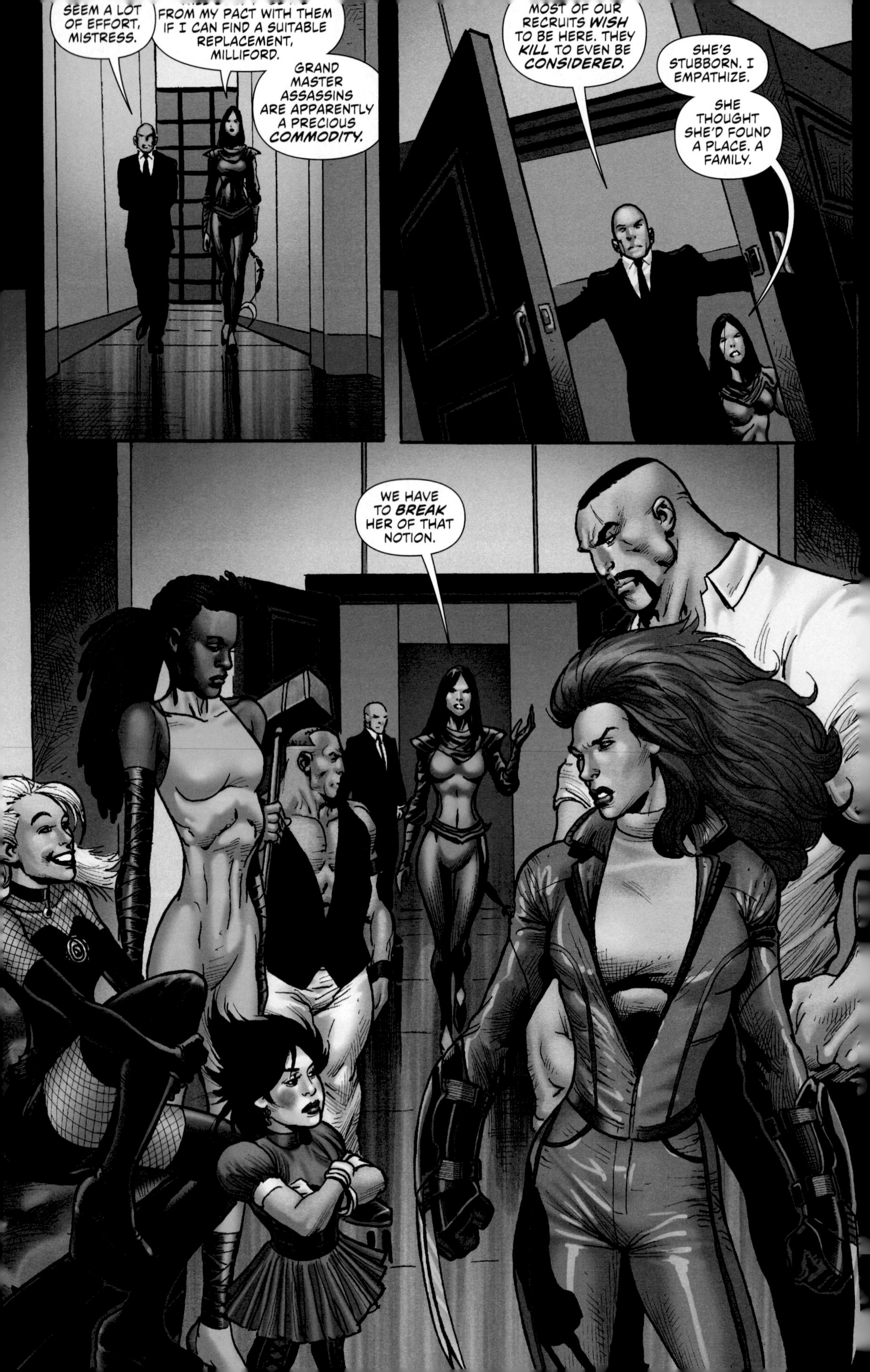
SEEM A LOT OF EFFORT, MISTRESS.
FROM MY PACT WITH THEM IF I CAN FIND A SUITABLE REPLACEMENT, MILLIFORD.
GRAND MASTER ASSASSINS ARE APPARENTLY A PRECIOUS COMMODITY.
MOST OF OUR RECRUITS WISH TO BE HERE. THEY KILL TO EVEN BE CONSIDERED.
SHE'S STUBBORN. I EMPATHIZE.
SHE THOUGHT SHE'D FOUND A PLACE. A FAMILY.
WE HAVE TO BREAK HER OF THAT NOTION.

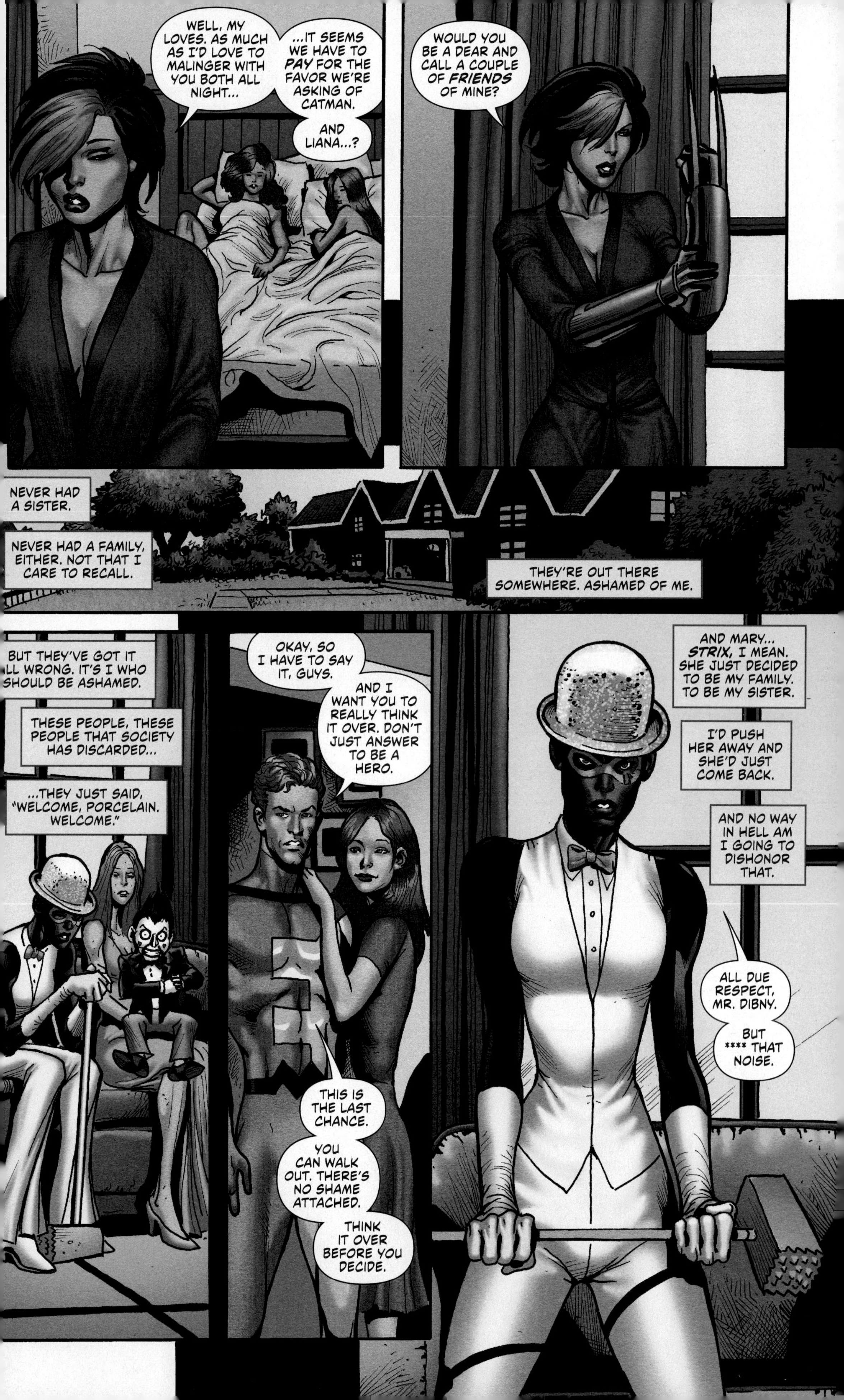
WELL, MY LOVES. AS MUCH AS I'D LOVE TO MALINGER WITH YOU BOTH ALL NIGHT...
...IT SEEMS WE HAVE TO PAY FOR THE FAVOR WE'RE ASKING OF CATMAN.
AND LIANA...?
WOULD YOU BE A DEAR AND CALL A COUPLE OF FRIENDS OF MINE?
NEVER HAD A SISTER.
NEVER HAD A FAMILY, EITHER. NOT THAT I CARE TO RECALL.
THEY'RE OUT THERE SOMEWHERE. ASHAMED OF ME.
BUT THEY'VE GOT IT LL WRONG. IT'S I WHO SHOULD BE ASHAMED.
THESE PEOPLE, THESE PEOPLE THAT SOCIETY HAS DISCARDED...
...THEY JUST SAID, "WELCOME, PORCELAIN. WELCOME."
OKAY, SO I HAVE TO SAY IT, GUYS.
AND I WANT YOU TO REALLY THINK IT OVER. DON'T JUST ANSWER TO BE A HERO.
THIS IS THE LAST CHANCE.
YOU CAN WALK OUT. THERE'S NO SHAME ATTACHED.
THINK IT OVER BEFORE YOU DECIDE.
AND MARY... STRIX, I MEAN. SHE JUST DECIDED TO BE MY FAMILY. TO BE MY SISTER.
I'D PUSH HER AWAY AND SHE'D JUST COME BACK.
AND NO WAY IN HELL AM I GOING TO DISHONOR THAT.
ALL DUE RESPECT, MR. DIBNY.
BUT **** THAT NOISE.

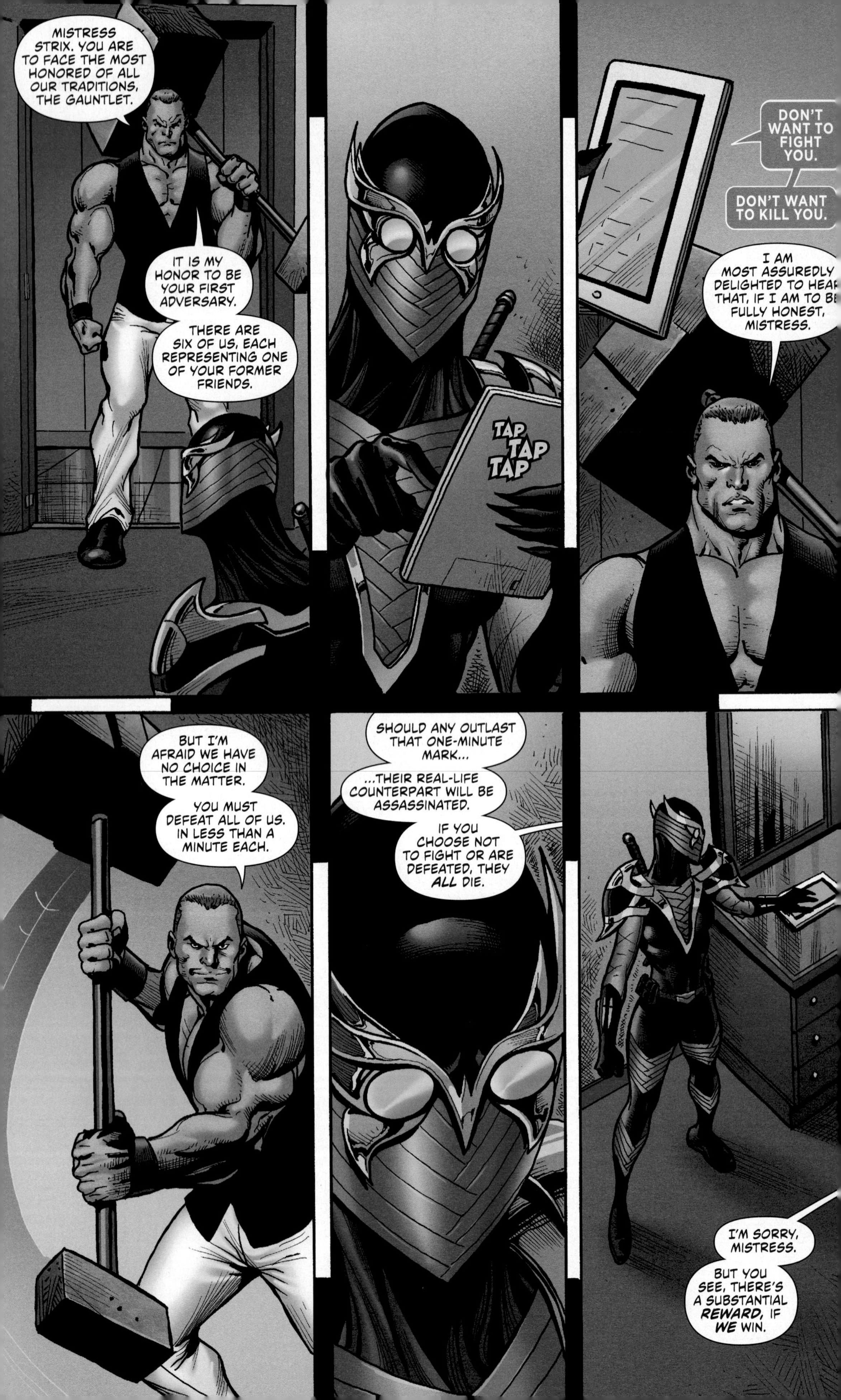

MISTRESS STRIX. YOU ARE TO FACE THE MOST HONORED OF ALL OUR TRADITIONS, THE GAUNTLET.
IT IS MY HONOR TO BE YOUR FIRST ADVERSARY.
THERE ARE SIX OF US, EACH REPRESENTING ONE OF YOUR FORMER FRIENDS.
TAP TAP TAP
DON'T WANT TO FIGHT YOU.
DON'T WANT TO KILL YOU.
I AM MOST ASSUREDLY DELIGHTED TO HEAR THAT, IF I AM TO BE FULLY HONEST, MISTRESS.
BUT I'M AFRAID WE HAVE NO CHOICE IN THE MATTER.
YOU MUST DEFEAT ALL OF US. IN LESS THAN A MINUTE EACH.
SHOULD ANY OUTLAST THAT ONE-MINUTE MARK...
...THEIR REAL-LIFE COUNTERPART WILL BE ASSASSINATED.
IF YOU CHOOSE NOT TO FIGHT OR ARE DEFEATED, THEY ALL DIE.
I'M SORRY, MISTRESS.
BUT YOU SEE, THERE'S A SUBSTANTIAL REWARD, IF WE WIN.

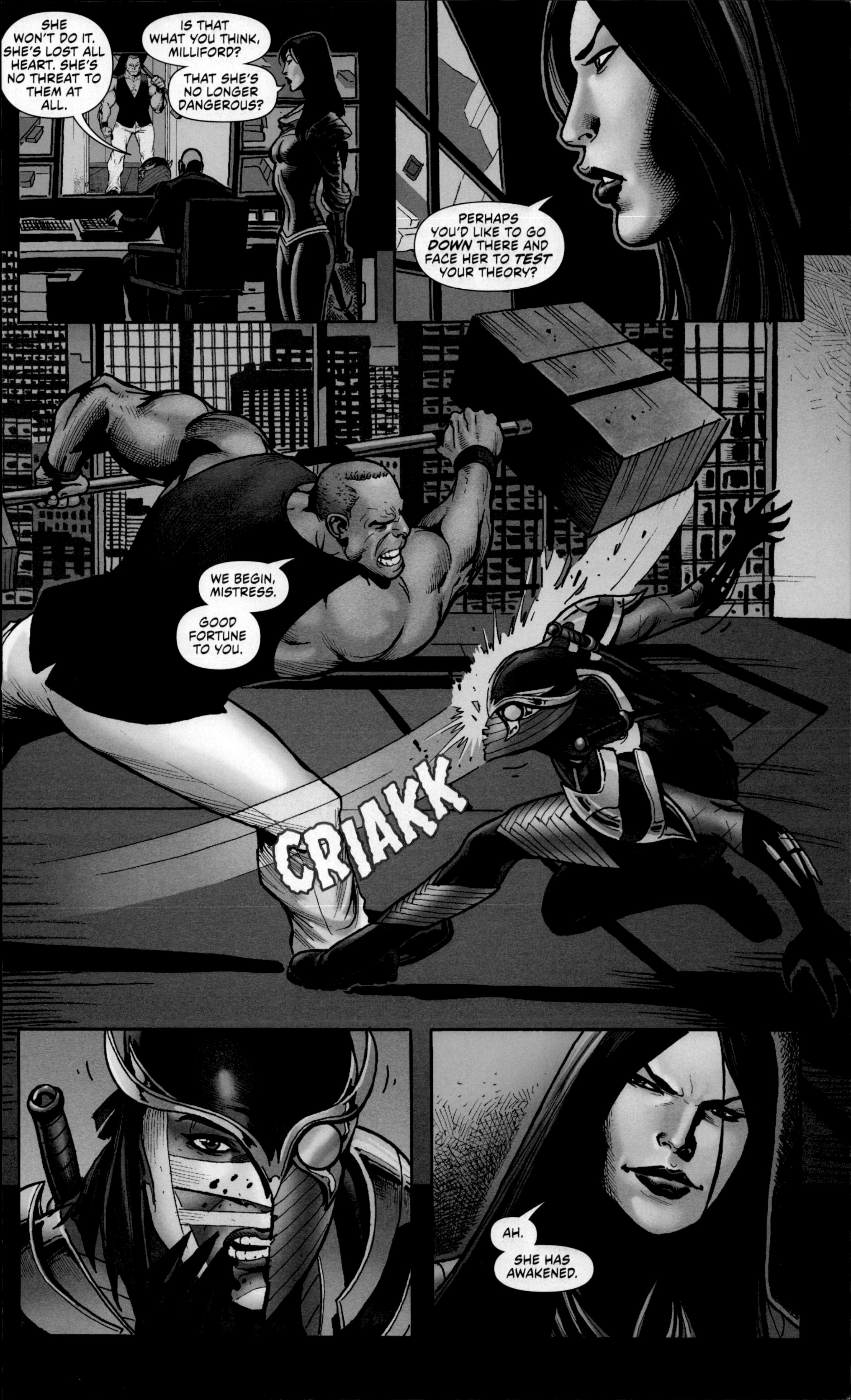
SHE WON'T DO IT. SHE'S LOST ALL HEART. SHE'S NO THREAT TO THEM AT ALL.
IS THAT WHAT YOU THINK, MILLIFORD?
THAT SHE'S NO LONGER DANGEROUS?
PERHAPS YOU'D LIKE TO GO DOWN THERE AND FACE HER TO TEST YOUR THEORY?
WE BEGIN, MISTRESS.
GOOD FORTUNE TO YOU.
CRIAKK
AH.
SHE HAS AWAKENED.

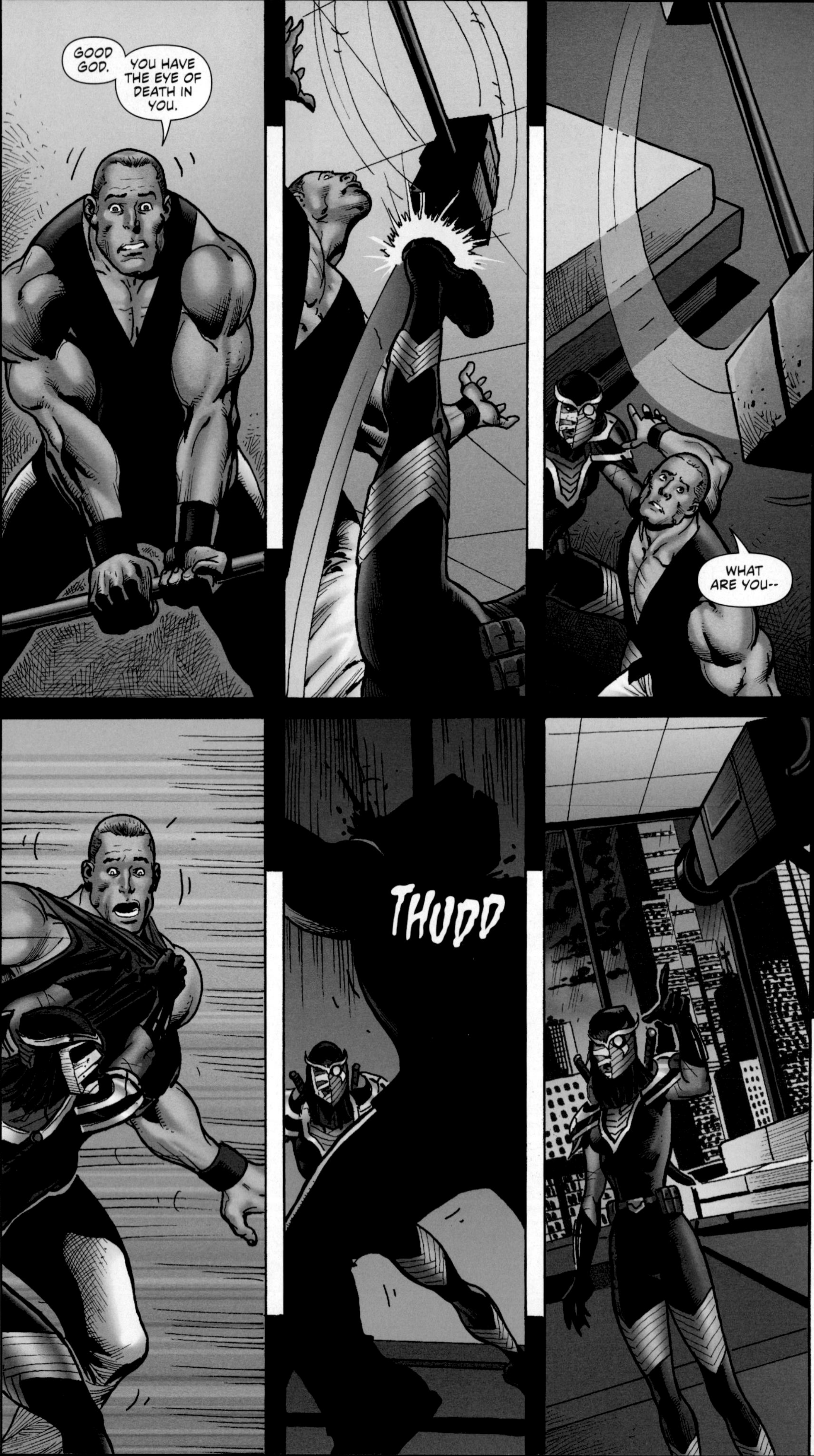
GOOD GOD.
YOU HAVE THE EYE OF DEATH IN YOU.
WHAT ARE YOU--
THUDD

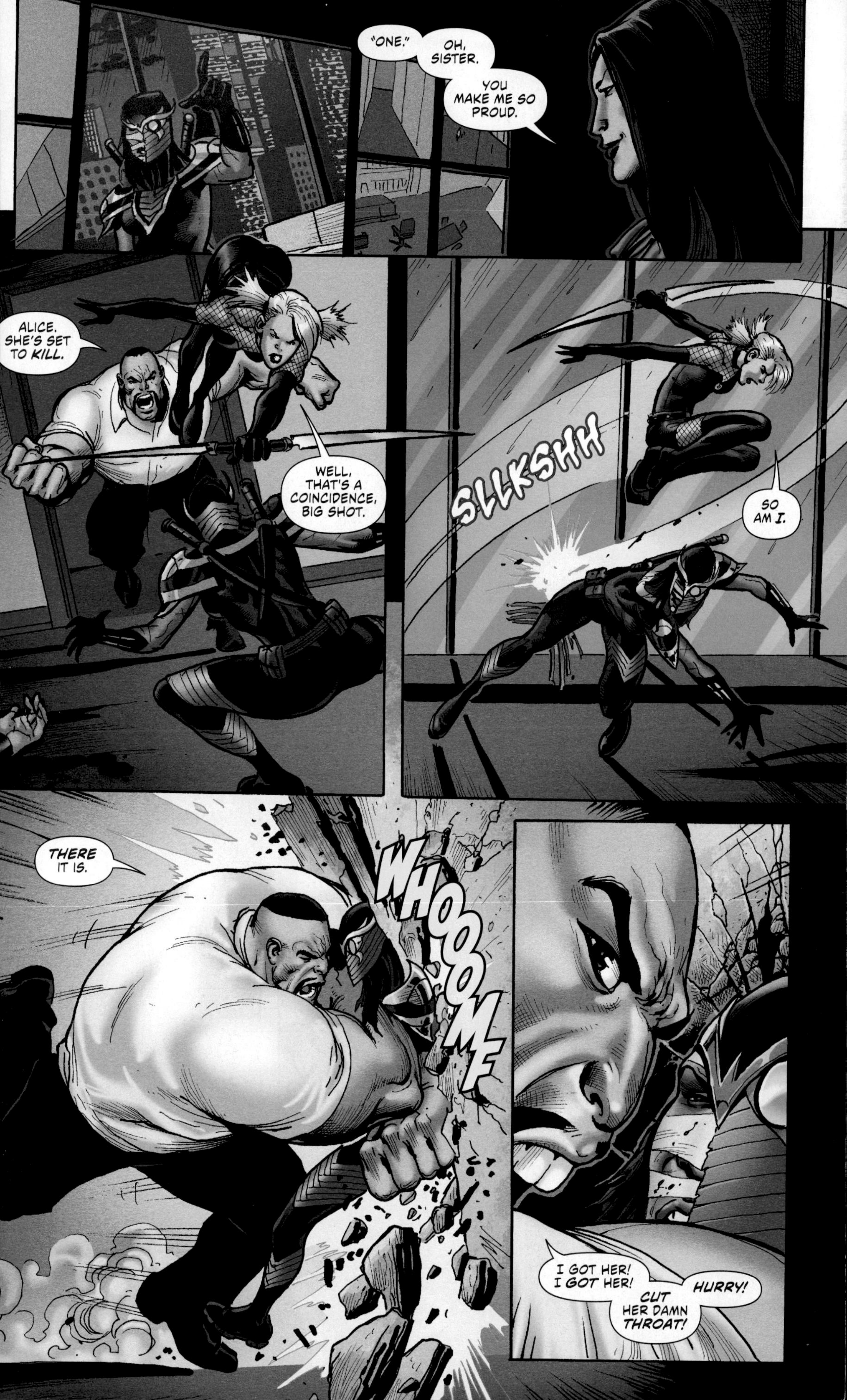
"ONE."
OH, SISTER.
YOU MAKE ME SO PROUD.
ALICE. SHE'S SET TO KILL.
WELL, THAT'S A COINCIDENCE, BIG SHOT.
SLLKSHH
SO AM I.
THERE IT IS.
WHOOOOMF
I GOT HER! I GOT HER!
HURRY!
CUT HER DAMN THROAT!

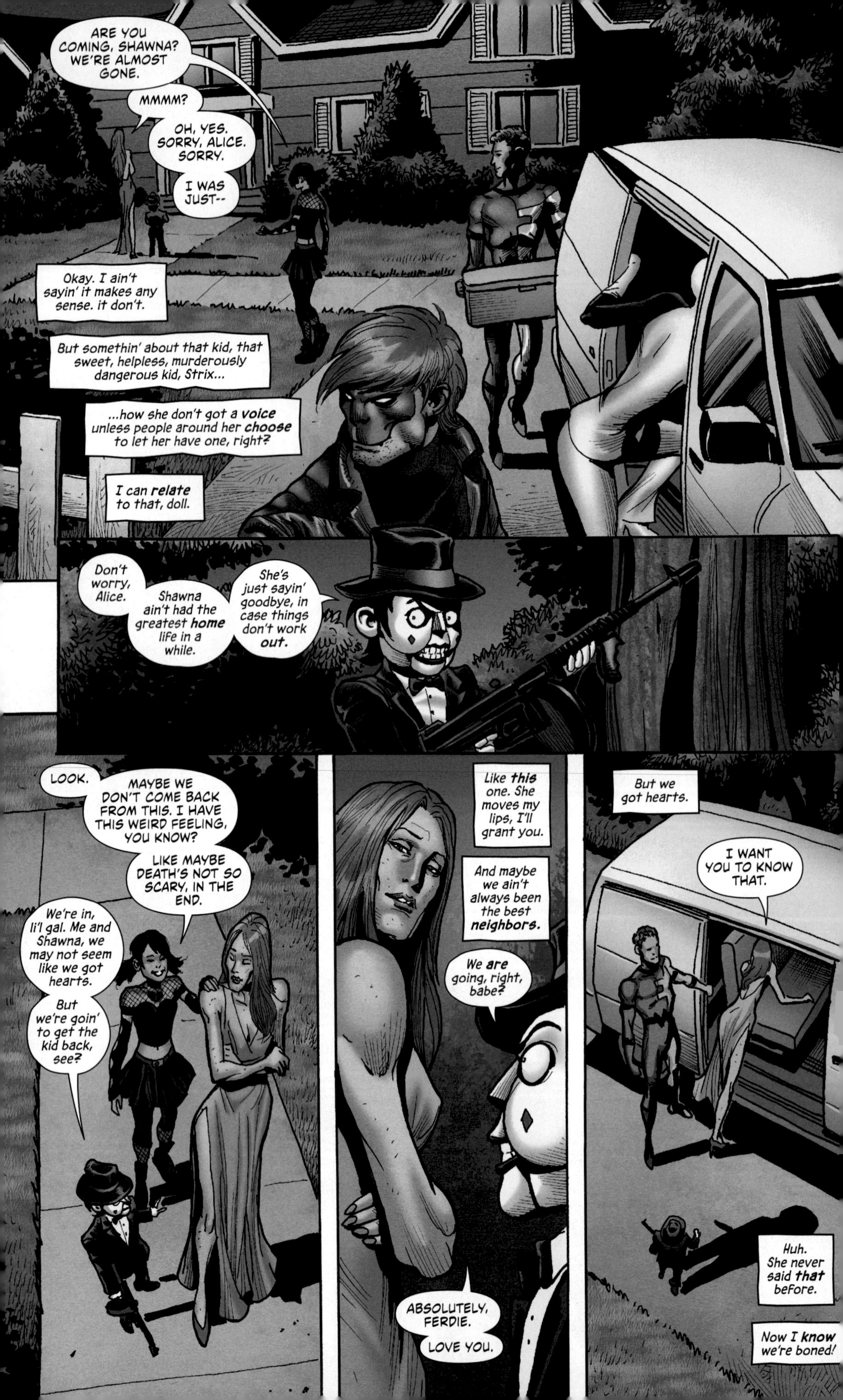
ARE YOU COMING, SHAWNA? WE'RE ALMOST GONE.
MMMM?
OH, YES. SORRY, ALICE. SORRY.
I WAS JUST--
Okay. I ain't sayin' it makes any sense. it don't.
But somethin' about that kid, that sweet, helpless, murderously dangerous kid, Strix...
...how she don't got a voice unless people around her choose to let her have one, right?
I can relate to that, doll.
Don't worry, Alice.
Shawna ain't had the greatest home life in a while.
She's just sayin' goodbye, in case things don't work out.
LOOK.
MAYBE WE DON'T COME BACK FROM THIS. I HAVE THIS WEIRD FEELING, YOU KNOW?
LIKE MAYBE DEATH'S NOT SO SCARY, IN THE END.
We're in, li'l gal. Me and Shawna, we may not seem like we got hearts.
But we're goin' to get the kid back, see?
Like this one. She moves my lips, I'll grant you.
And maybe we ain't always been the best neighbors.
We are going, right, babe?
ABSOLUTELY, FERDIE.
LOVE YOU.
But we got hearts.
I WANT YOU TO KNOW THAT.
Huh. She never said that before.
Now I know we're boned!

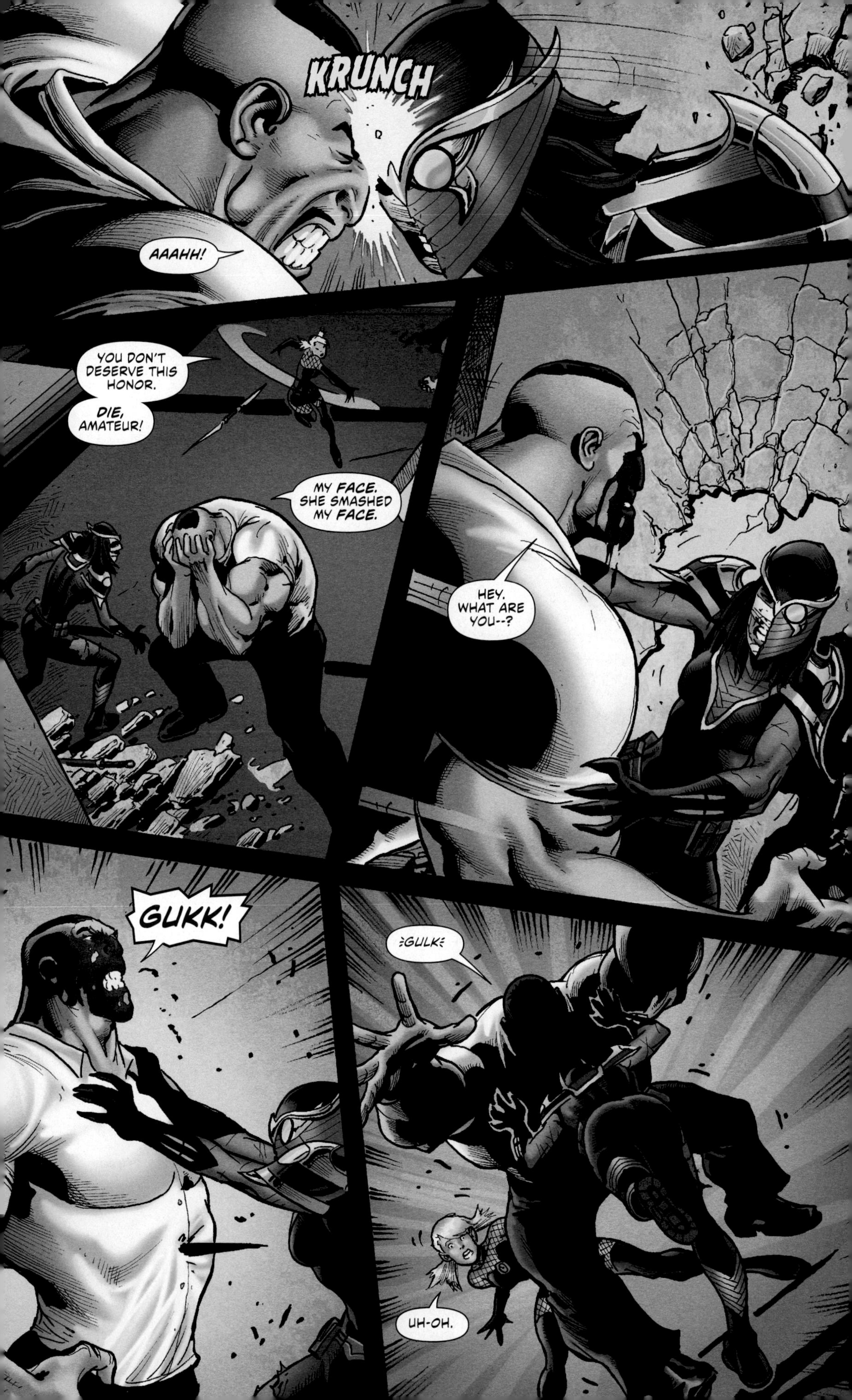
KRUNCH
AAAHH!
YOU DON'T DESERVE THIS HONOR.
DIE, AMATEUR!
MY FACE. SHE SMASHED MY FACE.
HEY. WHAT ARE YOU--?
GUKK!
GULK
UH-OH.

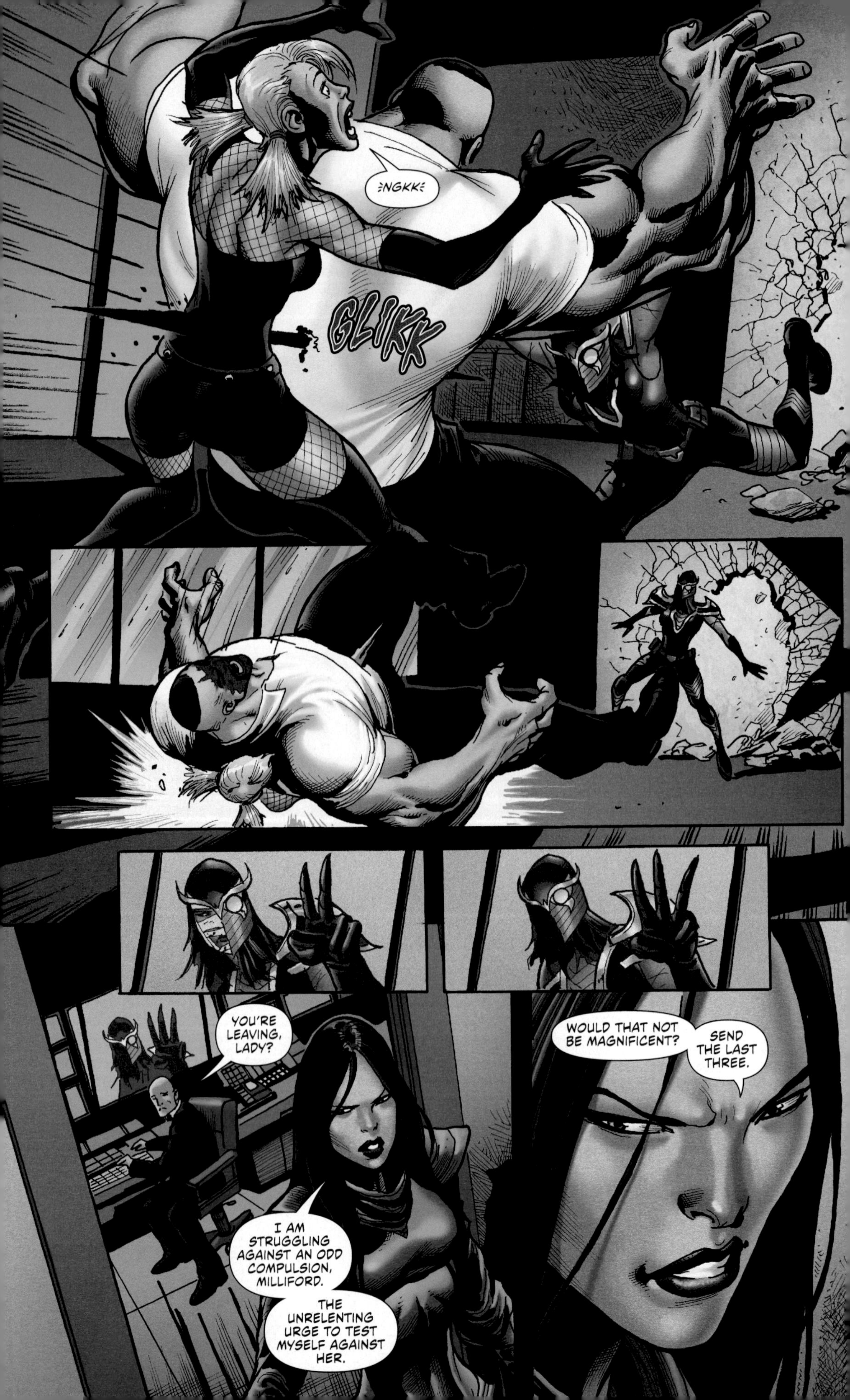
NGKK
GLIKK
YOU'RE LEAVING, LADY?
I AM STRUGGLING AGAINST AN ODD COMPULSION, MILLIFORD.
THE UNRELENTING URGE TO TEST MYSELF AGAINST HER.
WOULD THAT NOT BE MAGNIFICENT?
SEND THE LAST THREE.

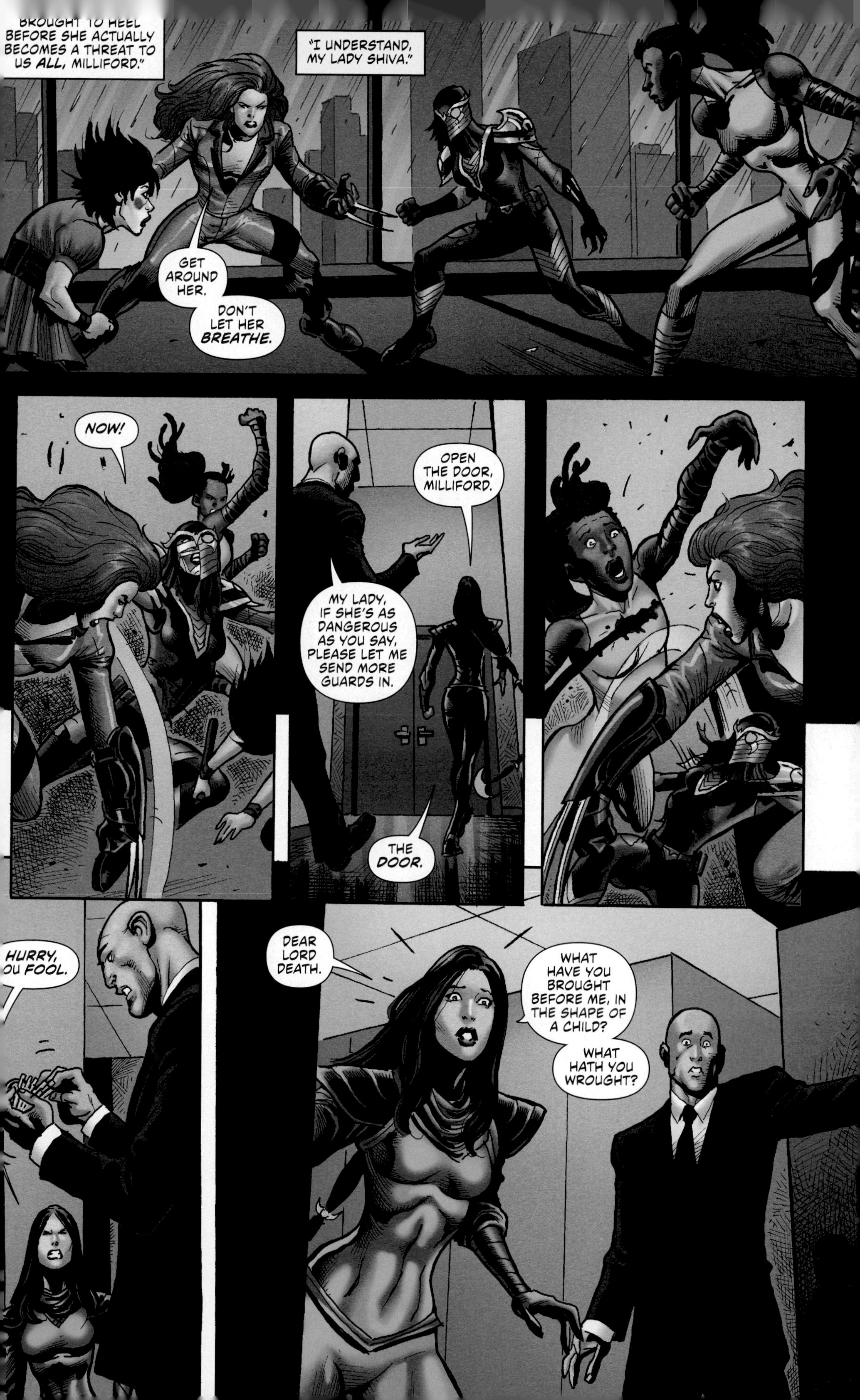
BROUGHT TO HEEL BEFORE SHE ACTUALLY BECOMES A THREAT TO US *ALL*, MILLIFORD."
"I UNDERSTAND, MY LADY SHIVA."
GET AROUND HER.
DON'T LET HER *BREATHE*.
NOW!
OPEN THE DOOR, MILLIFORD.
MY LADY, IF SHE'S AS DANGEROUS AS YOU SAY, PLEASE LET ME SEND MORE GUARDS IN.
THE *DOOR*.
HURRY, OU *FOOL*.
DEAR LORD DEATH.
WHAT HAVE YOU BROUGHT BEFORE ME, IN THE SHAPE OF A CHILD?
WHAT HATH YOU WROUGHT?

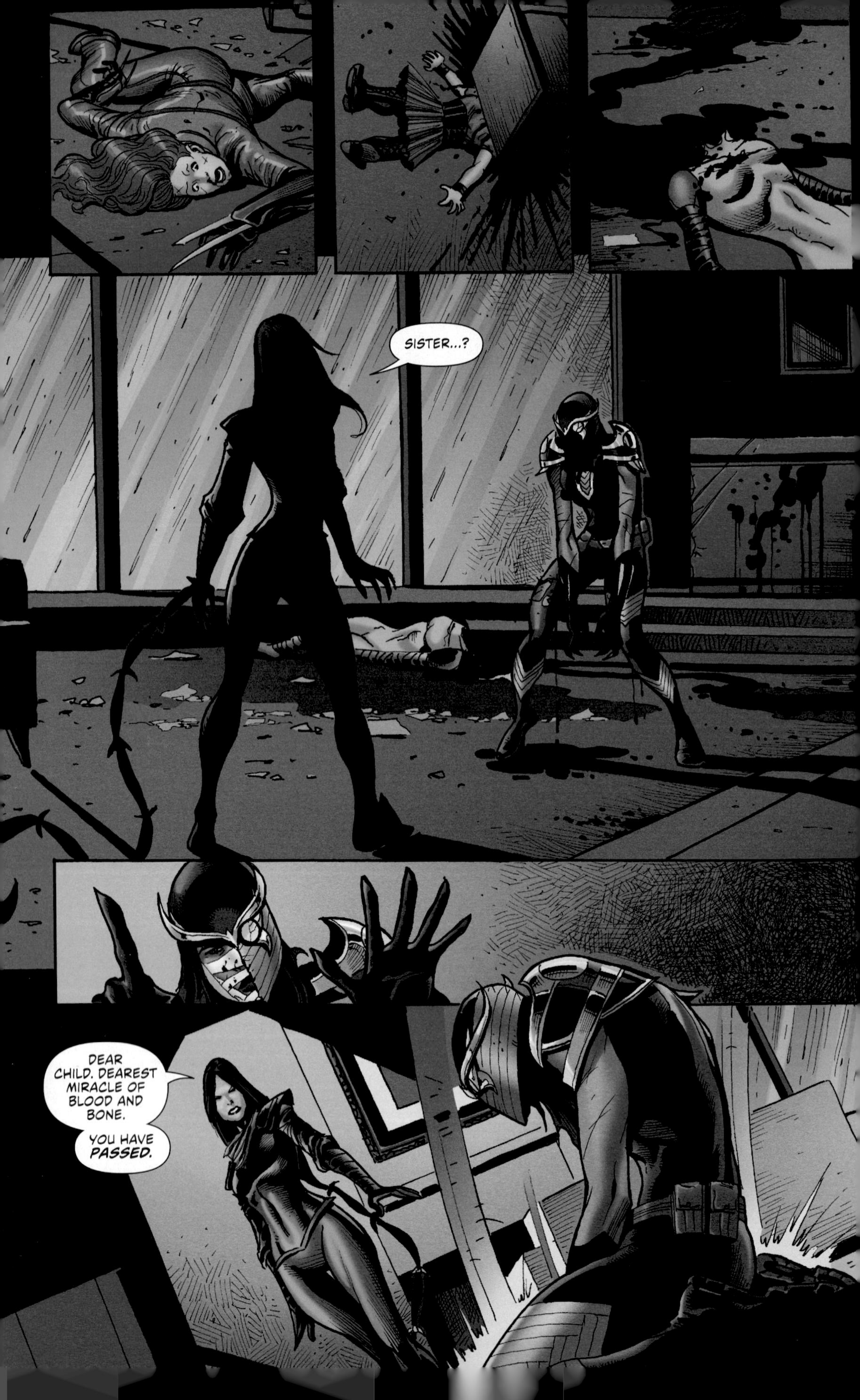
SISTER...?
DEAR CHILD. DEAREST MIRACLE OF BLOOD AND BONE.
YOU HAVE *PASSED.*

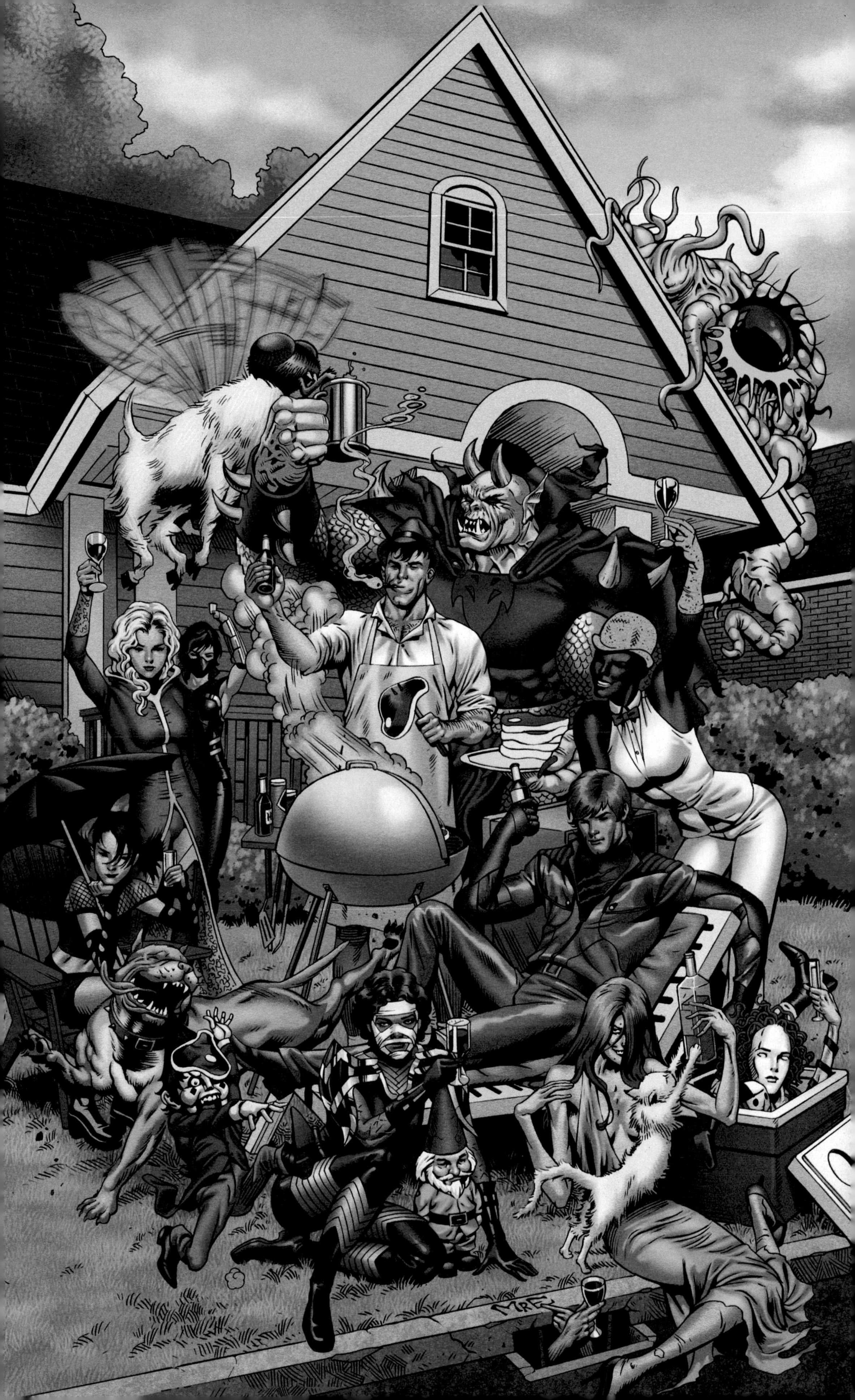

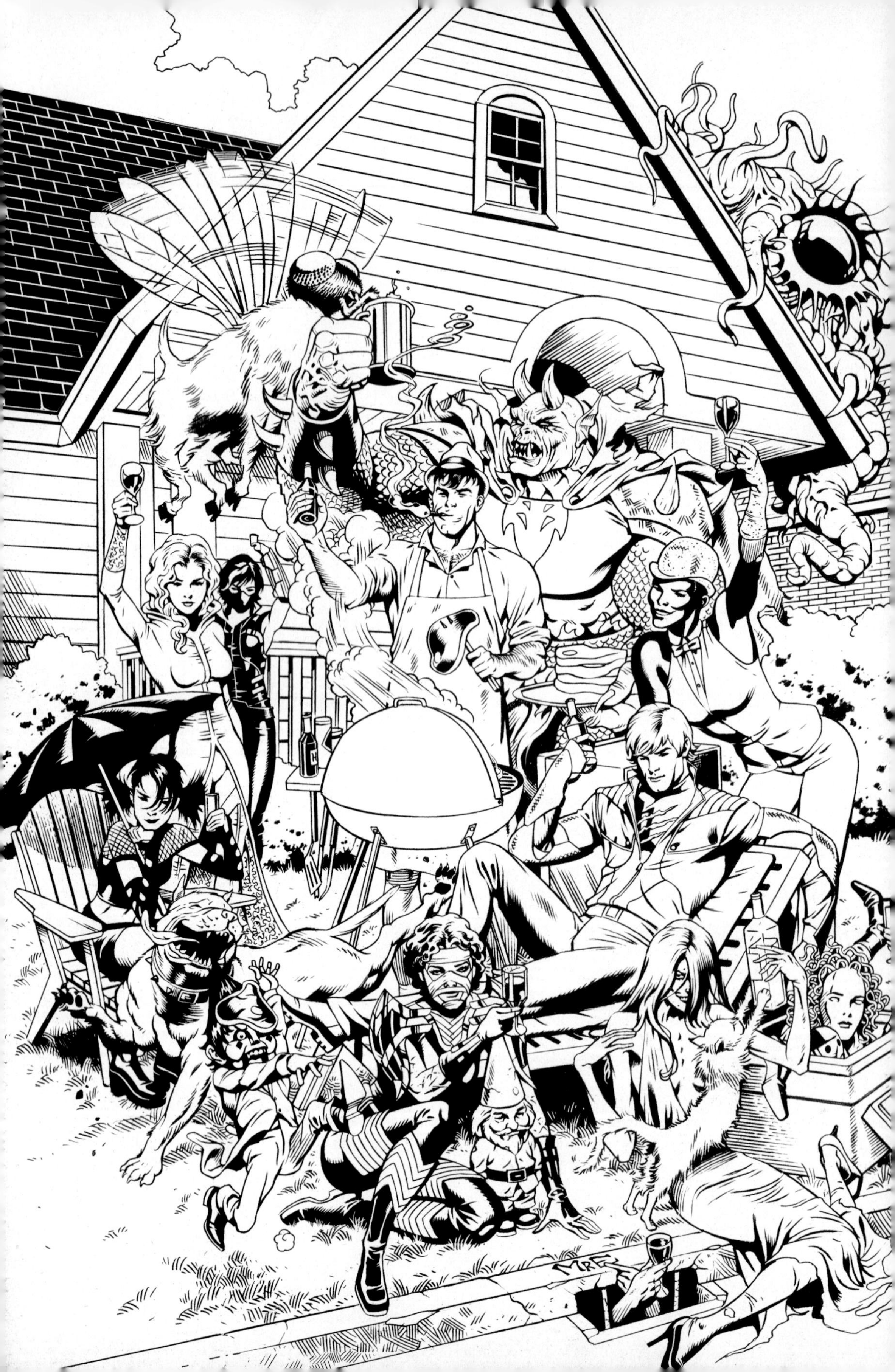

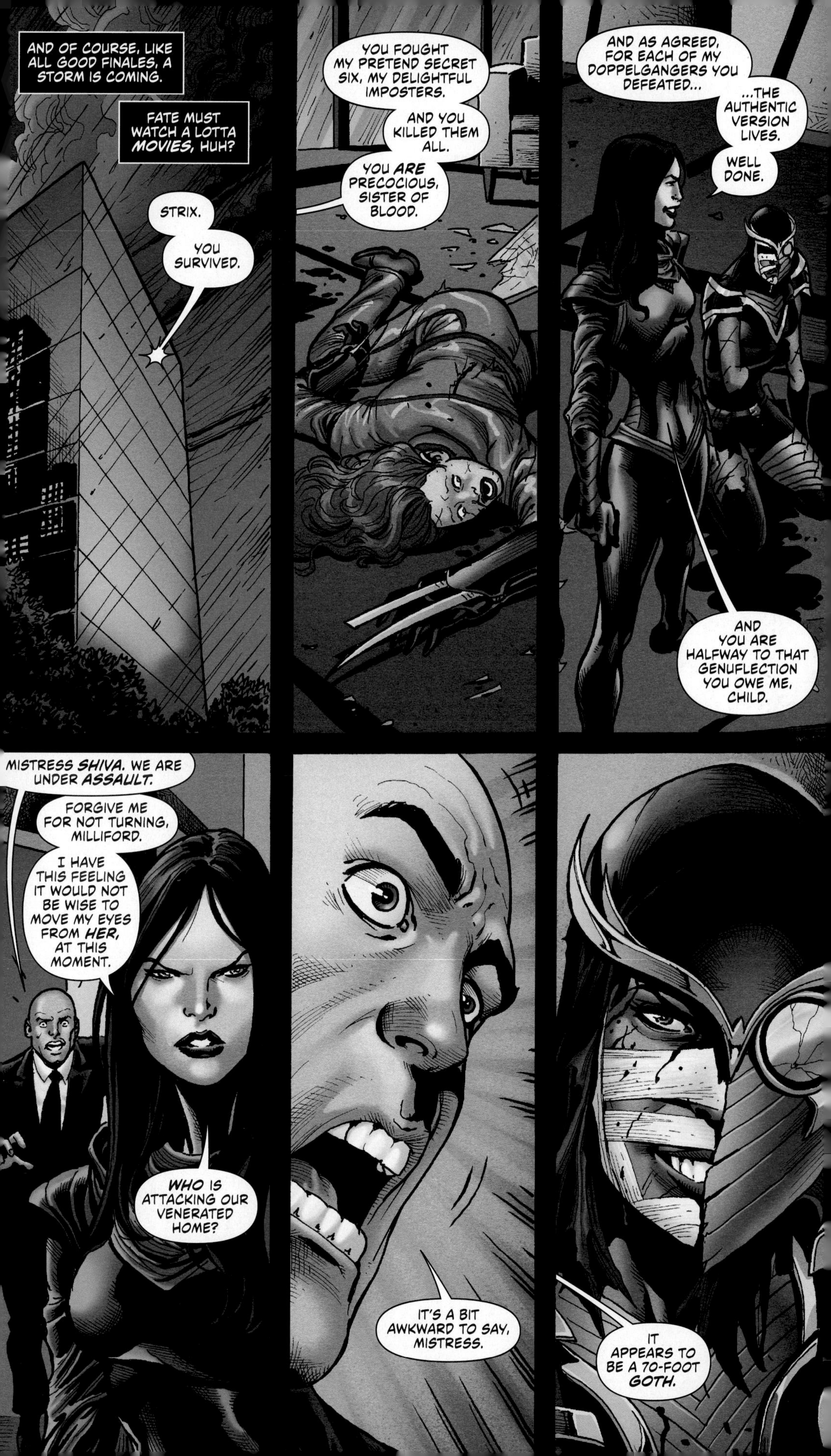
AND OF COURSE, LIKE ALL GOOD FINALES, A STORM IS COMING.
FATE MUST WATCH A LOTTA MOVIES, HUH?
STRIX.
YOU SURVIVED.
YOU FOUGHT MY PRETEND SECRET SIX, MY DELIGHTFUL IMPOSTERS.
AND YOU KILLED THEM ALL.
YOU ARE PRECOCIOUS, SISTER OF BLOOD.
AND AS AGREED, FOR EACH OF MY DOPPELGANGERS YOU DEFEATED...
...THE AUTHENTIC VERSION LIVES.
WELL DONE.
AND YOU ARE HALFWAY TO THAT GENUFLECTION YOU OWE ME, CHILD.
MISTRESS SHIVA. WE ARE UNDER ASSAULT.
FORGIVE ME FOR NOT TURNING, MILLIFORD.
I HAVE THIS FEELING IT WOULD NOT BE WISE TO MOVE MY EYES FROM HER, AT THIS MOMENT.
WHO IS ATTACKING OUR VENERATED HOME?
IT'S A BIT AWKWARD TO SAY, MISTRESS.
IT APPEARS TO BE A 70-FOOT GOTH.

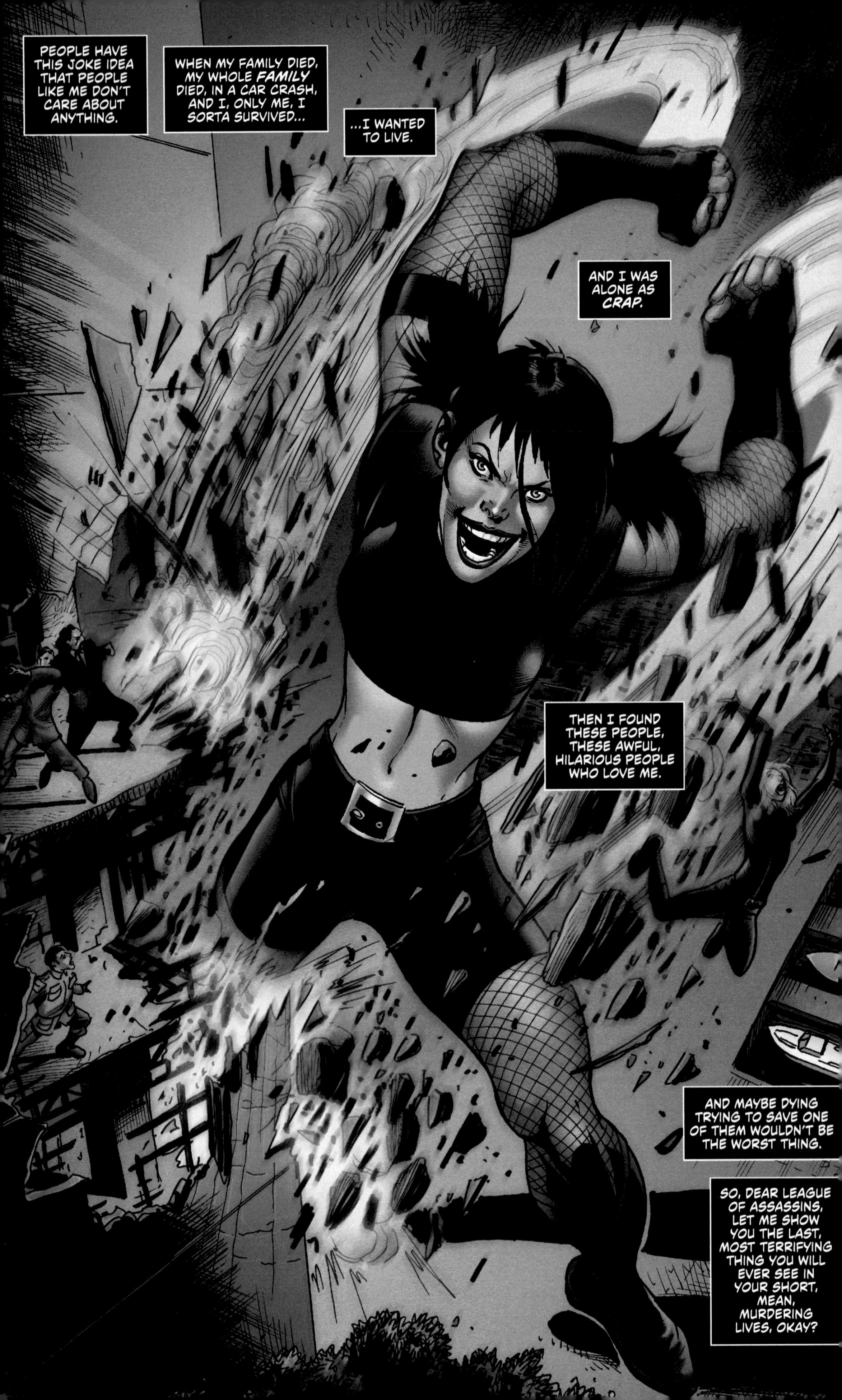
PEOPLE HAVE THIS JOKE IDEA THAT PEOPLE LIKE ME DON'T CARE ABOUT ANYTHING.
WHEN MY FAMILY DIED, MY WHOLE *FAMILY* DIED, IN A CAR CRASH, AND I, ONLY ME, I SORTA SURVIVED...
...I WANTED TO LIVE.
AND I WAS ALONE AS *CRAP.*
THEN I FOUND THESE PEOPLE, THESE AWFUL, HILARIOUS PEOPLE WHO LOVE ME.
AND MAYBE DYING TRYING TO SAVE ONE OF THEM WOULDN'T BE THE WORST THING.
SO, DEAR LEAGUE OF ASSASSINS, LET ME SHOW YOU THE LAST, MOST TERRIFYING THING YOU WILL EVER SEE IN YOUR SHORT, MEAN, MURDERING LIVES, OKAY?

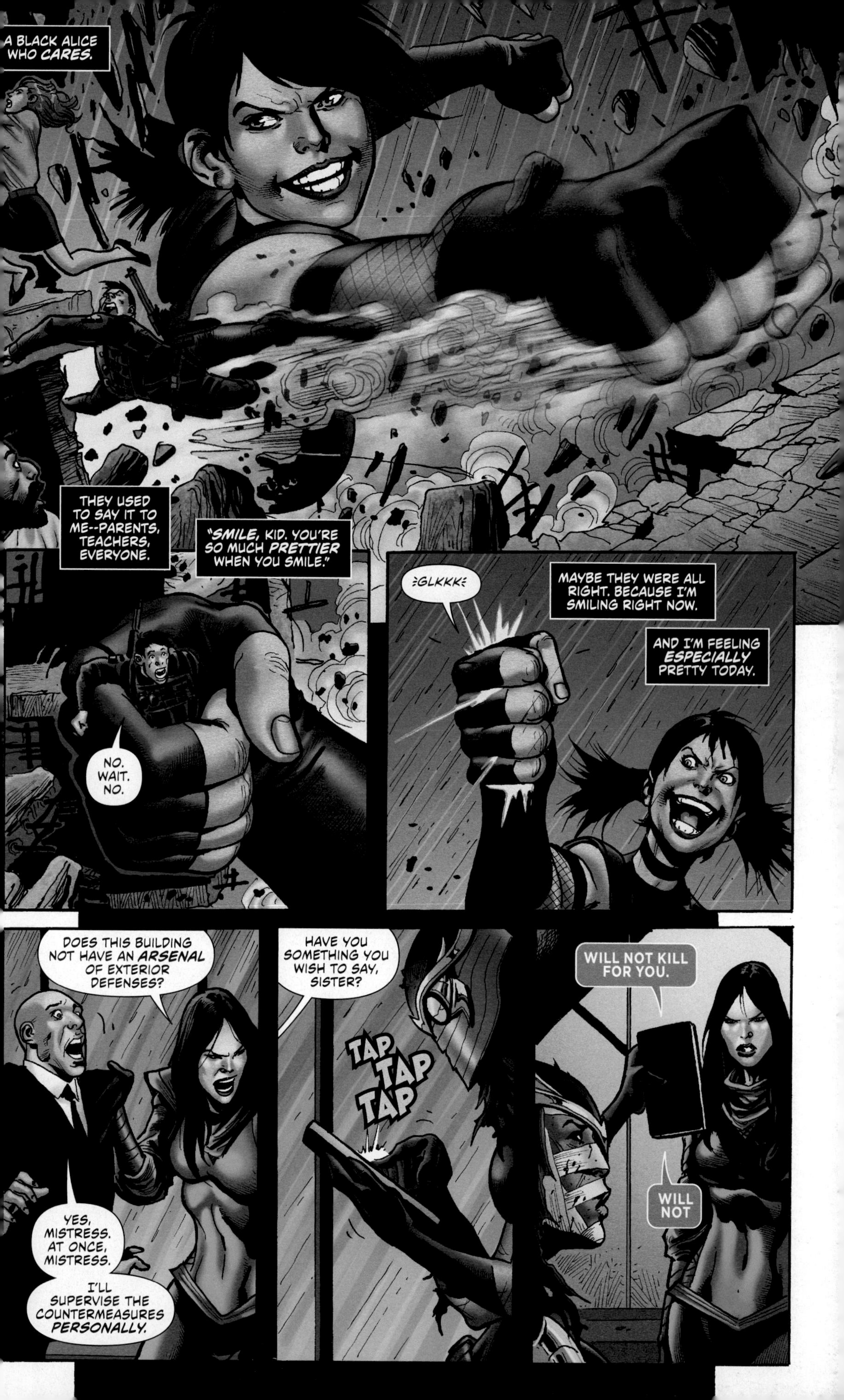
A BLACK ALICE WHO CARES.
THEY USED TO SAY IT TO ME--PARENTS, TEACHERS, EVERYONE.
"SMILE, KID. YOU'RE SO MUCH PRETTIER WHEN YOU SMILE."
NO. WAIT. NO.
GLKKK
MAYBE THEY WERE ALL RIGHT. BECAUSE I'M SMILING RIGHT NOW.
AND I'M FEELING ESPECIALLY PRETTY TODAY.
DOES THIS BUILDING NOT HAVE AN ARSENAL OF EXTERIOR DEFENSES?
YES, MISTRESS. AT ONCE, MISTRESS.
I'LL SUPERVISE THE COUNTERMEASURES PERSONALLY.
HAVE YOU SOMETHING YOU WISH TO SAY, SISTER?
TAP TAP TAP
WILL NOT KILL FOR YOU.
WILL NOT

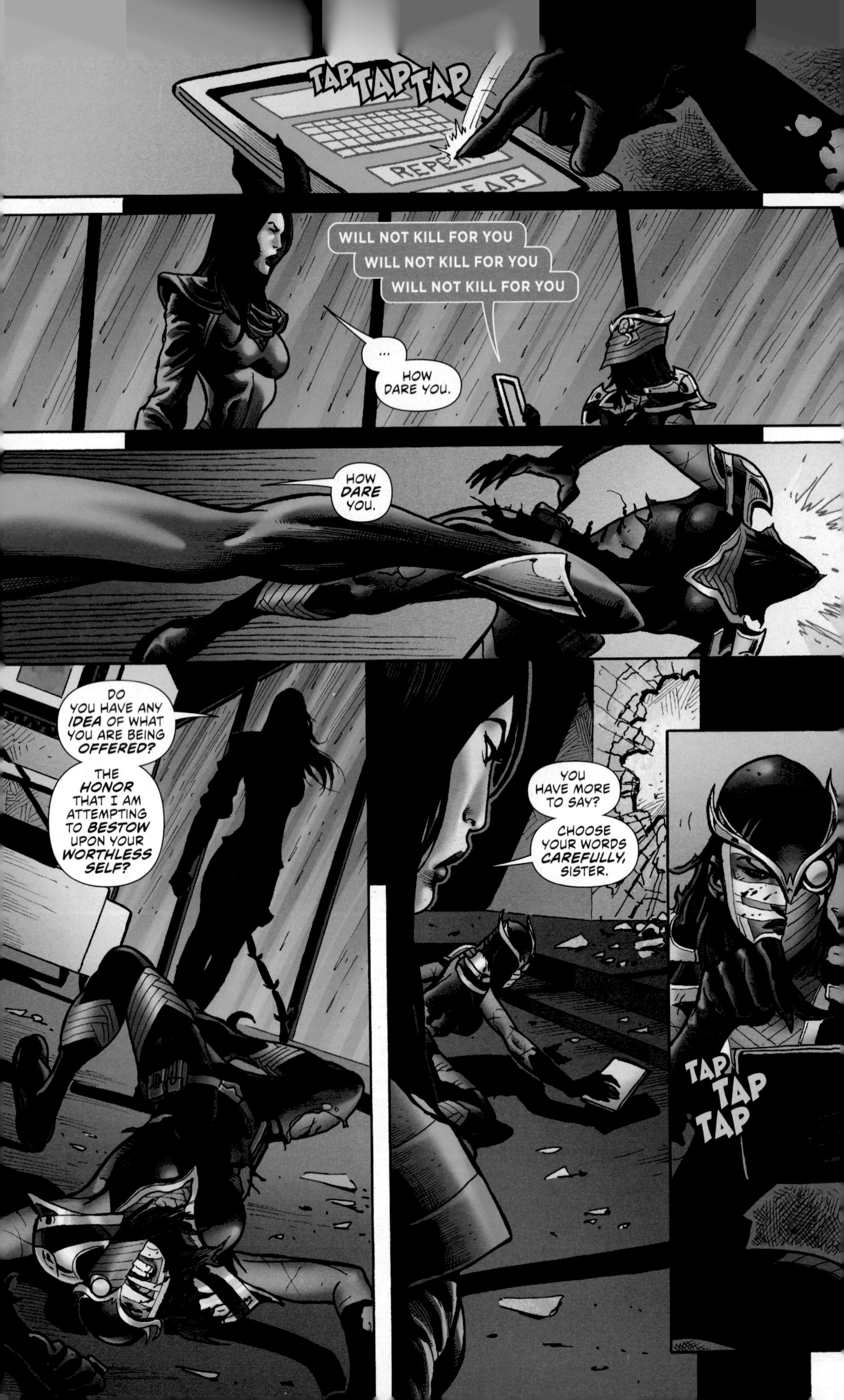
TAP TAP TAP
REPEA
WILL NOT KILL FOR YOU
WILL NOT KILL FOR YOU
WILL NOT KILL FOR YOU
... HOW DARE YOU.
HOW DARE YOU.
DO YOU HAVE ANY IDEA OF WHAT YOU ARE BEING OFFERED?
THE HONOR THAT I AM ATTEMPTING TO BESTOW UPON YOUR WORTHLESS SELF?
YOU HAVE MORE TO SAY?
CHOOSE YOUR WORDS CAREFULLY, SISTER.
TAP TAP TAP

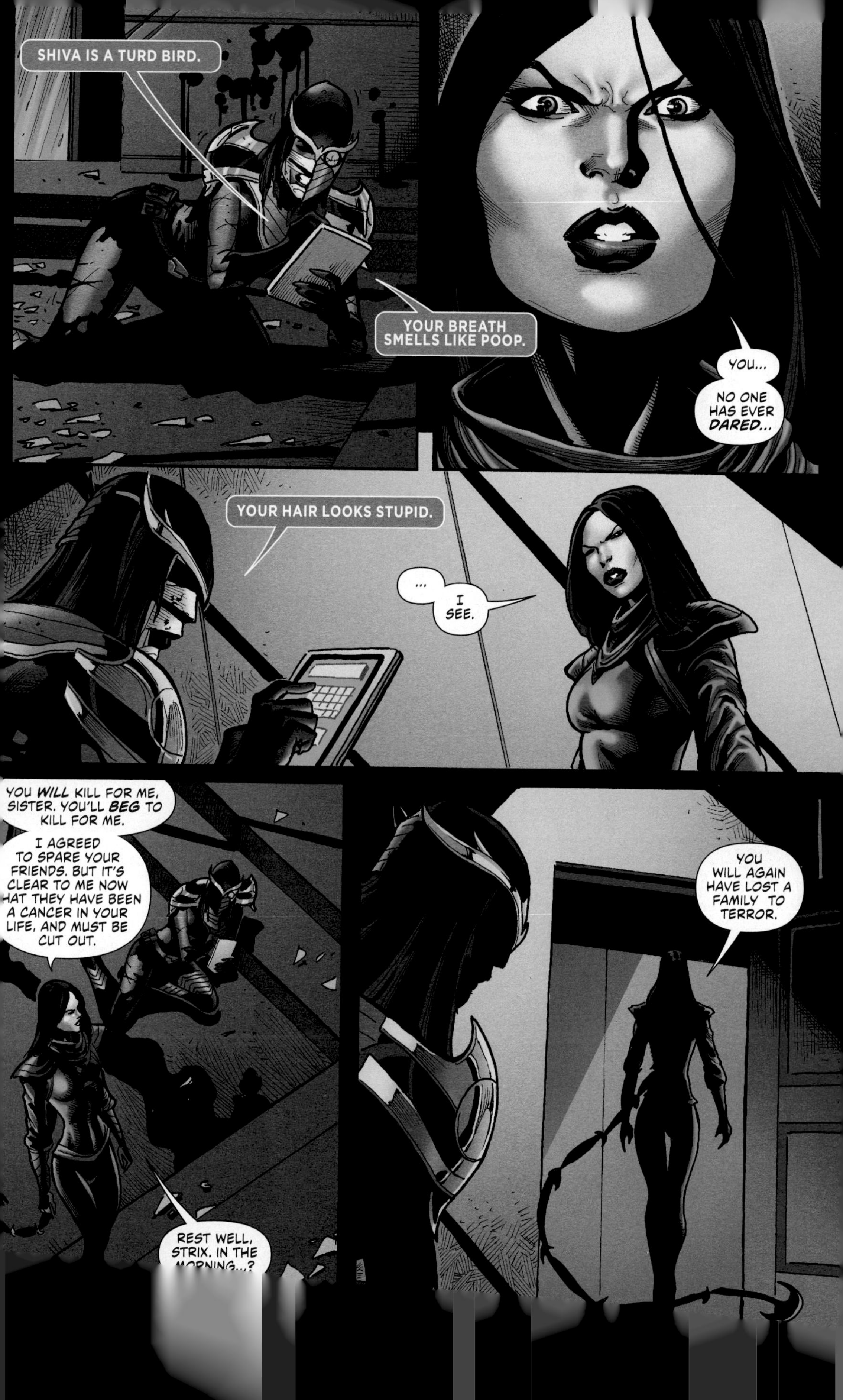
SHIVA IS A TURD BIRD.
YOUR BREATH SMELLS LIKE POOP.
YOU...
NO ONE HAS EVER *DARED*...
YOUR HAIR LOOKS STUPID.
...
I SEE.
YOU *WILL* KILL FOR ME, SISTER. YOU'LL *BEG* TO KILL FOR ME.
I AGREED TO SPARE YOUR FRIENDS. BUT IT'S CLEAR TO ME NOW HAT THEY HAVE BEEN A CANCER IN YOUR LIFE, AND MUST BE CUT OUT.
REST WELL, STRIX. IN THE
YOU WILL AGAIN HAVE LOST A FAMILY TO TERROR.

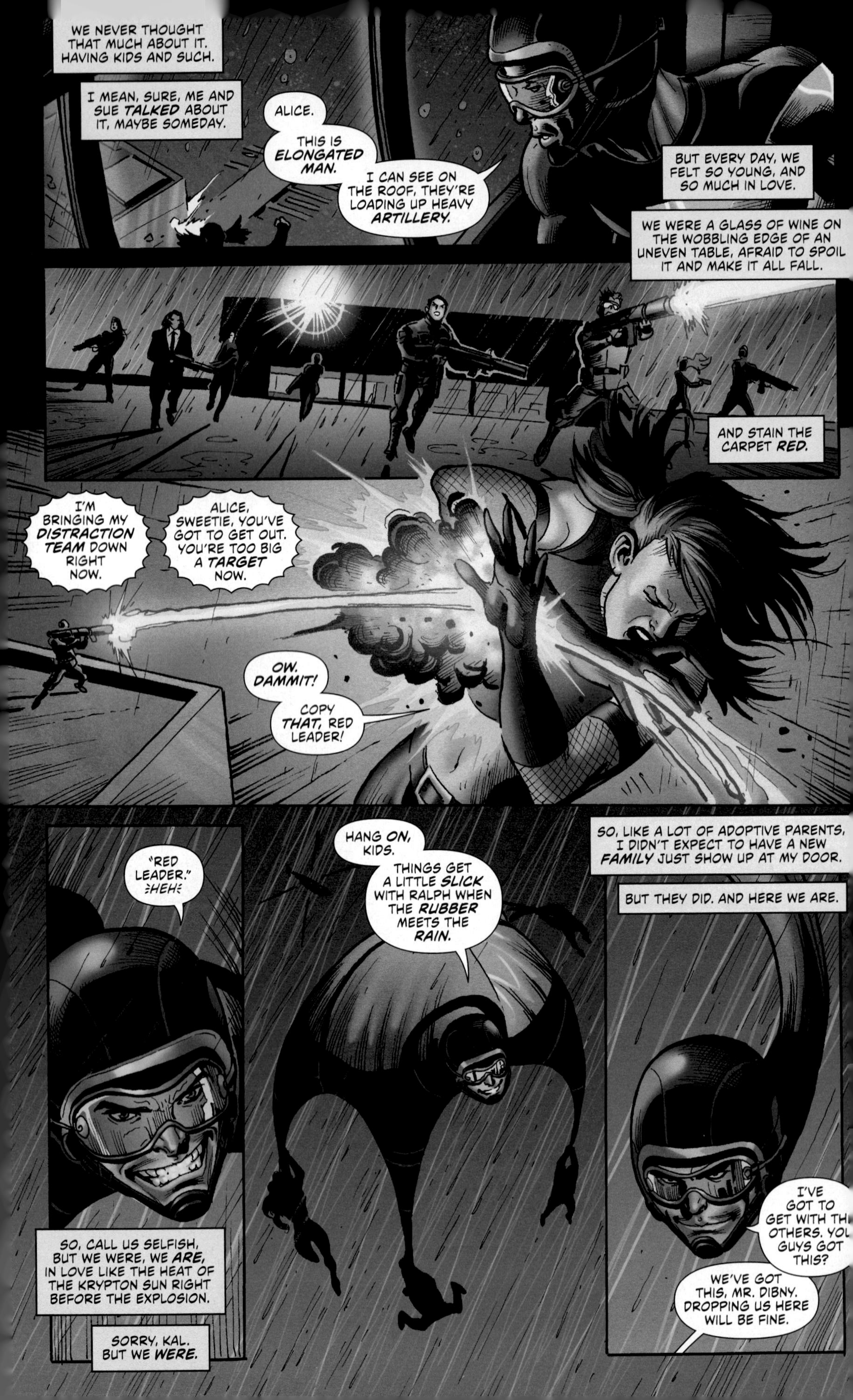

WE NEVER THOUGHT THAT MUCH ABOUT IT. HAVING KIDS AND SUCH.
I MEAN, SURE, ME AND SUE TALKED ABOUT IT, MAYBE SOMEDAY.
ALICE.
THIS IS ELONGATED MAN.
I CAN SEE ON THE ROOF, THEY'RE LOADING UP HEAVY ARTILLERY.
BUT EVERY DAY, WE FELT SO YOUNG, AND SO MUCH IN LOVE.
WE WERE A GLASS OF WINE ON THE WOBBLING EDGE OF AN UNEVEN TABLE, AFRAID TO SPOIL IT AND MAKE IT ALL FALL.
AND STAIN THE CARPET RED.
I'M BRINGING MY DISTRACTION TEAM DOWN RIGHT NOW.
ALICE, SWEETIE, YOU'VE GOT TO GET OUT. YOU'RE TOO BIG A TARGET NOW.
OW. DAMMIT!
COPY THAT, RED LEADER!
"RED LEADER." HEH
SO, CALL US SELFISH, BUT WE WERE, WE ARE, IN LOVE LIKE THE HEAT OF THE KRYPTON SUN RIGHT BEFORE THE EXPLOSION.
SORRY, KAL. BUT WE WERE.
HANG ON, KIDS.
THINGS GET A LITTLE SLICK WITH RALPH WHEN THE RUBBER MEETS THE RAIN.
SO, LIKE A LOT OF ADOPTIVE PARENTS, I DIDN'T EXPECT TO HAVE A NEW FAMILY JUST SHOW UP AT MY DOOR.
BUT THEY DID. AND HERE WE ARE.
I'VE GOT TO GET WITH TH OTHERS. YO GUYS GOT THIS?
WE'VE GOT THIS, MR. DIBNY. DROPPING US HERE WILL BE FINE.

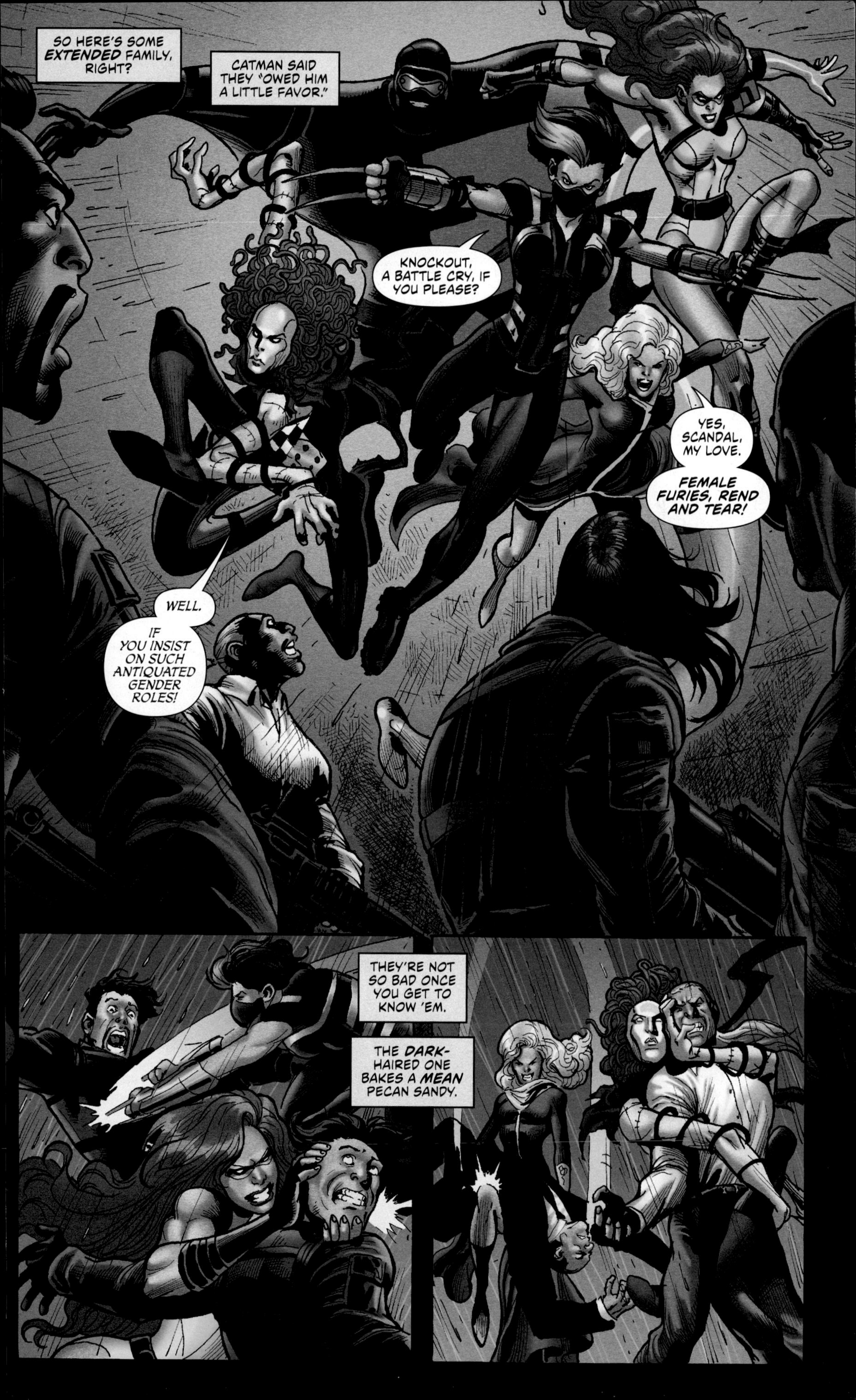
SO HERE'S SOME EXTENDED FAMILY, RIGHT?
CATMAN SAID THEY "OWED HIM A LITTLE FAVOR."
KNOCKOUT, A BATTLE CRY, IF YOU PLEASE?
YES, SCANDAL, MY LOVE.
FEMALE FURIES, REND AND TEAR!
WELL.
IF YOU INSIST ON SUCH ANTIQUATED GENDER ROLES!
THEY'RE NOT SO BAD ONCE YOU GET TO KNOW 'EM.
THE DARK-HAIRED ONE BAKES A MEAN PECAN SANDY.

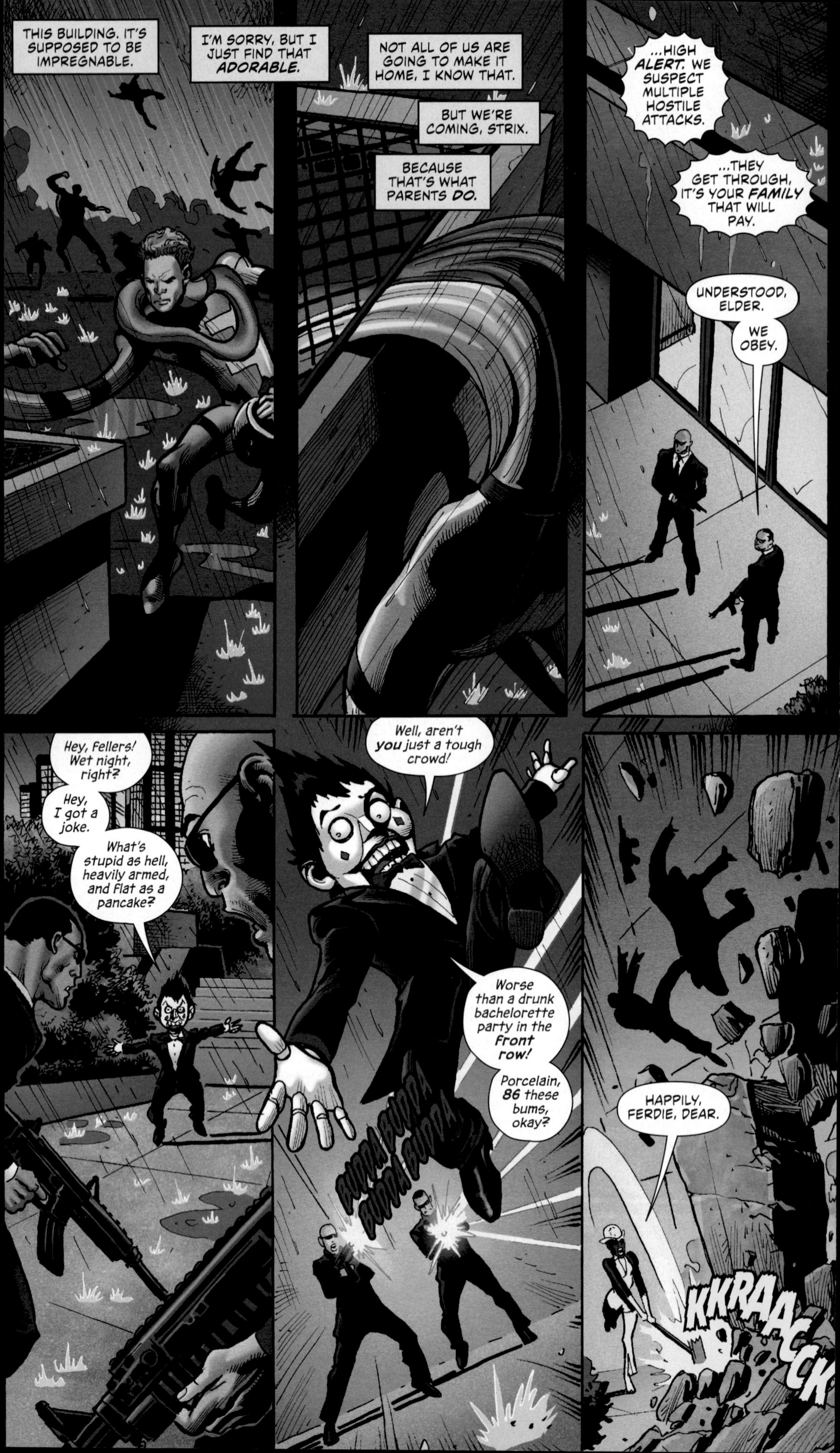
THIS BUILDING. IT'S SUPPOSED TO BE IMPREGNABLE.
I'M SORRY, BUT I JUST FIND THAT ADORABLE.
NOT ALL OF US ARE GOING TO MAKE IT HOME, I KNOW THAT.
BUT WE'RE COMING, STRIX.
BECAUSE THAT'S WHAT PARENTS DO.
...HIGH ALERT. WE SUSPECT MULTIPLE HOSTILE ATTACKS.
...THEY GET THROUGH, IT'S YOUR FAMILY THAT WILL PAY.
UNDERSTOOD, ELDER.
WE OBEY.
Hey, Fellers! Wet night, right?
Hey, I got a joke.
What's stupid as hell, heavily armed, and flat as a pancake?
Well, aren't you just a tough crowd!
Worse than a drunk bachelorette party in the Front row!
Porcelain, 86 these bums, okay?
BUDDA BUDDA BUDDA BUDDA
HAPPILY, FERDIE, DEAR.
KKRAACCK

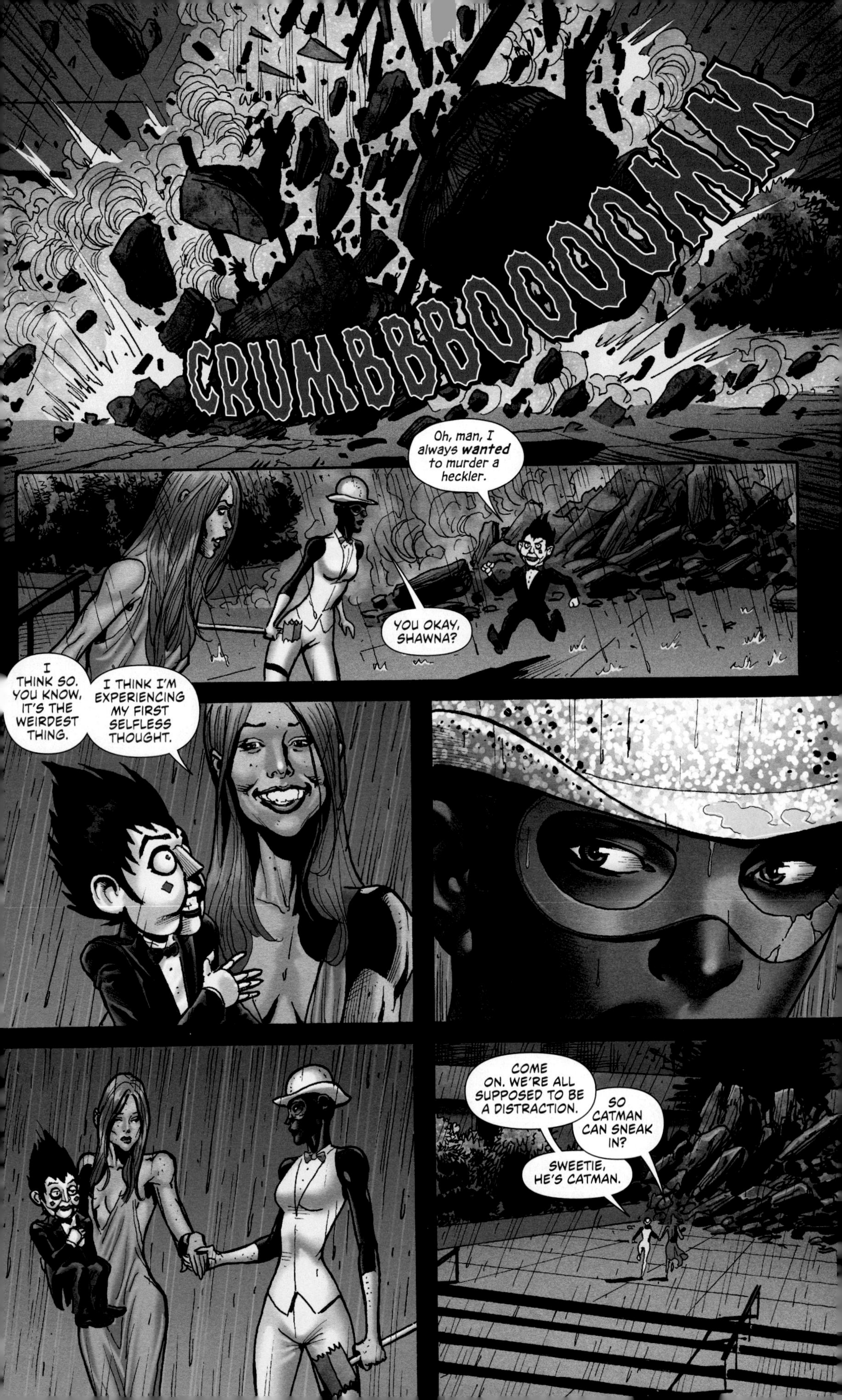
CRUMBBBOOOOOMM
Oh, man, I always **wanted** to murder a heckler.
YOU OKAY, SHAWNA?
I THINK SO. YOU KNOW, IT'S THE WEIRDEST THING.
I THINK I'M EXPERIENCING MY FIRST SELFLESS THOUGHT.
COME ON. WE'RE ALL SUPPOSED TO BE A DISTRACTION.
SO CATMAN CAN SNEAK IN?
SWEETIE, HE'S CATMAN.

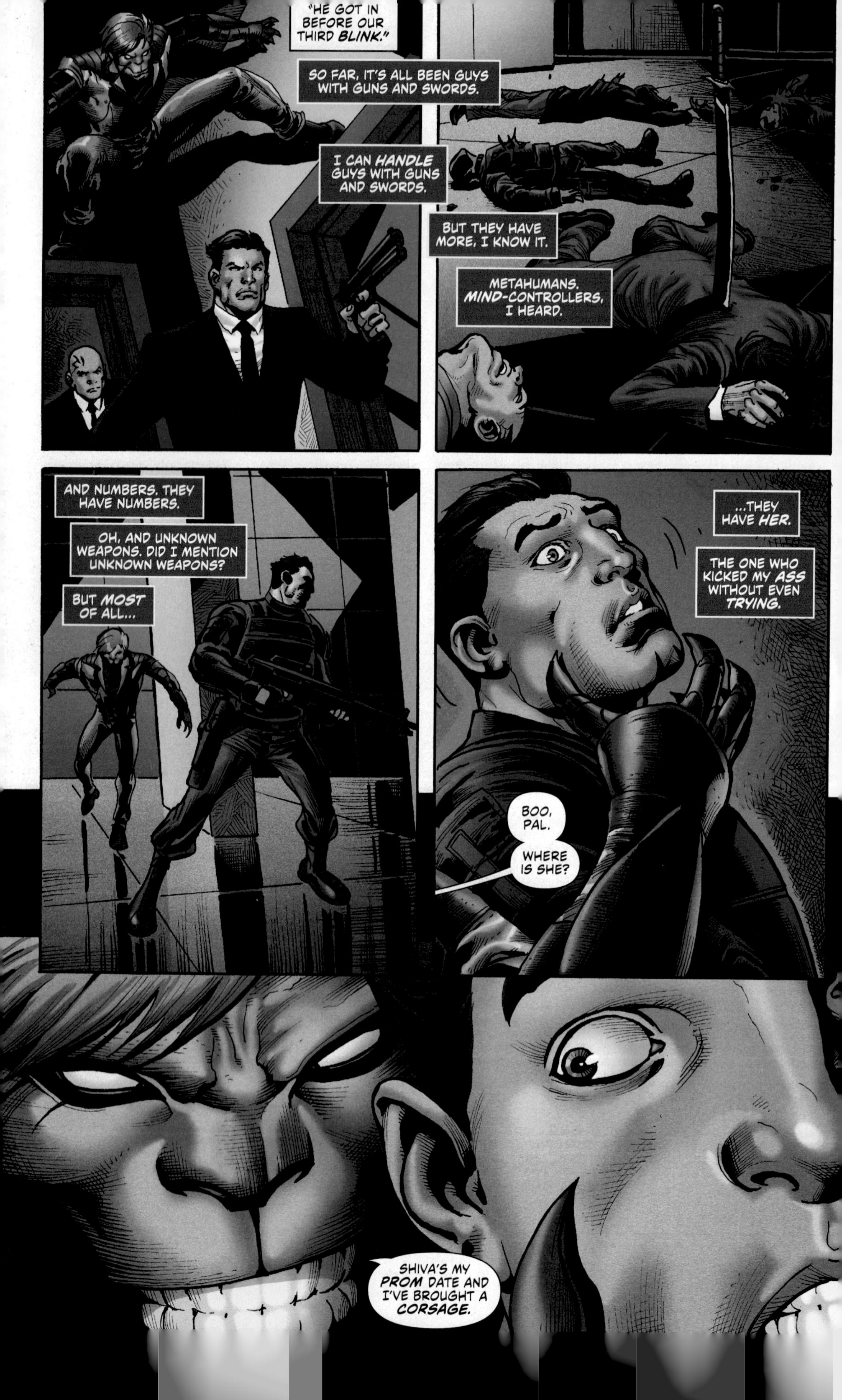
"HE GOT IN BEFORE OUR THIRD BLINK."
SO FAR, IT'S ALL BEEN GUYS WITH GUNS AND SWORDS.
I CAN HANDLE GUYS WITH GUNS AND SWORDS.
BUT THEY HAVE MORE, I KNOW IT.
METAHUMANS. MIND-CONTROLLERS, I HEARD.
AND NUMBERS. THEY HAVE NUMBERS.
OH, AND UNKNOWN WEAPONS. DID I MENTION UNKNOWN WEAPONS?
BUT MOST OF ALL...
...THEY HAVE HER.
THE ONE WHO KICKED MY ASS WITHOUT EVEN TRYING.
BOO, PAL.
WHERE IS SHE?
SHIVA'S MY PROM DATE AND I'VE BROUGHT A CORSAGE.

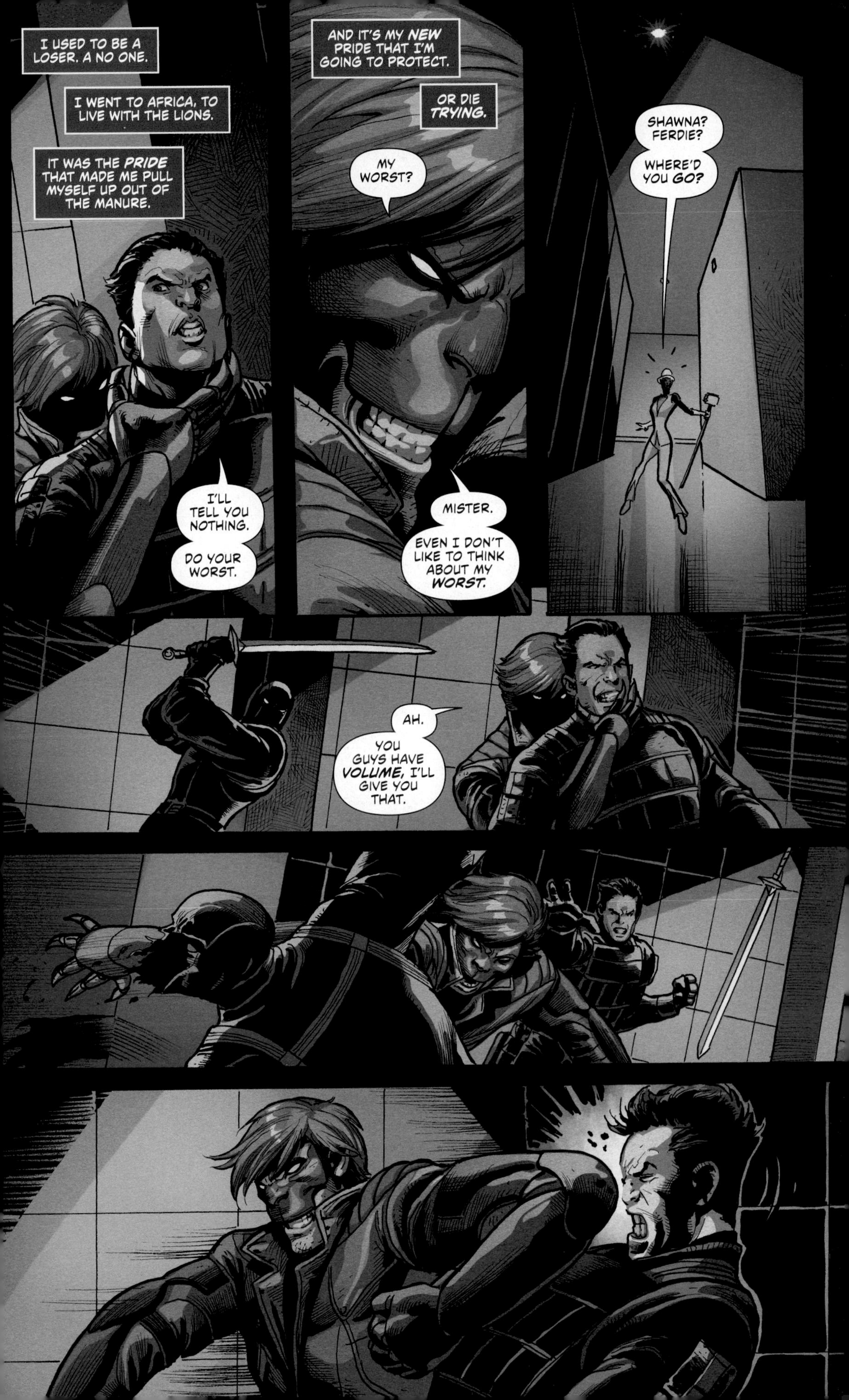
I USED TO BE A LOSER. A NO ONE.
I WENT TO AFRICA, TO LIVE WITH THE LIONS.
IT WAS THE PRIDE THAT MADE ME PULL MYSELF UP OUT OF THE MANURE.
I'LL TELL YOU NOTHING.
DO YOUR WORST.
AND IT'S MY NEW PRIDE THAT I'M GOING TO PROTECT.
OR DIE TRYING.
MY WORST?
MISTER.
EVEN I DON'T LIKE TO THINK ABOUT MY WORST.
SHAWNA? FERDIE?
WHERE'D YOU GO?
AH.
YOU GUYS HAVE VOLUME, I'LL GIVE YOU THAT.

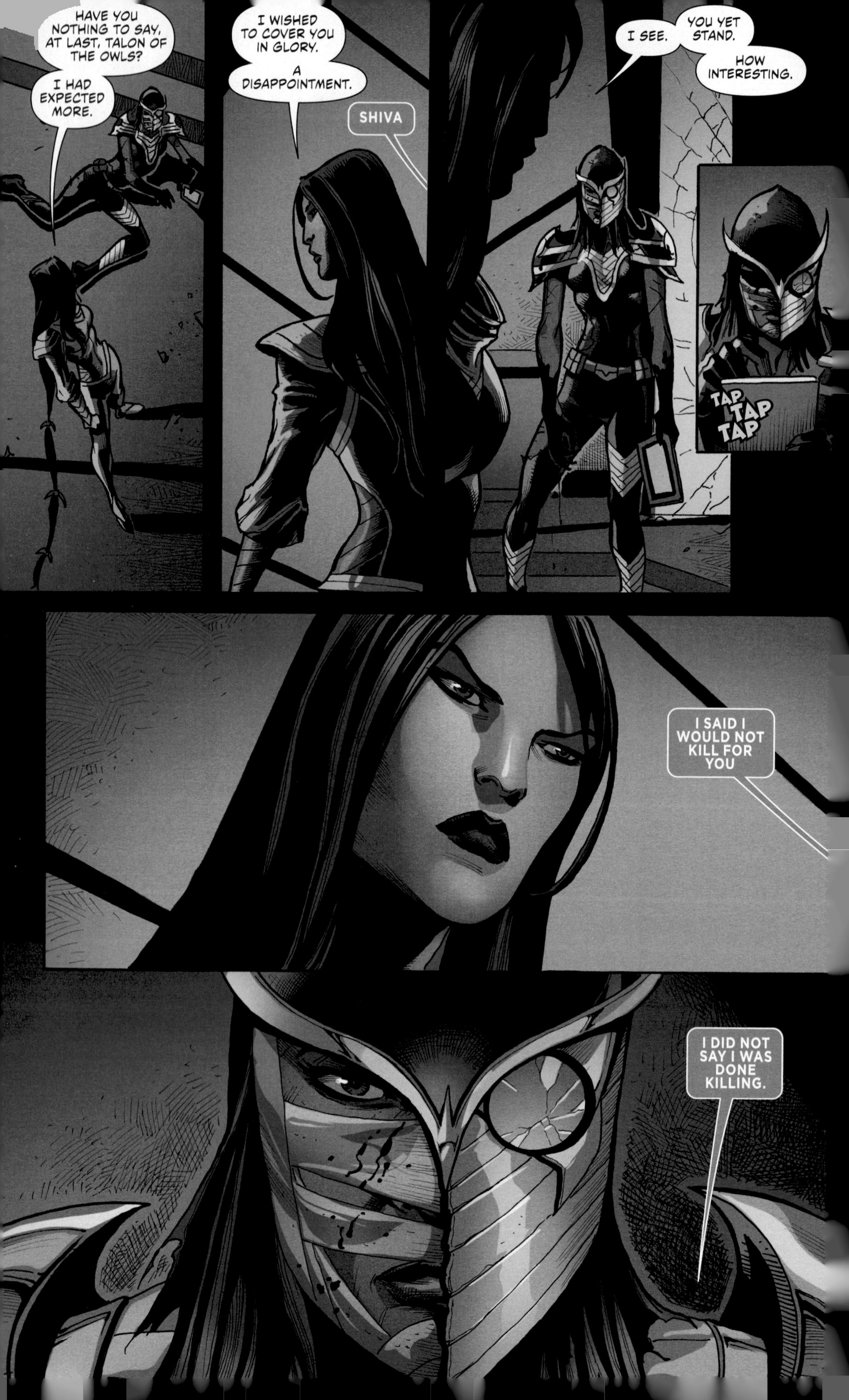
HAVE YOU NOTHING TO SAY, AT LAST, TALON OF THE OWLS?
I HAD EXPECTED MORE.
I WISHED TO COVER YOU IN GLORY.
A DISAPPOINTMENT.
SHIVA
I SEE.
YOU YET STAND.
HOW INTERESTING.
TAP TAP TAP
I SAID I WOULD NOT KILL FOR YOU
I DID NOT SAY I WAS DONE KILLING.

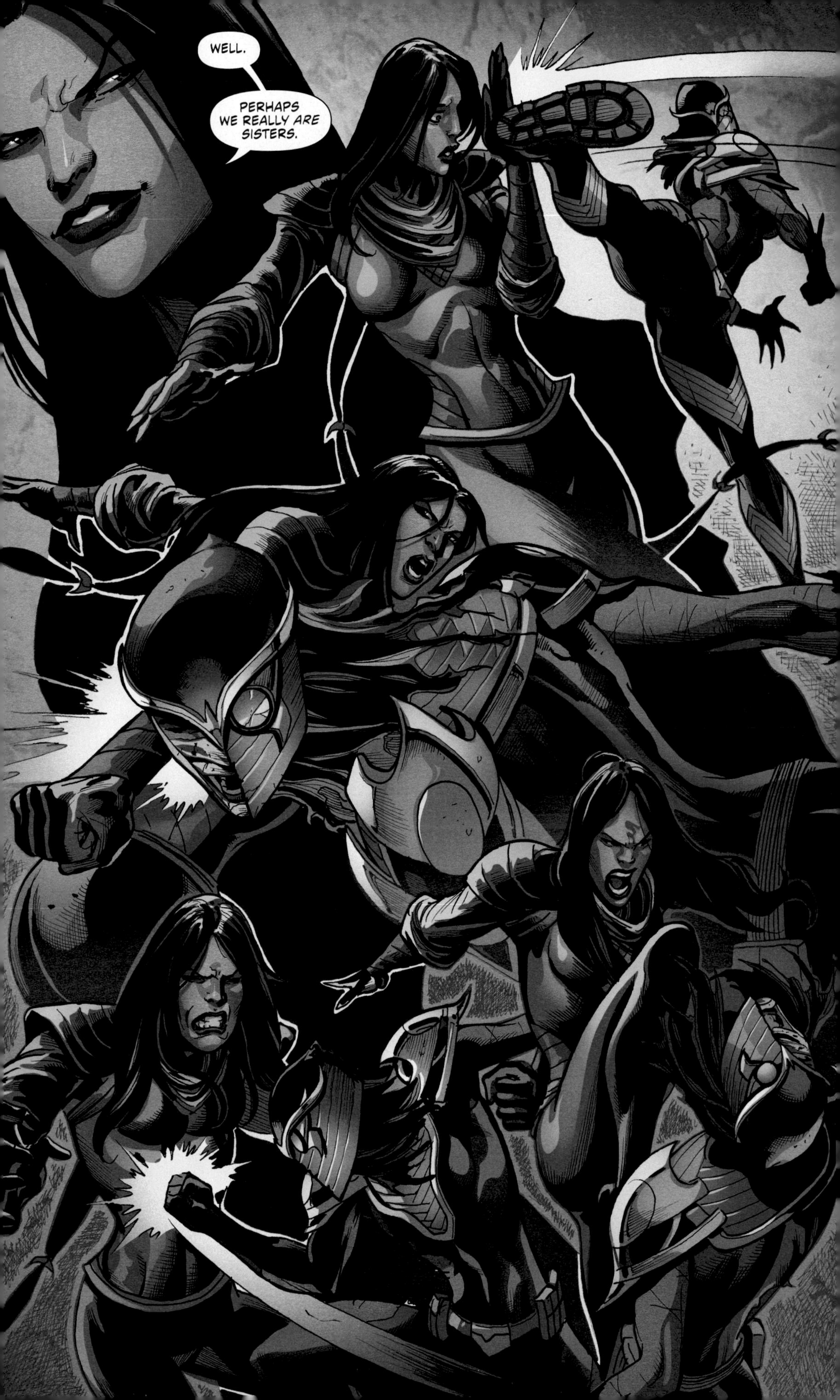
WELL.
PERHAPS WE REALLY ARE SISTERS.

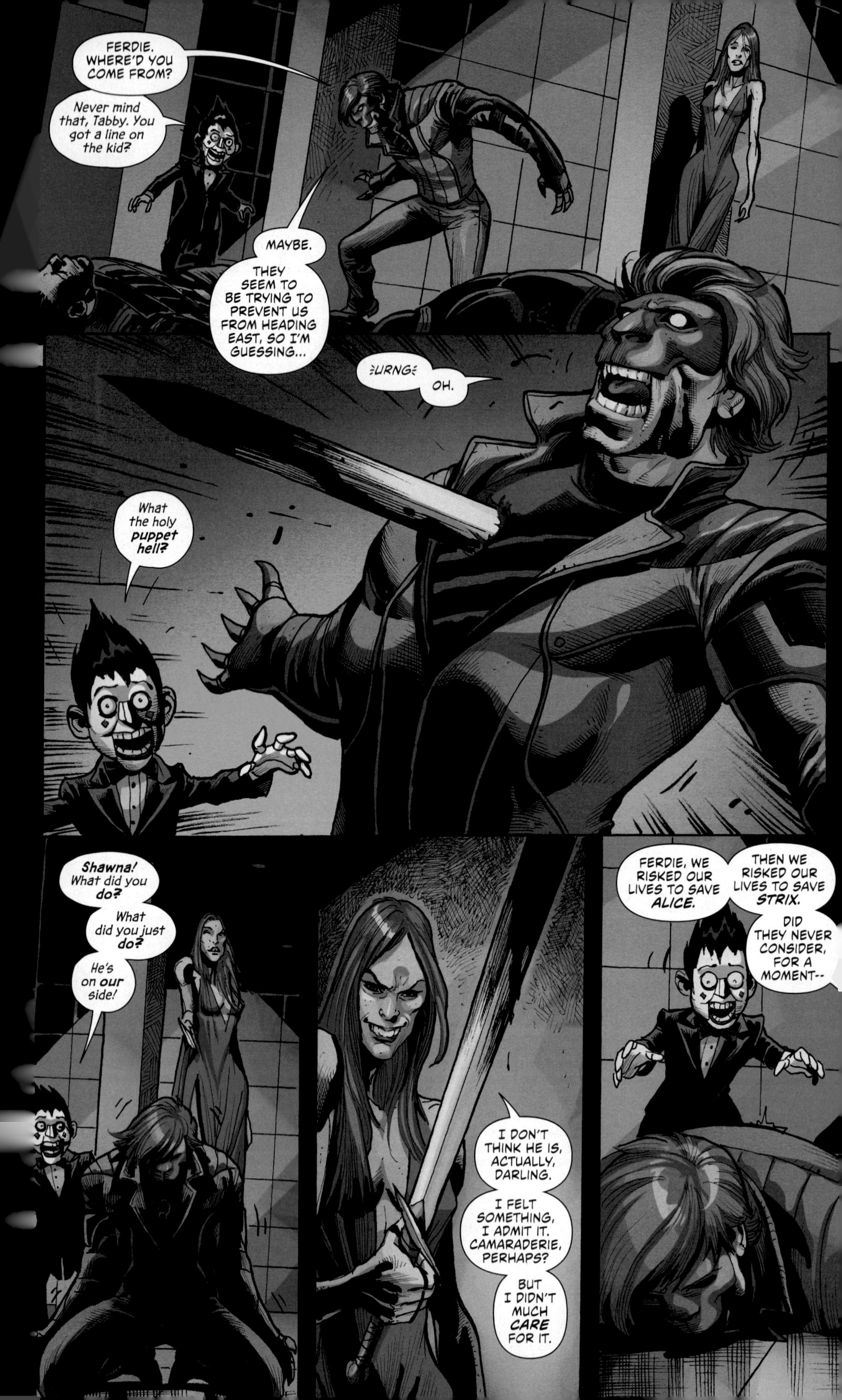
FERDIE. WHERE'D YOU COME FROM?
Never mind that, Tabby. You got a line on the kid?
MAYBE.
THEY SEEM TO BE TRYING TO PREVENT US FROM HEADING EAST, SO I'M GUESSING...
URNG
OH.
What the holy puppet hell?
Shawna! What did you do?
What did you just do?
He's on our side!
I DON'T THINK HE IS, ACTUALLY, DARLING.
I FELT SOMETHING, I ADMIT IT. CAMARADERIE, PERHAPS?
BUT I DIDN'T MUCH CARE FOR IT.
FERDIE, WE RISKED OUR LIVES TO SAVE ALICE.
THEN WE RISKED OUR LIVES TO SAVE STRIX.
DID THEY NEVER CONSIDER, FOR A MOMENT--

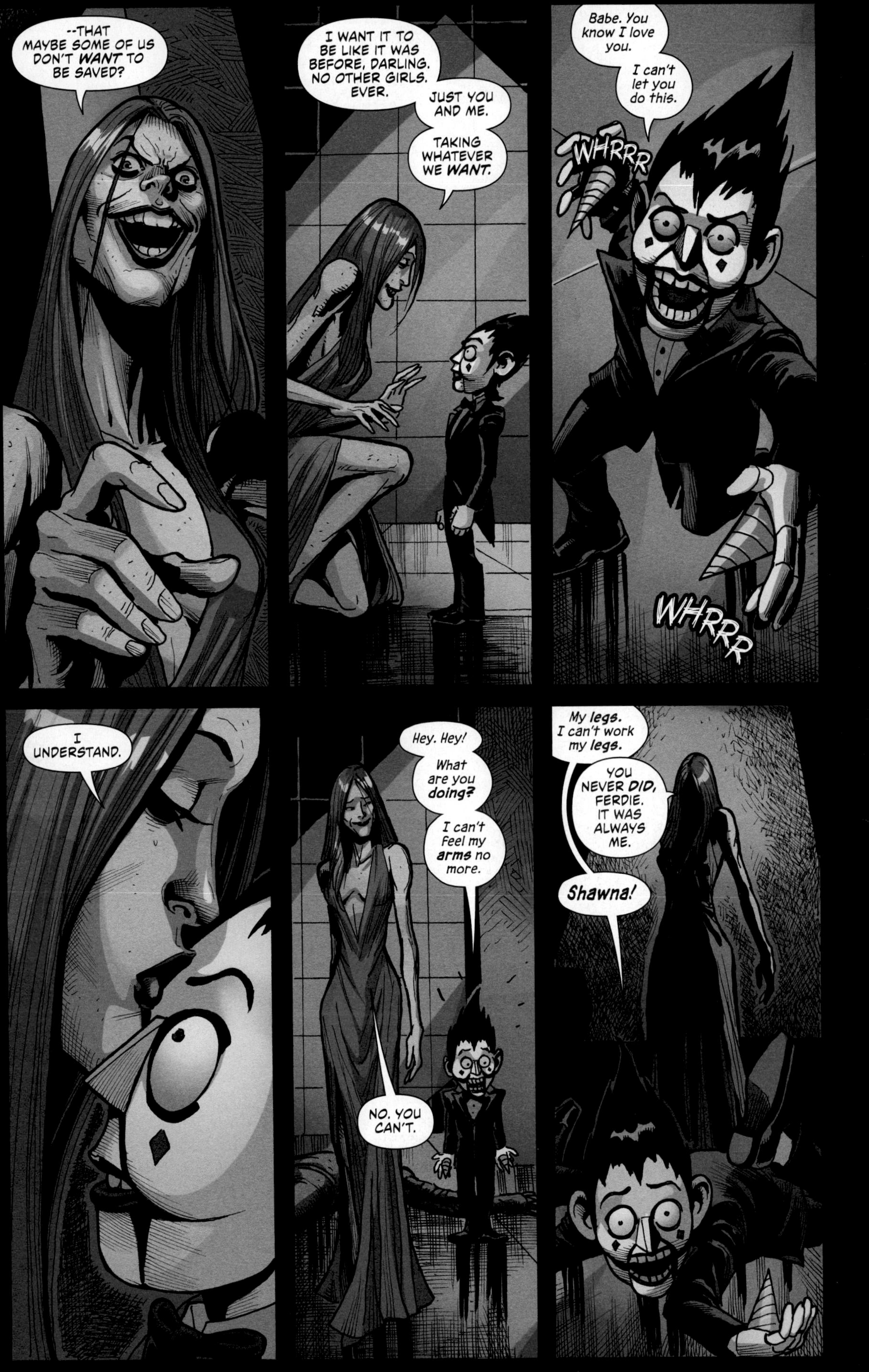
--THAT MAYBE SOME OF US DON'T WANT TO BE SAVED?
I WANT IT TO BE LIKE IT WAS BEFORE, DARLING. NO OTHER GIRLS. EVER.
JUST YOU AND ME.
TAKING WHATEVER WE WANT.
Babe. You know I love you.
I can't let you do this.
WHRRR
WHRRR
I UNDERSTAND.
Hey. Hey!
What are you doing?
I can't feel my arms no more.
NO. YOU CAN'T.
My legs. I can't work my legs.
YOU NEVER DID, FERDIE. IT WAS ALWAYS ME.
Shawna!

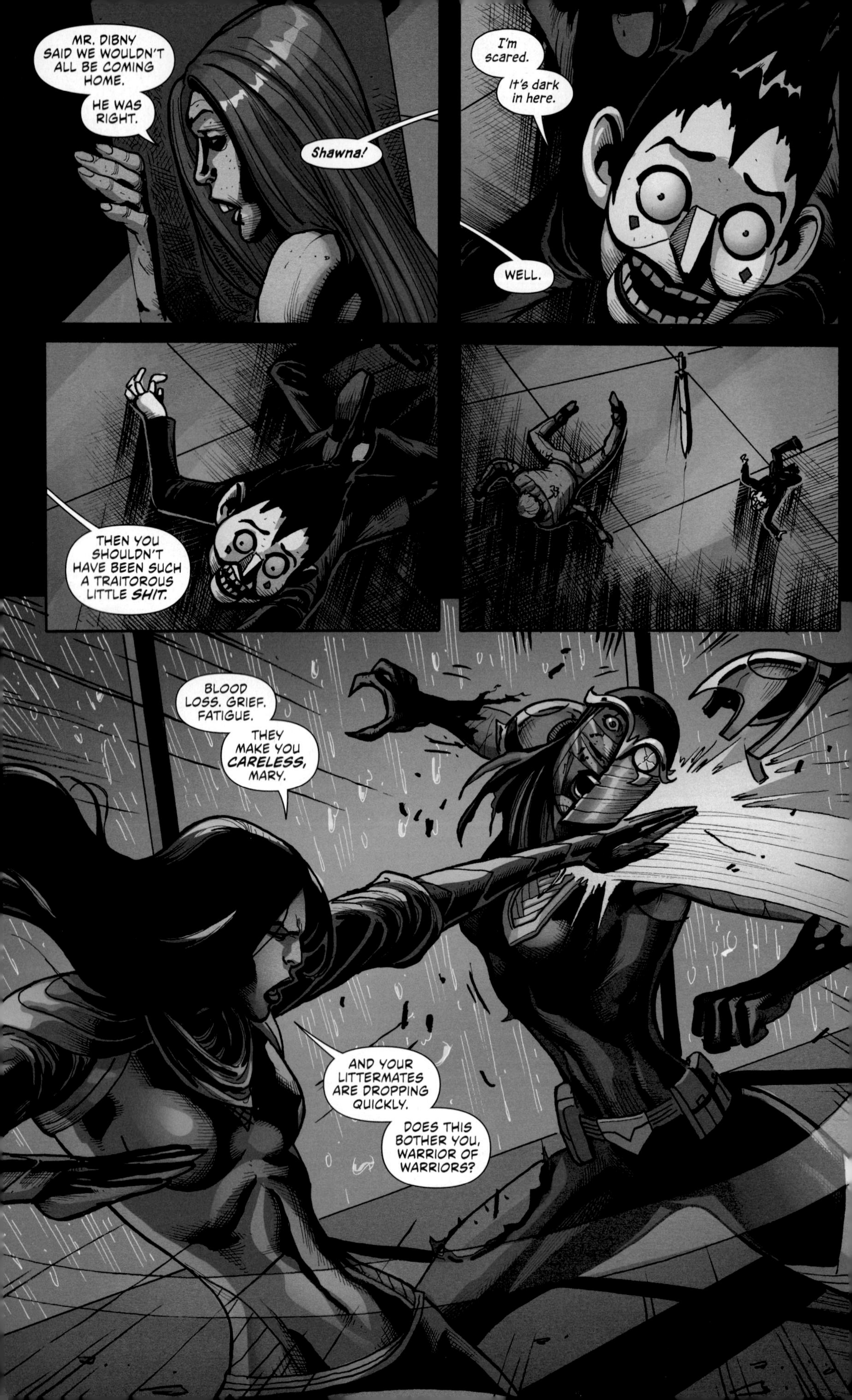
MR. DIBNY SAID WE WOULDN'T ALL BE COMING HOME.
HE WAS RIGHT.
Shawna!
I'm scared.
It's dark in here.
WELL.
THEN YOU SHOULDN'T HAVE BEEN SUCH A TRAITOROUS LITTLE SHIT.
BLOOD LOSS. GRIEF. FATIGUE.
THEY MAKE YOU CARELESS, MARY.
AND YOUR LITTERMATES ARE DROPPING QUICKLY.
DOES THIS BOTHER YOU, WARRIOR OF WARRIORS?

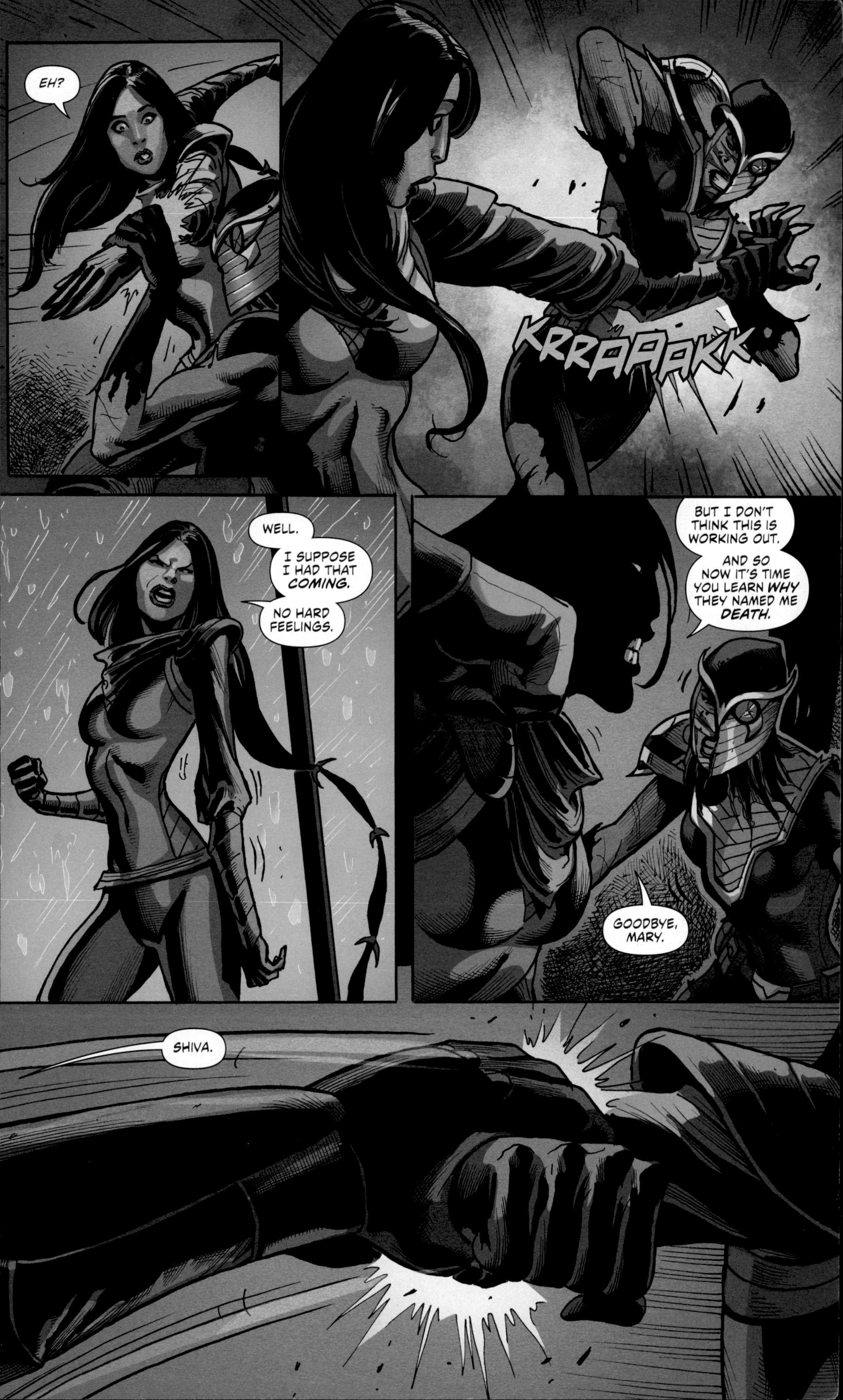
EH?
KRRAAAKK
WELL.
I SUPPOSE I HAD THAT *COMING*.
NO HARD FEELINGS.
BUT I DON'T THINK THIS IS WORKING OUT.
AND SO NOW IT'S TIME YOU LEARN ***WHY*** THEY NAMED ME ***DEATH***.
GOODBYE, MARY.
SHIVA.

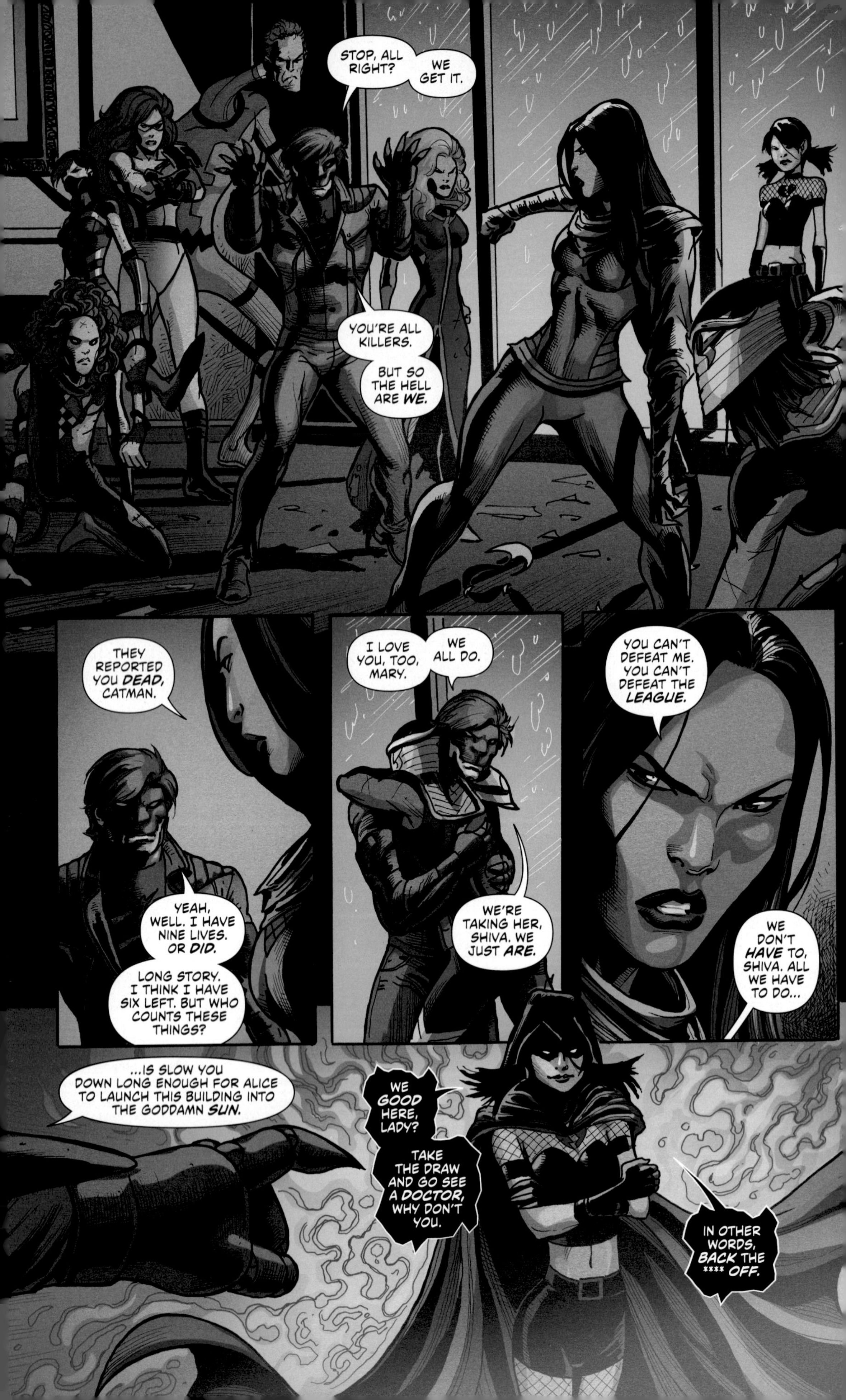
STOP, ALL RIGHT?
WE GET IT.
YOU'RE ALL KILLERS.
BUT SO THE HELL ARE *WE*.
THEY REPORTED YOU *DEAD*, CATMAN.
YEAH, WELL. I HAVE NINE LIVES. OR *DID*.
LONG STORY. I THINK I HAVE SIX LEFT. BUT WHO COUNTS THESE THINGS?
I LOVE YOU, TOO, MARY.
WE ALL DO.
WE'RE TAKING HER, SHIVA. WE JUST *ARE*.
YOU CAN'T DEFEAT ME. YOU CAN'T DEFEAT THE *LEAGUE*.
WE DON'T *HAVE* TO, SHIVA. ALL WE HAVE TO DO...
...IS SLOW YOU DOWN LONG ENOUGH FOR ALICE TO LAUNCH THIS BUILDING INTO THE GODDAMN *SUN*.
WE *GOOD* HERE, LADY?
TAKE THE DRAW AND GO SEE A *DOCTOR*, WHY DON'T YOU.
IN OTHER WORDS, *BACK* THE **** *OFF*.

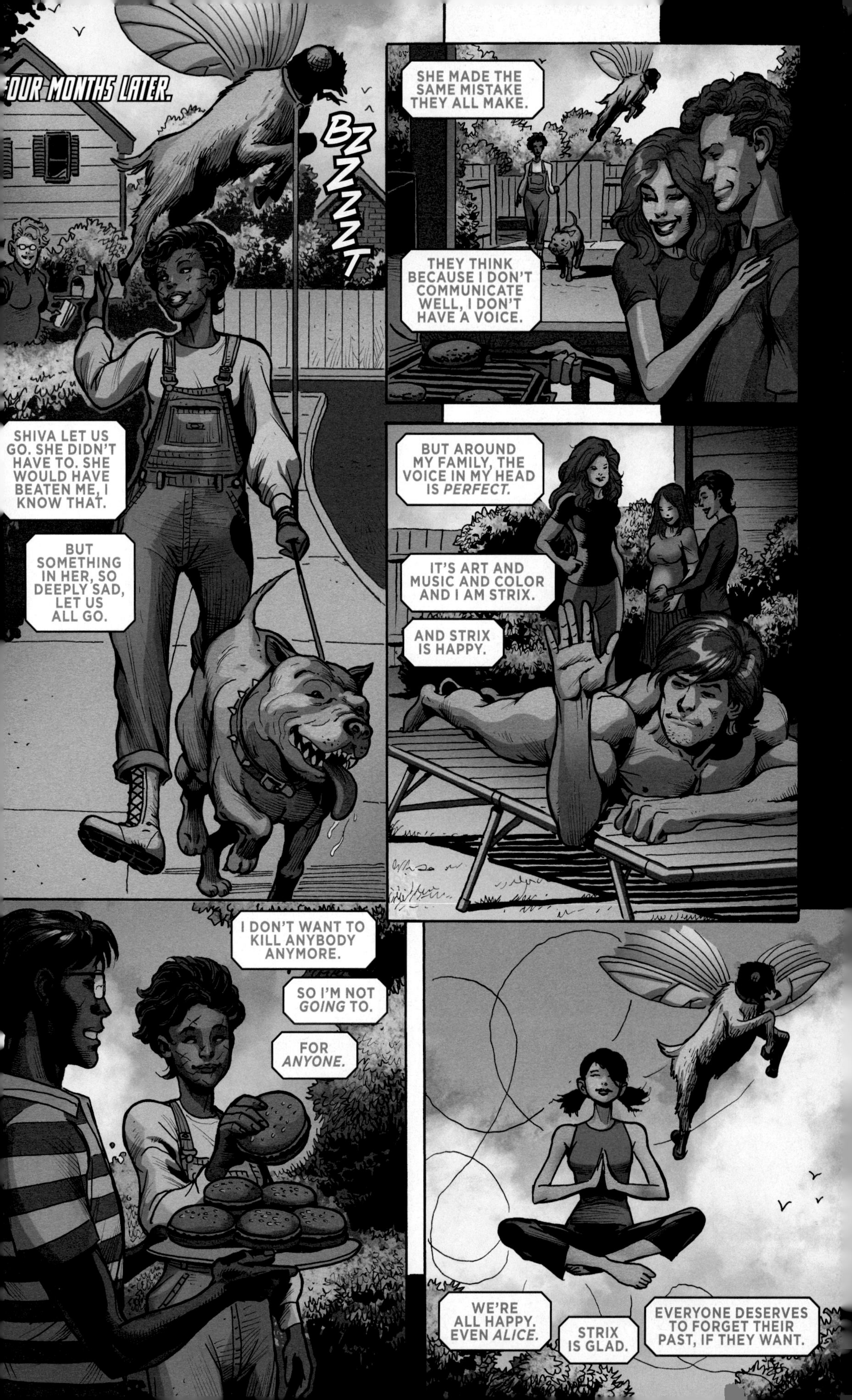

FOUR MONTHS LATER.
BZZZZZT
SHIVA LET US GO. SHE DIDN'T HAVE TO. SHE WOULD HAVE BEATEN ME, I KNOW THAT.
BUT SOMETHING IN HER, SO DEEPLY SAD, LET US ALL GO.
SHE MADE THE SAME MISTAKE THEY ALL MAKE.
THEY THINK BECAUSE I DON'T COMMUNICATE WELL, I DON'T HAVE A VOICE.
BUT AROUND MY FAMILY, THE VOICE IN MY HEAD IS *PERFECT.*
IT'S ART AND MUSIC AND COLOR AND I AM STRIX.
AND STRIX IS HAPPY.
I DON'T WANT TO KILL ANYBODY ANYMORE.
SO I'M NOT *GOING* TO.
FOR *ANYONE.*
WE'RE ALL HAPPY. EVEN *ALICE.*
STRIX IS GLAD.
EVERYONE DESERVES TO FORGET THEIR PAST, IF THEY WANT.

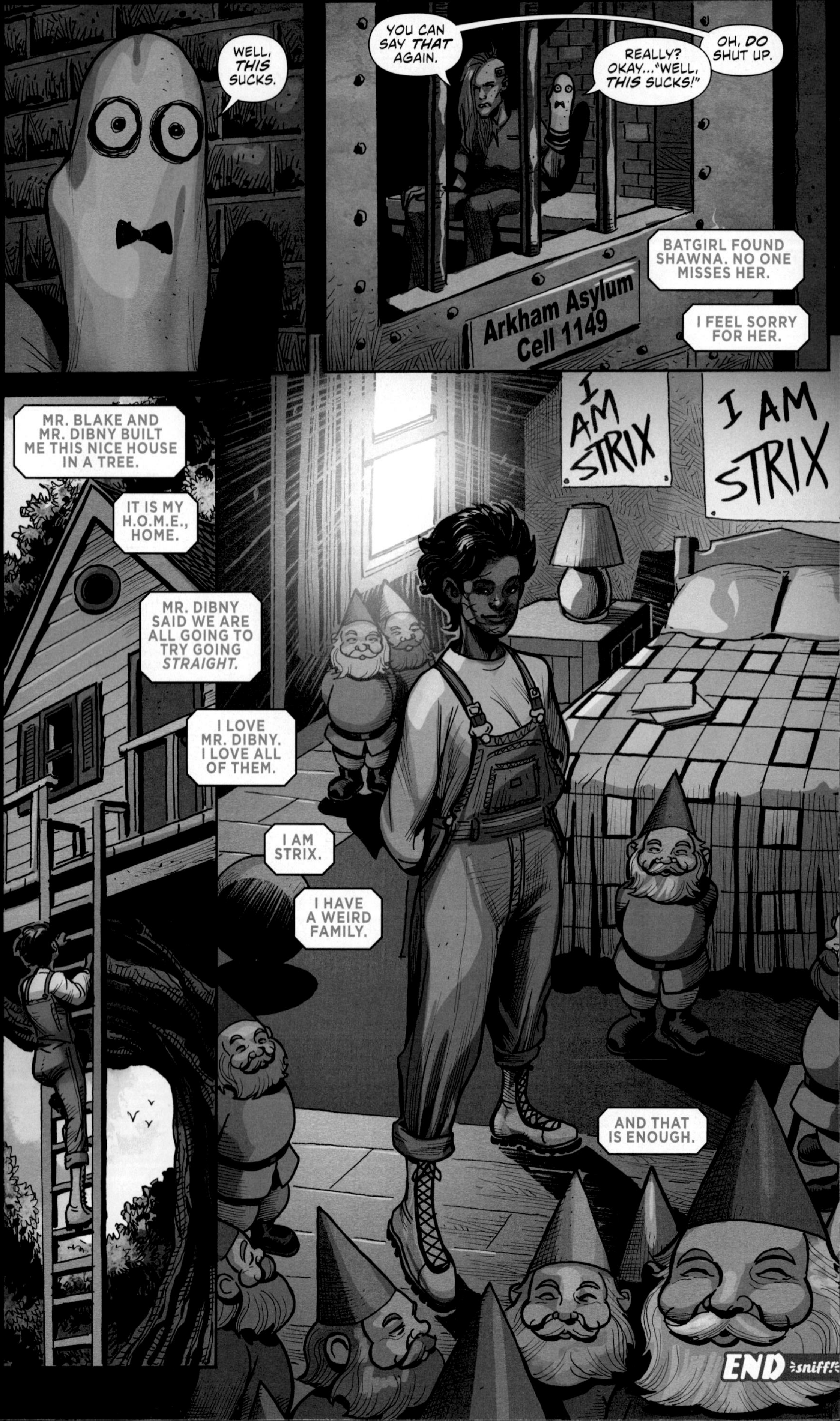
WELL, THIS SUCKS.
YOU CAN SAY THAT AGAIN.
REALLY? OKAY..."WELL, THIS SUCKS!"
OH, DO SHUT UP.
Arkham Asylum Cell 1149
BATGIRL FOUND SHAWNA. NO ONE MISSES HER.
I FEEL SORRY FOR HER.
MR. BLAKE AND MR. DIBNY BUILT ME THIS NICE HOUSE IN A TREE.
IT IS MY H.O.M.E., HOME.
MR. DIBNY SAID WE ARE ALL GOING TO TRY GOING STRAIGHT.
I LOVE MR. DIBNY. I LOVE ALL OF THEM.
I AM STRIX
I AM STRIX
I AM STRIX.
I HAVE A WEIRD FAMILY.
AND THAT IS ENOUGH.
END sniff!

"A pretty irresistible hook. What if the good guys assembled a bunch of bad guys to work as a Dirty Dozen-like superteam and do the dirty work traditional heroes would never touch (or want to know about)?"—THE ONION/AV CLUB

START AT THE BEGINNING!

SUICIDE SQUAD
VOLUME 1: KICKED IN THE TEETH

SUICIDE SQUAD
VOL. 2: BASILISK
RISING

SUICIDE SQUAD
VOL. 3: DEATH IS FOR
SUCKERS

DEATHSTROKE VOL. 1:
LEGACY

"A CLEVERLY WRITTEN, OUTSTANDING READ FROM BEGINNING TO END." — USA Today

THE NEW 52!

DC COMICS™

SUICIDE SQUAD™

VOLUME 1
KICKED IN
THE TEETH

ADAM **GLASS**   Federico **DALLOCCHIO**   Clayton **HENRY**

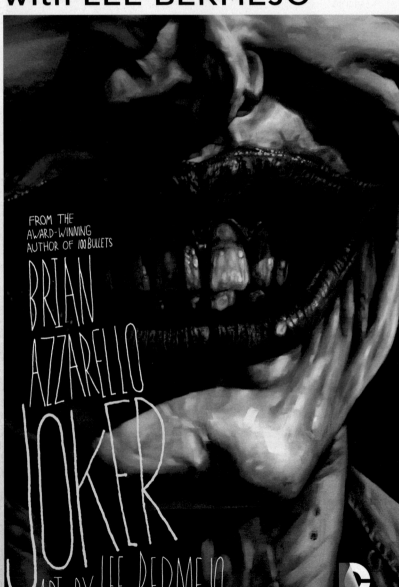

HARLEY QUINN
VOLUME 1: HOT IN THE CITY

AMANDA **CONNER**   JIMMY **PALMIOTTI**   CHAD **HARDIN**
STEPHANE **ROUX**   ALEX **SINCLAIR**   PAUL **MOUNTS**

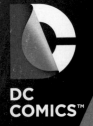

"Chaotic and unabashedly fun."—IGN

"I'm enjoying HARLEY QUINN a great deal; it's silly, it's funny, it's irreverent."
—COMIC BOOK RESOURCES

HARLEY QUINN

VOLUME 1: PRELUDES AND KNOCK-KNOCK JOKES

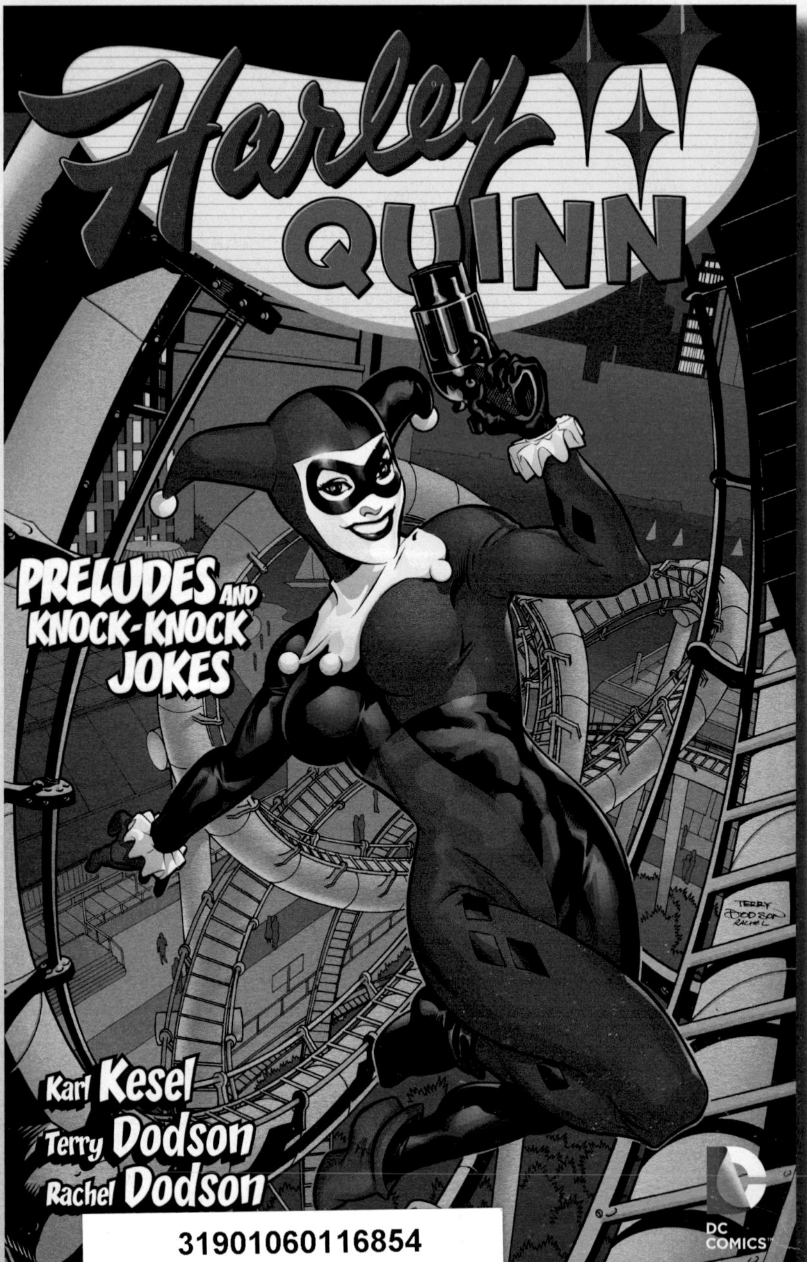

Harley QUINN
PRELUDES AND KNOCK-KNOCK JOKES
Karl Kesel
Terry Dodson
Rachel Dodson
DC COMICS

HARLEY QUINN VOL. 2: NIGHT AND DAY

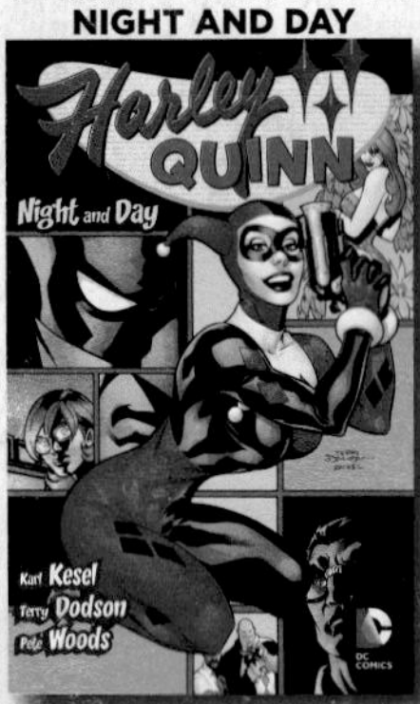

Harley QUINN
Night and Day
Karl Kesel
Terry Dodson
Pete Woods

with KARL KESEL, TERRY DODSON, and PETE WOODS

HARLEY QUINN VOL. 3: WELCOME TO METROPOLIS

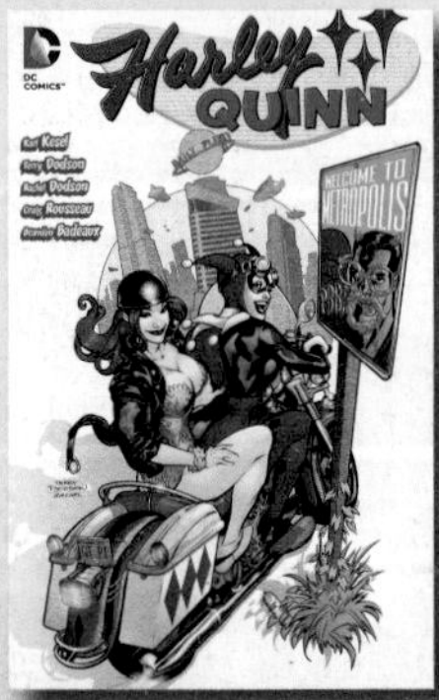

Harley QUINN
WELCOME TO METROPOLIS

with KARL KESEL, TERRY DODSON and CRAIG ROUSSEAU

HARLEY QUINN VOL. 4: VENGEANCE UNLIMITED

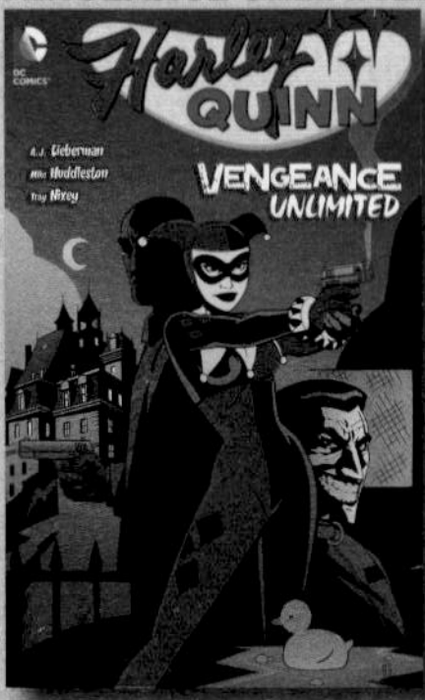

Harley QUINN
VENGEANCE UNLIMITED

with A.J. LIEBERMAN and MIKE HUDDLESTON